W9-CAN-230

MICROSOFT® OFFICE 2013
QuickSteps®

Carole B. Matthews

Marty Matthews

Bobbi Sandburg

New York Chicago San Francisco
Athens London Madrid Mexico City
Milan New Delhi Singapore Sydney Toronto

Cataloging-in-Publication Data is on file with the
Library of Congress

005.5
MICROSOFT OFFICE 2013

Microsoft® Office 2013 QuickSteps®

1234567890   WCK WCK   109876543

ISBN   978-0-07-180587-2
MHID   0-07-180587-7

SPONSORING EDITOR / Roger Stewart
EDITORIAL SUPERVISOR / Janet Walden
PROJECT MANAGER / Nidhi Chopra, Cenveo® Publisher Services
ACQUISITIONS COORDINATOR / Amanda Russell
TECHNICAL EDITOR / John Cronan
COPY EDITOR / William McManus
PROOFREADER / Claire Splan
INDEXER / Valerie Haynes Perry
PRODUCTION SUPERVISOR / George Anderson
COMPOSITION / Cenveo Publisher Services
ILLUSTRATION / Erin Johnson
ART DIRECTOR, COVER / Jeff Weeks
COVER DESIGNER / Pattie Lee
SERIES CREATORS / Marty and Carole Matthews
SERIES DESIGN / Mary McKeon

Contents at a Glance

1
2
3
4
5
6
7
8
9

Contents

Chapter 10   **Polishing and Publishing Your Presentations** 233

Chapter 11   **Using Outlook** 269

12

About the Authors

Carole and **Marty Matthews** have used computers for over 40 years, as programmers, systems analysts, managers, and company executives. They have been on both sides of using computers, both designing software and using it. For the last 30 years they have authored, co-authored, or managed the writing and production of more than 100 books, including: *Windows 8 QuickSteps, Facebook for Seniors QuickSteps, Genealogy for Seniors QuickSteps, Microsoft Office Excel 2013 QuickSteps*, and *Microsoft Word 2013 QuickSteps*.

Bobbi Sandburg has long been involved with computers, accounting, and writing. She is a retired accountant currently filling her time as a trainer, technical writer, and small-business consultant. She teaches at several venues, offering step-by-step instruction in a variety of computer applications. Her extensive background, coupled with her ability to explain complex concepts in plain language, has made her a popular instructor, consultant, and speaker. She has authored and co-authored more than a dozen computer books, including *Quicken 2013: The Official Guide, Genealogy for Seniors QuickSteps*, and *Computing for Seniors Quicksteps*.

About the Technical Editor

John Cronan has over 30 years of computer experience and has been writing and editing computer-related books for over 20 years. His writings include *Microsoft Office Excel 2010 QuickSteps* and *Microsoft Office Access 2010 QuickSteps*. He recently tech edited *Microsoft Windows 8 QuickSteps*. John and his wife Faye (and cat Little Buddy) reside in Everett, Washington.

Acknowledgments

This book is a team effort of truly talented people. Among them are

Roger Stewart, sponsoring editor, believed in us enough to sell the series, and continues to stand behind us as we go through the fourth edition. Thanks, Roger!

Janet Walden and **Nidhi Chopra**, project editors, greased the wheels and straightened the track to make a very smooth production process. Thanks, Janet and Nidhi!

John Cronan, technical editor, made sure our text was accurate and complete. It is a better book because of his excellence. Thanks, John!

William McManus, copy editor, added greatly to the readability and understandability of the book with excellence and intelligence. Thanks, Bill!

Claire Splan, proofreader, found all those sneaky discrepancies and typos, and errors that the rest of us missed and that make us crazy. Thanks, Claire!

Valerie Haynes Perry, indexer, who added so much to the usability of the book, and did so quickly and without notice. Thanks, Valerie!

Introduction

QuickSteps® books are recipe books for computer users. They answer the question "How do I…?" by providing quick sets of steps to accomplish the most common tasks in a particular program. The sets of steps ("QuickSteps") are the central focus of the book and show you how to quickly perform many functions and tasks. "QuickFacts" sidebars contribute supporting information that add to your overall understanding of the topic at hand. Notes, Tips, and Cautions augment the steps, and are presented next to the text they relate to. The introductions are minimal rather than narrative, and numerous illustrations and figures, many with callouts, support the steps.

QuickSteps® books are organized by function and the tasks needed to perform that function. Each function is a chapter, and each chapter begins with a list of the QuickSteps tasks covered. Each task contains the steps needed for accomplishing the function, along with relevant QuickFacts sidebars, Notes, Tips, Cautions, and screenshots.

Conventions Used in This Book

Microsoft® Office 2013 QuickSteps® uses several conventions designed to make the book easier for you to follow:

- A ✔ in the table of contents references a QuickFacts sidebar in a chapter.
- **Bold** type is used for words on the screen that you are to do something with, such as click **Save As** or **Open**.
- *Italic* type is used for a word or phrase that is being defined or otherwise deserves special emphasis.
- <u>Underlined</u> type is used for text that you are to type from the keyboard.
- SMALL CAPITAL LETTERS are used for keys on the keyboard, such as ENTER and SHIFT. When two or more keys are combined into a command (meaning you press them at the same time), they are designated with a plus sign, such as CTRL+SHIFT.
- When you are expected to enter a command, you are told to press the key(s). If you are to enter text or numbers, you are told to type them. Specific letters or numbers to be entered will be underlined.

QuickSteps to...

Chapter 1 _____

Stepping into Office

Microsoft Office is the most widely used of all Office Suite offerings. Most personal computers (PCs) have some version of Office installed, and most people who use a PC probably have Office available to them as well as some experience in its use. The upgrade of Office 2010 to Office 2013 has been a significant event. New features include touch mode, a flatter look of the ribbon, online picture support, resume reading mode, and better PDF support.

As you may know, Office is both simple to use and highly sophisticated, offering many features that commonly go unused. Office delivers a high degree of functionality even when only a small percentage of its capabilities are used. The purpose of this book is to acquaint you with how to use the upgrade to Office 2013 within four primary Office programs: Word, Excel, PowerPoint, and Outlook. You will learn not only how to access the newly placed common, everyday features, but also about many of those additional features that can enhance your experience with using Office.

In this chapter you will familiarize yourself with Office; see how to start and leave programs; discover how to use the Office 2013 windows, panes, ribbon, toolbars, and menus; learn how to get help, use the Clipboard, and check your spelling and find out how to customize the Office program to best meet your needs.

> **NOTE** We explain how to open an Office program using either Windows 7 or Windows 8. Thereafter, we'll assume you have Windows 8. You'll find that the instructions are usually the same, except when you're interfacing with the operating system, such as saving or opening a file. In Windows 8, the touch feature for newer computers is available. In this chapter, you'll find out how to use that feature. Thereafter, we'll assume you will interpret our instructions for using the keyboard and mouse accordingly if you are using the touch feature.

OPEN AND CLOSE AN OFFICE PROGRAM

An Office program can be opened using several methods, depending on which operating system you have, which method you consider to be convenient, your personal style, and the appearance of your Desktop. In this section you'll see several ways to start an Office application using either Windows 7 or Windows 8. You'll also see how to exit Office.

▷▷ Start an Office Program in Windows 7

If you are using Windows 7, you can open an Office program from the Start menu or from a shortcut that you place on the taskbar and/or Desktop.

Open an Office Program from the Start Menu

1. Start your computer, if it is not already running, and log on to Windows if necessary.

2. Click **Start** to open the Start menu.

3. Click **All Programs**, scroll down the menu if needed by clicking the scroll bar on the right, click **Microsoft Office 2013**, and click the program you want to launch.

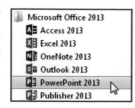

Pin an Office Program Shortcut to the Start Menu, Taskbar, or Desktop

When you *pin* something, you place a shortcut icon to it in a menu or taskbar. For instance, you can pin a shortcut to Word to the Start menu itself or to the taskbar at the bottom of your screen, and then use either of the shortcut icons to open Word with a single click.

Here is how to pin an Office program to the Start menu, the taskbar, or the Desktop using Windows 7:

1. Click **Start** to open the Start menu, click **All Programs**, scroll down (if needed), and click **Microsoft Office 2013**.

2. Right-click (click the right mouse button) the Office program for which you want to create a shortcut and then choose one of the following options:

   - Click **Pin To Start Menu** to place a shortcut on the Start menu itself.

   - Click **Pin To Taskbar** to place a shortcut on the taskbar.

   - Click **Send To**, and click **Desktop (Create Shortcut)** to place a shortcut on the Desktop.

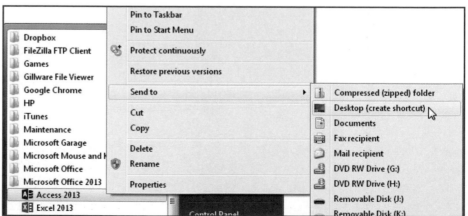

The Office program can then be started using one of these shortcuts, as described in the next section.

 TIP The Start menu's contents and sequence of items change depending on how often you use the various programs. The icons of the programs you use most often are automatically displayed on the left side of the Start menu. You can also pin items to the Start menu list, as just described, which is a great way to make your favorite programs easily accessible.

Start an Office Program Using a Shortcut

If you have pinned an Office program's shortcut to the Start menu (or use the program frequently enough that it is placed there automatically), to the taskbar, or to the Desktop, you'll find the Office program's icon displayed there. To use the shortcut to start your program:

- To open a program using the Start menu shortcut, click **Start**. The Start menu opens. Mouse over the icon and then click the icon or a recent file, depending on the Office program.

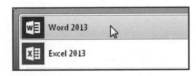

- To open an Office program using the taskbar shortcut, click its icon on the taskbar.
- To open a shortcut on the Desktop, double-click (press the mouse button twice in rapid succession) to start the program.

Start an Office Program in Windows 8

If you are using Windows 8, you can open an Office program from the Start screen or from a shortcut that you place on the taskbar and/or Desktop. Figure 1-1 shows an example of a Start screen that has been modified to show the Office tiles.

Open an Office Program from the Start Screen

With a normal installation of Office 2013 on Windows 8, you should see a tile for each of the Office programs on the Start screen. You may have to scroll to the right to see the tiles. (If you don't see the tiles, refer to the next topic.)

Then, click or tap the tile for the Office program you want to start. It will open on the Desktop.

 TIP If you want to position the tiles on the Start screen where you can more easily find them, simply drag them to a different position, such as was done in Figure 1-1. Click and drag the tile to the left of the Trending tiles.

Pin an Office Program Shortcut to the Start Screen or Taskbar

If you don't see the tile for the Office program you want to start on the Start screen:

1. Right-click and drag up with your pointer, or swipe up from the bottom of the screen if you are using touch, and click or tap **All Apps**. In the resulting list of programs, you should see the Office program tiles under Microsoft Office 2013. You may have to scroll right a bit.

2. Before you click or tap a tile to open the corresponding Office program, right-click the tile, or touch and hold the tile for a moment and then swipe down, to open the command bar across the bottom of the screen.

Figure 1-1: Windows 8 displays your programs as tiles or icons that you click or tap to open the programs.

3. If you will be using the Office program a great deal, click or tap **Pin To Start** and/or **Pin To Taskbar** to pin the program tile either to the Start screen or to the Desktop's taskbar, so you can start it in the future with fewer steps.

Start an Office Program Using a Shortcut

To start the Office program using a shortcut:

- From the shortcut on the Desktop, double-click or tap the program icon.
- From the shortcut on the taskbar, click or tap the program icon.

 NOTE If you find you want to remove the shortcut after you have pinned a program tile to the Start menu or taskbar, right-click the tile to see a context menu, or touch, hold, and swipe it to see the command bar again. You'll see an Unpin From Start Menu or Unpin From Taskbar option on the menu or bar. Click the option you want to remove the shortcut.

Close an Office Program

To exit any of the Office programs, click the **Close** icon on the right end of the title bar.

OPEN, CLOSE, AND SAVE AN OFFICE DOCUMENT

 NOTE In this chapter we are using the term "document" as a general term to cover files created in each program—Word documents, Excel workbooks, PowerPoint presentations, and, to some degree, Outlook items such as mail messages and contacts.

You may open an existing document or a new one in Word, Excel, or PowerPoint. (This section doesn't apply to Outlook.) If you are opening

 **QuickFacts**

Using Touch

Many newer computers running Windows 8 have a touch-sensitive screen that can be used in place of the mouse and occasionally the keyboard. In the earlier part of this chapter, we've included both mouse and touch commands to perform the steps. To keep this from getting laborious, from here on we'll just refer to the mouse commands, but you can use this table for the relevant touch command for each mouse command.

Table 1-1: Touch vs. Mouse Commands for Various Actions

Action	With a Mouse	With Touch
Select an object or start an app in the Start screen	**Click** the object	**Tap** the object
Open an object or start an app on the Desktop	**Double-click** the object	**Double-tap** the object
Open an object's context menu or the app bar for an app	**Right-click** the object	**Touch and hold** for a moment, then swipe down
Move an object on the screen	**Drag** the object with the mouse	**Drag** the object with your finger

For further information on using touch and/or the keyboard in place of or in addition to the mouse, see *Windows 8 QuickSteps*. That book has tear-out tables inside the back cover that compare the mouse, touch, and keyboard commands. These tables, which refer to general operating system functions, not Office program–specific functions, are also available at http://quicksteps.org/windows8cheats. On that site, click **Download Tables**.

a new file, you have an additional choice of which template to use (even a blank document is based on a "normally formatted" template; see the "Using Templates" QuickFacts, a bit later in the chapter, for more details). If you are starting one of these three Office programs for the first time during a computer session, you'll see the initial Office screen, shown for Word in Figure 1-2, which displays the files and templates that you may

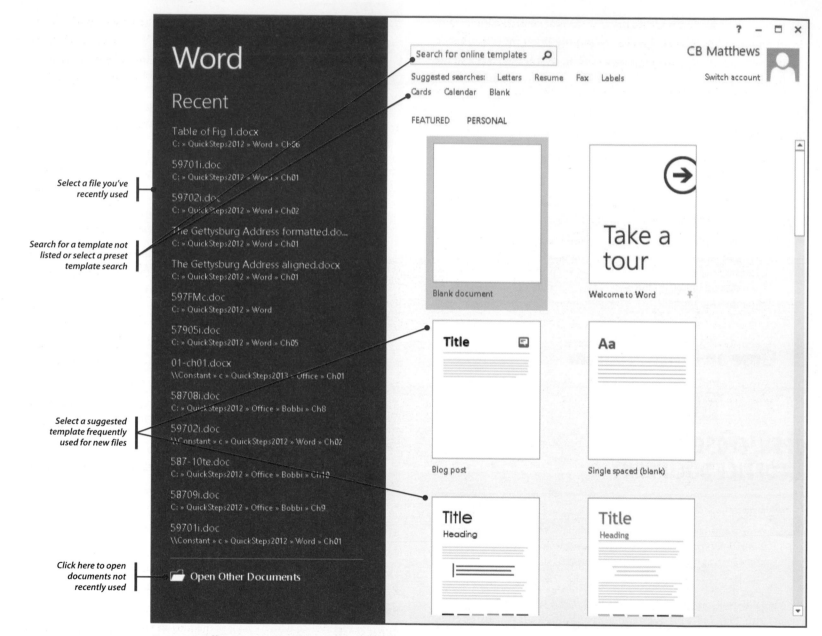

Select a file you've recently used

Search for a template not listed or select a preset template search

Select a suggested template frequently used for new files

Click here to open documents not recently used

Figure 1-2: Office presents you with access to recent files, older files, and templates to create new ones.

open and options for finding other documents and templates. If you have already used a program in this computer session, you will also see a blank document. Here, briefly, are your options of how to open a document:

1. Open your Office program using one of the techniques described earlier.

2. Do one of the following to open a new or existing document:

   - **Existing, recent**   From the initial Office screen, under Recent, click a filename to open a recently used document.

   - **New**   From the initial Office screen, click one of the templates listed in the right pane to open a new file.

   - **Existing, not recent**   From the initial Office screen, click **Open Other Documents** beneath the Recent list to search for an existing document not recently used.

   - **Existing, recent or not**   From a document window, click the **File** tab and then click **Open**, click **Recent Documents** to view them, or click the document location and search through recent folders or click **Browse** to find another one. (Perhaps you want to find an older file to use to start a new one, or maybe you've just opened an incorrect document.)

   - **New**   From a document window, click **File** and then click **New**. Click one of the listed templates or search for another one.

▷▷ Open a New Office Document

As you just read, when you start an Office program, you can immediately choose which kind of a document to open—a new one or an existing one (as shown in Figure 1-2). When you open a new file, you must first select a template. For instance, if you click Blank Document, you'll open a document with a "normally" formatted template. If you open any other document in the right pane (other than Take A Tour), you'll open a document with a template that has a specific design or format. See the "Using Templates" QuickFacts. Regardless of the template applied,

opening a new document displays a blank document pane in which you can start creating the new content immediately—be it a Word document, an Excel workbook, or a PowerPoint presentation. If you don't see a template you like, you can search Office Online for more suggestions (http://office.microsoft.com/en-us/templates/).

You can create a new document when you open one of the three Office programs:

1. From the initial Office screen or the document window (click **File** and then **New**), scroll through the list of available templates to view the options. Here are a few offered in Word, as shown in Figure 1-2— the other Office programs offer templates suitable for their uses:

   - **Blank Document**   Template for a blank document to which you can apply your own formatting and design from scratch

   - **Blog Post**   Template for a simple blog post

   - **Single Spaced (Blank)**   Template for a single-spaced modern document

   - **Ion Design (Blank)**   Template for a document featuring the Ion design, a clean look with a touch of personality

2. When you find a design you'd like to see more of, click it. You'll see the design expanded with a short description of what the template offers, such as shown in Figure 1-3.

3. When you find a template you want, click **Create**. A document based on the selected template will open.

▷▷ Locate and Open an Existing Document

You may also want to open and work on an Office document that has already been created (by you or someone else) in the same Office program or in a different Office program. To do this, you must first locate the document and then open it in the appropriate Office program. You can either locate the document directly from the Office program or search for it.

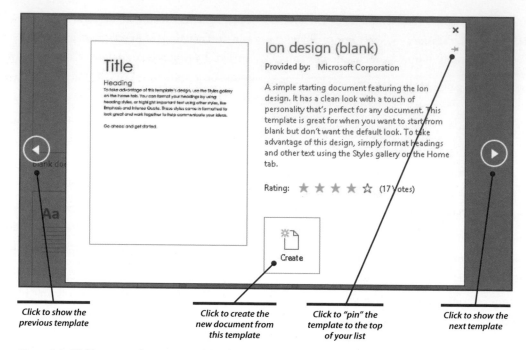

Click to show the previous template

Click to create the new document from this template

Click to "pin" the template to the top of your list

Click to show the next template

Figure 1-3: Clicking a template opens a view of it, allowing you to scroll through other templates.

 **QuickFacts**

Using Templates

A *template* is a special kind of document that is used as a pattern or the basis for other documents you create. For instance, you might want to create a business letter, marketing presentation, or budget with the appropriate design and format already applied. The template is said to be "attached" to the document, and every Office document must have a template attached to it. The template acts as the framework around which you create your document. The document that is opened automatically when you start an Office blank document uses a default template called Normal.dotm (versions of Word prior to 2007 used Normal.dot). This is referred to as "the Normal template" and contains standard formatting settings. (Excel uses a file extension of .xltx for its templates; PowerPoint uses .potx.) Other templates can contain boilerplate text, design or formatting options for the types of documents they create, and even automating procedures. Word, Excel, and PowerPoint are installed on your computer with a number of templates that you can use, and you can access other templates, both on your computer and through Office Online. You can create for your business or organization your own templates that make all your documents similar in appearance, regardless of the program.

When you first open an Office program, you'll see a screen similar to the one shown earlier in Figure 1-2 (for Word). If the file is one you've used recently, it will be listed on the left beneath Recent. If the file has not been opened recently with the program, you'll have to search for it.

1. To open a file from the initial Office screen, as shown in Word in Figure 1-2, look through the files listed under Recent and click the one you want to open. The document pane opens with the selected document present.

–Or–

If the list of recent documents doesn't contain the one you want, click **Open Other Documents** at the bottom of the list and go to step 2.

2. You have a choice of five sources of where the document might be found:

- **Recent Documents** Lists the documents that have been opened recently. If you see the one you want, just click it and it will open in the document pane.

- **SkyDrive** Click this if your document is stored on the SkyDrive rather than on your computer. (See the "Using SkyDrive" QuickFacts for more information.)

- **Other Web Locations** Allows you to locate a document on another website. If this is what you want, click and use your browser to find and open the file. (You may not see this on your screen if you have no web-based files other than SkyDrive.)

- **Computer** Allows you to search using File Explorer if the document is stored on your hard disk or on your network.

- **Add A Place** Allows you to specify a new location where your document may be found if you use SharePoint or another SkyDrive, for instance.

3. Select the location where the file is stored. Double-click the drive, folder, or sequence of folders you need to open in order to find the document.

4. When you have found the document you want to open, double-click it. It will appear in your Office program, ready for you to begin your work.

If you have a hard time finding a document using the direct approach just described, you can search for it either in the Office program or in Windows.

 **QuickFacts**

Using SkyDrive

We've all heard of "the cloud," where you can store your documents, videos, and photos online rather than on a hard disk. SkyDrive is the cloud for Microsoft Office. You can easily store and retrieve documents from SkyDrive in Office 2013 using Windows Explorer. On your hard disk, you establish a SkyDrive folder. Everything you want on SkyDrive is put there. Everything in the folder is automatically uploaded to SkyDrive, and Microsoft synchronizes the content between your computer and SkyDrive. That is, every time you change something in the computer folder, it is also changed in the SkyDrive copy, and vice versa. Your documents are always updated. SkyDrive is structured similarly to what you would find on your hard disk, with files and folders. See "Get SkyDrive for Your Files" later in the chapter to create an online folder.

Using SkyDrive has several advantages. If you are traveling, for instance, you can access your files from anywhere (even from an unfamiliar computer), such as a laptop or Internet café. If you have a document you want to share with someone else, you can make it available just to them. This is particularly handy for larger files, where you can bypass e-mail delivery, downloading documents more rapidly without requiring storage space on a computer. If anyone changes the SkyDrive document, everyone sees the updates.

▷▷ Save a Document for the First Time

As you are working with your document, you'll want to save it to avoid the chance of losing your work. Then, when you're finished, you'll need to save it one more time to disk. You can save it to your computer, the SkyDrive, or another web location.

The first time you save a document, you have to specify where you want to save it—that is, the disk drive and the folder or subfolder in which you want it saved. If this is your first time saving the file, the Save As page will appear so that you can specify the location and enter a file name.

1. Click the **File** tab and click **Save As**.

2. On the Save As page, click the destination location:

   - Click **SkyDrive** to save the file online in the cloud.

   - Click **Computer** to save the file on your hard disk or a network location.

   - Click **Add A Place** "to add a SharePoint location or another SkyDrive location to your Save As places and then save the file there.

3. Continue with the selected destination as described next.

Save to SkyDrive

1. On the Save As page, click *yourname's* **SkyDrive** and then click **Browse**. A dialog box is displayed listing the folders and files on SkyDrive.

2. If you already have an appropriate folder you want to use for this document within the SkyDrive folder, double-click that folder and click **Save**. Your document is added to the online folder.

3. If you do not have a folder in which you want to store your document, click **New Folder**, name the new folder, press **ENTER**, and click **Open** or double-click it to select it.

4. Click **Save** to save the document.

Get SkyDrive for Your Files

If you want to store your files online in the "cloud," you first need to establish a Windows Live ID, and then an account with SkyDrive and create a SkyDrive folder on your computer. Then, you can easily store and retrieve your files online, with all the benefits (see the "Using SkyDrive" QuickFacts).

1. Click the **File** tab, click **Open**, and then click **SkyDrive**.

2. Click **Learn More**. Read the privacy statement and the service agreement, and if you agree to the terms and conditions, click **Download**.

3. Click **Run** to run SkyDrive, and then click **Yes** to allow Microsoft to access your computer. A SkyDrive folder will be installed on your computer. It is now available for you to store and retrieve documents, photos, videos, and other content.

 NOTE After you have established your SkyDrive account, you can access it from anywhere with a web browser by going to https://skydrive.live.com/ and logging in. You can then download files to your computer or mobile phone.

Save to Your Computer

On the Save As page, click **Computer**. You then have several options:

- Under Recent Folders, find the one you want, if it is listed, and double-click it. In the Save As dialog box (a Word example is shown in Figure 1-4), verify the file name is what you want and click **Save**.

- If the folder you want is not listed under Recent Folders, click **Browse**, find the folder in which to save the file and double-click it. Then click **Save**.

- If you want to store your new document in a new folder, open the Save As dialog box by using either of the previous actions, click **New Folder** in the toolbar, type the name of the new folder, and press **ENTER**. Click **Open** and then click **Save**.

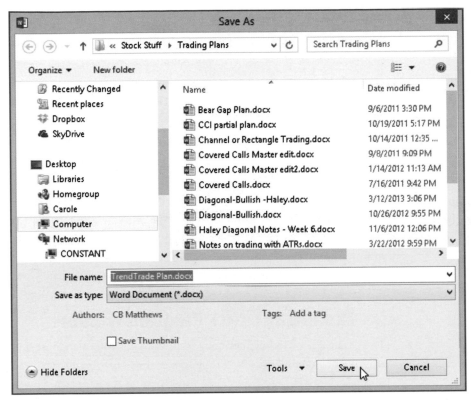

Figure 1-4: Saving a file insures that your work will not be lost—do it often.

 TIP When saving a file, you don't have to enter a file extension in the Save As Type field unless you want to change the default. For example, the .docx extension will be supplied by Word automatically.

Add Another New Place

You can add another place to save and retrieve your files with the Add A Place option. You are given two initial possibilities: a SharePoint destination, and SkyDrive. In both cases, you'll have to sign in with your Windows Live ID before you can access the files.

1. Click **Office 365 SharePoint** or **SkyDrive**. A Sign-in To Office dialog box is displayed.
2. Click **Sign In** and follow the prompts to enter your ID and password.

 Save a Document Automatically

It is important to save a document periodically as you work. Having an Office program save it automatically will reduce the chance of losing data in case of a power failure or other interruption. Although the option to save automatically is turned on by default, as well as a default time interval for saving , you can change these.

1. Click the **File** tab, click **Options**, and click the **Save** option on the left.
2. Beneath Save Documents (or Presentations or Files, depending on the program), make sure the **Save AutoRecover Information Every** *x* **Minutes** check box is selected.

3. The save interval is initially set at 10 minutes. To change it, click the **Minutes** arrows to select a time interval for how often the Office program should save your document.
4. Click **OK** to close the dialog box.

CAUTION As good as Office's automatic saving feature is, it won't be of help if your hard disk fails. If you are working on an important document, consider manually saving your document to a separate disk drive as well, such as a USB drive, periodically while you work.

Save a Document as a Copy or as a Template

After you have initially saved a document and specified its location, you can quickly use it to create a copy or a template.

Save a Copy of Your Document

When you save a document under a different name, you create a copy of it.

1. Click the **File** tab and then click **Save As**. Click the destination drive, Computer or SkyDrive (or another place if you added one, or click **Add A Place** to add a new one, as described earlier). Click the folder name under Recent Folders, or click **Browse**.

2. In the Save As dialog box, enter the new name in the File Name text box.

3. Click **Save**.

Save a Document as a Template

To save a document as a template from which to create new documents:

1. Click the **File** tab and then click **Save As**. Click the destination drive, Computer or SkyDrive (or another place if you added one, or click **Add A Place** to add a new one, as described earlier).

2. Click the folder name under Recent Folders, or click **Browse**. Select the folder(s) in which to store the template, and enter a name (without an extension) for the template in the File Name text box.

3. In the Save As dialog box, click the **Save As Type** drop-down list box, and click the Office program template, such as Word Template (*.dotx), Excel Template (*.xltx), or PowerPoint Template (*.potx).

4. Click **Save**.

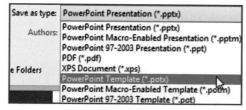

Close an Office Document

To close a document in Word, Excel, or PowerPoint, click the **File** tab in the upper-left corner of the Office program window, and click **Close**.

EXPLORE AN OFFICE PROGRAM

Office 2013 provides a wide assortment of windows, ribbon tabs, toolbars, menus, and special features to help you accomplish your tasks. Much of this book explores how to find and use all of those items. In this section you'll see and learn how to use the most common features of the default window, including the various parts of the window, the tabs on the ribbon, and the task pane. (We are using Word for our examples, but most of the Office programs are similar. Specific differences in similar programs will be pointed out in the individual program chapters.)

Explore an Office Program Window

The Office 2013 window has many features to aid you in creating and editing documents. Figure 1-5 shows an example of what is presented to you by Word (front), Excel, and PowerPoint (back) when you open a new document and click the Home tab. You can see the primary parts of the ribbon in Figure 1-6. Although we are using Word as our example, the principal features of the window, including the various ribbon tabs, are similar throughout the Office programs, so we are describing those common features in this section; specific differences for each program are explained in the corresponding chapters of this book.

> **TIP** To gain working space in the document pane, you can minimize the size of the ribbon. To do this, double-click the active tab name. Click it again to restore the size of the ribbon.

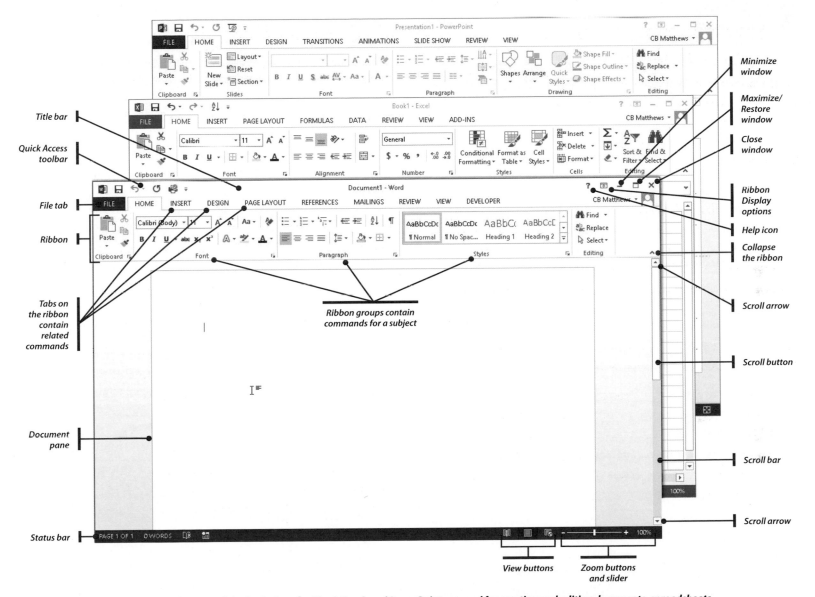

Title bar

Quick Access toolbar

File tab

Ribbon

Tabs on the ribbon contain related commands

Document pane

Status bar

Minimize window

Maximize/ Restore window

Close window

Ribbon Display options

Help icon

Collapse the ribbon

Scroll arrow

Scroll button

Scroll bar

Scroll arrow

Ribbon groups contain commands for a subject

View buttons

Zoom buttons and slider

Figure 1-5: The Office 2013 default windows for Word, Excel, and PowerPoint are used for creating and editing documents, spreadsheets, and slide shows, respectively.

Understanding the Ribbon

The *ribbon*, the container at the top of most Office program windows, holds the tools and features you are most likely to use (see Figure 1-6, which uses Word as an example). The ribbon collects tools for a given function into *groups*—for example, the Font group provides the tools to work with text. Groups are then organized into tabs for working on likely tasks. For example, the Insert tab contains groups for adding components, such as tables, links, and charts, to your slide, spreadsheet, or document. Each Office program has a default set of tabs with additional *contextual* tabs that appear as the context of your work changes. For instance, when you select a picture, a Format tab containing shapes and drawing tools that you can use with the particular object appears beneath the defining tools tab (such as the Picture Tools tab); when the object is unselected, the Format tab disappears. Depending on the tool, you are then presented with additional options in the form of a list of commands, a dialog box or task pane, or galleries of choices that reflect what you'll see in your work. Groups that contain several more tools than can be displayed in the ribbon include a *dialog box launcher* icon that takes you directly to these other choices.

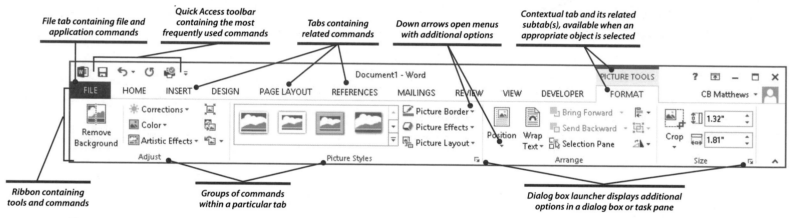

File tab containing file and application commands

Quick Access toolbar containing the most frequently used commands

Tabs containing related commands

Down arrows open menus with additional options

Contextual tab and its related subtab(s), available when an appropriate object is selected

Ribbon containing tools and commands

Groups of commands within a particular tab

Dialog box launcher displays additional options in a dialog box or task pane

Figure 1-6: Organized into tabs and then groups, the commands and tools on the ribbon are how you create, edit, and otherwise work with documents and Outlook items.

Use the Mouse

A *mouse* is any pointing device—including trackballs, pointing sticks, and graphic tablets—with one or more buttons. This book assumes a two-button mouse. Moving the mouse moves the pointer on the screen. You *select* an object on the screen by moving the pointer so that it is on top of the object and then pressing the left button on the mouse.

Five actions can be accomplished with the mouse:

- **Point** at an *object* on the screen (a button, an icon, a menu or one of its options, or a border) to highlight it. To *point* means to move the mouse so that the tip of the pointer is on top of the object.

- **Click an object** on the screen to select it, making that object the item that your next actions will affect. Clicking will also open a menu, select a menu option, or activate a button or "tool" on a toolbar or the ribbon. *Click* means to point at an object you want to select and quickly press and release the left mouse button.

- **Double-click** an object to open or activate it. *Double-click* means to point at an object you want to select, then press and release the left mouse button twice in rapid succession.

- **Right-click** an object to open a context menu containing commands used to manipulate that object. *Right-click* means to point at an object you want to select, then quickly press and release the right mouse button. For example, right-clicking selected text opens the adjacent context menu.

- **Drag** an object to move it on the screen to where you want it moved within the document. *Drag* means to point at an object you want to move and then press and hold the left mouse button while moving the mouse. The pointer will morph into an arrow and rectangle and as you drag it, the insertion point is moved so you can precisely place the object. When the insertion point is where you want it, release the mouse button.

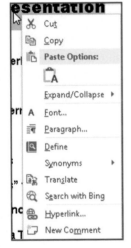

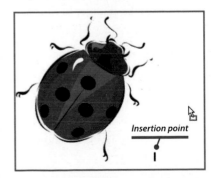

Insertion point

Place the Insertion Point by dragging the mouse to the position in the text or textbox where you want the insertion point placed, and then clicking it. The insertion point is moved to where you click.

Use the Mini Toolbar

When you select text, a mini text toolbar is displayed that allows you to perform a function directly on the text, such as making text bold or centering a paragraph. This toolbar contains a subset of the tools contained in the Font and Paragraph groups of the Home tab.

Display and Use the Text Toolbar

1. Select text by double-clicking it or dragging over the text.

2. Place the pointer over the text, and the mini toolbar is displayed. If it fades, move the mouse over it to make it clearer.

3. Click a button or icon on the mini toolbar that represents the tool to do something. For instance, click **Bold** to make the selected text boldface.

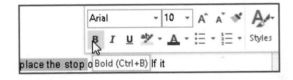

TIP If the mini toolbar starts to fade, you can make it clearer by placing the pointer over it.

Hide or Show the Mini Toolbar

You can hide the mini toolbar by changing the default setting.

1. Click the **File** tab, and click **Options**.

2. Click the **General** option.

3. Under User Interface Options, click the **Show Mini Toolbar On Selection** check box to remove the check mark, which hides the mini toolbar.

4. Click **OK** to finalize the choice.

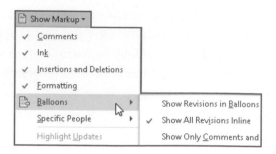

> **TIP** If you decide you want to see the mini toolbar, follow these steps again and replace the check mark in the **Show Mini Toolbar On Selection** check box.

▷▷ Use Tabs and Menus

Tabs are displayed at the top of the ribbon or a dialog box. Menus are displayed when you click a down arrow on a ribbon button, in a dialog box, or on a toolbar. Here are some of the ways to use tabs and menus:

- To open a tab or menu with the mouse, click the tab or menu.

- To open a tab or menu with the keyboard, press **ALT** followed by the highlighted letter in the tab or menu name. For example, press **ALT** followed by **F** to open the File menu. The identifying keys are displayed when you press **ALT** by itself, as shown here.

- To select a tab or menu command, click the tab or menu to open it, and then click the option.

- A number of menu options have a right-pointing arrow on their right to indicate that a submenu is associated with that option. To open the submenu, move the mouse pointer to the menu option with a submenu (it will have a right-pointing arrow). The submenu will open. Move the mouse pointer to the submenu, and click the desired option.

> **NOTE** To help clarify things later—some options have dual functionality; that is, you can click the option label to perform the stated action, or you can click its down arrow to have other choices. To "Click *Labelname*" means the former; to "Click the *Labelname* down arrow" means the latter.

▷▷ Use Various Views

Each of the Office programs presents documents in several views, allowing you to choose which view facilitates the task you are doing. To access a view, click the **View** tab and then click a Views group button. Here are the various views for Word, Excel, and PowerPoint (Outlook handles its views differently and is explained in Chapter 11):

Word displays five possible views:

Word Document Views group

- **Read Mode** displays the text without the ribbon and more like a book, giving you a larger reading space where you can "turn" to the next page. Click the **View** menu on the top of the window to change to another view or to make changes to the page layout or color.

- **Print Layout** displays the text as it looks on a printed page and is the default view. This is also how you edit the document normally.

- **Web Layout** shows how the text will look as a web page.

- **Outline** displays the text in outline form with a contextual Outlining tab on the ribbon. You can use this view to promote and demote levels of text and rearrange levels, as shown in the Outline Tools group. With the Show Document button, you can toggle commands to extend your ability to create, insert, link, merge, split, and lock the document. Click **Close Outline View** to return to the Print Layout view.

- **Draft** displays the text of the document in draft status for quick and easy editing. Headings and footings may not be visible.

Excel displays five possible views:

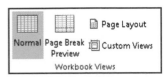

Excel Workbook Views group

- **Normal** displays the normal spreadsheet view with numbered rows and lettered columns and is the default view.
- **Page Layout** displays the spreadsheet as it looks on a printed page.
- **Page Break Preview** displays where the spreadsheet has page breaks and allows you to change them.
- **Custom Views** allows you to select a custom view or add the current view to the list of custom views.

PowerPoint contains four possible views:

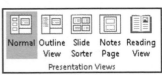

PowerPoint Presentation Views group

- **Normal** displays the currently selected slide in the Presentation pane on the right, and displays the Slides pane on the left.
- **Outline View** displays the slide presentation in outline format in the Outline pane on the left, and displays the currently selected slide in the Presentation pane on the right.
- **Slide Sorter** displays thumbnails of slides in the Slides pane.

- **Notes Page** displays a "split" page showing the slide and any notes that have been entered for that slide.
- **Reading View** displays a slide show that fits within the window, as opposed to the full screen you see when you start the slide show.

PERSONALIZE AND CUSTOMIZE OFFICE 2013 PROGRAMS

You can personalize your Office program, or make it your own, by changing its default settings for options such as which tools are available on the Quick Access toolbar, which color scheme is used for the screen background, and which user name and initials are displayed for you when you revise or add comments to a document. You can customize your Office program by customizing the general defaults on editing, proofing, display, and other options. Many of these options will be discussed in the appropriate chapters for the corresponding Office programs. In this section we will look at how you can personalize the Quick Access toolbar, the display, and other popular options.

Work with the Quick Access Toolbar

The Quick Access toolbar that appears by default in the upper-left corner of the Word, Excel, Outlook, and PowerPoint windows can become your "best friend" if you modify it so that it fits your own way of working.

> **TIP** You can add a command to the Quick Access toolbar from the ribbon by right-clicking the button and choosing **Add To Quick Access Toolbar**.

Add a Command to the Quick Access Toolbar

The Quick Access toolbar contains the commands that are most commonly used. The default commands for all Office programs are Save, Undo, and Redo (and Next Item and Previous Item in Outlook).

You can add to the Quick Access toolbar the commands that you use on a regular basis as follows:

1. Click the **File** tab, and click **Options**.

2. Click the **Quick Access Toolbar** option. If you are using Word, you will see the dialog box shown in Figure 1-7.

3. Open the **Choose Commands From** drop-down list box on the left, and select the type of command you want from the listed options.

4. In the list box on the left, find and click the command you want to add to the toolbar, and then click **Add** to move its name to the list box on the right. Repeat this for all the commands you want to add to the Quick Access toolbar.

5. Click **OK** when you are finished.

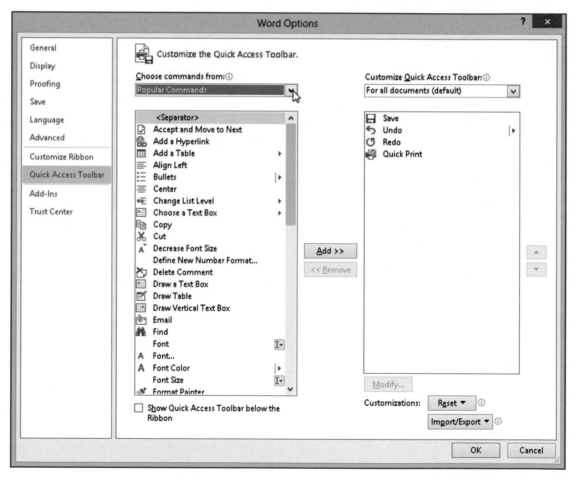

Figure 1-7: You can customize the Quick Access toolbar by adding and removing commands for easy and quick access using the options, such as these for Word.

NOTE To remove a tool from the Quick Access Toolbar, right-click the tool to be removed and click **Remove From Quick Access Toolbar** on the context menu.

Move the Quick Access Toolbar

To move the Quick Access toolbar beneath the ribbon, right-click anywhere on the **Quick Access toolbar**, and click **Show Quick Access Toolbar Below The Ribbon**.

Show or Hide ScreenTips

When you hold your pointer over a command or tool, a screen tip is displayed by default. The screen tip may be just the name of the tool or command, or it may be enhanced with a small feature description. You can hide the ScreenTips or choose not to see the feature descriptions.

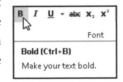

1. Click the **File** tab in Word, Excel, Outlook, or PowerPoint, and click **Options**.
2. Click the **General** option.
3. Under User Interface Options, click the **ScreenTip Style** drop-down list, and choose the option you want.
4. Click **OK** to finalize the choice.

Change the Screen Color

The theme color of the Office program screen is set to white by default. You can change the screen to light gray or dark gray.

1. Click the **File** button in Word, Excel, Outlook, or PowerPoint, and click **Options**.
2. Click the **General** tab.

3. Under Personalize Your Copy Of Microsoft Office, click the **Office Theme** down arrow, and click the color you want. The default is White.

White   Light Gray   Dark Gray

4. Click **OK** to save the change.

Add Identifying Information

You can add identifying information to a document to make it easier to organize your information and to find it during searches, especially in a shared environment. In Word, Excel, and PowerPoint (Outlook doesn't have this capability):

1. Click the **File** tab, click **Info**, click **Properties** in the right pane, and then click **Show Document Panel**. A Document Properties panel containing standard identifiers displays under the ribbon, as shown for Word in Figure 1-8.
2. Type identifying information, such as title, subject, and keywords (words or phrases that are associated with the document).
3. To view more information about the document, click the **Document Properties** down arrow in the panel's title bar, and click **Advanced Properties**. Review each tab in the Properties dialog box to see the information available, and make any changes or additions. Close the Properties dialog box when you're finished by clicking **OK**.

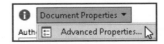

4. Close the Document Properties panel by clicking **X** in the upper-right corner of the panel.

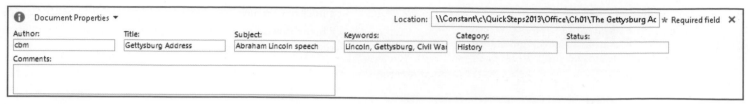

Figure 1-8: A Document Properties panel beneath the ribbon allows you to add identifying data to your document so that it is easier to locate using search tools.

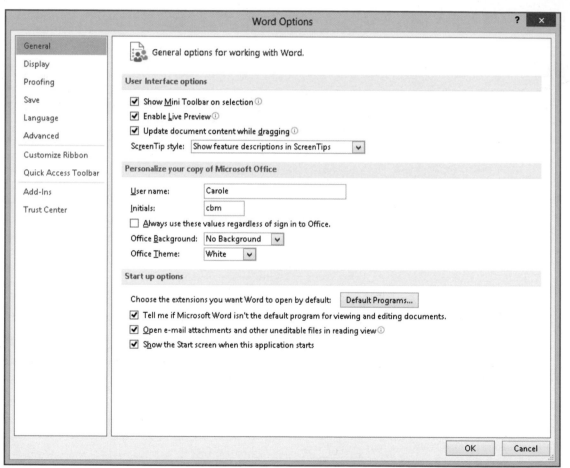

Figure 1-9: Some basic preferences used in Word are set in the General options view.

Set General Preferences

Setting preferences allows you to adapt your Office program to your needs and inclinations. The Word, Excel, Outlook, or PowerPoint Options dialog box provides access to these settings.

1. Click the **File** tab, and then click **Options**.

2. Click the General options (see Figure 1-9 for Word's General options, which are discussed in the following list; the specific options available differ from program to program).

   • Review and select the options that you prefer by clicking to put a check mark in the corresponding check box. Earlier in this chapter, you saw how to disable the mini toolbar, show and hide ScreenTips, and change the color scheme of the Word window. If you are unsure about other options, keep the default settings and see how well those settings work for you.

- In the User Name text box, type the user name you want displayed in documents that you revise using Track Changes.

- In the Initials text box, type the initials associated with the user name that will be displayed in comments you insert into a document.

- Under Start Up Options, check the **Open E-mail Attachments And Other Uneditable Files In Reading View** check box if you want to open Word e-mail attachments in full-screen Read Mode view.

3. When you have set the General options you want, click each of the other categories of options (such as Display or Proofing), reviewing the settings and making the changes you want. These are discussed further in the applicable chapters.

4. When you have finished selecting your preferences, click **OK** to close the Office program Options dialog box.

⟩⟩ Use AutoCorrect

AutoCorrect is a feature that helps you type information correctly. For example, it corrects simple typing errors and makes certain assumptions about what you want to type. You can turn it off or change its rules.

Turn AutoCorrect Options On or Off

The AutoCorrect feature assumes that you will always want certain corrections made while you type. Among these corrections, AutoCorrect by default changes the second of two initial capital letters in a word to lowercase; capitalizes the first letter of each sentence; capitalizes the first letter of table cells and names of days; corrects the accidental use of the CAPS LOCK key; and replaces misspelled words with the results it assumes you want. (See "Change AutoCorrect Spelling Corrections" later in this chapter to retain the correction of misspelled words but change the corrections that are made.) To turn off the automatic spelling corrections that an Office program makes:

Figure 1-10: The AutoCorrect dialog box is where you change the automatic corrections.

1. Click the **File** tab, and click **Options**.

2. Click **Proofing**, and then click **AutoCorrect Options** to open the AutoCorrect Options dialog box, shown in Figure 1-10.

3. Find the option you want to turn off or on, and click the relevant check box. If a check mark is in the box, the option is enabled; otherwise, the option is turned off.

Change AutoCorrect Spelling Corrections

Your Office program may automatically correct spellings that are not really incorrect. You can add a new spelling correction, replace a current spelling correction with a new one, or replace the result that is now used. You do this by replacing one word with another in the AutoCorrect dialog box. When you first open the dialog box, both the Replace and With boxes are blank. In this case, you simply add what you want. Here are the directions for how you add and replace AutoCorrect entries.

1. Click the **File** tab, and click the **Options** button. Then click **Proofing**.

2. Click the **AutoCorrect Options** button to open the AutoCorrect dialog box. If it is not already selected, click the **AutoCorrect** tab, as shown in Figure 1-10.

   - To add new entries when both the Replace and With boxes are blank, fill in the **Replace** and **With** boxes, and click **Add**.

   - To replace entries in the Replace and With boxes, click in the appropriate box and type your new text. If you type over the Replace box contents click **Add**. If you type over the With text contents, click **Replace**. The "old" text will not be deleted; it is still in the list. To eliminate an entry in the list, you must select it and then click the **Delete** button.

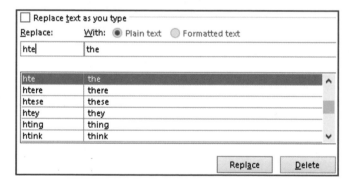

   - To delete and replace an entry in the AutoCorrect list, click the entry to be replaced, and click **Delete**. Then type the new spelling option. Click **Add**.

USE COMMON OFFICE TOOLS

Office offers many common tools and commands among its programs. This section presents the following five tools that you may find handy:

- Help
- Thesaurus
- Translate
- Clipboard
- Spell checker

▷▷ Open Help

The Office Help system is maintained online at Microsoft. It is easily accessed.

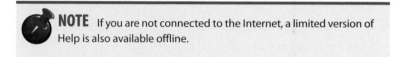
NOTE If you are not connected to the Internet, a limited version of Help is also available offline.

Click the **Help** icon [**?**] to open the Office program Help window, shown in Figure 1-11 for Word.

- Find the topic for which you want help, and click it.

   –Or–

- Type words in the Search text box, and click the **Search Online Help** icon.

On the toolbar at the top of the Office program Help window are several options for navigating through the topics and printing one out, as shown in Figure 1-12.

▷▷ Use the Thesaurus

You can find synonyms for words with the Thesaurus feature in all Office programs.

1. To use the Thesaurus, first select the word for which you want to search for synonyms.

Figure 1-11: When you click the Help icon, you will see the Office program Help dialog box, where you can click the topic for which you want help or search for more specific words.

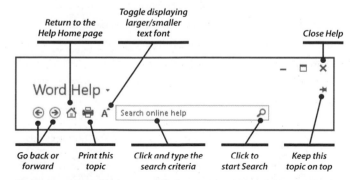

Return to the Help Home page

Toggle displaying larger/smaller text font

Close Help

Go back or forward *Print this topic* *Click and type the search criteria* *Click to start Search* *Keep this topic on top*

Figure 1-12: The Help toolbar helps you navigate through the topics and then print them out.

2. Click the **Review** tab, and in the Proofing group, click **Thesaurus**. The Thesaurus task pane will appear with the most likely synonyms listed.

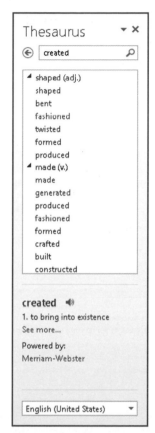

3. Move your pointer over a word in the list, click its down arrow, and click either **Insert** to replace the selected text with the synonym or **Copy** to copy the synonym but leave the selected text intact.

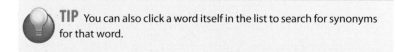

TIP You can also click a word itself in the list to search for synonyms for that word.

4. Click **Close** to remove the task pane.

Translate a Document

The options for Translate differ slightly between Word, Excel, Outlook, and PowerPoint. In this section we use Word to explain this function, but Excel, Outlook, and PowerPoint are similar.

Translate Selected Words

You can translate selected words in two ways: selecting specific words to be translated or relying on the mini translator.

1. Click the **Review** tab, and in the Language group, click the **Translate** down arrow.

2. Click **Choose Translation Language**, and in the dialog box that opens, choose your language preferences. Click **OK** to close the dialog box.

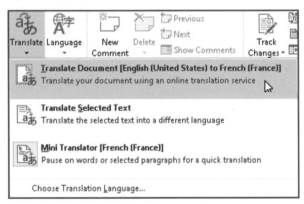

3. Again click the **Translate** down arrow, and then click either of the following options:

   • **Translate Selected Text**   Click this option if you have specific text selected that you want to translate. The Research task pane will appear with the translation as its source reference, as shown in Figure 1-13. If the languages are not correct in the task pane, click the **From** and **To** down arrows, and click the appropriate languages. The translation will be automatically displayed beneath the Bilingual Dictionary label and your selected word or phrase.

   • **Mini Translator [***Language (Country)***]**   Click this option if you want to be able to move your mouse over a word or phrase and see its translation displayed in a pop-up translation box.

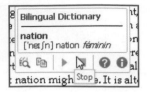

Translate a Whole Document

Translating a whole document requires that the document be sent online to a translating service. It is an unsecured site, so if you are concerned about the privacy of a document, don't send it for translation.

To translate a whole document from one language to another:

1. Click the **Review** tab, and in the Language group, click the **Translate** down arrow.

2. Click **Translate Document**. You'll see a cautionary message about the security of the process. If you want to proceed, click **Send**. If not, click **Don't Send**. Alternatively, to translate the whole document, you can open the Research task pane (as described in the previous section and shown in Figure 1-13), and click the green **Search** arrow under Translate The Whole Document.

3. Your document will open in a browser. You are offered several views: Side By Side (shown in Figure 1-14),

Figure 1-13: You can use the Research task pane to translate selected words into other languages.

The browser window shows the Microsoft Translator page with the URL http://www.microsofttranslator.com/bv.aspx?&lo=SS&frc and the following content:

Translate URL http:// **English** → **French** Views Report a problem w

Translated 100%

THE GETTYSBURG ADDRESS

Gettysburg, Pennsylvania
November 19, 1863

Abraham Lincoln

Four score and seven years ago our fathers brought forth on this continent, a new nation, conceived in Liberty, and dedicated to the proposition that all men are created equal. Now we are engaged in a great civil war, testing whether that nation or any nation so conceived and so dedicated, can long endure. We are met on a great battle-field of that war. We have come to dedicate a portion of that field, as a final resting place for those who here gave their lives that that nation might live. It is altogether fitting and proper that we should do this.

But, in a larger sense, we cannot dedicate -- we cannot consecrate -- we elected hallow -- this ground. The brave men, living and dead, who struggled here, have consecrated it, far above our poor power to add or detract. The world will little note, nor long remember what we say here, but it can never forget what they did here. It is for us the living, rather, to be dedicated here to the unfinished work which they who fought here have thus far so nobly advanced. It is rather for us to be here dedicated to the great task remaining before us -- that from these honored dead we take increased devotion to that cause for which they gave the last full measure of devotion -- that we here highly resolve that these dead shall not have died in vain --

LE DISCOURS DE GETTYSBURG

Gettysburg, Pennsylvanie
19 Novembre 1863

Abraham Lincoln

F notre score et il y a sept ans, nos pères enfantés sur ce continent, une nouvelle nation, conçue dans la liberté et dédié à la proposition voulant que tous les hommes sont créés égaux. Maintenant, nous sommes engagés dans une guerre civile, essai si cette nation ou n'importe quelle nation ainsi conçue et tellement dévoués, peut longtemps supporter. Nous sommes rencontré sur un grand champ de bataille de cette guerre. Nous sommes arrivés à consacrer une partie de ce domaine, comme un dernier lieu de repos pour ceux qui ici ont donné leurs vies que cette nation peut vivre. Il est tout à fait juste et bon que nous devrions le faire.

B ut, dans un sens plus large, nous ne pouvons pas consacrer-- nous ne pouvons pas consacrer--nous avons élu hallow--ce motif. Les braves, les vivants et les morts, qui se sont battus ici, ont consacré, bien au-delà de notre faible pouvoir d'ajouter ou non. Le monde sera peu noter, ni longtemps, n'oubliez pas ce que nous disons ici, mais il ne peut jamais oublier ce qu'ils faisaient ici. C'est pour nous les vivants, plutôt, de se consacrer ici à le œuvre inachevée qui eux qui se sont battus ici ont avancé jusqu'à présent si noblement. C'est plutôt pour nous ici consacrée à la grande tâche restant devant nous--que ces morts

Figure 1-14: You can translate a document using an Internet service as the translator.

Top/Bottom, Original With Hover Interpretation, and Translation With Original Hover. Select the view you want.

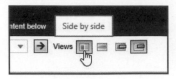

4. To save the translation, click **File** and then **Save As**. Find your path to the folder in which you want to save the translation, as described earlier in this chapter. Type in a name and click **Save**. Follow any other prompts in the browser's dialog box that you may encounter.

5. Close your browser when you're finished.

 NOTE You can translate a word or phrase by highlighting the text and then right-clicking the selection. Click **Translate** from the context menu. The word or phrase will be copied into the Research task pane and translated. Click the green **Search** arrow to initiate the translation for the whole document.

▷▷ Use the Office Clipboard

The Office Clipboard is shared by all Microsoft Office products. You can copy objects and text from any Office application and paste them into another Office application. The Clipboard can contain up to 24 items. The 25th item copied to the Clipboard will overwrite the first one.

Open the Clipboard

To display the Office Clipboard, click the **Home** tab, and then click the dialog box launcher in the lower-right corner of the Clipboard group. The Clipboard pane opens.

Add to the Clipboard

When you cut or copy text or a selected object, it is automatically added to the top of the Office Clipboard.

Copy Clipboard Items to a Placeholder

To paste one item from the Clipboard:

- Click to place the insertion point in the text, text box, or placeholder where you want to paste an item from the Clipboard. On the Clipboard, click the item that you want to paste at the insertion point.

  –Or–

- On the Clipboard, select the item to be inserted. Right-click the document where you want to paste the item, and click **Paste**.

To paste all items:

1. Click to place the insertion point in the text, text box, or placeholder where you want the items on the Office Clipboard inserted.

2. Click **Paste All** on the Clipboard.

Delete Items on the Clipboard

- To delete all items, click **Clear All** on the Clipboard pane.

- To delete a single item, click the arrow next to the item (displayed when you mouse over the item), and click **Delete**.

Set Clipboard Options

1. On the Clipboard pane, click the **Options** down arrow at the bottom. A context menu is displayed.

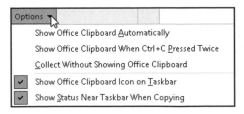

2. Click an option to select it (indicated with a check mark) or deselect it.

- **Show Office Clipboard Automatically** always shows the Office Clipboard when copying more than one item. When this option is checked, the following option is also selected automatically.

- **Show Office Clipboard When CTRL+C Pressed Twice** shows the Office Clipboard when you press **CTRL+C** twice to make two copies (in other words, copying two items to the Clipboard will cause the Clipboard to be displayed). This option will be automatically selected when the previous option is chosen.

- **Collect Without Showing Office Clipboard** copies items to the Clipboard without displaying the task pane.

- **Show Office Clipboard Icon On Taskbar** displays the icon when the Clipboard is being used. This option is checked by default.

- **Show Status Near Taskbar When Copying** displays a message about the items being added to the Clipboard as copies are made. This option is checked by default.

▷▷ Check Spelling

With its default settings, the spelling checker automatically runs in the background and flags (with a red underline) as potential misspellings any words that it can't find in its internal dictionary. If you prefer not to see the red underlining below potentially misspelled words, you can change the default setting so that it doesn't appear. Changing this setting doesn't turn off the spell checker—it's simply waiting for you to prompt it manually.

When you launch the spelling checker manually, it searches for words that are not in its internal dictionary. When it finds one, it displays the Spelling pane, shown in Figure 1-15.

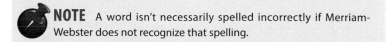

NOTE A word isn't necessarily spelled incorrectly if Merriam-Webster does not recognize that spelling.

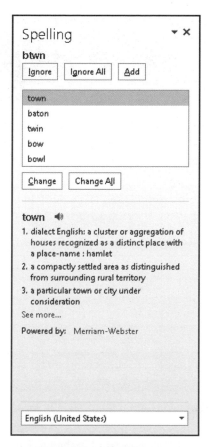

Figure 1-15: Use the Spelling pane to look for misspellings, correct them with suggested words or your own, and add words to the dictionary.

1. Click in the document where the spelling checker should begin.

2. To display the spelling checker, click **Spelling** (**Spelling and Grammar** in Word) in the Review tab Proofing group. The Spelling pane will appear when the spelling checker finds a word that is not in its internal dictionary.

TIP To use the spelling checker to quickly check an individual word that has been flagged as misspelled (with a red underline), right-click the word. A context menu will display one or more options for correct spellings, as shown next. Click the correct word if it is on the list. If the spelling checker has incorrectly flagged a word as being misspelled, you can either click **Ignore All** to ignore all occurrences of the word in the current document, or click **Add To Dictionary** so that the spell checker doesn't flag that word ever again in the current Office program.

- If the word is spelled incorrectly, look at the suggestions list, and click the suggestion you want to use. Click **Change** to change the one occurrence of the word, or click **Change All** to change all occurrences of that same word in the present document.

- If the identified word is spelled correctly but is not in the spell checker's internal dictionary, you can add the word to a custom dictionary by clicking **Add**, or you can skip the word by clicking **Ignore** or **Ignore All** (to skip all occurrences of the same word). The spelling checker will continue to the next misspelled word.

- Select one of the options below the selected word for synonyms of the word.

3. Click **Close** to end the search for spelling errors. When the spelling check is finished, a message will be displayed to that effect. Click **OK**.

⫸ Make Accessibility Changes

To ensure that everyone, including those with disabilities, will be able to enjoy your presentation:

1. Click the **File** tab, and click **Info**.

2. Click **Check For Issues** in the Inspect Presentation section in PowerPoint (or Inspect Workshop for Excel, or Inspect Document for Word).

3. Click **Check Accessibility** to open the Accessibility Checker as a pane in the PowerPoint window, as shown in Figure 1-16.

4. Review each item shown in the Inspection Results and follow any suggestions to fix the issue.

5. After you have completed your fixes, you will see a message stating no accessibility issues are found.

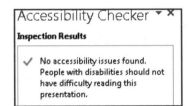

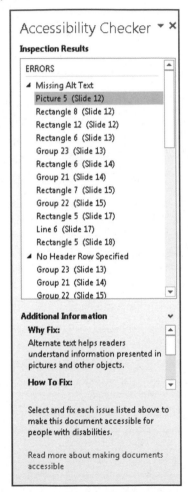

Figure 1-16: Use the Accessibility Check to ensure everyone can enjoy your presentation.

Chapter 2

Working with Documents in Word

Microsoft Office Word 2013 allows you to create and edit *documents*, such as letters, reports, invoices, plays, and books. Documents come in many forms these days, from the hard-back printed book, to ebooks on tablets and headlines on iPhones. This book itself was written in Word 2013. You may be viewing it in book form or on a tablet.

In the computer, a document is called a *file*, an object that has been given a name and is stored on a disk drive. For example, the name given to the file for this chapter is Chap02.docx. "Chap02" is the file name, and ".docx" is the file extension. By default, documents saved in Word 2013 are saved with the .docx extension.

In this chapter you'll briefly review from Chapter 1 how to create new documents and find existing ones. Then you'll see how to enter, change, and delete text; find and replace text; and select, copy, and move text. You'll also learn how to use some special tools, such as Building Blocks, highlighting, and hyphenation.

STEP INTO WORD

If you are already accustomed to working with Word, this section will serve as a review. If you are not acquainted with Word, this section will serve to introduce you to the important terms and concepts you need to understand to work with Word. Then it will give you a brief look at the different views you can use when creating a document, and introduce you to other important concepts and tools you'll find in Word.

Refer to Chapter 1 for instructions on how to open Word and customize your Desktop with shortcuts placed on your taskbar or Start menu so you can get to your documents with ease. Return here to learn "the rest of the story" about Word.

Use the Start Screen for Word

When you first open Word 2013, you'll see the Start screen, as shown in Figure 2-1. From here, you can start your document with one of the many listed templates, search online for additional choices, or base your new document on either a recent document or one you've created some time ago. You can also choose a blank template to start your document "from scratch." See Chapter 1 for information on how to start Word and choose your beginning document or template. This chapter contains only a brief review of opening a document and working with templates.

> **NOTE** To bypass the Start screen when you open Word 2013, open a document in Word, click **File**, and then click **Options**. On the General tab, under Start Up Options, clear the **Show The Start Screen When This Application Starts** check box. Click **OK** to save your selection.

Create a New Document

In the days before computers, creating a new document was termed "starting with a clean sheet of paper." Today, it is called "starting with a

blank screen"—which actually refers to a blank area within a window on the screen, as shown in Figure 2-2. Simply starting Word opens a blank document pane into which you can start typing a new document immediately.

The blinking bar in the upper-left corner of the document pane, called the *insertion point*, indicates where the text you type will appear. The I-beam mouse pointer shows you where the mouse pointer is, and where the insertion point will be relocated if you click the mouse. Your mouse pointer can be pointing to a different place than the insertion point. If the two point to different places in your text, you need to be aware that text you type will be inserted at the insertion point, not where the mouse pointer is pointing. However, the problem is solved when you click the mouse, which moves the insertion point to where you click.

> **TIP** Your ribbon options may vary depending on the size of your window. Windows that are not maximized in size display abbreviated options, such as the Editing group in Figure 2-2, on the right end of the ribbon.

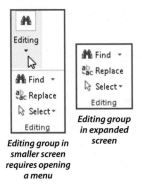

Editing group in smaller screen requires opening a menu

Editing group in expanded screen

You can create a new document in two ways: using the default, or "normal," blank document (the Normal.dotx template) or using a unique template on which to base the document. A template, as you learned in Chapter 1, acts as the framework around which you create your document. Every Word document must have a template attached to it.

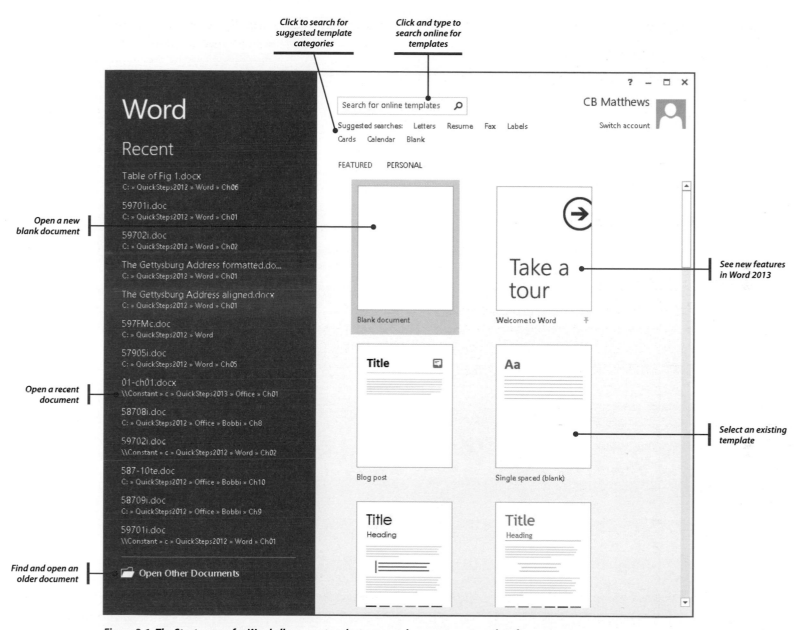

Figure 2-1: The Start screen for Word allows you to select a recent document or a template for a new one.

Click to search for suggested template categories

Click and type to search online for templates

Open a new blank document

Open a recent document

Find and open an older document

See new features in Word 2013

Select an existing template

Word

Recent

Table of Fig 1.docx
C: » QuickSteps2012 » Word » Ch06

59701i.doc
C: » QuickSteps2012 » Word » Ch01

59702i.doc
C: » QuickSteps2012 » Word » Ch02

The Gettysburg Address formatted.do...
C: » QuickSteps2012 » Word » Ch01

The Gettysburg Address aligned.docx
C: » QuickSteps2012 » Word » Ch01

597FMc.doc
C: » QuickSteps2012 » Word

57905i.doc
C: » QuickSteps2012 » Word » Ch05

01-ch01.docx
\\Constant » c » QuickSteps2013 » Office » Ch01

58708i.doc
C: » QuickSteps2012 » Office » Bobbi » Ch8

59702i.doc
\\Constant » c » QuickSteps2012 » Word » Ch02

587-10te.doc
C: » QuickSteps2012 » Office » Bobbi » Ch10

58709i.doc
C: » QuickSteps2012 » Office » Bobbi » Ch9

59701i.doc
\\Constant » c » QuickSteps2012 » Word » Ch01

📁 Open Other Documents

Search for online templates 🔍

Suggested searches: Letters   Resume   Fax   Labels
Cards   Calendar   Blank

FEATURED   PERSONAL

CB Matthews

Switch account

Blank document

Take a tour

Welcome to Word

Title

Blog post

Aa

Single spaced (blank)

Title
Heading

Title
Heading

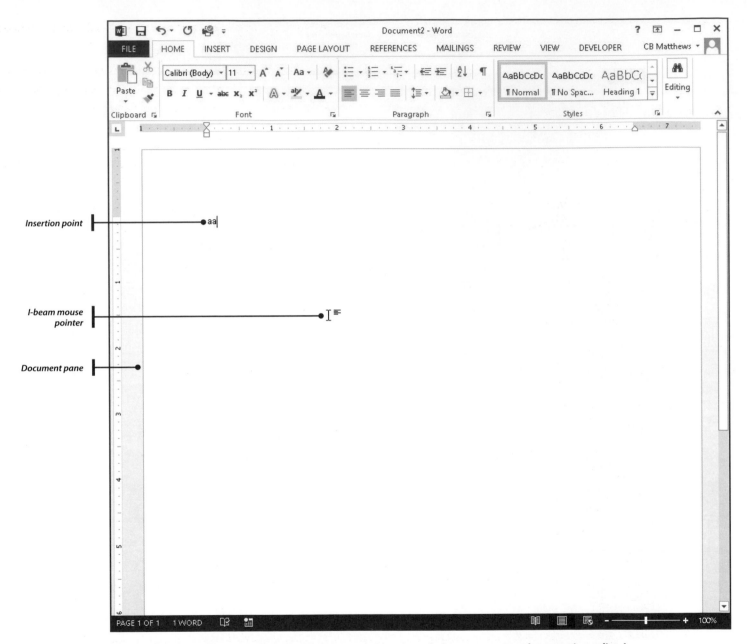

Insertion point

I-beam mouse pointer

Document pane

Figure 2-2: When you first start Word, the blank document pane is ready for you to create a document immediately.

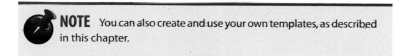

NOTE You can also create and use your own templates, as described in this chapter.

Use a Template on Your Computer

With Word open on your computer:

1. Click the **File** tab, and then click **New**. The New document page will open, as shown in Figure 2-3.

2. Scroll and find the template you want. Click it. For some templates, such as Blank Document, a blank document will open immediately in Word. For others, a preview of the selected template will open, as shown in Figure 2-4.

3. You can scroll through the previews by clicking the **Next** and **Previous** arrows. When you find the right template, click **Create**. A document with the selected template opens.

TIP As good as Word's automatic saving is, it is a great idea to manually save your document frequently (like a couple of times an hour). Doing this can save you the frustration of working several hours on a document only to lose it. See Chapter 1 for how to save a document or set the time interval for automatic saving.

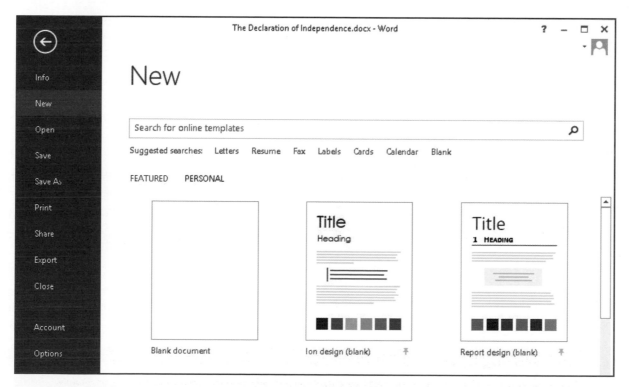

Figure 2-3: The New document page gives you choices for how to start a document.

Figure 2-4: When you open the template pane, you can scroll back and forward for more options or click Create to create a beginning document with a template you like.

Use an Office Online Template

When you download an Office Online template, it will be stored on your computer, available to you in the Template pane of the New document page, ready for your next use without needing to be downloaded again. To use an Office Online template, with Word open on your computer:

1. Click the **File** tab, and then click **New**. The New document page will appear.

2. In the Templates pane immediately beneath the Search text box is a Suggested Searches list of categories of templates (such as Letters and Resume). Click the category you want to see, and you'll see the possibilities for that category, as shown in Figure 2-5.

—Or—

Type a category of template you'd like to use in the Search text box and click **Search** (the magnifying glass icon).

3. Find the template you want to use, click it, and in the preview pane click **Create**. A new document is opened with the template in Word.

Create a Template

If you don't find a template that meets your needs, you can create your own. To do this, it's easiest to start with an existing template and modify it to suit your ongoing needs. Be sure to change the name of the template when you save it so that the original template is not modified.

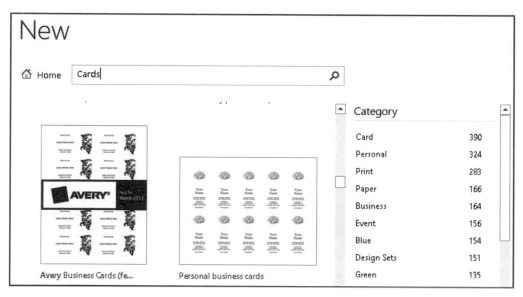

Figure 2-5: When you click a Suggested Search category of templates, you will have access to thousands of templates, organized by category for easier access.

This is particularly important if you are basing your new template on the Normal.dotx template.

1. Find the template you want to use as the basis for your new template and create a new document with it.

2. Add the recurring text, images, and formatting that you want to include in the new template (and, therefore, in each document that you create based upon that template).

3. Click the **File** tab and then click **Save As**.

4. On the Save As page, click the destination (Computer, for instance) and click **Browse**.

5. In the Save As dialog box enter the name for the new template file in the File Name box, set the Save As Type field to **Word Template (*.dotx)**, and click **Save**. The template should be saved in the default Custom Office Templates subfolder located in the My Documents folder.

 CAUTION If you use the Normal.dotx template as the basis for your new template but fail to save it under a different name after you make changes to it, those changes will be applied to all documents you create with Normal.dotx in the future. When you click **Save As**, make sure to change the name in the File Name box. If the Normal .dotx template is renamed, damaged, or moved, Word automatically creates a new version (with the original, default settings) the next time you start Word. The new version will not include any changes or modifications you made to the version that you renamed or moved.

Search for Existing Templates

When you first upgrade to Word 2013, templates from your previous version of Word are retained on your computer. Existing templates are often stored under %appdata%\Microsoft\Templates\. To find them:

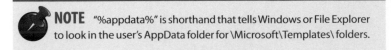

NOTE "%appdata%" is shorthand that tells Windows or File Explorer to look in the user's AppData folder for \Microsoft\Templates\ folders.

1. Copy and paste **%appdata%\Microsoft\Templates** into your Windows or File Explorer window address box and click the **Go** icon. You'll see a list of templates on the Templates screen.

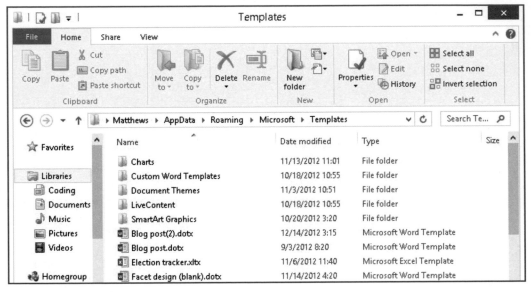

2. Click the template you want to use.

Change the Default Storage Folder for Templates

You can establish your own folder destination for new templates, rather than the default Custom Office Templates subfolder in the My Documents folder.

1. Click the **File** tab, click **Options**, and then click **Save**.

2. Under Save Documents, to the right of Default Local File Location, click **Browse**. In the Modify Location dialog box, find and click the folder you want to use to store the templates.

3. In the address box, click the folder icon to the left of the address to convert the contents to a valid URL. Then copy the address of the desired template folder from the address box in the Modify Location dialog box, and paste it into the **Default Personal Templates Location** text box.

4. Click **OK** to save the setting and close the dialog box.

New templates will be saved to the default location.

Locate and Open an Existing Document

After you create, save, and close a document, you may want to reopen it later, either to read it or to make further revisions. Similarly, you may want to open a Word document created by someone else, or open a document created in another program (as described in the following section). In either case, you must first locate the document, and then open it in Word. You can locate the document either directly from Word or by searching for it using Windows Explorer or File Explorer.

You'll find the steps to locate and open a document in Chapter 1. Refer there for the details of how to do it.

Import a Document

If you have a word-processing document created in a program other than Word, you can most likely open it and edit it in Word.

1. Click the **File** tab, and click **Open**. On the Open page, click the source location of the word-processing document (Computer, SkyDrive, or Other Web Locations) and click **Browse** to open the Open dialog box.

2. At the bottom of the Open dialog box, click the **File Name** drop-down list box to display the list of file types that you can directly open in Word (see Table 2-1 for a complete list). Click the one you want.

3. Navigate to the folder in which the document is located. Having selected the correct file type, the Open dialog box will list only files of that type.

4. Double-click the file you want to open. Depending on the file type, you may see a message stating Word needs to convert your file to an editable Word document. In that case, just click **OK**.

 TIP To return to the Word screen from a File menu page (such as the Open page), click the left-pointing arrow in the upper-left corner of the page.

Table 2-1: File Types That Word Can Open Directly

File Type	Extension
Plain text files	.txt
Rich Text Format files	.rtf
Web page files	.htm, .html, .mht, .mhtml
Word 97 to 2003 files	.doc
Word 97 to 2003 template files	.dot
Word 2007 to 2013 document files (macro-enabled)	.docx (.docm)
Word 2007 to 2013 template files	.dotx
WordPerfect 5.x and 6.x files	.doc, .wpd
Works 6.0 to 9.0 files	.wps
XML files	.xml
Open Document Text files	.odt
PDF files	.pdf

 QuickFacts

Using View Buttons

Word 2013 offers five views that you can use to display your document in different ways.

To display any of these views, click the **View** tab, and then click a Views group button:

You can immediately switch to Print Layout view, Web Layout view, or Read Mode by using the Views toolbar on the status bar:

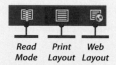

You can choose a view based on which best facilitates the task that you are performing:

● **Print Layout** is the default view in Word and displays the text as it will look when the document is printed.

● **Read Mode** displays the document as a "book" with facing pages. You can "flip" through the pages rather than scroll through them. To display as much of the document as possible onscreen, Read Mode hides the ribbon. At the top of the screen is a toolbar with limited options for using the document. Click **Edit Document** if you want to change back to Print Layout view.

● **Web Layout** shows how the text will look as a web page and displays a document in a larger font size and wraps to fit the window rather than the page margins.

● **Outline** displays the document's framework in outline mode, showing headers, indented text, levels of heads, and bulleted lists. It reveals the structure imposed by styles assigned to the text. This view also has an Outline tab that allows you to work with the outline. See Chapter 4 for more details. This view is accessible from the View tab but not from the status bar.

● **Draft** suppresses headings and footers and other design elements in order to display the text in draft form so that you have an unobstructed view of the contents. This view is accessible only from the View tab.

WRITE A DOCUMENT

Whether you create a new document or open an existing one, you will likely want to enter and edit text. Editing, in this case, includes adding and deleting text as well as selecting, moving, and copying it.

Enter Text

To enter text in a document that you have newly created or opened, simply start typing. The characters you type will appear in the document pane at the insertion point and in the order that you type them.

Determine Where Text Will Appear

The *insertion point*, the blinking vertical bar shown earlier in Figure 2-2, determines where text that you type will appear. In a new document, the insertion point is located in the upper-left corner of the document pane, and remains there until you enter text. It is also placed there by default when you open an existing document. When you enter text, the insertion point moves, or is pushed, to the right, staying to the right of the last character you typed. However, you can move the insertion point within or to the end of existing text using either the keyboard or the mouse.

New text pushes the insertion point to the right |

Move the Insertion Point with the Keyboard

When Word is open and a document is active, the insertion point moves every time you press a character or directional key on the keyboard (unless a menu or dialog box is open or the task pane is active). The directional keys include TAB, BACKSPACE, and ENTER, as well as the four arrow keys, and HOME, END, PAGE UP, and PAGE DOWN.

Move the Insertion Point with the Mouse

When the mouse pointer is in the document pane, it appears as an I-beam, as you saw in Figure 2-2. The I-beam shape is used because it fits between characters on the screen. You can move the insertion point by moving the I-beam mouse pointer to where you want the insertion point and then clicking.

Place the pointer within text to insert characters.

Insert Text or Type Over It

When you press a letter, symbol, or number key with Word in its default mode (as it is when you first start it), the insertion point and any existing text to the right of the insertion point is pushed to the right and down on a page. This is also true when you press the TAB or ENTER key. This is called *insert* mode.

In versions of Word prior to 2007, if you press the INSERT (or INS) key, Word is switched to *overtype* mode, and the OVR indicator is enabled in the status bar. In overtype mode, any character key you press types over (replaces) the existing character to the right of the insertion point. In Word 2007–2013, this capability is turned off by default, and pressing the INSERT key does nothing. The reason for the change is that, more often than not, users would press the INSERT key by mistake and then discover the mistake only after typing over a lot of text they didn't want to type over. If you prefer, you can turn on overtype mode capability:

1. Click the **File** tab, click **Options**, and click **Advanced**.

2. Under Editing Options, click **Use The Insert Key To Control Overtype Mode**.

3. Click **OK**.

Overtype mode does not affect the ENTER key, which continues to push existing characters to the right of the insertion point to the next line. The TAB key in overtype mode does replace characters to the right, *unless* it is pressed at the beginning of the line, in which case it is treated as an indent and pushes the rest of the line to the right.

Insert Line or Page Breaks

In Word, simply keep typing and the text will automatically wrap around to the next line. Only when you want to break a line before it would otherwise end must you manually intervene. There are four instances where manual line breaks are required:

- At the **end of a paragraph** To start a new paragraph, press **ENTER**.

- At the **end of a short line** within a paragraph To start a new line, press **SHIFT+ENTER**. This new line is considered part of the previous paragraph and retains its formatting. When you create a new line in the normal way, by pressing **ENTER**, the new paragraph can be formatted differently.

- At the **end of a page** To force the start of a new page anywhere on the page, press **CTRL+ENTER**. You may want to do this, for instance, at the end of a major part of the document when it occurs before the natural end of the page.

- At the **end of a section** To start a new section, press **CTRL+SHIFT +ENTER**.

You can also enter a page break using the mouse. With the insertion point positioned where you want the break to occur, click the **Insert** tab, and click **Page Break** in the Pages group. A page break will be inserted in the text. (If your screen is small-sized, you'll have to click **Pages** and select from the menu.)

Select Text

In order to copy, move, or delete text, you first need to select it. *Selecting text* means to identify it as a separate block from the rest of the text in a document. You can select any amount of text, from a single character up to an entire document. As text is selected, it is highlighted with a colored background, as you can see in Figure 2-6, and a mini toolbar for character editing appears. You can select text with either the mouse or the keyboard.

Select Text with the Mouse

You can select varying amounts of text with the mouse.

- **Select a single word** by double-clicking it.

- **Select a single line** by moving the I-beam mouse pointer to the left of the line until it changes to an arrow pointer and then clicking (this area on the left where the mouse pointer becomes an arrow is called the *selection bar*).

- **Select a single sentence** by pressing and holding **CTRL** while clicking in the sentence.

- **Select a single paragraph** by double-clicking in the selection bar opposite the paragraph, or by rapidly clicking three times in the paragraph.

- **Select an entire document** by pressing and holding **CTRL+SHIFT** while clicking in the selection bar anywhere in the document. Alternatively, in the Home tab Editing Group, click **Select** and then click **Select All**.

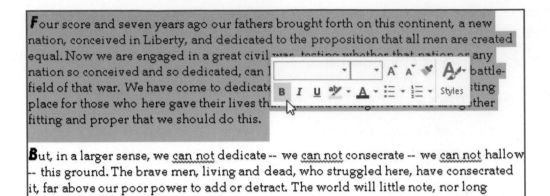

Figure 2-6: You will always know what you are moving, copying, or deleting because it is highlighted on the screen.

- **Select one or more characters** in a word, or **select two or more words**, by clicking:

  1. Click to place the insertion point to the left of the first character or word.

  2. Press and hold **SHIFT** while clicking to the right of the last character or word. The selected range of text will be highlighted.

- **Select one or more characters** in a word, or **select two or more words**, by dragging:

  1. Move the mouse pointer to the left of the first character.

  2. Press and hold the mouse button while dragging the mouse pointer to the right or left. The selected text will be highlighted.

> **NOTE** You select a picture by clicking it. Once selected, a picture can be copied, moved, or deleted from a document in the same ways as text, using the Office Clipboard (see Chapter 1 for more details on the Clipboard).

Select Text with the Keyboard

You can also select varying amounts of text using only the keyboard.

- To **select one or more characters or words**, use the arrow keys to move the insertion point to the left or right of the first character you want to select, and then press and hold **SHIFT** while using the arrow keys to move the insertion point to the right or left.

- **To select a paragraph,** click the pointer to the left of the first word in the paragraph, press **SHIFT**, click the pointer to the right of the last word in the paragraph.

- To **select a line**, place the pointer at the beginning of a line by pressing **HOME**, and then press **SHIFT+END**.

- To **select an entire document**, press **CTRL+A**.

⪢ Copy and Move Text

Copying and moving text are similar actions. Think of copying text as moving it and leaving a copy behind. Both copying and moving are done in two steps.

1. Selected text is copied or cut (removed) from its current location and placed automatically on the Clipboard.

2. The contents of the Clipboard are pasted to a new location, as identified by the insertion point.

 NOTE The Office Clipboard is shared by all Office products. You can copy or cut objects and text from any Office application and paste it into another Office application. The Clipboard is used within Word when you copy or cut a section of text and paste it into another place within the same document or into another Word document. Refer to Chapter 1 to find out more about the Office Clipboard.

Cut Text

When you *cut* text, you place it on the Clipboard and delete it from its current location. After you paste the text from the Clipboard to a new location, the text has been *moved* and no longer exists in its original location. To cut and place text on the Clipboard, select it and then use one of these techniques:

- Press **CTRL+X**.
- Right-click the text and choose **Cut** from the context menu.
- In the Home tab Clipboard group, click **Cut**.

Copy Text

When you *copy* text to the Clipboard, you also leave it in its original location. After you paste the text from the Clipboard to a new location in the document, you have the same text in two places in the document. To copy text to the Clipboard, select it and then use one of these techniques:

- Press **CTRL+C**.
- Right-click the text and click **Copy** from the context menu.
- In the Home tab Clipboard group, click **Copy**.

Paste Text

To complete a copy or a move, you must *paste* the text from the Clipboard to either the same or another document where the insertion point is located. A copy of the text stays on the Clipboard and can be pasted again. To paste the contents of the Clipboard at the insertion point:

- Press **CTRL+V**.
- Right-click and choose one of the options under Paste Options on the context menu: paste the text using the source formatting (the original formatting of the text—leftmost icon), merge formatting (change the formatting to that of the surrounding text—middle icon), or keep text only (strip any formatting to retain only the text—rightmost icon).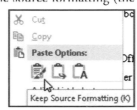

- In the Home tab Clipboard group, click **Paste**.

Use the Paste Options Smart Tag

The Paste Options smart tag appears when you paste text. Like the context menu that appears when you right-click at the insertion point (described in the previous section), the Paste Options smart tag gives you choices to keep source formatting, merge formatting, or keep text only. The Paste Options smart tag also gives you a Set Default Paste option, which you can click to display the Word Options dialog box so that you can set defaults for pasting text during a cut or copy action. The Paste Options smart tag is most valuable when you can see that the paste operation has resulted in formatting that you don't want.

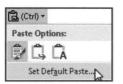

Undo a Move or Paste Action

You can undo a move or paste action with one of these techniques:

- Press **CTRL+Z**.
- Click **Undo** in the Quick Access toolbar. (Click the down arrow to see a list of actions to undo.)

Redo an Undo Action

You can redo many undo actions with one of these techniques:

- Press **CTRL+Y**.
- Click **Redo** in the Quick Access toolbar.

 NOTE Under certain circumstances, especially while formatting, the Redo option becomes Repeat.

Delete Text

Deleting text removes it from its current location *without* putting it on the Clipboard. To delete selected text, press **DELETE** (or **DEL**).

 NOTE You can recover deleted text by clicking **Undo** in the Quick Access toolbar.

Enter Symbols and Special Characters

Entering a keyboard character into your document takes only a keystroke, but many other characters and symbols exist beyond those that appear on the keyboard (for example, ©, £, Ã, 'Ω, Љ, and •). You can enter these characters and symbols using either the Symbol dialog box or a sequence of keys (also called a keyboard shortcut).

Enter Symbols and Special Characters from the Symbol Dialog Box

To enter a symbol or special character via the Symbol dialog box:

1. Move the insertion point to where you want to insert the symbol or special character.
2. In the Insert tab Symbols group, click **Symbol**. A Symbol menu will open containing the symbols you most commonly use.

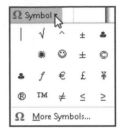

3. If the symbol you want is on the menu, click it to insert the symbol in the document.
4. If the symbol you want is not on the menu, click **More Symbols**. The Symbol dialog box appears.
   - Click the **Symbols** tab for characters within various font styles.
   - Click the **Special Characters** tab for common standard characters, as shown in Figure 2-7.
5. Click the character you want, click **Insert**, and then click **Close**. The special character or symbol is inserted where the insertion point is located.

If you want to insert multiple special characters or symbols, do not click Close in step 5 and continue to use the Symbol dialog box as instructed.

 TIP The AutoCorrect As You Type option of the AutoCorrect feature, which is discussed in Chapter 1, also provides a quick way of entering commonly used special characters, such as copyright, trademark, and registered symbols, and en and em dashes.

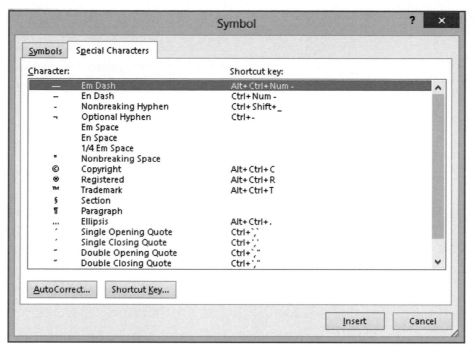

Symbol

Symbols | Special Characters

Character: Shortcut key:

—   Em Dash   Alt+Ctrl+Num -
–   En Dash   Ctrl+Num -
‐   Nonbreaking Hyphen   Ctrl+Shift+_
¬   Optional Hyphen   Ctrl+-
     Em Space
     En Space
     1/4 Em Space
°   Nonbreaking Space
©   Copyright   Alt+Ctrl+C
®   Registered   Alt+Ctrl+R
™   Trademark   Alt+Ctrl+T
§   Section
¶   Paragraph
…   Ellipsis   Alt+Ctrl+.
'   Single Opening Quote   Ctrl+`,`
'   Single Closing Quote   Ctrl+','
"   Double Opening Quote   Ctrl+`,"
"   Double Closing Quote   Ctrl+','"

AutoCorrect...   Shortcut Key...

Insert   Cancel

Figure 2-7: The Symbol dialog box contains special characters as well as several complete alphabet and symbol sets.

Enter Symbols and Special Characters from the Keyboard

You can use keyboard shortcut keys to enter symbols and special characters. If a keyboard shortcut includes numerals, they must be entered on the numeric keypad. The following steps describe that situation. Of course, if the keyboard shortcut doesn't use numerals, you don't need the numeric keypad.

1. Move the insertion point to where you want to insert the symbol or special character.

2. Press **NUM LOCK** to put the numeric keypad into numeric mode.

3. Press and hold **ALT** while pressing all four digits (including the leading zero) on the numeric keypad, not the regular numeric keys above the keypad.

4. Release **ALT**. The symbol or special character is inserted where the insertion point is located.

The shortcut keys for some of the more common special characters are shown in Table 2-2 ("NUM" means to press the following key on the numeric keypad, so NUM- simply means to press - in the upper-right corner of the numeric keypad).

Table 2-2: Shortcut Keys for Common Characters

Character	Name	Shortcut Keys
•	Bullet	ALT+0149
©	Copyright	ALT+CTRL+C
™	Trademark	ALT+CTRL+T
®	Registered	ALT+CTRL+R
£	Pound	ALT+0163
€	Euro	ALT+CTRL+E
–	En dash	CTRL+NUM-
—	Em dash	ALT+CTRL+NUM-

NOTE When you click a common symbol or special character in the Symbol dialog box, you'll see the shortcut keys for the character.

NAVIGATE A DOCUMENT

Understanding how to navigate a document is essential to being able to work with it. *Navigating* in this context refers both to moving around in a document and to finding the text you need (and perhaps replacing it with something else).

⮞⮞ Move Around in a Document

Word provides a number of ways to move around in a document using the mouse and the keyboard.

Use the Mouse and Scroll Bars

There are two scroll bars: one for moving vertically within the document, and one for moving horizontally. These are only displayed when your text is too wide or too long to fit completely on the screen. Each scroll bar contains four controls for getting you where you want to go. Using the vertical scroll bar, shown in Figure 2-8, you can

- **Move upward one line** by clicking the upward-pointing *scroll arrow*.
- **Move upward or downward** by clicking and dragging the *scroll button* in the corresponding direction.
- **Move up or down the screen's height** by clicking in the *scroll bar* above the scroll button to move toward the beginning of the document, or by clicking below the scroll button to move toward the end of the document.
- **Move downward one line** by clicking the downward-pointing *scroll arrow*.

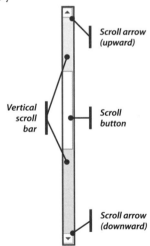

Figure 2-8: The vertical scroll bar and its button and arrows allow you to move easily to different locations within your document.

The horizontal scroll bar has similar controls, only these are used to move horizontally on the screen.

Move with the Keyboard

The following keyboard commands, used for moving around in your document, also move the insertion point:

- One character left or right using the **LEFT** or **RIGHT ARROW**
- One line up or down using the **UP** or **DOWN ARROW**
- One word left or right using **CTRL+LEFT ARROW** or **CTRL+RIGHT ARROW**
- One paragraph up or down using **CTRL+UP ARROW** or **CTRL+DOWN ARROW**
- To the beginning or end of a line using **HOME** or **END**
- To the beginning or end of a document using **CTRL+HOME** or **CTRL+END**
- One screen up or down using **PAGE UP** or **PAGE DOWN**

- To the previous or next page in the same relative location using **CTRL+PAGE UP** or **CTRL+PAGE DOWN**
- To the top or bottom of the window using **CTRL+ALT+PAGE UP** or **CTRL+ALT+PAGE DOWN**

Go to a Particular Location

The Go To command opens the Find And Replace dialog box with the Go To tab displayed, as shown in Figure 2-9. This allows you to go immediately to the location of some object, such as a page, a footnote, or a table. You can open the dialog box with the Go To tab displayed via any of the following actions:

- Press **CTRL+G**.
- Click the left end of the status bar (the Page *X* Of *Y* area). In the Navigation task pane that opens, click the down arrow in the Search text box and click **Go To**.
- In the Home tab Editing group, click the **Find** down arrow and click **Go To**. If your window is reduced in size, you may have to click **Editing** in the Editing group for a menu with the Find down arrow.

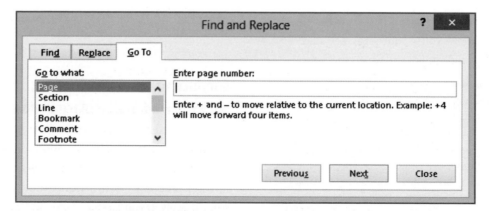

Figure 2-9: The Go To tab contains commands for you to go to a particular page as well as to other particular items within a document.

After opening the dialog box, select from the **Go To What** list the object you want to go to, and then enter the number or name of the object in the text box on the right. For example, select **Page** on the left and enter 5 on the right to go to page 5.

NOTE You can also move by a number of items relative to your current position by entering a plus sign (+) or a minus sign (–) and a number. For example, if you select **Page** and enter -3, you will be moved backward three pages.

Find and Replace Text

Often, you'll want to find particular text in a document, but you may not know where, or even how many times, that text occurs. This is especially true when you want to locate names or words that are sprinkled throughout a document. For example, if you had repeatedly referred to a table on page 4 and the table was subsequently moved to page 5, you would need to search for all occurrences of "page 4" and change them to "page 5." In this example, you not only want to *find* "page 4," but also want to *replace* it with "page 5."

In addition to allowing you to do a simple search for a word or phrase, as in the previous example, Word allows you to conduct an advanced search for parts of words, particular capitalization, and words that sound alike.

TIP If you want your search to find just the word "ton" and not words like "Washington" or "tonic," you can either put a space at both the beginning and end of the word in the Find What field (ton) or click **More** in the Find And Replace dialog box and then click **Find Whole Words Only**. The latter is the preferred way to do this, because putting a space after the word would not find the word followed by a comma or a period. (To use the latter search method from the Navigation task pane, click the down arrow in the Search text box, click **Options**, and then click **Find Whole Words Only** in the Find Options dialog box.)

Conduct a Simple Search with the Navigation Task Pane

If you just want to search for a word or phrase:

1. In the Home tab Editing group, click **Find**. The Navigation task pane opens.

2. In the Search box, type the word or phrase for which you want to search. As you type, the results are displayed below the Search box, as shown in Figure 2-10.

3. Click an individual search result in the Navigation task pane and the document will be repositioned so that you can see the search result in the document. Beneath the search box will be a list of page thumbnails, each page containing the searched-for text. Click a page to see the specific occurrence of the search criteria on that page.

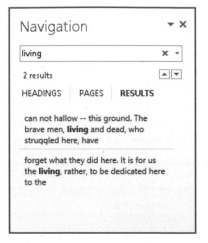

Figure 2-10: When you search for a word or phrase, the Find command in the Navigation task pane displays a list of results beneath the search criteria as you type.

Conduct an Advanced Search with the Find And Replace Dialog Box

If you need to conduct a more advanced search, such as to find whole words only, particular capitalization, or words that sound alike, open the Find And Replace dialog box by clicking the **Find** down arrow in the Home tab Editing group and then clicking **Advanced Find**. Alternatively, if you already have the Navigation task pane open, click the **Search** down arrow and then click **Advanced Find**. Click **More** to see all the options (see Figure 2-11), described next.

Find and Replace

Find | Replace | Go To

Find what: living

Options: Search Down

<< Less   Reading Highlight ▾   Find In ▾   Find Next   Cancel

Search Options

Search: Down

☐ Match case
☐ Find whole words only
☐ Use wildcards
☐ Sounds like (English)
☐ Find all word forms (English)

☐ Match prefix
☐ Match suffix

☐ Ignore punctuation characters
☐ Ignore white-space characters

Find

Format ▾   Special ▾   No Formatting

Figure 2-11: Word offers a number of advanced ways to search a document, and find and replace text.

- **Match Case**   Find a specific capitalization of a word or phrase.
- **Find Whole Words Only**   Find whole words only, so when searching for "equip," for example, you don't get "equipment."
- **Use Wildcards**   Find words or phrases that contain a set of characters by using wildcards to represent the unknown part of the word or phrase (see the "Using Wildcards" QuickFacts).
- **Sounds Like**   Find words that sound alike but are spelled differently (homonyms).

- **Find All Word Forms**   Find a word in all its forms—noun, adjective, verb, or adverb (for example, for the search term "ski," you'd find ski, skier, and skiing).
- **Match Prefix or Match Suffix**   Find words containing a common prefix or suffix (for instance, if you searched for "anti" you'd find antipathy, antibiotic, and antidote).
- **Ignore Punctuation Characters**   Find words without regard for any punctuation. This is especially useful when a word you are searching for might contain a punctuation mark, such as a hyphen (for example, your search term is "rerun" and you also want to find instances of "re-run").
- **Ignore White-Space Characters**   Find words without regard to any internal characters such as spaces, tabs, or optional hyphens (for example, your search term is "basketball" and you also want to find any instances of "basket ball").
- **Format**   Find specific types of formatting, such as for fonts, paragraphs, etc.

- **Special**   Find specific special characters, such as paragraph marks, em dashes (—), or nonbreaking spaces (can't be the first or last character in a line).

QuickFacts

Using Wildcards

Wildcards are characters that are used to represent one or more characters in a word or phrase when searching for items with similar or unknown parts. To use wildcards, check the **Use Wildcards** check box in the Find And Replace dialog box, and then type in the Find What text box the known characters along with the wildcard character(s). For example, typing <u>page ?</u> will find both "page 4" and "page 5." The "?" stands for any single character.

Find	Replace	Go To
Find what:	page ?	
Options:	Use Wildcards	

Word has defined the characters shown in Table 2-3 as wildcard characters when used with the Find command to replace one or more characters.

NOTE In the Find And Replace dialog box, instead of repeatedly clicking **Find Next** to highlight each occurrence of an item, you can click **Reading Highlight** and then click **Highlight All**. All occurrences will be highlighted, and the first occurrence will be displayed. To further choose where you want to search, click **Find In** and click your choice of where in the document to search), then click **Find Next** to advance to the next occurrence. The highlights remain until you click **Reading Highlight** and then **Clear Highlighting**.

Note that when you choose to search with wildcards, the Find Whole Words Only and Match Case features are turned on automatically and cannot be turned off (their check boxes are cleared but dim). This applies to Match Prefix and Match Suffix as well.

Table 2-3: Wildcard Characters Used with the Find Command

Character	Used to Replace	Example	Will Find	Won't Find
?	A single character	Page ?	Page 4 or Page 5	Page1 (no space)
*	Any number of characters	Page *	Page 4 and Page 5	Pages1–5
<	The beginning of a word	<corp	Corporate	Incorporate
>	The end of a word	ton>	Washington	Toner
\	A wildcard character	What\?	What?	What is
[cc]	One of a list of characters	B[io]b	Bib or Bob	Babe
[c-c]	One in a range of characters	[l-t]ook	look or took	Book
[!c-c]	Any character except one in the range	[!k-n]ook	book or took	Look
{n}	n copies of the previous character	Lo{2}	Loo and Look (first two instances)	Lot
{n,}	n or more copies of the previous character	Lo{1,}	Lot or Look (first instance	Late
{n,m}	n to m copies of the previous character	150{1,3}	150 to 1500 (first three instances)	15
@	Any number of copies of the previous character	150@	150 or 1500	1400

Replace Text

Often, the purpose of searching for a word, phrase, or other text is to replace it with something else. Word lets you use all the features of Find and then replace what is found.

1. In the Home tab Editing group, click **Replace**. (You may have to click **Editing** and then **Replace** if your window is reduced in size.) The Find And Replace dialog box appears with the Replace tab selected, as shown in Figure 2-12.

2. Type in the **Find What** text box the text for which you want to search.

3. Type in the **Replace With** text box the text you want to replace the found item(s) with.

4. Click **Find Next**. The first occurrence in the document below the current insertion point will be highlighted.

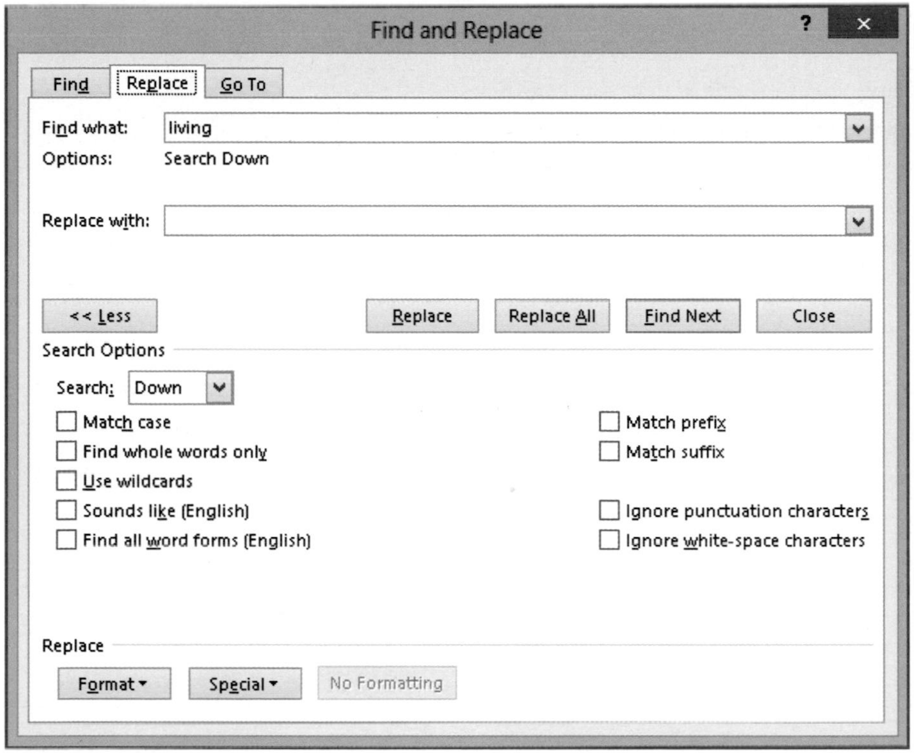

Find and Replace

| Find | Replace | Go To |

Find what: living

Options: Search Down

Replace with:

<< Less   Replace   Replace All   Find Next   Close

Search Options

Search: Down

☐ Match case
☐ Find whole words only
☐ Use wildcards
☐ Sounds like (English)
☐ Find all word forms (English)

☐ Match prefix
☐ Match suffix

☐ Ignore punctuation characters
☐ Ignore white-space characters

Replace

Format ▾   Special ▾   No Formatting

Figure 2-12: You can replace a single instance of text or replace all instances at once.

5. Choose one of the following options:

- Click **Replace** if you want to replace the current instance with the text you entered in the Replace With text box. Word replaces this instance and automatically finds the next instance.

- Click **Replace All** if you want to replace all occurrences of the text with the text you entered in the Replace With text box. Word replaces all instances at one time.

- Click **Find Next** if you don't want to replace the text that was found and want to find the next occurrence.

6. When you are done, click **Close**.

TIP You can generally undo the last several operations by repeatedly issuing one of the Undo commands. If you accidentally click Replace All instead of Replace, clicking Undo once will undo all changes.

USE WORD WRITING AIDS

Word 2013 provides several aids that can assist you not only in creating your document but also in making sure that it is as professional-looking as possible. These include building blocks, character and word counts, highlighting, and hyphenation. (Other aids, such as AutoCorrect and Thesaurus can be found in Chapter 1.)

Use Building Blocks

Building blocks are blocks of text and formatting that you can use repeatedly, such as cover pages, a greeting, phrases, headings, or a closing. You can insert specific styles of page numbers or unique math formulas. Word provides a number of these building blocks for you, but you can also identify and save your own building blocks and then use them in different documents.

Create a Building Block

1. Select the text or graphic, along with its formatting, that you want to store as a building block. (Include the paragraph mark in the selection if you want to store paragraph formatting.)

> **NOTE** The paragraph mark carries with it the formatting specifications for the paragraph. When you select a paragraph, or the end of one, to copy it and paste it elsewhere, pay attention to whether or not you also include the paragraph mark in your selection. If yes, when you paste the text, the source formatting will be carried into the destination paragraph and reformat it. If no, the destination paragraph (and the copied text) will retain its original formatting. See "Turn On Formatting Marks" in Chapter 3 for more details about the paragraph mark.

2. In the Insert tab Text group, click **Quick Parts**, and then click **Save Selection To Quick Part Gallery**.

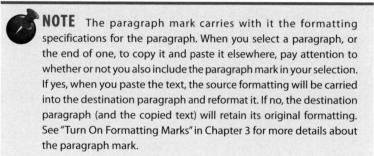

3. In the Create New Building Block dialog box, accept the suggested name for the building block, or type a short abbreviation for a new one (for example, change "Microsoft Office" to "msfto").

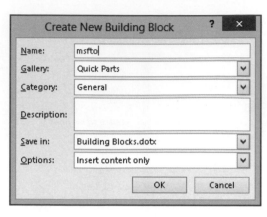

4. In most cases, you will accept the Quick Parts gallery, the General category, and the Building Blocks.dotx file name, since those provide for the easiest retrieval.

5. Click the **Options** down arrow, and, depending on what you are saving in your building block, click the option that is correct for you. If you want paragraph formatting, you must include the paragraph mark.

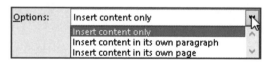

6. Click **OK**.

Insert One of Your Building Blocks

1. Place the insertion point in the document where you want to insert the building block.

2. In the Insert tab Text group, click **Quick Parts**, and then double-click the entry you want.

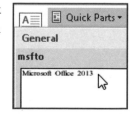

Insert One of Word's Building Blocks

1. Place the insertion point in the document where you want to insert the building block.

2. In the Insert tab Text group, click **Quick Parts**, and then click **Building Blocks Organizer**. The Building Blocks Organizer dialog box appears, as shown in Figure 2-13.

3. Scroll through the list of building blocks until you find the one that you want. Click the entry to see it previewed on the right, as shown in the example in Figure 2-13. Click **Insert** if you want to use it.

Delete a Building Block

1. In the Insert tab Text group, click **Quick Parts**, and then click **Building Blocks Organizer**. The Building Blocks Organizer dialog box appears.

2. Scroll through the list of building blocks until you find the one that you want to delete. Click the entry to see it previewed on the right. If you are certain that you want to delete it, click **Delete**, click **Yes** to confirm the deletion, and click **Close**.

CAUTION You cannot undo the deletion of a building block. The only way to restore it is to re-create it.

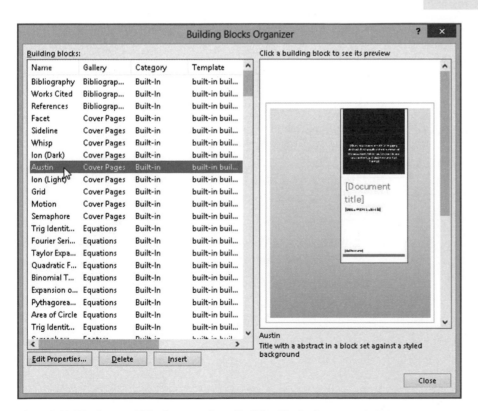

Figure 2-13: Word comes with a large number of building blocks that you can access.

⮞⮞ Count Characters and Words

Word can tell you the number of characters and words in a document or in just a portion of the document you select.

Click the **Review** tab, and then click **Word Count** in the Proofing group. The Word Count dialog box appears, displaying information about your document (see Figure 2-14).

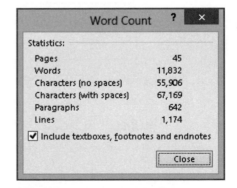

Figure 2-14: The Word Count feature is a quick and easy way to view the statistics of your document.

Use Highlighting

The Highlight feature is useful for marking important text in a document or text that you want to call a reader's attention to. Keep in mind, however, that highlighting parts of a document works best when the document is viewed on your screen or online. When printed, the highlighting marks often appear gray and may even obscure the text you're trying to call attention to.

Apply Highlighting

The Highlight button is a toggle that switches color highlighting on and off. First you choose a color, and then you apply the highlight to text or a graphic.

1. In the Home tab Font group, click the **Highlight** down arrow, and select a color from the menu. The cursor turns into a highlighter.

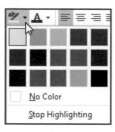

2. Drag the pointer over the text or graphic that you want to highlight. The highlighting is applied to your selection.

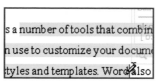

3. To turn off highlighting, click the **Highlight** icon or press **ESC**.

> **TIP** You can also apply highlighting by selecting the text first and then clicking **Highlight** in the Home tab Font group. The default highlight color is applied. Another alternative is to right-click selected text and use the Highlight button on the mini toolbar.

Remove Highlighting

1. Select the text that you want to remove highlighting from, or press **CTRL+A** to select all of the text in the document.

2. In the Home tab Font group, click the **Highlight** button. (This requires that the default be No Color.)

   –Or–

   In the Home tab Font group, click the **Highlight** drop-down arrow, and then click **No Color**.

Change Highlighting Color

1. Select the text for which you want to change the color of the highlight.

2. In the Home tab Font group, click the **Highlight** drop-down arrow, and click the color that you want to use.

Find Highlighted Text in a Document

1. In the Home tab Editing group, click the **Find** down arrow, and click **Advanced Find**. The Find And Replace dialog box appears. Clear any text in the Find What text box (unless you're searching for particular words that are highlighted.)

2. If you don't see the Format button, click the **More** button.

3. Click the **Format** button, and then click **Highlight**.

4. Click **Find Next**. Word displays the first occurrence of highlighted text in the document below the current insertion point. Repeat this until you reach the highlight you are looking for. Click **Cancel** if you want to close the Find And Replace dialog box at this spot. Otherwise, continue to click **Find Next** until you reach the end of the document.

5. Click **OK** when the message box is displayed indicating that Word has finished searching the document, and click **Close** in the Find And Replace dialog box.

 ## Add Hyphenation

The Hyphenation feature automatically hyphenates words at the ends of lines based on standard hyphenation rules. You might use this feature if you want words to fit better on a line, or if you want to avoid uneven margins in right-aligned text or avoid large gaps between words in justified text. (See Chapter 3 for information on text alignment.)

Automatically Hyphenate a Document

To automatically hyphenate a document, you must be in Print Layout format.

1. In the Page Layout tab Page Setup group, click **Hyphenation**. A drop-down menu appears.

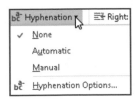

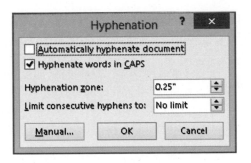

Figure 2-15: You can determine how Word will automatically hyphenate words.

2. Click **Hyphenation Options** to open the Hyphenation dialog box. Select the option you want (see Figure 2-15):

- **Automatically Hyphenate Document**   Either enables automatic hyphenation as you type or after the fact for selected text (this option is turned off in Word by default)

- **Hyphenate Words in CAPS**   Hyphenates words typed in all uppercase letters

- **Hyphenation Zone**   Sets the distance from the right margin within which you want to hyphenate the document (the lower the value, the more words are hyphenated)

- **Limit Consecutive Hyphens To**   Sets the maximum number of hyphens that can appear in consecutive lines

3. Click **OK** when finished.

 TIP You can also hyphenate existing text by selecting the text, clicking **Hyphenation** in the Page Layout tab, and clicking **Automatic** in the menu.

Manually Hyphenate Text

1. In the Page Layout tab Page Setup group, click **Hyphenation**. A drop-down menu appears.

2. Click **Manual**.

3. Word searches for possible words to hyphenate. When it finds one, the Manual Hyphenation dialog box appears.

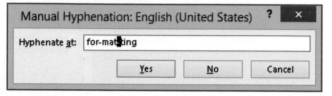

4. Do one of the following:

   • Click **Yes** to hyphenate the word at the suggested blinking hyphen.

   • Click one of the other hyphen choices (if any), and then click **Yes**.

   • Click **No** to continue without hyphenating the word.

5. Word will continue searching for words to hyphenate and display the Manual Hyphenation dialog box until the entire document has been searched (or you click **Cancel**). A message box is displayed to that effect. Click **OK**.

Chapter 3

Formatting a Document

Plain, unformatted text conveys information, but not nearly as effectively as well-formatted text, as you can see by the two examples in Figure 3-1. Word provides numerous ways to format your text. Most fall under the categories of text formatting, paragraph formatting, and page formatting, which are discussed in the following sections of this chapter. Additional formatting that can be applied at the document level is discussed in Chapter 4.

This chapter discusses the direct, or manual, application of formatting. Much of the character and paragraph formatting discussed in this chapter is commonly applied using styles that combine a number of different individual formatting steps, saving significant time over direct formatting. (Styles are discussed in Chapter 4.) Direct formatting is usually applied only to a small amount of text that needs formatting that is different from its style.

FORMAT TEXT

Text formatting is the formatting that you can apply to individual characters, and includes the selection of fonts, font size, color, character spacing, and capitalization.

 NOTE Prior to applying formatting, you must select the text to be formatted. Chapter 2 contains an extensive section on selecting text.

The Declaration of Independence
of the Thirteen Colonies In CONGRESS,
July 4, 1776

The unanimous Declaration of the Thirteen United States of America,

When in the Course of human events it becomes necessary for one people to dissolve the political bo
which have connecte
equal station to which
of mankind requires t

We hold these truths
Creator with certain u
That to secure these
consent of the goverr
the Right of the Peop
such principles and or
and Happiness. Prude
light and transient ca
suffer, while evils are
accustomed. But whe
design to reduce ther
Government, and to
these Colonies; and s
Government. The hist
usurpations, all havin
this, let Facts be subr

He has refused his As

The Declaration of Independence
of the Thirteen Colonies In CONGRESS,
July 4, 1776

The unanimous Declaration of the Thirteen United States of America,

When in the Course of human events, it becomes necessary for one people to dissolve the political bands which have connected them with another, and to assume among the powers of the earth, the separate and equal station to which the Laws of Nature and of Nature's God entitle them, a decent respect to the opinions of mankind requires that they should declare the causes which impel them to the separation.

We hold these truths to be self-evident, that all men are created equal, that they are endowed by their Creator with certain unalienable Rights that among these are Life, Liberty and the pursuit of Happiness. --That to secure these rights, Governments are instituted among Men, deriving their just powers from the consent of the governed, --That whenever any Form of Government becomes destructive of these ends, it is the Right of the People to alter or to abolish it, and to institute new Government, laying its foundation on such principles and organizing its powers in such form, as to them shall seem most likely to effect their Safety and Happiness. Prudence, indeed, will dictate that Governments long established should not be changed for light and transient causes; and accordingly all experience hath shewn, that mankind are more disposed to suffer, while evils are sufferable, than to right themselves by abolishing the forms to which they are accustomed. But when a long train of abuses and usurpations, pursuing invariably the same Object evinces a

Figure 3-1: Formatting makes text both more readable and more pleasing to the eye.

▷▷ Survey the Text-Formatting Tools

Text formatting can be applied using the Font dialog box, keyboard shortcuts, the Font group on the Home tab, and the mini toolbar that displays when you select text.

Access the Font Dialog Box

The Font dialog box provides the most comprehensive selection of text formatting and spacing alternatives. Click the **Font** dialog box launcher in the Home tab Font group to open the Font dialog box (see Figure 3-2). Alternatively, you can right-click the selected text you want to format and then click **Font**.

Use Keyboard Shortcuts

Using keyboard shortcuts to format text allows you to keep your hands on the keyboard. Table 3-1 summarizes the keyboard shortcuts for formatting text.

Access the Font Group

You'll find that for most of your text formatting, you'll simply use the Font group (see Figure 3-3). To display the Font group tools, click the **Home** tab.

Access the Mini Toolbar

The mini toolbar is displayed automatically when you select text. You can also see it when you right-click text (which also displays a context menu; see Tip on next page). The toolbar has several of the buttons also available in the Home tab's Font and Paragraph groups. Consequently, you can most likely access the same functions with the mini toolbar as you can with the Font and Paragraph groups. Therefore, to reduce repetition, using the mini toolbar to carry out these tasks will not be discussed in this chapter. See Chapter 1 for details on how to use the mini toolbar.

Table 3-1: Text Formatting Shortcut Keys

Apply Formatting	Shortcut Keys
Align left	CTRL+L
Align right	CTRL+R
All caps	CTRL+SHIFT+A
Bold	CTRL+B
Bulleted list	CTRL+SHIFT+L
Center	CTRL+E
Change case	SHIFT+F3
Decrease font size	CTRL+SHIFT+<
Increase font size	CTRL+SHIFT+>
Decrease font size one point	CTRL+[
Increase font size one point	CTRL+]
Open Font dialog box	CTRL+D
Font name	CTRL+SHIFT+F
Italic	CTRL+I
Reset character formatting	CTRL+SPACEBAR
Small caps	CTRL+SHIFT+K
Subscript	CTRL+=
Superscript	CTRL+SHIFT+=
Symbol font	CTRL+SHIFT+Q

 TIP The mini toolbar and a context menu with font and paragraph formatting options (and other options) are displayed when you select and right-click the text you want to format. You can then click the necessary commands.

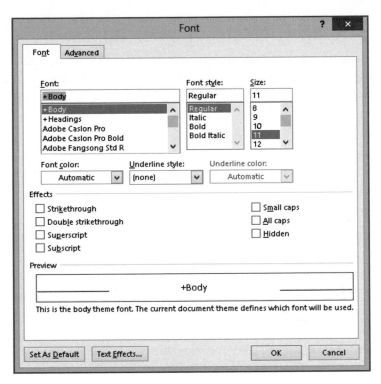

Figure 3-2: The Font dialog box provides the most complete set of text-formatting controls.

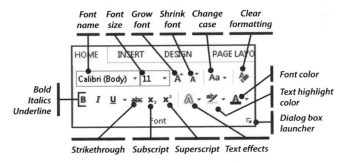

Figure 3-3: The Font group on the Home tab provides fast formatting with the mouse.

Apply Character Formatting

You apply character formatting by selecting text and then applying a characteristic to it. For instance, you can select and apply a font, change the font size, make text bold or italics, underline it, or change the text color. For many of the most common formatting options, using the Home tab Font group is easiest, or perhaps the mini toolbar that appears when you select text. The Font dialog box is used when you need a command not found in the ribbon or mini toolbar.

Select a Font

A *font* is a set of characters that share a particular design, which is called a *typeface*. When you install Windows, and again when you install Office, a number of fonts are automatically installed on your computer. You can see the fonts available by clicking the down arrow next to the font name in the Home tab Font group (shown next) and then scrolling through the list (your most recently used fonts are at the top, followed by all fonts listed alphabetically). You can also see the list of fonts in the Font dialog box, where you can select a font in the Font list and see what it looks like in the Preview area at the bottom of the dialog box.

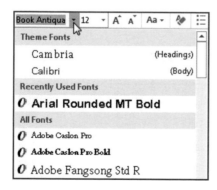

By default, the Calibri font is used for body text in all new documents using the default Normal template. To change this font:

1. Select the text to be formatted.

2. In the Home tab Font group, click the **Font** down arrow. Scroll through the list until you see the font that you want (your selected text changes as you point to each font), and then click it.

 NOTE Several types of fonts are included in the default set that is installed with Windows and Office. Alphabetic fonts come in two varieties: serif fonts, such as Times New Roman or Century Schoolbook, where each letter is designed with distinctive ends, or *serifs,* on each of the character's lines, and sans-serif ("without serifs") fonts, such as Arial and Century Gothic, without the ends. Sans-serif fonts are generally used for headings and lists, while serif fonts are generally used for body text in printed documents, but often the reverse is true in web pages. Finally, there are symbol fonts, such as Wingdings and Webdings, with many special characters, such as smiling faces ("smilies"), arrows, and pointing fingers.

Apply Bold or Italic Style

Fonts come in four styles: regular (or "roman"), bold, italic, and bold-italic. The default is, of course, regular, yet fonts such as Arial Black and Eras Bold appear bold. To make fonts bold, italic, or bold-italic:

1. Select the text to be formatted.

2. Press **CTRL+B** to make it bold, and/or press **CTRL+I** to make it italic.

    –Or–

    Click the **Bold** icon in the Font group, and/or click the **Italic** icon.

Change Font Size

Font size is measured in *points*, which is the height of a character, not its width. For most fonts, the width varies with the character, the letter "i" taking up less room than "w," for example. (The Courier New font is an exception, with all characters having the same width.) There are 72 points in an inch. The default font size is 11 points for body text, with standard headings varying from 11 to 14 points. The 8-point type is common for smaller print; anything below 6 point is typically unreadable. To change the font size of your text:

1. Select the text to be formatted.

2. In the Home tab Font group, click the **Font Size** down arrow, scroll through the list until you see the font size you want, and then click it (as you point to each size your selected text changes to reflect it).

   –Or–

   Press **CTRL+SHIFT+<** to decrease the font size, or press **CTRL+SHIFT+>** to increase the font size.

 TIP At the top of the Font Size list, you can type in half-point sizes, such as 10.5, as well as sizes that are not on the list, such as 15.

Underline Text

Several forms of underlining can be applied.

Select the text to be formatted. You have these options for underlining the selected text:

- In the Home tab Font group, click the **Underline** down arrow, and click the type of underline you want.

- Press **CTRL+U** to apply a continuous underline to the entire selection (including spaces).

- Press **CTRL+SHIFT+W** to apply an underline to just each word in the selection.

- Press **CTRL+SHIFT+D** to apply a double underline to the entire selection.

 TIP The Underline Style drop-down list in the Font dialog box, as with the Underline drop-down list in the Font group, contains underline choices beyond those the other methods provide—dotted, wavy, and so on.

Use Font Color

To change the color of text:

1. Select the text to be formatted.

2. In the Home tab Font group, click the **Font Color** button to apply the currently selected color, or click the **Font Color** down arrow and choose a color from the drop-down menu. You can mouse over the colors and see each reflected in the selected text.

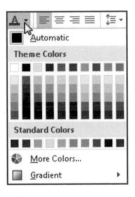

3. If, in selecting a color from the Home tab Font group, you do not find the color you want within the 40-color palette, click **More Colors** to open the Colors dialog box. In the Standard tab, you can pick a color from a 145-color palette, or you can use the Custom tab to choose from an almost infinite range of colors by clicking in the color spectrum or by entering the RGB (red, green, and blue) values, as you can see in Figure 3-4, or the HSL (hue, saturation, and luminescent) values.

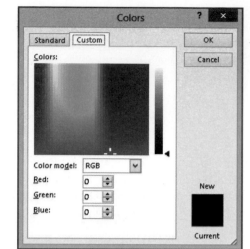

Figure 3-4: You can create any color you want in the Custom tab of the Colors dialog box.

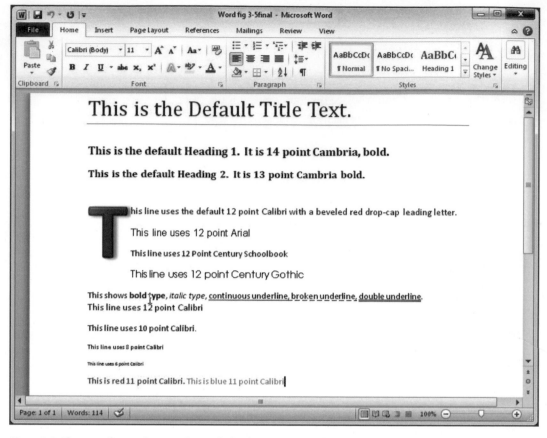

Figure 3-5: Character formatting must be applied judiciously, or it will detract from the appearance of a document.

Reset Text

Figure 3-5 shows some of the formatting that has been or will be discussed. All of that formatting can be reset to the plain text or the default formatting. To reset text to default settings:

1. Select the text to be formatted.

2. In the Home tab Font group, click the **Clear Formatting** button.

   –Or–

   Press **CTRL+SPACEBAR** to clear just the character formatting.

▷▷ Reset Font Defaults

Word comes with a default set of formatting parameters for body text composed of Calibri, 11-point regular type, and black color. You can change this in the Font dialog box.

1. Click the **Font** dialog box launcher on the Home tab.

2. In the Font dialog box, Font tab, select the font, style, size, and color you want.

3. Click **Set As Default**, and select either **This Document Only** or **All Documents Based On The Normal.dotm Template**.

4. Click **OK** to make those settings the new default set.

Change Character Spacing and OpenType Features

Word provides the ability to change two groups of advanced font features that deal with character spacing and OpenText features. Both of these are set in the Advanced tab of the Font dialog box, which is shown in Figure 3-6.

Figure 3-6: The Font dialog box, Advanced tab allows you to apply sophisticated formatting to text.

Set Character Spacing

Character spacing, in this case, is the amount of space between characters on a single line. Word enables you to increase and decrease character

spacing, scale the size of selected text, raise and lower vertically the position of text on the line, and determine when to apply kerning (how much space separates certain character pairs, such as "A" and "V," which can overlap). To apply character spacing:

1. Select the text to be formatted, click the **Font** dialog box launcher on the Home tab to open the Font dialog box, and click the **Advanced** tab. You have these character spacing options:

   - **Scale**   Select the percentage scale factor that you want to apply. (This is not recommended. It is better to change the font size so as not to distort the font.)

   - **Spacing**   Select the change in spacing (expanded or condensed) that you want and the amount of that change in points (pt).

   - **Position**   Select the change in position (raised or lowered) that you want and the amount of that change in points.

   - **Kerning For Fonts**   Determine if you want to apply kerning rules and, if so, the point size at which you want to do that (it becomes more important in larger point sizes).

2. Check the results in the Preview area, an example of which is shown in Figure 3-6. When you are satisfied, click **OK**.

 NOTE   Character spacing, especially kerning, is predominantly used when you are creating something like a brochure, flyer, or newspaper ad in which you want to achieve a professional look.

Use Text Effects

Word provides a number of text effects that can be applied directly from the Font group in the Home tab (see Figure 3-3), such as superscript, subscript, and strikethrough, or from the Font dialog box's Effects area (see Figure 3-2), such as double strikethrough, small caps, and hidden. In addition, Word 2013 has a Text Effects button and menu in the Font group that allows you to apply a number of visual effects to selected characters, such as shadow, glow, and bevel.

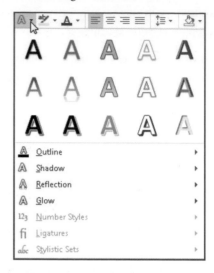

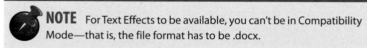

![NOTE icon] **NOTE** For Text Effects to be available, you can't be in Compatibility Mode—that is, the file format has to be .docx.

1. Select the text to which you want to apply the effect.

2. In the Home tab Font group, click the **Text Effects** down arrow to open the Text Effects drop-down menu.

3. Slowly hover the mouse pointer over the various effects to see the results on the selected text.

4. After looking at each of the 15 letter-style options, hover over each of the submenus at the bottom that are available with your selected text (not all submenus are available, depending on the font selected). Each contains a submenu with further choices.

5. Try various combinations of Outline, Shadow, Reflection, Glow, Number Styles, Ligatures, and Stylistic Sets. You have many possibilities. Depending on the active font selected, a submenu may not be available.

6. On most of the submenu items, the last item will be a "*named* Options," such as "Shadow Options." If you click that, you'll see a Format Text Effects task pane on the right with even more possibilities, shown in Figure 3-7.

7. Select the effects you want to use, previewing them on your page. When you are satisfied, if you are using the Format Text Effects task pane, click **Close** in the upper-right corner of the task pane to close it.

Set OpenType Features

OpenType is an open specification for defining computer fonts that is quite flexible, both in its ability to represent a great many of the world's alphabets and in its ability to be easily scaled or sized.

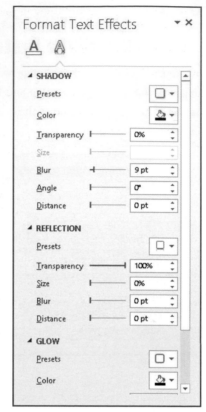

Figure 3-7: Using either the Text Effects drop-down menu or the Format Text Effects task panes, such as the one shown here, you can make characters look any way you want.

OpenType was started by Microsoft and added to by Adobe Systems and others to create a substantial enhancement to its predecessor, TrueType. OpenType is the predominant method used to create fonts on most computers today.

The Advanced tab of Word's Font dialog box contains a group of settings that provides stylistic alternatives for certain OpenType fonts, in addition to the control of the use of ligatures (stylistic pairs of letters like Æ) and the spacing and forms of numbers. These settings are applicable to fonts in which the font designer has added these options. One such font that is available with Windows 7, Windows 8, and Office 2013 is Gabriola. Figure 3-8 shows the Gabriola font at 20 points with various OpenType features selected.

1. Select the text to be formatted, click the **Home** tab, click the **Font** dialog box launcher, and click the **Advanced** tab, shown in Figure 3-6. The OpenType features available are (see the upcoming Note at the end of this section):

   - **Ligatures**   Select from among None, Standard, Standard And Contextual, Historical And Discretionary, or All on various levels of styling pairs of letters like Æ.

   - **Number Spacing**   Retain Default or Tabular, or select Proportional, depending on whether you are using the number in a sentence, where you might want proportional spacing, or in a tabular list, where you want the numbers to line up. The Proportional setting tends to take less horizontal space, but Tabular is the default. Try this with the Calibri font.

- **Number Forms**   Retain Default or Lining, where the tops and bottoms of the numbers line up, or select Oldstyle, where the tops and bottoms of the numbers don't line up. Lining is the default, shown on the top in this example of Calibri numbers.

> 123,456,789
>
> 123,456,789

- **Stylistic Sets**   Select from up to 20 alternative embellishments to a font that have been added by the font designer.

- **Use Contextual Alternatives**   When checked, this applies added flourishes that the designer wants used in only certain contextual circumstances, such as the first character in some lines, as you can see in example (c) in Figure 3-8.

2. After making a selection, click **OK** and look at the effect on your page. The Preview area does not do justice to these changes.

(a)

(b)

(c)

> When in the Course of human events, it becomes necessary for one people to dissolve the political bands which have connected them with another, and to assume among the powers of the earth, the

Figure 3-8: OpenType fonts give the font designer many added features that can be used in a given font. Here the Gabriola font is shown: (a) in its default configuration, (b) with stylistic set 5, and (c) with stylistic set 7 with Use Contextual Alternates checked.

Change Capitalization

You can, of course, capitalize a character you are typing by holding down SHIFT while you type. You can also press CAPS LOCK to have every letter that you type be capitalized and then press CAPS LOCK again to turn off capitalization. You can also change the capitalization of existing text.

1. Select the text whose capitalization you want to change.
2. In the Home tab Font group, click **Change Case**. Select one of these options:

   - **Sentence case** capitalizes the first letter of the first word of every selected sentence.
   - **lowercase** displays all selected words in lowercase.
   - **UPPERCASE** displays all selected words in all caps. All the characters of every selected word will be capitalized.
   - **Capitalize Each Word** puts a leading cap on each selected word.
   - **tOGGLE cASE** changes all lowercase characters to uppercase and all uppercase characters to lowercase.

Create a Drop Cap

A *drop cap* is an enlarged capital letter at the beginning of a paragraph that extends down over two or more lines of text (see the red "T" in Figure 3-5 earlier in this chapter). To create a drop cap:

1. Select the character or word that you want to be formatted as a drop cap.

2. In the Insert tab Text group, click **Drop Cap**. A menu will open. You have these choices:

   - **None**, the default, keeps a standard letter.
   - Click **Dropped** to have the first letter dropped within the paragraph text.
   - Click **In Margin** to set the capital letter off in the margin.
   - Click **Drop Cap Options** to see further options in the Drop Cap dialog box. You can change the font, specify how many lines will be dropped (3 is the default), and specify how far from the text the dropped cap will be placed. Click **OK** to close the Drop Cap dialog box.

3. Make the choice you want to use.

The paragraph will be reformatted around the enlarged capital letter. Here are the two examples of putting the dropped cap in the paragraph or in the margin.

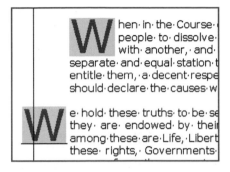

 NOTE To remove a drop cap, select the character or word, in the Insert tab, click **Drop Cap** in the Text group, and click **None** on the menu.

FORMAT A PARAGRAPH

Paragraph formatting, which you can apply to any paragraph, is used to manage alignment, indentation, line spacing, bulleted or numbered lists, and borders. In Word, a paragraph consists of a paragraph mark (created by pressing **ENTER**) and any text or objects that appear between that paragraph mark and the previous paragraph mark. A paragraph can be empty, or it can contain anything from a single character to as many characters as you care to enter.

⯈⯈ Survey the Paragraph-Formatting Tools

Text formatting can be applied using the Paragraph dialog box, keyboard shortcuts, the Paragraph group on the Home tab, and the mini toolbar that displays when you select or right-click text. (See "Access the Mini Toolbar" earlier in the chapter.)

Access the Paragraph Dialog Box

The Paragraph dialog box provides the most comprehensive selection of paragraph formatting and spacing alternatives. Click the **Paragraph** dialog box launcher 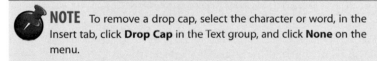 in the Home tab Paragraph group to open the Paragraph dialog box (see Figure 3-9). Alternatively, you can right-click the selected text you want to format and then click **Paragraph**. Even though the Paragraph dialog box is the most comprehensive source of Paragraph formatting commands, you'll find that using the commands on the ribbon (Home tab Paragraph group) or the mini toolbar will be quicker and easier for most formatting tasks.

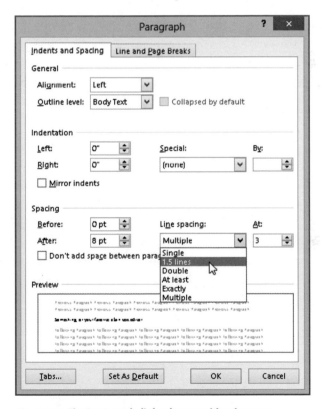

Figure 3-9: The Paragraph dialog box provides the most complete set of text-formatting controls.

Use Keyboard Shortcuts for Paragraphs

Using keyboard shortcuts to format paragraphs allows you to keep your hands on the keyboard. Table 3-2 summarizes the keyboard shortcuts for formatting a paragraph.

Table 3-2: Keyboard Shortcuts for Working with Paragraphs	
Hang paragraph	CTRL+T
Unhang paragraph	CTRL+SHIFT+T
Heading level 1	ALT+CTRL+1
Heading level 2	ALT+CTRL+2
Heading level 3	ALT+CTRL+3
Indent paragraph	CTRL+M
Unindent paragraph	CTRL+SHIFT+M
Reset paragraph formatting	CTRL+Q
Line space—single	CTRL+1
Line space—1.5 lines	CTRL+5
Line space—double	CTRL+2
Normal style	CTRL+SHIFT+N
Left Align	CTRL+L
Right Align	CTRL+R
Center Align	CTRL+E
Justified	CTRL+J

Access the Paragraph Group

You'll find that for most of your paragraph formatting, you'll simply use the Paragraph group (see Figure 3-10). To display the Paragraph group tools, click the **Home** tab. You can also open the Paragraph dialog box by right-clicking the paragraph you want to format and clicking **Paragraph**.

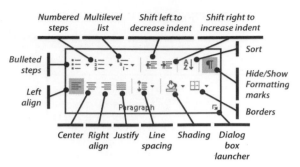

Figure 3-10: The Paragraph group in the Home tab contains many of the tools you need for formatting paragraphs.

▷▷ Set Paragraph Alignment

Four types of paragraph alignment are available in Word (see Figure 3-11): left aligned, centered, right aligned, and justified. Left aligned, right aligned, and centered are self-explanatory. Justified means that the text in a paragraph is spread out between the left and right margins. Word does this by adding space between words, except for the last line of a paragraph. To apply paragraph alignment, click in the paragraph you want to align (you don't need to select the entire paragraph) and then choose one of the following options:

- In the Home tab Paragraph group, click the **Paragraph** dialog box launcher to open the Paragraph dialog box. On the Indents And Spacing tab, click the **Alignment** down arrow, click the type of alignment you want, and click **OK**. See Figure 3-11.

- There are several keyboard shortcuts available. Refer to Table 3-2.

- In the Home tab Paragraph group, click the **Align Left**, **Center**, **Align Right**, or **Justify** button, depending on what you want to do. See Figure 3-11.

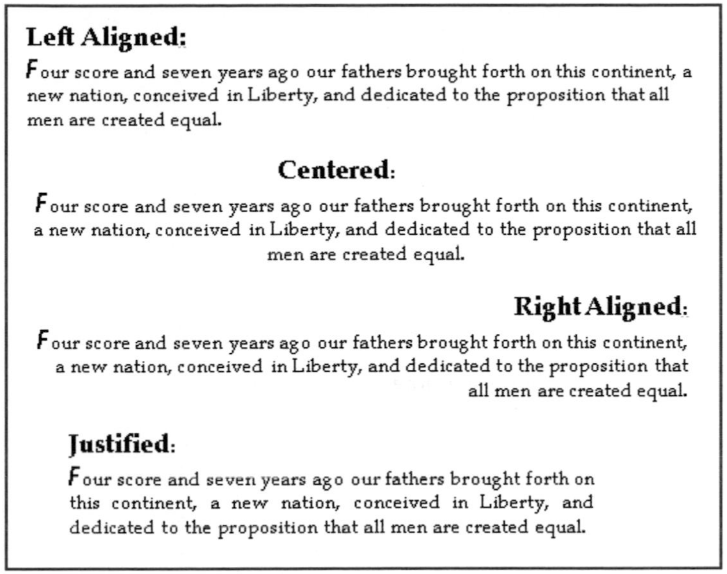

Left Aligned:

ℱour score and seven years ago our fathers brought forth on this continent, a new nation, conceived in Liberty, and dedicated to the proposition that all men are created equal.

Centered:

ℱour score and seven years ago our fathers brought forth on this continent, a new nation, conceived in Liberty, and dedicated to the proposition that all men are created equal.

Right Aligned:

ℱour score and seven years ago our fathers brought forth on this continent, a new nation, conceived in Liberty, and dedicated to the proposition that all men are created equal.

Justified:

ℱour score and seven years ago our fathers brought forth on this continent, a new nation, conceived in Liberty, and dedicated to the proposition that all men are created equal.

Figure 3-11: Paragraph alignment provides both visual appeal and separation of text.

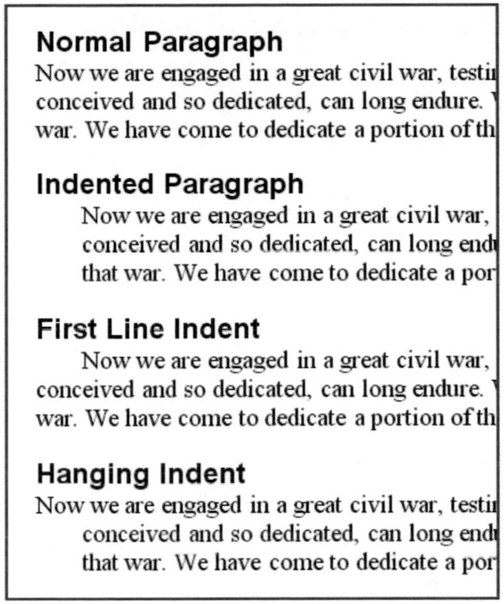

Normal Paragraph

Now we are engaged in a great civil war, testi conceived and so dedicated, can long endure. war. We have come to dedicate a portion of th

Indented Paragraph

Now we are engaged in a great civil war, conceived and so dedicated, can long end that war. We have come to dedicate a por

First Line Indent

Now we are engaged in a great civil war, conceived and so dedicated, can long endure. war. We have come to dedicate a portion of th

Hanging Indent

Now we are engaged in a great civil war, testi conceived and so dedicated, can long end that war. We have come to dedicate a por

Figure 3-12: Indenting allows you to separate a block of text visually.

✓ **QuickFacts**

Indenting a Paragraph

As illustrated in Figure 3-12, indenting a paragraph in Word means to move the left or right edge (or both) of the paragraph inward toward the center. You can also move the left side of the first line away from the center, for a *hanging indent*.

The three types of indenting shown in Figure 3-12 serve particular purposes, such as:

- An **indented paragraph**, either just on the left or on both the left and right, is used to separate and call attention to a piece of text.

- **Indenting the first line** of a paragraph is used to indicate the start of a new paragraph.

- A **hanging indent** indents all of the lines in a paragraph except the first line, which hangs out to the left. This is a unique way to start a new paragraph and provides an outlining look to the paragraph. Bullets and numbered lists are an example of hanging indents.

There are also other types of paragraph indentations, such as:

- **Bulleted and numbered lists** are used to organize and group pieces of text so they can be viewed as elements within a given topic. These are special kinds of hanging indents.

- An **outline** is used to provide a hierarchical structure.

▷▷ Change and Remove Indents

Indentation is a powerful formatting tool when used correctly. Like other formatting, it can also be overused and make text hard to read or to understand. Ask yourself two questions about indentation: Do I have a good reason for it? Does it improve the readability and/or understanding of what is being said?

In all cases, unless otherwise noted, first click the paragraph for which you want to change or remove the indentation.

Increase or Decrease the Left Indent

To move the left edge of an entire paragraph to the right, or to move it back to the right, you have the following choices:

- In the Home tab Paragraph group, click **Increase Indent** one or more times to indent the left edge a half-inch each time (the first click will move the left paragraph edge to the nearest half-inch or inch mark). To decrease the left indent, click **Decrease Indent** one or more times.

Decrease Indent   Increase Indent

- Press **CTRL+M** one or more times to indent the left edge a half-inch each time. Press **CTRL+SHIFT+M** one or more times to unindent the left edge.

- In the Page Layout tab Paragraph group, under Indent, click the **Left** spinner's up arrow until you get the amount of indentation you want. To remove or reduce the indent, click the **Left** spinner's down-arrow.

- On the Home tab, click the **Paragraph** dialog box launcher. On the Indents And Spacing tab, under Indentation, click the **Left** spinner's up arrow until you get the amount of indentation you want, and

then click **OK**. To reduce or remove the indentation, click the **Left** spinner's down-arrow.

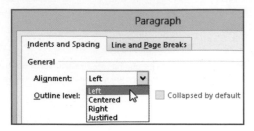

Increase or Decrease the Right Indent

To move the right edge of an entire paragraph to the left, you have these choices:

- In the Page Layout tab Paragraph group, under Indent, click the **Right** spinner's up arrow until you get the amount of indentation you want. To remove or reduce the right indent, click the **Right** spinner's down-arrow.

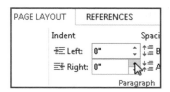

- On the Home tab, click the **Paragraph** dialog box launcher. On the Indents And Spacing tab, under Indentation, click the **Right** spinner's up arrow until you get the amount of indentation you want, and then click **OK**. To remove or reduce the right indentation, click the **Right** spinner's down-arrow.

Indent the First Line

When indenting the first line, you can either move the first line only or move the entire paragraph except for the first line (see "Make and

Remove a Hanging Indent"). To move only the first line of a paragraph to the right or left, you have these choices:

- Click on the left edge of the first line of the paragraph and press **TAB**.

- Click the paragraph, click the **Home** tab, and then click the **Paragraph** dialog box launcher. On the Indents And Spacing tab, under Indentation, click the **Special** down arrow, and click **First Line**. If you want an indent different than the .5" default, click the **By** spinner to set the amount of indentation you want, and click **OK**.

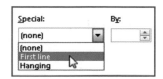

Make and Remove a Hanging Indent

To indent all of a paragraph except for the first line, you have these choices:

- Press **CTRL+T** one or more times to indent the left edge of all but the first line each time. To unindent the hanging indent, press **CTRL+SHIFT+T** one or more times.

- On the Home tab, click the **Paragraph** dialog box launcher. On the Indents And Spacing tab, under Indentation, click the **Special** down arrow, and select **Hanging**. Enter the amount of the indent, and click **OK**. To remove the hanging indent, on the Indents And Spacing tab, under Indentation, click the **Special** down arrow, and click **None**. Click **OK**.

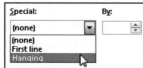

 TIP You can reset *all* paragraph formatting, including indents, hanging indents, alignment, and paragraph spacing, to their default settings by clicking in a paragraph (or selecting multiple paragraphs) and pressing **CTRL+Q**.

Set Indents for Lists

To set the indents for a bulleted or numbered list:

1. Select the list to be indented and right-click the list and select **Adjust List Indents**. The Adjust List Indents dialog box appears.

   - To set the bullet distance from the margin, click the **Bullet Position** spinners.

   - To change the distance between the bullet and the text, click the **Text Indent** spinner.

   - To identify which character is to follow the bullet or number, click the **Follow Number With** down-arrow and select between a tab character, a space, or nothing.

   - To set a tab stop, click the **Add Tab Stop At** check box and click the spinner beneath it to set the tab stop.

2. Click **OK**.

Change the Level of Indents for Lists

You can change the level number for bulleted and numbered lists. Each level has its own style or image of a bullet or number.

1. Click in the text for the bullet or number you want to change.

2. In the Home tab, Paragraph group, click the **Bullets** or **Numbering** down-arrow, and click **Change List Level**.

3. Click the level where you want the bullet or number.

⏵⏵ Use the Ruler for Indents

You can use the horizontal ruler to set tabs and indents.

Display the Rulers

To display the rulers, if they are not already visible, in the View tab Show group, check the **Ruler** check box. Vertical and horizontal rulers will be displayed on the top and left sides of the document window.

Set a Paragraph Indent on the Left

To move the paragraph to the left:

1. Click the paragraph to be indented.

2. Drag the **Left Indent** tab (the small box) to where you want the paragraph indented.

Set a Paragraph Indent on the Right

To move the right side of the paragraph to the left:

1. Click to select the paragraph to be indented.

2. Drag the **Right Indent** tab on the right of the ruler to where you want the paragraph indented.

Set a First-Line Indent

To indent the first line to the right of the rest of the paragraph:

1. Click to select the paragraph to be indented.

2. Drag the **First Line Indent** tab on the left of the ruler to where you want the paragraph indented.

Set a Hanging Indent

To indent all but the first line of a paragraph to the right of the first line:

1. Click to select the paragraph to be indented.

2. Drag the **Hanging Indent** tab on the left of the ruler to where you want the paragraph indented.

UNDERSTAND LINE AND PARAGRAPH SPACING

The vertical spacing of text is determined by the amount of space between lines, the amount of space added before and after a paragraph, and where you break lines and pages.

 ## Set Line Spacing

The amount of space between lines is most often set in terms of the line height, with *single spacing* being one times the current line height, *double spacing* being twice the current line height, and so on. You can also specify line spacing in points, as you do the size of type. Single spacing is approximately 14 points for 12-point type. To set line spacing for an entire paragraph, click the paragraph for which you want to set the line spacing, and then choose one of these options:

- In the Home tab Paragraph group, click **Line Spacing**, and then click the line spacing, in terms of lines, that you want to use.

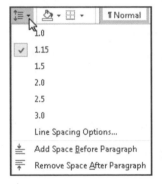

- Press **CTRL+1** for single-line spacing, press **CTRL+5** for one-and-a-half-line spacing, and press **CTRL+2** for double-line spacing.

- On the Home tab, click the **Paragraph** dialog box launcher. On the Indents And Spacing tab, under Spacing, click the **Line Spacing** down arrow. From the menu that appears, select the line spacing you want to use. Click **OK**.

Add Space Between Paragraphs

In addition to specifying space between lines, you can add extra space before and after paragraphs. With typewriters, many people would add an extra blank line between paragraphs. That has carried over to computers, but it does not always look good. If you are using single spacing, leaving a blank line will leave an extra 14 points (with 12-point type) between paragraphs. Common paragraph spacing is to leave 3 points before the paragraph and 6 points afterward, so if you have two of these paragraphs, one after the other, you would have a total of 9 points, in comparison to the 14 points from an extra blank line. To add extra space between paragraphs, click the paragraph to which you want to add space, and then choose one of these options:

- In the Page Layout tab Paragraph group, under Spacing, click the **Before** and **After** spinners to set the spacing before and after the paragraph.

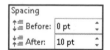

- On the Home tab, click the **Paragraph** dialog box launcher. On the Indents And Spacing tab, under Spacing, click the **Before** spinner or enter a number in points ("pt") for the space you want to add before the paragraph. If desired, do the same thing for the space after the paragraph. When you are ready, click **OK**.

> **NOTE** In the Paragraph dialog box, you can specify the amount of space between lines in a format other than the number of lines. From the Line Spacing drop-down list, click **Exactly**, and then enter or select the number of points to use between lines. With 12-point type, single-line spacing is about 14 points, one-and-a-half-line spacing (1.5) is about 21 points, and so on. With 11-point type, single spacing is about 12 points. If you reduce the line spacing below the size of the type (below 12 points for 12-point type, for example), the lines will begin to overlap and become hard to read.

Set Line and Page Breaks

The vertical spacing of a document is also affected by how lines and pages are broken and how much of a paragraph you force to stay together or be with text either before or after it.

You can break a line and start a new one, thereby creating a new line, a new paragraph, or a new page.

- To **create a new paragraph**, move the insertion point to where you want to break the line and press **ENTER**.

- To **advance to a new line while staying in the same paragraph**, move the insertion point to where you want to break the line and press **SHIFT+ENTER**.

- To **break a page and start a new one**, press **CTRL+ENTER**.

  –Or–

  In the Insert tab Pages group, click **Page Break**. (If your screen is smaller, you may have to click **Pages** first, and then click **Page Break** from the menu, as shown here.)

  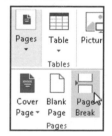

  –Or–

  In the Page Layout tab Page Setup group, click **Breaks** and then click **Page**.

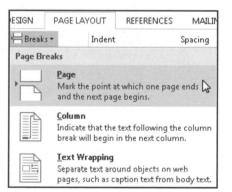

Handle Split Pages

When a paragraph is split over two pages, you have several ways to control how much of the paragraph is placed on which page.

1. Click the paragraph you want to change.

2. On the Home tab, click the **Paragraph** dialog box launcher, and click the **Line And Page Breaks** tab.

3. Check whichever of the following options are correct for your situation, and then click **OK**:

   • **Widow/Orphan Control** adjusts the pagination to keep at least two lines on one or both pages. For example, if you have two lines, without checking Widow/Orphan Control, one line is placed on the first page and the second is placed on the next page. When you check this option, all three lines are placed on the second page. Widow/Orphan Control is checked by default.

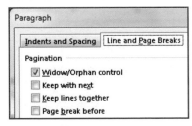

   • **Keep With Next** forces the entire paragraph to stay on the same page with the next paragraph. This option is used with paragraph headings that you want to keep with the first paragraph.

   • **Keep Lines Together** forces all lines of a paragraph to be on the same page. This option can be used for a paragraph title where you want all of it on one page.

• **Page Break Before** forces a page break before the start of the paragraph. This option is used with major section headings or titles that you want to start on a new page.

⏩ Use Numbered and Bulleted Lists

Word provides the means to automatically number or add bullets to paragraphs and then format the paragraphs as hanging indents so that the numbers or bullets stick out to the left (see Figure 3-13).

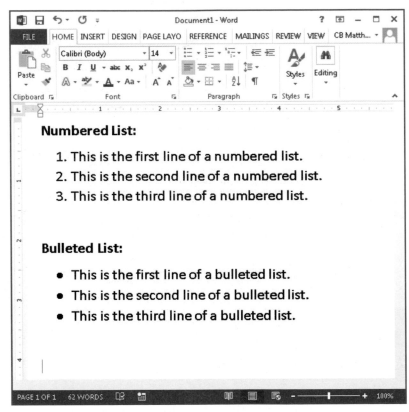

Figure 3-13: Bullets and numbering help organize thoughts into lists.

Create a Numbered List Using AutoCorrect

You can create a numbered list as you type, and Word will automatically format it according to your text. Word's numbered lists are particularly handy, because you can add or delete paragraphs in the middle of the list and have the list automatically renumber itself. To start a numbered list:

1. Press ENTER to start a new paragraph.

2. Type 1., press either the SPACEBAR *two* times or press TAB once, and then type the rest of what you want in the first item of the numbered list.

3. Press ENTER. The number "2." automatically appears, and both the first and the new lines are formatted as hanging indents. Also, the AutoCorrect lightning icon appears when you press ENTER on the first line.

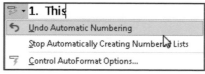

1. This is the first line in a new numbered list.
2. |

4. After typing the second item in your list, press ENTER once again. The number "3." automatically appears. Type the item and press ENTER to keep numbering the list.

5. When you are done, press ENTER twice. The numbering will stop and the hanging indent will be removed.

If you click the **AutoCorrect** icon, you may choose to undo the automatic numbering that has already been applied, stop the automatic creation of numbered lists, and control the use of AutoCorrect (see Chapter 1 for more information on AutoCorrect).

1. This
↶ Undo Automatic Numbering
Stop Automatically Creating Numbered Lists
⚡ Control AutoFormat Options...

 TIP You can type 1 with or without a period, and 2 will be formatted in the same way. If you type the period and press **TAB** or two spaces, the AutoCorrect icon appears immediately. It disappears when you press **ENTER**.

Create a Numbered, Bulleted, or Multilevel List Before You Type Text

You can also set up the formatting for a numbered, bulleted, or multilevel list before you start typing the text it will contain.

Bullets Numbering Multilevel list

1. Press ENTER to start a new paragraph.

2. In the Home tab Paragraph group, click **Numbering** to begin a numbered list; click **Bullets** to start a bulleted list; or click **Multilevel List** to start a multilevel tiered list. If you click Multilevel List, you'll need to also select a type of list from the menu.

 NOTE If you find your numbering "off"—for instance, a new list's numbering is continued from a previous list—right-click the first new numbered item and click **Restart At 1**, or the appropriate number.

3. Type the first item, and press ENTER to start the second numbered or bulleted item with the same style as the first. When you are done creating the list, press ENTER twice to stop the automatic list.

–Or–

Click the **Home** tab and then click **Numbering** (or Bullets or Multilevel List) in the Paragraph group to end the list.

TIP You can switch a numbered list to a bulleted one or vice versa by selecting the list and clicking the other icon in the Home tab Paragraph group.

Customize Bullets and Numbers

To select a bullet style other than the default, click the **Bullets** down arrow and click your choice from the seven options on the menu, as shown

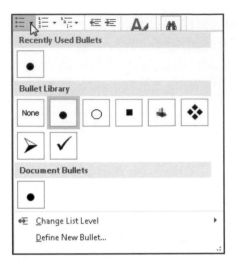

Figure 3-14: Clicking the Bullets down arrow displays a list of choices for formatting bullets.

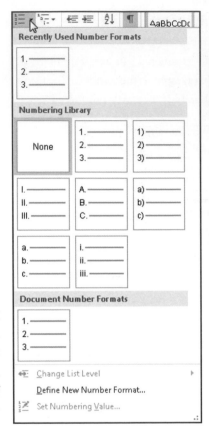

Figure 3-15: Numbered paragraphs can use numbers, letters, or even uppercase or lowercase roman numerals.

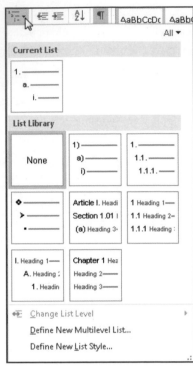

Figure 3-16: Multilevel paragraphs use a variety of characters to identify and format a multilevel list, including numbers, bullets, and text.

in Figure 3-14. Word also offers seven different styles for numbering paragraphs, as you can see in Figure 3-15, and seven styles for multilevel lists, as shown in Figure 3-16. For those who feel seven choices is not enough, there is a Define New option for bullets, numbering, and multilevel lists that includes the ability to select from hundreds of pictures and to import others to use as bullets. To use custom bullets or numbering (multilevel lists are handled separately later):

1. Click the **Home** tab and then click the **Bullets** or **Numbering** down arrow to open the Bullets or Numbering menu.

2. Depending on whether you are using bullets or numbering, you have the following choices.

   For bullets:

   Click **Define New Bullet**. The Define New Bullet dialog box appears (see Figure 3-17). Use one of the following:

   - Click **Font** and then select the font and other attributes in the dialog box for the character that you want to use. Click **OK** to close the Font dialog box when you are ready.

   - Click **Symbol** to select a symbol, and then click **OK**.

   - Click **Picture** to open the Insert Pictures dialog box (see Figure 3-18). To use your own picture, click **Browse** for either your computer or SkyDrive, select the picture from the files stored there, and click **Insert**. To use a picture from the Office.com Clip Art catalog or from the results of using Bing Image Search, in the Search Office.com text box or Search Bing text box, respectively,

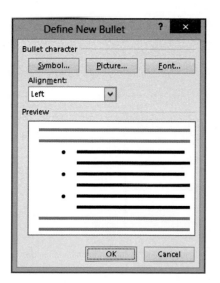

Figure 3-17: You can select any character in any font to use as a bullet.

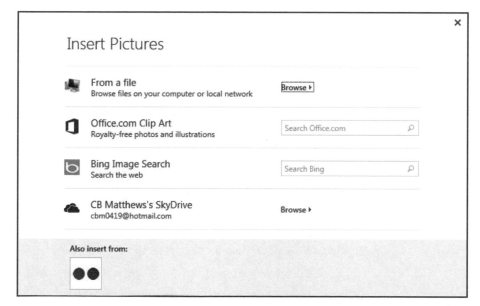

Figure 3-18: Word provides a number of ways for you to access your own pictures or those online.

type a keyword, such as <u>flowers</u>, and click the **Search** icon (as shown next). You'll see a collection of pictures you might use for the bullet image. Select an image and click **Insert**. Regardless of the source of the image, after clicking Insert, set the alignment in the Define New Bullet dialog box, and click **OK**. The new bullet will appear on your page.

For numbering:

Click **Define New Number Format**. The Define New Number Format dialog box appears. Click the **Number Style** down arrow to choose the style (numbers, capital letters, lowercase letters, roman numerals, and so on). Optionally, click **Font** to choose the numbers formatted with a particular font, and click **OK** to close the Font dialog box. Press **TAB** to make any additions to the number in the Number Format text box. For example, delete the period for a number without the period or add a prefix such as "A-" to produce numbers A-1, A-2, and so on, as shown in Figure 3-19. Click the **Alignment** down arrow to choose between right alignment, left alignment, or centered. Click **OK** to apply the customized numbering.

Remove Numbering and Bulleting

To remove the numbering or bulleting (both the numbers or bullets and the hanging indent):

1. Select the paragraphs from which you want to remove the numbering or bulleting.

2. In the Home tab Paragraph group, click **Numbering**, **Bullets**, or **Multilevel List**, as appropriate.

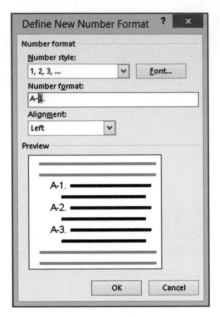

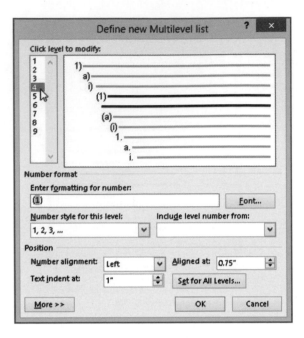

Figure 3-19: You can add a recurring prefix or suffix to automatically generated numbers.

Define New Multilevel Lists

Defining new multilevel lists is handled much like bullets and numbering, but is slightly more complicated.

1. In the Home tab Paragraph group, click the **Multilevel List** down arrow to open the menu.

2. Click **Define New Multilevel List**. The Define New Multilevel List dialog box opens. First, click the specific level to be modified. You have these choices:

- Click in the **Enter Formatting For Number** text box and modify the level if needed. An example would be to add a preface, such as "a-1," for instance.

- Click **Font** to select a specific font or make changes to the formatting, such as Bold or Small Caps. It will be reflected to the left.

- Click the **Number Style For This Level** down arrow and select a different numbering style if desired.

- Click the **Include Level Number From** down arrow and select another level to be attached to the selected numbering scheme. It will be placed before the current level number.

- Select a **Position** setting to align the level or indent it.

- Click **More** to open an additional group of modifications to refine the changes you can make to the multilevel list.

Add Horizontal Lines, Borders, and Shading

Borders and shading allow you to separate and call attention to text. You can place a border on any or all of the four sides of selected text, paragraphs, and pages; and you can add many varieties of shading to the space occupied by selected text, paragraphs, and pages—with or without a border around them (see Figure 3-20). You can create horizontal lines as you type, and you can add other borders from both the Home tab Paragraph group and the Borders And Shading dialog box.

Add a Horizontal Line

You can add a horizontal line between the left and right margins of your document if you want to indicate, for example, a clear transition between topics without adding a heading.

> Hyphens------
>
> Equal Signs ====
>
> Underscores _____

Press **ENTER** to create a new paragraph. You have these choices of horizontal lines:

- **A single, light horizontal line** Type --- (three hyphens) and press **ENTER**.
- **A double horizontal line** Type === (three equal signs) and press **ENTER**.
- **A single, heavy horizontal line** Type _ _ _ (three underscores) and press **ENTER**.
- **A graphic horizontal line** In the Home tab Paragraph group, click the **Borders** down arrow, and click **Horizontal Line**.

Add Borders and Shading to Text

Borders and shading can be added to any amount of text, from a single character to several pages.

1. Select the text for which you want to have a border or shading.

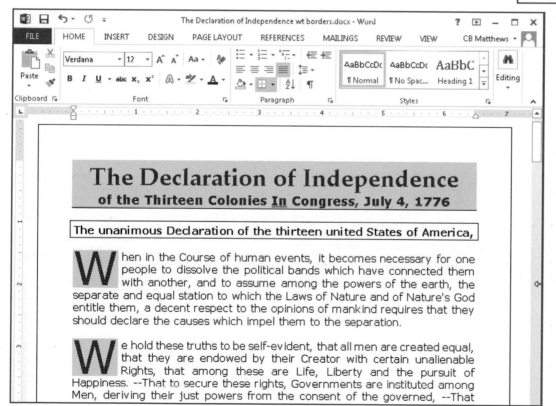

Figure 3-20: Borders and shading can be applied to text, blank paragraphs, phrases, characters, and words.

2. In the Home tab Paragraph group, click the **Borders** down arrow 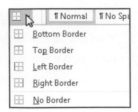, and then select the type of border you want to apply. If you have selected less than a full paragraph, you can only select a four-sided box (you actually can select less, but you will get a full box).

–Or–

In the Home tab Paragraph group, click the Borders down arrow, and click **Borders And Shading** on the menu. The Borders And Shading dialog box appears, as shown in Figure 3-21.

- To add text or paragraph borders, click the **Borders** tab, click the type of box (click **Custom** for fewer than four sides), choose the line style, color, and width you want. If you want fewer than four sides and are working with paragraphs, click the sides you want in the Preview area. Click **Options** to set the distance (in points) the border is away from the text.

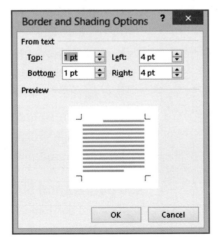

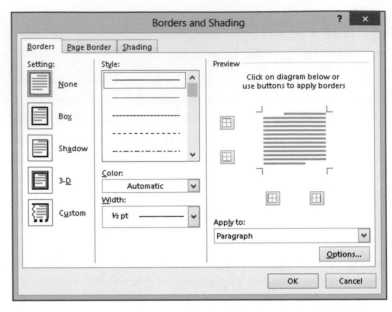

Figure 3-21: Borders can be created with many different types and widths of lines.

- To add page borders, click the **Page Border** tab, click the type of box (click **Custom** for fewer than four sides), and choose the line style, color, width, and art, if any, you want to use for the border, such as custom drawn lines or a row of miniature company logos. If you want fewer than four sides, click the sides you want in the Preview area. Click **Options** to set the distance the border is away from either the edge of the page or the text.

- To add shading, click the **Shading** tab, and click the color of shading, or *fill*, you want. If desired, select a pattern (this is independent of the fill), and choose whether to apply it to the entire page, to the paragraph, or just to the selected text.

When you are done with the Borders And Shading dialog box, click **OK** to close it.

FORMAT A PAGE

Page formatting has to do with the overall formatting of items, such as margins, orientation, size, and vertical alignment of a page. You can set options for page formatting either from the Page Layout tab or the Page Setup dialog box.

Turn On Formatting Marks

Turning on formatting marks helps you see what is making your document look the way it does. To make it easier to see any formatting and what is causing the spacing in a document, you can display some or all of the formatting marks.

- In the Home tab Paragraph group, click **Show/Hide Formatting Marks** [¶] to show all of the formatting marks—tabs, spaces, and paragraph marks, among other characters.

> → This·has·a·tab,·spaces··,·and·a·paragraph·mark¶

- To fine-tune exactly which formatting marks to display, click the **File** tab, click **Options**, and then click **Display**. Under Always Show These Formatting Marks On The Screen, you can choose which marks to display. The default is to show no formatting marks. Click **OK** when finished.

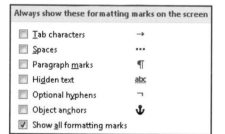

Set Margins

Margins are the space between the edge of the paper and the text. To set margins:

1. Open the document whose margins you want to set. If you want the margins to apply only to a selected part of a document, select that part now.

2. In the Page Layout tab Page Setup group, click **Margins** to open the menu shown in Figure 3-22.

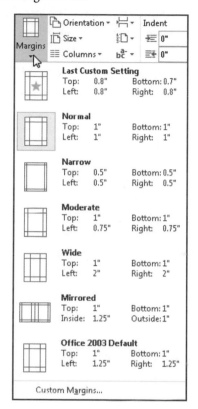

Figure 3-22: You can select from a group of predefined margins, according to the needs of your document, or you can create a custom set of margins.

3. Click the option you want.

> **CAUTION** Remember that page formatting changes the margins and other formatting for whole pages. If you select a part of the document to have special formatting, it will separate that section by pages. To change formatting for smaller sections of text, use indenting.

▷▷ Copy Formatting

Often, you'll want a word, phrase, or paragraph formatted like an existing word, phrase, or paragraph. Word allows you to copy just the formatting. You can copy a single occurrence or several scattered throughout the document. You can use the keyboard as well to do this.

Use the Format Painter for a Single Copy

1. Select the word, phrase, or paragraph from which you want to copy the formatting. In the case of a paragraph, make sure you have included the paragraph mark (see "Turn On Formatting Marks").

2. In the Home tab Clipboard group, click **Format Painter** .

3. With the special pointer (brush and I-beam), select the word, phrase, or paragraph (including the paragraph mark) you want formatted.

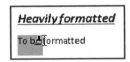

> **TIP** If you are copying the formatting for a whole paragraph, you can just click the source paragraph, click **Format Painter**, and then click the new paragraph to copy its formatting.

Copy Formatting to Several Places

To copy formatting to several separate pieces of text or paragraphs:

1. Drag across the source text with the formatting you want to copy.

2. In the Home tab Clipboard group, double-click **Format Painter**.

3. Simply select each piece of text or paragraph that you want to format (or click it). It will automatically be formatted.

4. When you are done, to remove the Format Painter action, click **Format Painter** or press **ESC**.

▷▷ Use the Page Setup Dialog Box to Format a Page

You can do a lot of page formatting using the Page Setup dialog box.

1. On the Page Layout tab, click the **Page Setup** dialog box launcher. The Page Setup dialog box appears, as shown in Figure 3-23.

Figure 3-23: Many page-formatting tasks can be done in the Page Setup dialog box.

2. Click the **Margins** tab, if it isn't already visible. You have these options:

   • Under Margins, click the spinners or manually enter the desired distance in inches between the particular edge of the paper and the start or end of text.

- Under Orientation, click either **Portrait** or **Landscape**, depending on which you want.

- Under Pages, click the **Multiple Pages** down arrow, and select an option: click **Mirror Margins** when the inside gutter (the combined inside margin of two bound pages) is larger (if you will be printing and binding the document, for example); click **2 Pages Per Sheet** when a normal sheet of paper is divided into two pages; and click **Book Fold** when you are putting together a section of a book ("a signature") with four, eight, or more pages in the signature.

- If you want these changes to apply only to the selected part of a document, under Preview, click the **Apply To** down arrow and click **Selected Text**.

3. When you are done setting margins, click **OK**.

If you want to further differentiate between the left and right pages, you need to use sections (described in Chapter 4).

 TIP If you are going to bind the document and want to add an extra amount of space on one edge for the binding, click the **Gutter** spinner to set the extra width you want, and click the **Gutter Position** down arrow to select the side that the gutter is on.

Use Mirror Margins with the Menu

Mirror margins allow you to have a larger "inside" margin, which would be the right margin on the left page and the left margin on the right page, or any other combination of margins that are mirrored between the left and right pages. To create mirror margins:

1. Open the document whose margins you want mirrored.

2. In the Page Layout tab Page Setup group, click **Margins**.

3. Click **Mirrored**. When you do that, the left and right margins change to inside and outside margins.

Determine Page Orientation

Page orientation specifies whether a page is taller than it is wide ("portrait") or wider than it is tall ("landscape"). For 8½-inch by 11-inch letter size paper, if the 11-inch side is vertical (the left and right edges), which is the standard way of reading a letter, then it is a portrait orientation. If the 11-inch side is horizontal (the top and bottom edges), then it is a landscape orientation. Portrait is the default orientation in Word and most documents. To change it:

1. Open the document whose orientation you want to set. If you want the orientation to apply only to a selected part of a document, select that part now; but you can only select whole pages to have a particular orientation.

2. In the Page Layout tab Page Setup group, click **Orientation**.

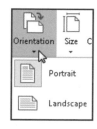

3. On the menu, click the option you want.

Specify Paper Size

Specifying the paper size gives you the starting perimeter of the area within which you can set margins and enter text or pictures.

1. In the Page Layout tab Page Setup group, click **Size**. A menu will open, shown in Figure 3-24.

2. Click the size of paper you want.

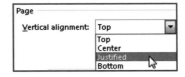

Figure 3-24: Choose the paper size from a selection of popular sizes in the Page Layout tab.

1. Click the **File** tab, click **Options**, and then click **Advanced** in the left pane.

2. Under Editing Options, check both **Keep Track Of Formatting** and **Mark Formatting Inconsistencies**.

Set Vertical Alignment

Just as you can right align, center, left align, and justify text between margins (see "Set Paragraph Alignment"), you can also specify vertical alignment so that text is aligned with the top, bottom, or center of the page or justified between the top and bottom.

1. On the Page Layout tab, click the **Page Setup** dialog box launcher.

2. On the Layout tab, under Page, click the **Vertical Alignment** down arrow, and click the vertical alignment that you want to use.

3. Click **OK** when you are done.

 Track Inconsistent Formatting

When you turned on the formatting marks (see "Turn On Formatting Marks" earlier in the chapter), you might have felt a bit disappointed that they didn't tell you more. You can direct Word to track inconsistencies in your formatting as you type.

Chapter 4

Customizing a Document

Microsoft Word 2013 provides a number of tools that combine text creation, layout, and formatting features that you can use to customize your documents. Two of the most common tools used at a broad level are styles and themes.

This chapter discusses creating documents through the use of styles and themes; formatting your documents using tabs, headers and footers, and outlines; and inserting front and end matter, such as tables of contents and indexes.

USE STYLES

Word 2013 provides a gallery of styles that provides you with sets of canned formatting choices, such as font, bold, and color, that you can apply to headings, titles, text, and lists. You use styles by identifying what kind of formatting a selected segment of text needs, such as for a header or title. Then, using style sets, you select the style of formatting you want to apply to the document. Formatting will be applied to the whole document smoothly and easily. You can easily change style sets and create new ones.

 NOTE Many of the tools in Word, such as creating tables of contents, are only available after you have identified the style of the text. For instance, you cannot create a table of contents if you have not identified which lines of text are headings and subheadings.

Understanding Themes and Styles

Word allows you to quickly and easily apply formatting to your documents to make them look professional and consistent by using ready-made themes, styles, and templates. A *theme* changes the background, color, fonts, and effects used in a document. Themes are similar throughout most of the Office suite, so if you choose a theme in Word, you likely will be able to apply that theme to Excel or PowerPoint documents as well. Every document has a theme as defined by its template.

A *style* applies a specific set of formatting characteristics to individual characters or to entire paragraphs within the theme. For example, you can apply styles to headings, titles, lists, and other text components. Consequently, styles determine how the overall design comes together in its look and feel. Styles are beneficial to document creation, because they provide an integrated and consistent platform to all text selected for formatting. Every theme has a certain set of styles assigned to it. You can change styles within a theme and change themes within a document.

A *template* contains a theme, with its unique style of formatting, and is used to set up a document for the first time. You can create your own templates and in this way, you can standardize the look of all documents that are based on a given template. Templates are discussed in Chapter 2.

▷▷ Identify Text with a Style

Within your document you have components, such as headings, titles, lists, regular paragraphs, and so on. For Word to know how to format these according to a given style, each component must be identified. You can do this by selecting text and clicking the matching style.

1. Select the text to be formatted as, for example, a title or heading.

2. In the Home tab Styles group, click the **More** down arrow. The Styles gallery is displayed, as shown in Figure 4-1.

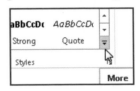

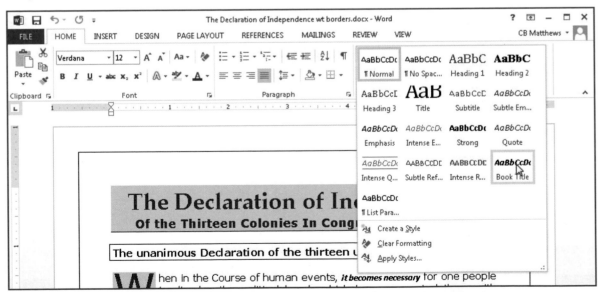

Figure 4-1: The Styles gallery shows you ready-made options for formatting headings, text, and paragraphs.

3. Point at the thumbnail of the component that matches the type of style you want to assign to the selected text. For example, select your main heading text, and then click **Heading 1** in the Styles gallery.

▷▷ Apply Predefined Style Sets to a Document

A predefined *style set* is a group of styles that has been defined and made available to you in the Design tab. You can apply a style set to a new document before you begin entering text, or you can apply a new style set to an existing document or change it from its current style set.

You will not see all the effects of a style set until you have identified the components in your document, such as headings or titles. You can see how a style set will affect a document by selecting it and seeing what happens to the color, styles, and fonts of the document.

1. Open the document to which you want to apply a style set. It can be either a blank document or one that already has the components identified, such as title, headings, and lists. (You can define the components later, but you won't be able to see the effects of the style sets until they are defined.)

2. In the Design tab Document Formatting group, mouse over a style set you want to consider and you'll see it reflected in the document. Figure 4-2 shows an example. To review the whole document with

Point to a style set in the menu list to see its effects in a document

The first style set in the menu shows the style currently active for a document

The document shows the effects of a selected style set

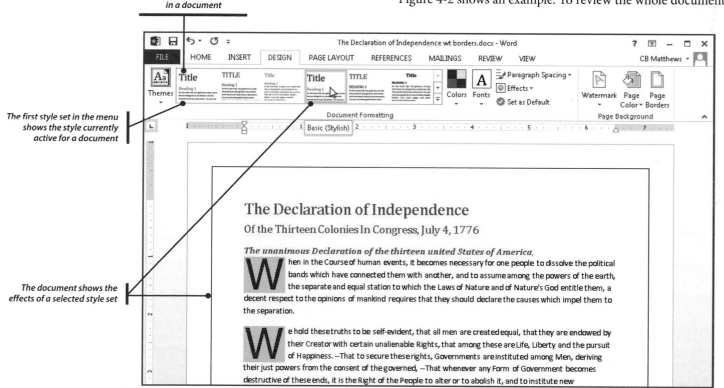

Figure 4-2: Style sets are used to provide consistent styles throughout a document.

the style set applied or to apply the one you want, click the style set. Remember that if you have components that are not identified with the styles, such as headings, they will not receive the formatting properly.

3. If you decide that you don't want to apply that particular style set to your document, simply click **Undo** in the Quick Access toolbar and it will be removed.

Create a New Style

You may want to create a new style that is immediately available to you for your documents. To create a new style option that will appear in the Style gallery:

1. Format the text using the mini formatting toolbar (see Chapter 1) or the commands in the Home tab Font and Paragraph groups (see Figure 3-3 in Chapter 3 for a visual guide).

2. Select the newly formatted text that represents the new style.

3. Click the **Home** tab and then click the **Styles** task pane launcher to open the Styles task pane.

4. Click the **New Style** icon on the bottom of the task pane. The Create New Style From Formatting dialog box is displayed.

5. Type the name you want for the style, verify the settings, and click **OK**. It will appear in the Style gallery in the Home in the Styles group.

> **NOTE** You can also create a new style by selecting the formatted text containing the new style, clicking the **More** down arrow in the Home tab Styles group, and clicking **Create A Style** in the expanded Styles menu. You can name and modify the style as you wish.

Modify a Style

You can modify an existing style. To do this:

1. In the Home tab Styles group, click the **More** down arrow . The Styles gallery is displayed.

2. Right-click the style to be changed, and click **Modify** (note that some styles cannot be changed). The Modify Style dialog box appears, as shown in Figure 4-3.

–Or–

At the bottom of the expanded Quick Style gallery, click **Apply Styles**. The Apply Styles task pane appears. Click the **Style Name** down arrow, and select the name of the style you wish to change (note that some styles cannot be changed). Click **Modify** to open the Modify Style dialog box.

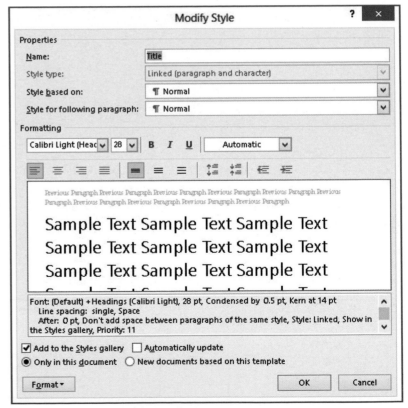

Figure 4-3: You can change a style by altering it in the Modify Style dialog box.

3. Change any formatting options you want. Here are some choices you have:

- To display more options, click **Format** in the bottom-left corner, and then click the attribute—for example, **Font** or **Numbering**—that you want to modify. Make that change and click **OK**. Repeat this step for any additional attributes you want to change, clicking **OK** each time you are finished.

- To add a modified style to the Styles gallery, check the **Add To The Styles Gallery** check box.

- To automatically apply updates to the document, check the **Automatically Update** check box. Word will automatically update the document with the modifications for the defined styles.

- To determine whether this style will be redefined for this document only, or for all new documents with this style, click the appropriate radio button.

- To create a new style, type a new name for the style, unless you want to change the formatting for the currently named style.

4. Click **OK** to close the Modify Style dialog box.

> **NOTE** To change your style to another one, in the Home tab Styles group, click the **More** down arrow and choose an alternative style from the Styles gallery.

▷▷ Clear a Style from Text or a Document

When you clear or delete a style from text, the text is reformatted with the Normal style. To clear the formatting of a whole document or of certain text, perhaps because you have applied the wrong style or wish to change it, follow these options.

Delete Style from Selected Text

Select specific text that you wish to clear of formatting. You then have these choices:

- In the Home tab Font group, click **Clear All Formatting** .

- In the Home tab Styles group, click the **More** down arrow and click **Clear Formatting**.

- On the Home tab, click the **Styles** task pane launcher to open the Styles task pane. Find the style to be removed, click the **down arrow** to the right of the style, and click **Clear Formatting of *n* Instance(s)**. (Clear the **Show Preview** check box to see the Clear Formatting option.)

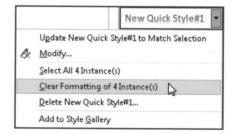

Delete Style from the Whole Document

To delete a style from a whole document:

1. Click the **Home** tab and then click the **Styles** task pane launcher to open the Styles task pane.

2. Select the style to be removed, click the down arrow to the right of the style, and click **Delete *name of style***. (You can also right-click the style to be removed and click **Delete *name of style*.**)

3. Click **Yes** to confirm that you want to remove the formatting from the whole document.

▷▷ Delete/Restore a Style from the Gallery

Styles are kept in the Styles task pane and displayed in the Styles gallery. You can delete styles from the gallery, but they will remain in Styles task pane unless you specifically delete them. If you delete any style from a document, the text formatted with that style will be reformatted with the Normal style. However, some styles cannot be deleted; the command to delete them will be unavailable (or grayed out), such as with the Normal style.

To delete a style from the gallery, perhaps that you created for a one-time-use document and don't ever plan to use again, or to restore it in case of a mistake or change of mind:

1. In the Home tab Styles group, click the **More** down arrow to display the Styles gallery.

2. Right-click the style you want to delete, and click **Remove From Style Gallery**. The style will be removed from the Style gallery. However, this does not mean that the style is gone; it is still in the Styles task pane.

To restore the style to the gallery:

1. On the Home tab, click the **Styles** task pane launcher to open the Styles task pane.

2. Right-click the style that you want to restore, and click **Add To Style Gallery**.

▷▷ Examine Current Styles

The Styles task pane contains a couple of ways you can look at the content of styles. For instance, you may wish to see what a style looks like before applying it, or see what styles have been applied to selected text.

Show a Preview of Styles

In addition to looking at the Styles gallery to see an example of what the style looks like, you can see an example in the Styles task pane.

1. On the Home tab, click the **Styles** task pane launcher to open the Styles task pane.

2. Check the **Show Preview** check box to see how the styles will appear.

3. If you want to apply a style to selected text, click the style.

4. Click the **Close** button (**X**) to close the task pane.

Inspect a Style

Perhaps you want to see what formatting has been applied to selected text.

1. Select the text whose style you want to inspect.

2. On the Home tab, click the **Styles** task pane launcher to open the Styles task pane.

3. Click the **Style Inspector** icon to open the Style Inspector task pane, shown on the left in Figure 4-4. You can see the essential formatting of the selected text. You have these choices:

   - To the right of a formatting style, click a **Reset** or **Clear** icon to reset or clear one component's formatting.

   - Click **Clear All** to reset or clear all the formatting for this style.

   - Click the **New Style** icon to create a new style from the one currently selected. The Create New Style From Formatting dialog box is displayed (introduced in the "Create a New Style" section earlier in the chapter).

   - Click the **Reveal Formatting** icon to see further detail of the selected formatting, as shown on the right in Figure 4-4. Check the **Distinguish Style Source** check box in the Reveal Formatting task pane to see where a style originates.

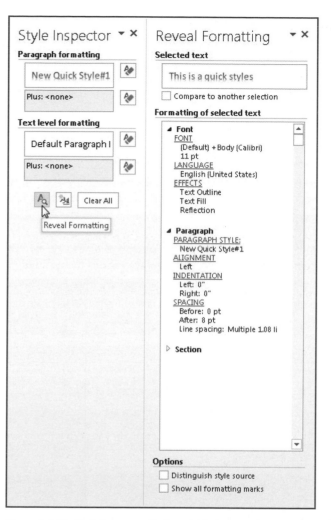

Figure 4-4: The Style Inspector displays the formatting for the style of selected text (left), and allows you to reveal formatting in more detail (right).

USE THEMES

Using a theme is another way that you can make a document look professional. Themes contain styles with coordinated colors, fonts (for body text and headings), and design effects (such as special-effect

uses for lines and fill effects) to produce a unique look. You can use the same themes with PowerPoint and Excel as well, thereby standardizing a look. All documents have themes; one is assigned to a new document by default.

⟩⟩ Assign a Theme to Your Document

To apply a theme to a document:

1. In the Design tab Document Formatting group, click **Themes** to display a gallery of themes, as shown in Figure 4-5. (This option is not available in Compatibility Mode.)

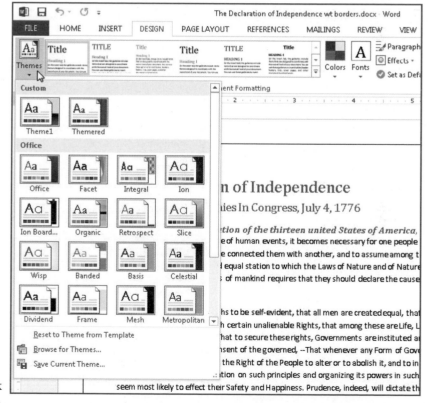

Figure 4-5: Use themes to standardize your documents with other Office products, such as PowerPoint and Excel.

2. Mouse over the menu of themes to see how each will look in your current document.

3. Click the theme you want, and it will be applied to the current document.

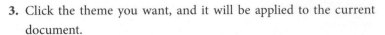

Change a Theme

In addition to changing the overall theme of a document, you can customize a theme by altering the fonts, color, and design effects.

Change the Color of a Theme

Each theme consists of a set of four colors for text and background, six colors for accents, and two colors for hyperlinks. (Only 8 colors are shown in the Colors drop-down menu; all 12 colors are available when you choose Custom Colors.) You can change any single color element or all of them. When you change the colors, the font styles and design elements remain the same.

1. In the Design tab Document Formatting group, click **Colors**. The Theme Colors menu of color combinations will be displayed, as shown in Figure 4-6.

2. As you point at the rows of color combinations, you can see how the colors will change the document beneath. Mouse over the colors to see which ones appeal to you.

3. When you find the one you want, click it.

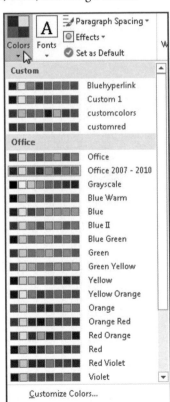

Figure 4-6: The menu of color combinations offers alternatives for your theme colors.

Change Theme Fonts

Each theme includes two fonts: the *body* font is used for general text entry, and a *heading* font is used for headings. The default fonts used in Word for a new document are Calibri for body text and Cambria for headings. After you have assigned a theme to a document, the fonts may be different, and they can be changed.

1. In the Design tab Document Formatting group, click **Fonts**. The Theme Fonts drop-down list displays various theme fonts. Custom Font Themes will be displayed above other Office Font Themes. The current theme font combination is highlighted in its place in the list.

2. Point to each font combination to see how the fonts will appear in your document.

3. Click the font name combination you decide upon. When you click a font name combination, the fonts will replace both the body and heading fonts in your whole document.

Create a Custom Font Theme Set

You may also decide that you want a unique set of fonts for your document. You can create a custom font set that is available in the list of fonts for your current and future documents.

1. In the Design tab Document Formatting group, click **Fonts** and then click **Customize Fonts**. The Create New Theme Fonts dialog box is displayed.

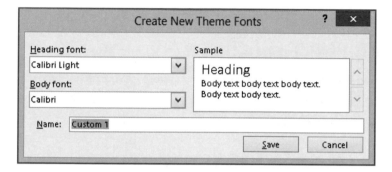

2. Click either or both the **Heading Font** and **Body Font** down arrows to select a new font combination. Click your choice(s) to view the new combination in the Sample area on the right.

3. Type a new name for the font combination you've selected, and click **Save**. Custom fonts are displayed at the top of the Theme Fonts drop-down list.

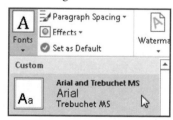

 TIP Remember that you can preview what a theme, color, or font looks like by simply selecting your text, opening one of the menus described here, and hovering your mouse over an option to see how it looks with your text.

Change Themed Graphic Effects

Shapes, illustrations, pictures, and charts include graphic effects that are controlled by themes. Themed graphics are modulated in terms of their lines (borders), fills, and effects (such as shadowed, raised, and shaded). For example, some themes simply change an inserted rectangle's fill color, while other themes affect the color, the weight of the border, and whether it has a 3-D appearance. Theme effects do not affect text.

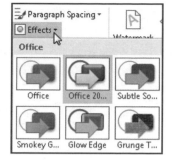

1. In the Design tab Document Formatting group, click **Effects** to open the Theme Effects drop-down list, which displays a gallery of effects combinations. The current effects combination is highlighted.

2. Point to each combination to see how the effects will appear in your document, assuming you have a graphic or chart inserted on the document page (see Chapter 12 for information on inserting these into your document).

3. Click the effects combination you want.

▷▷ Create a Custom Theme

You can create a new theme, save it, and use it for documents that you want to be unique and distinctively yours. You do so by selecting a group of text, background, accent, and hyperlink colors, and then giving them a collective name.

1. In the Design tab Document Formatting group, click **Colors** and then click **Customize Colors**. The Create New Theme Colors dialog box appears, as shown in Figure 4-7.

Type a name and click Save
to create a custom theme

Click a menu of colors
for the named elements

Selected colors are reflected
in the Sample area

Create New Theme Colors   ?   ×

Theme colors

Text/Background - Dark 1

Text/Background - Light 1

Text/Background - Dark 2

Text/Background - Light 2

Accent 1

Accent 2

Accent 3

Accent 4

Accent 5

Accent 6

Hyperlink

Followed Hyperlink

Sample

Text   Text

Hyperlink
Hyperlink

Name: Custom 2

Reset   Save   Cancel

Figure 4-7: The Create New Theme Colors dialog box allows you to create a new theme to use with multiple documents.

2. To select a color for one of the color groups, click the text/background, accent, or hyperlink down arrow, and click the color you want to test. It will be displayed in the Sample area.

Theme Colors

Standard Colors

More Colors...

3. Go through each set of colors that you want to change.

4. When you have selected a group of colors that you like, type a name in the Name text box, and click **Save**.

5. To restore the original colors in the Sample area in the Create New Theme Colors dialog box and start over, click **Reset**.

> **NOTE** You may find that you want to change something in a custom theme after you've been using it for a while. To edit a custom theme, in the Design tab Document Formatting group, click the **Colors** button, right-click the custom theme you want to edit, and click **Edit**. The Edit Theme Colors dialog box, similar to that shown in Figure 4-7, will appear.

WORK WITH DOCUMENTS

In addition to using styles and themes to format your documents, you can use section breaks, columns, tabs, headers and footers, tables of contents, and indexes to further refine your documents.

Create Section Breaks

A *section break* indicates the end of a section in a document. You can use section breaks to vary the layout of a document within a page or between pages. For example, you might choose to format the introduction of a magazine article in a single column and format the body of the article in two columns. You must separately format each section, but the section break allows them to be different. Section breaks allow you to change the number of columns, page headers and footers, page numbering, page borders, page margins, and other characteristics and formatting within a section. The section break retains the formatting above it, not after it.

Insert a Section Break

1. Click the place in the document where you want to insert a section break.

2. In the Page Layout tab Page Setup group, click **Breaks** to open the Breaks menu, as shown in Figure 4-8.

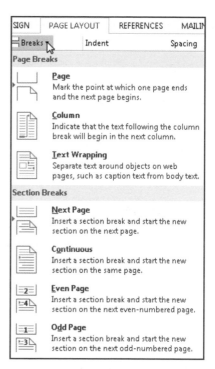

Figure 4-8 Insert breaks in a document to separately format sections of text.

3. To create a new section, in the Section Breaks area, select what comes after the break. You have the following options:

- Click **Next Page** to begin a new section on the next page.

- Click **Continuous** to begin a new section on the same page.

- Click **Even Page** to start the new section on the next even-numbered page.

- Click **Odd Page** to start the new section on the next odd-numbered page.

When you click the option you want, the section break is inserted. If the Show/Hide Formatting feature is turned on (in the Home tab Paragraph group), you'll be able to see the section breaks in the text.

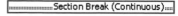

TIP If you don't see section breaks displayed in your document, click the **Home** tab and then click **Show/Hide** ¶ in the Paragraph group.

Delete a Section Break

When you delete a section break, you also delete the specific formatting for the text in the paragraphs immediately above that break. That text becomes part of the following section and assumes the relevant formatting of that section. When a section break is inserted on a page, you will see a note to that effect if the Show/Hide Formatting feature is turned on. You can delete the break by selecting that note.

1. Click the note for section break that you want to delete.

2. Press **DELETE**.

TIP You can also set or change a section break from the Page Setup dialog box. On the Page Layout tab, click the **Page Setup** dialog box launcher. In the Page Setup dialog box, click the **Layout** tab to see the section settings.

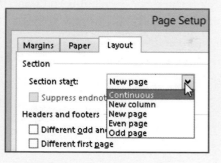

Create and Use Columns

You can format your documents in a single column or in two or more columns, like text found in newspapers or magazines. You must first create either a continuous break or a page break, not a column break, before you create the columns. This prevents them from forming in the previous section. To create columns in a document:

1. Place the insertion point at the place where you want the columns to begin. In the Page Layout tab Page Setup group, click **Breaks**, and then **Continuous** (or select **Page** instead of Continuous if the columns are to start on the next page).

2. To define the columns, click **Columns** in the Page Setup group to display a menu.

3. Click the thumbnail option that corresponds to the number or type of columns you want.

   –Or–

   If you do not see what you want, click **More Columns** at the end of the menu to display the Columns dialog box (see Figure 4-9). Then:

   • Click an icon in the Presets area, or type a number or click the spinner in the Number Of Columns box, to set the number of columns you want. If you click One in the Presets area, the Equal Column Width check box is not meaningful and is therefore dim. (Clicking any other preset will make the check box available; clicking Left or Right will clear it.)

   • Use the options in the Width And Spacing area to manually determine the dimensions of your columns and the amount of space between columns.

   • Check the **Line Between** check box if you want Word to insert a vertical line between columns.

   • Use the **Apply To** drop-down list box to select the part of the document to which you want your selections to apply: Whole Document, This Section, or This Point Forward. Click **This Point Forward**, and then check the **Start New Column** check box if you want to insert a column break at an insertion point. If the text is selected, you'll see an option for Selected Text that is the default.

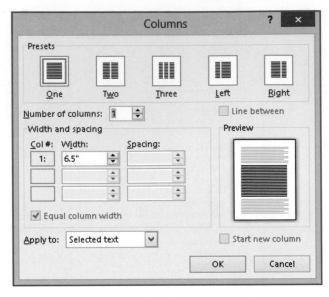

Figure 4-9: Use the Columns dialog box to create and format columns in your documents.

4. Click **OK** when finished.

TIP The Preview area in the Columns dialog box displays the effects as you change the various column settings.

Use Tabs

A *tab* is a type of formatting usually used to align text and create simple tables. By default, Word has *tab stops* (the horizontal positioning of the insertion point when you press TAB) every half-inch. Tabs are better than space characters to create constant positioning, because tabs are set to specific measurements, while spaces may not always align the way you intend due to the size and spacing of individual characters in a given font.

To align text with a tab, click to the left of the text that you want aligned and press the TAB key.

Set Tabs Using the Ruler

To set tabs using the ruler at the top of a page, you click the tab area to the left of the ruler.

Word supports five kinds of tabs:

- **Left tab** left-aligns text at the tab stop.
- **Center tab** centers text at the tab stop.
- **Right tab** right-aligns text at the tab stop.
- **Decimal tab** aligns the decimal point of tabbed numbers at the tab stop.
- **Bar tab** left-aligns text with a vertical line that is displayed at the tab stop.

1. Select the text, from one line to an entire document, in which you want to set one or more tab stops.

2. To the left of the horizontal ruler, click the **Left Tab** icon until it changes to the type of tab you want: Left Tab, Center Tab, Right Tab, Decimal Tab, or Bar Tab. (First Line Indent and Hanging Indent icons are also found here. See Chapter 3 for how to work with them.)

3. Click the bottom edge of the horizontal ruler approximately where you want to set a tab stop. After the tab icon is on the ruler, you can drag it to the intended position.

4. Once you have the tabs set, you can
   - Drag a tab off the ruler to get rid of it.
   - Drag a tab to another spot on the ruler to change its position.

Set Tabs Using Measurements

To set tabs according to specific measurements:

1. On the Home tab, click the **Paragraph** dialog box launcher, and click the **Tabs** button in the bottom-left corner of the Paragraph dialog box that appears.

   –Or–

   Double-click a tab in the ruler and then click the **Tabs** button in the Paragraph dialog box.

   In either case, the Tabs dialog box opens, as shown in Figure 4-10.

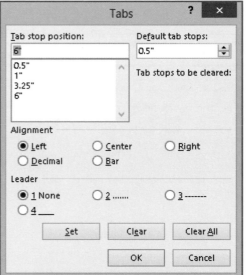

2. Enter the measurements you want in the Tab Stop Position text box, and choose an **Alignment** radio button to specify the alignment for text typed at the tab stop.

3. Click **Set**.

4. Repeat steps 2 and 3 for as many tabs as you want to set. Click **OK** to close the dialog box.

Figure 4-10: From the Tabs dialog box, you can format specific tab measurements and set tab leaders.

Set Tabs with Leaders

You can also set tabs with *tab leaders*—characters that fill the space otherwise left by a tab—a dotted line, a dashed line, or a solid underscore.

This line has no leader
.... This line has a dotted leader
-------- This has a dashed-line leader
_____ This has a solid-line leader

1. Open the Tabs dialog box shown in Figure 4-10 using either method described in the previous section.

2. In the Tab Stop Position text box, type the position for a new tab, or select an existing tab stop to which you want to add a tab leader.

3. In the Alignment area, select the alignment for text typed at the tab stop.

4. In the Leader area, select the leader option you want, and then click **Set**.

5. Repeat steps 2–4 for additional tabs. When you are done, click **OK** to close the dialog box.

> **TIP** When working with tabs, it's a good idea to display text formatting so that you can distinguish tabs from spaces. To display formatting, click the **Home** tab and then click **Show/Hide** in the Paragraph group.

Add Headers and Footers

Headers and footers are parts of a document that contain information such as page numbers, revision dates, the document title, and so on. The header appears at the top of every page, and the footer appears at the bottom of every page. Figure 4-11 shows the buttons available on the Header & Footer Tools Design tab.

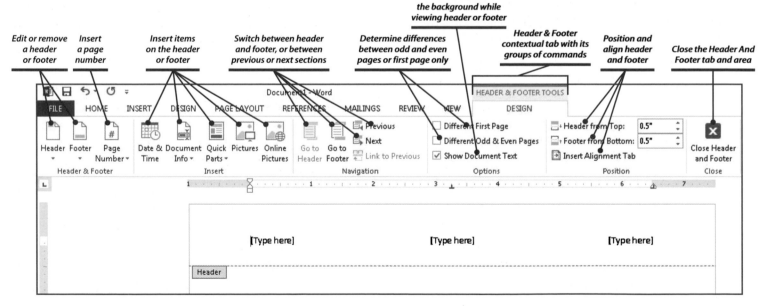

Figure 4-11: Headers and footers provide consistent information across the tops and bottoms of your document pages. These areas can also have unique tabs and other formatting.

You can enter a header or footer using a predefined header format.

d. Click in the rightmost **Type Here** area and, if desired, type Page, and leave a space. With the insertion point immediately after "Page" and the space in the tab, click **Page Number** in the Header & Footer group, click **Current Position**, and click **Plain Number**. If desired, adjust the tab marks in the ruler.

e. Format the text as desired using the Home tab.

5/14/2013   **My Company Name**   Page 1

Header

Create a Header or Footer from Menus

You can create or edit a header or footer for an open document as follows:

1. In the Insert tab Header & Footer group, click **Header** or **Footer**. Click one of the predefined headers or footers in the list. A preformatted header or footer area will be displayed (without content) with the special contextual Header & Footer Tools Design tab, shown earlier in Figure 4-11.

2. Click in the predefined areas and type your text. If you want something different than the predefined content, click in the area and use the elements contained within the Design tab, such as Page Number in the Header & Footer group, or Date & Time in the Insert group, to select content.

3. To enter a left-aligned date, a centered title, and a right-aligned page number, use the following steps as an example of how to proceed:

    a. Select the **Blank (Three Columns)** item from the Header menu.

    b. Click in the first **Type Here** area to select it, and either type the date or click **Date & Time** in the Insert group and click one of the formats.

    c. Click in the next **Type Here** area and type the title.

4. When finished, double-click in the document area or click **Close Header And Footer** in the Close group.

Edit a Header or Footer

1. Open the header or footer area by double-clicking the header area. (Alternatively, in the Insert tab Header & Footer group, click **Header** and then click **Edit Header** or **Footer,** and then click **Edit Header** or **Edit Footer**.) The header or footer area will be displayed along with the special contextual Header & Footer Tools Design tab, as shown earlier in Figure 4-11.

2. If necessary, click **Previous** or **Next** in the Navigation group to display the header or footer section you want to edit.

Previous
Next

3. Edit the header or footer. For example, you might revise text, change the font, apply bold formatting, or add a date or time.

4. When finished, double-click in the document area or click **Close Header And Footer** in the Close group.

 NOTE When you edit a header or footer, Word automatically changes the same header or footer throughout the document, unless the document contains different headers or footers in different sections.

Delete a Header or Footer

1. Double-click the header or footer area of the document. Or, if you can't see the header or footer, first double-click the split between pages, and then double-click the header or footer area. The header or footer area will be displayed along with the Header & Footer Tools Design tab, shown in Figure 4-11.

2. If necessary, click **Previous** or **Next** in the Navigation group to move to the header or footer section you want to delete.

3. Select the text or graphics you want to delete, and press **DELETE**.

–Or–

Click **Header** or **Footer** in the Header & Footer group, and then click **Remove Header** or **Remove Footer**.

In either case, the *content* of the header or footer will be removed, but the blank header or footer area will remain. To remove the area itself, you need to hide the white space. Place your pointer on the white space above or between pages. An icon with an up and down arrow within two lines will appear. This toggles the display of the white space on and off. Double-click the pointer to hide the white space. To redisplay the white space, simply double-click it again.

 NOTE When you delete a header or footer, Word automatically deletes the same header or footer throughout the entire document. To delete a header or footer for part of a document, you must first divide the document into sections, and then create a different header or footer for part of a document. (See "Create Section Breaks" earlier in this chapter for more information.)

Use Different Left and Right Page Headers and Footers

When you choose different left and right pages for your headers or footers, section breaks are used to allow different margins and tabs. Sometimes, you might want to create a document that has different left and right headers and/or footers. For example, you might have a brochure, pamphlet, or manuscript in which all odd-numbered pages have a title in the header and all even-numbered pages have the section name or other information.

To create different left and right headers and/or footers:

1. Display the header and/or footer and its Design tab by either double-clicking in the header area or clicking the appropriate option in the Insert tab, as explained in previous sections.

2. In the Options group, check **Different First Page** to enter a separate title or no title for the first page. Create a different first page in the First Page Header area, create the normal header in the Header area of the second page, and so on.

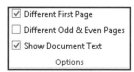

–And/Or–

Check **Different Odd & Even Pages** to have a different heading on the odd- and even-numbered pages. For instance, perhaps your page number is on the left for even-numbered pages and on the right for odd-numbered pages. Create the header or footer for odd-numbered pages in the Odd Page Header or Odd Page Footer area, and create the header or footer for even-numbered pages in the Even Page Header or Even Page Footer area.

3. Type the text of the footnote or endnote.

4. When you're finished, click in the document to continue working in the text.

This Is an Odd Page Header 1

Odd Page Header

3. When finished, double-click in the document area or click **Close Header & Footer** in the Close group.

 ## Add Footnotes and Endnotes

Footnotes and *endnotes* are types of annotations in a document, usually used to provide citation information or to provide additional information for readers. The difference between the two is where they appear in a document. Footnotes appear either after the last line of text on the page or at the bottom of the page on which the annotated text appears. Endnotes appear either at the end of the section in which the annotated text appears or at the end of the document.

Insert a Footnote or Endnote

1. Position the insertion point immediately after the text you want to annotate.

2. In the References tab Footnotes group, click **Insert Footnote** or **Insert Endnote**. For a footnote, the insertion point will be positioned at the bottom of the page; for an endnote, it will be positioned at the end of the document.

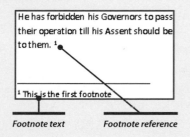

TIP Sometimes it is easier to see a footnote or endnote than the text to which it refers. To quickly find the text in the document that a footnote or endnote refers to, either double-click the reference number in the endnote or footnote or place the pointer to the right of the note and right-click the footnote or endnote, and click **Go To Footnote** or **Go To Endnote**. The insertion point will be positioned at that location in the text.

He has forbidden his Governors to pass their operation till his Assent should be to them. [1]

[1] This is the first footnote

Footnote text   Footnote reference

TIP If you find that your footnotes skip pages, make sure you have enough room on the bottom of the page for the notes.

Change Footnotes or Endnotes

If you want to change the numbers or formatting of footnotes or endnotes, or if you want to add a symbol to the reference, use the Footnote And Endnote dialog box.

1. In the References tab Footnotes group, click the **Footnotes** dialog box launcher to open the Footnote And Endnote dialog box (see Figure 4-12).

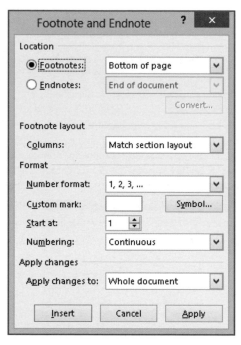

Figure 4-12: Footnotes and endnotes provide supplemental information to the body of your document. Use the dialog box to control location and formatting.

2. You have these options:

   - Under Location box, click the **Footnotes** or **Endnotes** option, and click the down arrow to the right to choose where the footnote or endnote will be placed.

   - Under Footnote Layout, click the **Columns** down arrow and select an option if it applies.

   - Under Format, click the **Number Format** down arrow, and select the type of numbering you want from the drop-down list.

   - To choose a custom mark (a character that uniquely identifies a footnote or endnote), click the **Symbol** button. A Symbol dialog box appears. Scroll through the symbols, and double-click the one you want to use. It will be displayed in the Custom Mark text box. You can also just type a character into the Custom Mark text.

   - Click the **Start At** spinner to alter the starting number of the footnote or endnote.

   - Click the **Numbering** down arrow, and choose how the numbering is to start.

   - Click the **Apply Changes To** down arrow to select the part of the document that will contain the changes.

3. Click **Insert**. Word makes the changes you made.

4. Type the note text.

5. When finished, return the insertion point to the body of your document, and continue typing.

Delete a Footnote or Endnote

In the document, select the number of the note you want to delete, and then press **DELETE**. Word automatically deletes the footnote or endnote and renumbers the notes.

When deleting an endnote or footnote, make sure to delete the number corresponding to the annotation in your main text and not the number and text in the footnote. If you delete the endnote or footnote, the placeholder for the annotation will remain.

Convert Footnotes to Endnotes or Endnotes to Footnotes

1. Select the reference number or symbol in the body of a document for the footnote or endnote.

2. On the References tab, click the **Footnotes** dialog box launcher to open the Footnote And Endnote dialog box.

3. Click **Convert** to open the Convert Notes dialog box.

4. Select the option you want, and then click **OK**.

5. Click **Close**.

Create an Index

An *index* is an alphabetical list of words or phrases in a document and the corresponding page references. Indexes created using Word can include main entries and subentries as well as cross-references. When creating an index in Word, you first need to tag the index entries in the document and then generate the index.

Tag Index Entries

1. In the document in which you want to build an index, select the first word or phrase that you want to use as an index entry. If you want an index entry to use text that you separately enter instead of using existing text in the document, just place the insertion point in the document where you want your new index entry to reference.

2. In the References tab Index group, click **Mark Entry** (you can also press **ALT+SHIFT+X**). The Mark Index Entry dialog box appears (see Figure 4-13).

3. The selected word will be in the Main Entry text box. If you want to rename it or enter another word, click in the **Main Entry** text box and type or edit the entry as you want it in the index. You can customize the entry by creating a subentry.

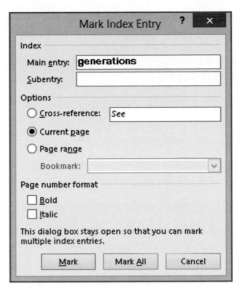

Figure 4-13: You need to tag index entries before you can generate an index.

4. Under Options, you can choose how the index entry will be indexed: as a cross-reference, with the page number, or with a previously bookmarked page range (for example, "insert themes" under "Use Themes" a range of pages previously bookmarked).

5. Check the **Bold** and/or **Italic** check box in the Page Number Format area to determine how the page numbers will appear in the index.

6. Click **Mark**. To mark all occurrences of this text in the document, click **Mark All**.

7. Repeat steps 3–6 to mark additional index entries on the same page.

8. Click **Close** to close the dialog box when finished. The field containing the information for the index is inserted into the text.

9. Repeat steps 1–8 for the remaining entries in the document.

Generate an Index

1. Position the insertion point where you want to insert the finished index (this will normally be at the end of the document).

2. In the References tab Index group, click **Insert Index** to open the Index dialog box (see Figure 4-14).

3. On the Index tab of the Index dialog box, set the formatting for the index. You have these options:

- For the Type option, click **Indented** to indent subentries beneath the main entry, or click **Run-In** to print subentries beside the upper-level category.

- Click the **Columns** spinner to set the number of columns in the index page.

- Click the **Language** down arrow to set the language for the index.

- Check **Right Align Page Numbers** to right-align the numbers. This will allow a leader to be printed.

- Click the **Tab Leader** down arrow to select the type of leader between the entry and the page number.

- Click the **Formats** down arrow to use an available design template, such as Classic or Fancy.

4. Click OK when finished. Word generates the index.

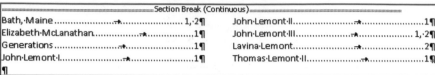

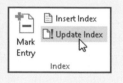

TIP If you add more index items after the index has been created, you'll have to update the index to add them. Either click the index and press **F9** or click the index, click the **References** tab, and click **Update Index** in the Index group.

▷▷ Create a Table of Contents

A *table of contents* is a list of the headings in the order in which they appear in the document. If you have formatted paragraphs with heading styles, you can automatically generate a table of contents based on those headings. If you have not used the heading styles, then, as with indexes, you must first tag table of contents (or TOC) entries and then generate the table of contents. (See "Use Styles" earlier in this chapter.)

Tag Entries for the Table of Contents

Use the Quick Style gallery to identify a segment of text within your document so that it can contain a consistent style for headings and other text that you want contained in a table of contents.

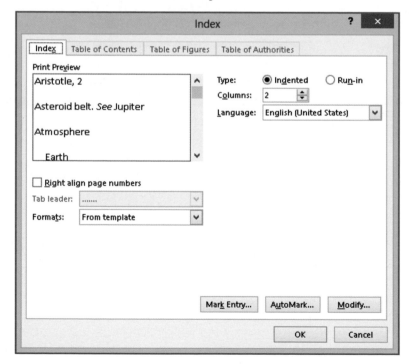

Figure 4-14: Use the options and settings in the Index dialog box to determine how your index will look.

1. Select the text to be formatted as a title or heading.

2. In the Home tab Styles group, click the **More** down arrow to open the Styles gallery.

3. Point at each thumbnail to determine which style it represents, and then click the thumbnail of the style you want to apply, such as Heading 1, Heading 2, or Title.

Place Other Text in a Table of Contents

To add text other than identified headings in a table of contents:

1. Select the text or phrase to be shown in the table of contents.

2. In the References tab Table Of Contents group, click **Add Text**. A menu is displayed.

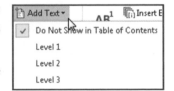

3. Click the option you want. You have these choices:

- **Do Not Show In Table Of Contents** removes the identification that something should be included in the TOC.

- **Level 1**, **Level 2**, or **Level 3** assigns selected text to a level similar to Heading 1, Heading 2, or Heading 3.

 TIP Another way to tag TOC entries is to select the text that you want to include in your table of contents, press **ALT+SHIFT+O** to open the Mark Table Of Contents Entry dialog box, click the **Level** spinner to choose the level, and click **Mark**. If you have multiple tables of contents, you can identify to which TOC the current entry belongs by using the Table Identifier feature. To mark additional entries, select the text, click in the **Entry** box, and click **Mark**. When you have finished adding entries, close the dialog box.

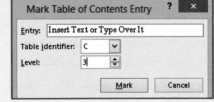

Use the Outlining Tab for the Table of Contents

The Outlining tab contains an easy way to tag or identify entries for the table of contents (see "Create and Use Outlines" later in this chapter). For a table of contents, use the Promote and Demote controls to create a hierarchy of headings in your document that can be used for a table of contents.

1. In the View tab Views group, click **Outline**. An Outlining page and tab becomes available (see Figure 4-15). In the Outlining tab Master Document group, click **Show Document** to access the options to insert and manipulate subdocuments, as shown in Figure 4-16.

✓ QuickFacts

Handling Subdocuments

A document is considered a *master document* when it contains either embedded files or links to subdocuments. *Subdocuments* are documents that pertain or contribute to the master document. Perhaps the master document is being created by several people, each "owning" a particular topic. The Outlining tab contains commands for managing the master documents and its subdocuments.

- **Create** Allows you to create a subdocument by embedding a file with a link back to its source. Subdocuments must be positioned in the master document following a heading; a subdocument cannot be inserted in the body text without a heading.

- **Insert** Allows you to browse and then insert a subdocument. It must follow the same rules as creating a subdocument.

- **Unlink** Deletes the link from a subdocument back to its source, and makes the subdocument part of the master document. It does not delete the subdocument itself, only the link to its source document.

- **Merge** Merges several subdocuments into one.

- **Split** Separates two subdocuments into two.

- **Lock Document** Locks the path to the source so that changes to the master document and its subdocuments will not flow back to the linked subdocuments.

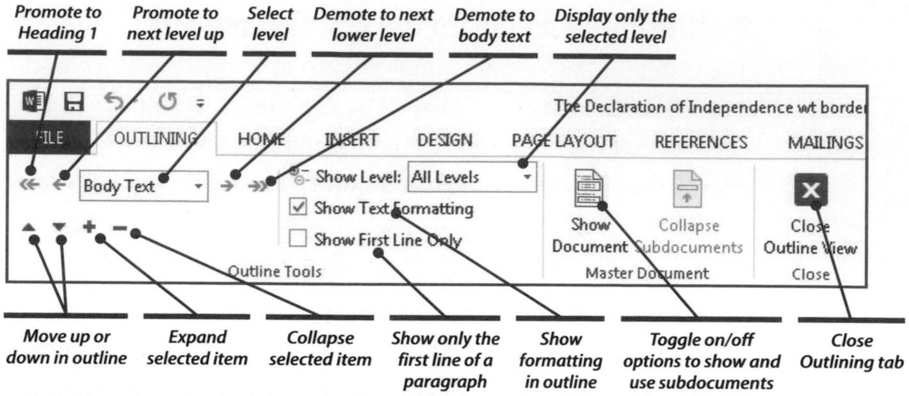

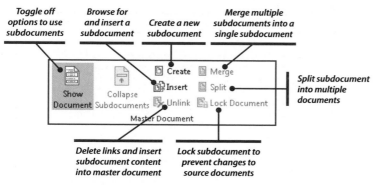

Promote to Heading 1 · Promote to next level up · Select level · Demote to next lower level · Demote to body text · Display only the selected level

Move up or down in outline · Expand selected item · Collapse selected item · Show only the first line of a paragraph · Show formatting in outline · Toggle on/off options to show and use subdocuments · Close Outlining tab

Figure 4-15: Use the Outlining tab to mark entries for a table of contents. The Outlining ribbon provides a number of ways to work with outlines.

Toggle off options to use subdocuments · Browse for and insert a subdocument · Create a new subdocument · Merge multiple subdocuments into a single subdocument

Split subdocument into multiple documents

Delete links and insert subdocument content into master document · Lock subdocument to prevent changes to source documents

Figure 4-16: The subdocument commands appear when Show Documents on the Outlining tab is clicked. These commands allow subdocuments to be inserted and manipulated.

2. Click the right or left arrows to promote or demote the levels, respectively.

3. Click **Close Outline View** when you are finished and ready to generate the table of contents.

Generate a Table of Contents

1. Place the insertion point where you want to insert the table of contents (normally, at the beginning of the document).

2. In the References tab Table Of Contents group, click **Table Of Contents** to open the menu shown in Figure 4-17. You have these options:

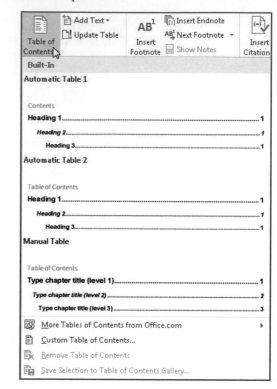

Figure 4-17: A table of contents can have several formats.

- Click one of the two built-in styles, **Automatic Table 1** or **Automatic Table 2**, which automatically inserts the assigned titles and indented levels. Just pick the format you prefer. (They are the same except for the heading.)

- Click the **Manual Table** option for a formatted structure, and then fill in the headings yourself.

- Click **Custom Table Of Contents** to automatically generate a table of contents with formatting that you specify in the Table Of Contents dialog box, shown in Figure 4-18.

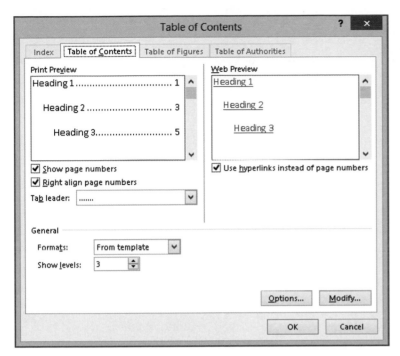

Figure 4-18: Use the options and settings in the Table Of Contents dialog box to determine how your table of contents will look.

- Under **General**, click the **Formats** down arrow to use one of the available designs.
- Click the **Show Levels** spinner and set it to the highest level of heading you want to display in the TOC.

4. Click **OK** when finished.

▷▷ Create and Use Outlines

An *outline* is a framework upon which a document is based. It is a hierarchical list of the headings in a document. You might use an outline to help you organize your ideas and thoughts when writing a speech, a term paper, a book, or a research project. The Outlining tab in Word makes it easy to build and refine your outlines, as shown in Figure 4-19.

⊕ **Working with Illustrations**
  ○ Table of Contents
  ○ *Illustration* is a term used to describe several forms of visual enhancements that can be added to a document. Illustrations include pictures, clip art, drawings, shapes, SmartArt, charts, and Screenshots. In this chapter you will learn how to insert, format, and manage illustration files, such as digital photos and clip art images.
⊕ **(1)Work with Pictures**
  ○ *Pictures*, which include both digital photos and *clip art* (small drawings or commercial photos), are separate files that can be manipulated in a number of ways once you have them within Word. You can organize your picture collections, resize images, and move them into the exact positions that you want.
    ⊕ *(2)Linking Picture Files*
      ○ 1.   To link a picture file when you are inserting a picture into a document, click the **Insert** tab, and click **Picture** in the Illustrations group to open the Insert Picture dialog box.
      ○ 2.   Click the **Insert** down arrow in the lower-right corner, and click **Link To File**.
      ○ **Illustration 1 [Insert button context menu]**
    ⊕ *(2)Add Pictures*
      ○ You can browse for picture files, use the Clip Art task pane to assist you, drag them from other locations, or import them directly from a scanner or digital camera.
        ⊕ *(3)Browse for Pictures*
          ○ 1.   Place your insertion point in the Word paragraph or table where you want to insert the picture.
          ○ 2.   In the Insert tab, click **Picture** in the Illustrations group. The Insert Picture dialog box appears, as shown in Figure 7-1.

Figure 4-19: Outlines are an excellent way to begin writing a document. Start with the overall ideas and drill down to your core thoughts.

3. If you clicked Custom Table Of Contents, the Print Preview and Web Preview list boxes in the dialog box show how the TOC will appear based on the options selected. You have these options:

- Clear the **Show Page Numbers** check box to suppress the display of page numbers.

- Clear the **Right Align Page Numbers** check box to allow page numbers to follow the text immediately. When this is checked, the Tab Leader drop-down list box becomes available.

- Click the **Tab Leader** down arrow, and click **(None)** or another option for a leader between the text in the TOC and the page number.

- Clear the **Use Hyperlinks Instead Of Page Numbers** check box to use page numbers in place of hyperlinks.

1. Open a new blank document (see Chapter 1). Click the **View** tab and then click **Outline** in the Views group. Word switches to the Outlining tab, displayed earlier in Figures 4-15 and 4-16.

2. Type your first-level heading text, and press ENTER. Word formats the headings using the built-in heading style Heading 1. Demote your heading level and type your second-level heading text, and continue throughout the document. You have these ways of setting the levels:

- Assign a heading to a different level by clicking the **Level** *no* drop-down list box.

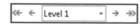

–Or–

Place the insertion point in the text, and then click the **Promote** or **Demote** button on the Outlining toolbar until the text is at the level you want.

- To move a heading to a different location (the heading retains its level), place the insertion point in the heading, and then click the **Move Up** or **Move Down** button in the Outlining tab Outline Tools group until the heading is where you want it. (If a heading is collapsed, the subordinate text under the heading moves with it.)

3. You can display as much or as little of the outline as you want by collapsing or expanding it. To collapse the sublevels under a heading in the outline, double-click the plus sign opposite the heading. To expand the same heading, double-click the plus sign again.

–Or–

Select the heading and click the **Expand** or **Collapse** button in the Outlining tab Outline Tools group.

4. When you're satisfied with the organization, click **Close Outline View** in the Close group, which automatically switches to Print Layout view (see the "Using View Buttons" QuickFacts in Chapter 2 for more information).

Chapter 5

Entering and Editing Data in Excel

Data is the heart and soul of Excel, yet before you can calculate data, chart it, analyze it, and otherwise *use* it, you have to place it on a worksheet. Data comes in several forms—such as numbers, text, dates, and times—and Excel handles the entry of each form uniquely. After you enter data into Excel's worksheets, you might want to make changes. Simple actions—such as removing text and numbers, copying and pasting data, and moving data— are much more enhanced in Excel than the standard actions most users are familiar with.

In addition, Excel provides several tools to assist you in manipulating your data. You can have Excel intelligently continue a series so that you don't have to manually enter the sequential numbers or text. Automatic tools that provide pop-ups—small toolbars related to the Excel task you're working on—are available to help you verify accuracy. These, and other ways of entering and editing data, are covered in this chapter.

Understanding Data Types

Cells in Excel are characterized by the type of data they contain. *Text* is composed of characters that cannot be used in calculations. For example, "Quarterly revenue is not meeting projection." is text, and so is "1302 Grand Ave." *Numbers* are just that: numerical characters that can be used in calculations. *Dates* and *times* occupy a special category of numbers that can be used in calculations, and are handled in a variety of ways. Excel lets you know what it thinks a cell contains by its default alignment of a cell's contents; that is, text is left-aligned and numbers (including dates and times) are right-aligned by default (of course, you can change these, as described later in the chapter).

Text: left-aligned   *Number: right-aligned*

	A	B	C
1	Supplies	23567	
2			
3			

ENTER DATA

An Excel worksheet is a matrix, or grid, of lettered *column headings* across the top and numbered *row headings* down the side. The first row of a typical worksheet is used for column *headers*. The column headers represent categories of similar data. The rows beneath a column header contain data that is further categorized by a row header along the leftmost column. Figure 5-1 shows examples of two common worksheet arrangements. Worksheets can also be used to set up *tables* of data, where columns are sometimes referred to as *fields* and each row represents a unique *record* of data.

Each intersection of a row and column is called a *cell*, and is referenced first by the column location and then by the row location. The combination of a column letter and row number assigns each cell an *address*. For example,

the cell at the intersection of column D and row 8 is called D8. A cell is considered *active* when it is clicked or otherwise selected as the place in which to place new data.

▷▷ Enter Text

In an Excel worksheet, text is used to identify, explain, and emphasize numeric data. It comprises characters that cannot be used in calculations. You enter text by typing, just as you would in a word-processing program.

💡 **TIP** Excel provides several highly visible identifiers for the active cell: the Name box to the left of the Formula bar displays the address; the column and row headings are highlighted in color; the Formula bar displays cell contents; and the cell borders are bold.

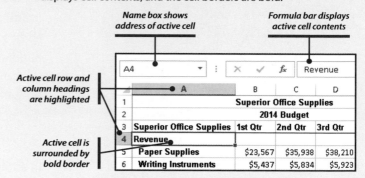

Enter Text Continuously

Text (and numbers) longer than one cell width will appear to cover the adjoining cells to the right of the active cell. The covered cells have not been "used;" their contents have just been hidden, as shown in Figure 5-2. To enter text on one line:

1. Click the cell in which you want the text to start.

2. Type the text. The text displays in one or more cells (see rows 2 and 4 in Figure 5-2).

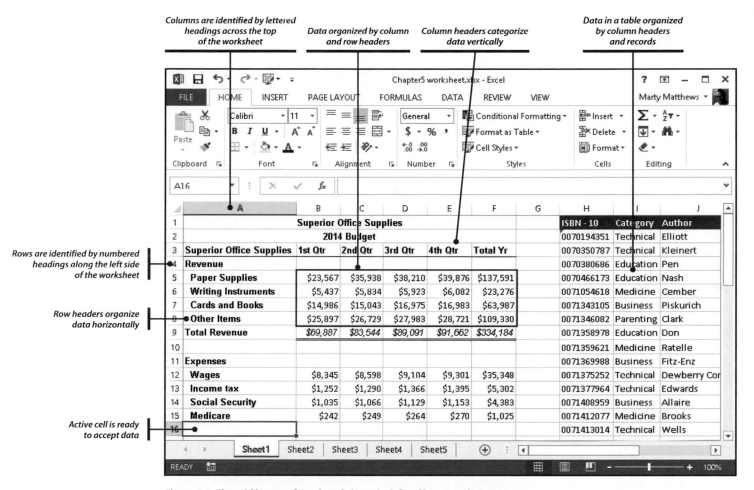

Columns are identified by lettered headings across the top of the worksheet

Data organized by column and row headers

Column headers categorize data vertically

Data in a table organized by column headers and records

Rows are identified by numbered headings along the left side of the worksheet

Row headers organize data horizontally

Active cell is ready to accept data

	A	B	C	D	E	F	G	H	I	J
1			Superior Office Supplies					ISBN - 10	Category	Author
2			2014 Budget					0070194351	Technical	Elliott
3	Superior Office Supplies	1st Qtr	2nd Qtr	3rd Qtr	4th Qtr	Total Yr		0070350787	Technical	Kleinert
4	Revenue							0070380686	Education	Pen
5	Paper Supplies	$23,567	$35,938	$38,210	$39,876	$137,591		0070466173	Education	Nash
6	Writing Instruments	$5,437	$5,834	$5,923	$6,082	$23,276		0071054618	Medicine	Cember
7	Cards and Books	$14,986	$15,043	$16,975	$16,983	$63,987		0071343105	Business	Piskurich
8	Other Items	$25,897	$26,729	$27,983	$28,721	$109,330		0071346082	Parenting	Clark
9	Total Revenue	$69,887	$83,544	$89,091	$91,662	$334,184		0071358978	Education	Don
10								0071359621	Medicine	Ratelle
11	Expenses							0071369988	Business	Fitz-Enz
12	Wages	$8,345	$8,598	$9,104	$9,301	$35,348		0071375252	Technical	Dewberry Cor
13	Income tax	$1,252	$1,290	$1,366	$1,395	$5,302		0071377964	Technical	Edwards
14	Social Security	$1,035	$1,066	$1,129	$1,153	$4,383		0071408959	Business	Allaire
15	Medicare	$242	$249	$264	$270	$1,025		0071412077	Medicine	Brooks
16								0071413014	Technical	Wells

Figure 5-1: The grid layout of Excel worksheets is defined by several components.

3. Complete the entry. (See "Complete an Entry" later in the chapter for several ways to do that.)

NOTE See Chapter 6 for ways to increase column width to accommodate the length of text in a cell.

Wrap Text on Multiple Lines

You can select a cell and wrap text at the end of its column width, much like how a word-processing program wraps text to the next line when entered text reaches its right margin.

1. Click the cell in which you want to enter text.

2. Type all the text you want to appear in a cell. The text will continue to the right, overlapping as many cells as its length dictates (see row 4 in Figure 5-2).

3. Press **ENTER** to complete the entry. (See "Complete an Entry" later in the chapter.) Click the cell a second time to select it.

4. Click the **Home** tab at the left end of the ribbon. In the Alignment group, click the **Wrap Text** button. The text wraps within the confines of the column width, increasing the row height as necessary (see row 6 in Figure 5-2).

Constrain Text on Multiple Lines

When you want to constrain the length of text in a cell:

1. Click the cell in which you want to enter text.

2. Type the text you want to appear on the first line.

B4			×	✓	fx	Costs of Goods Sold (Se
	A	B	C	D	E	F
1						
2		Supplies				
3						
4		Costs of Goods Sold (Seattle property)				
5						
6		Costs of Goods Sold (Seattle property)				
7						
8		Costs of Goods Sold (Seattle property)				
9						

Figure 5-2: Text in a cell can cover several cells or be placed on multiple lines.

3. Press **ALT+ENTER**. The insertion point moves to the beginning of a new line.

4. Repeat steps 2 and 3 for any additional lines of text. (See row 8 in Figure 5-2.)

5. Complete the entry. (See "Complete an Entry.")

⮞⮞ Complete an Entry

You can complete an entry using the mouse or the keyboard and control where the active cell goes next.

Stay in the Active Cell

To complete an entry and keep the current cell active, click **Enter** (the check mark icon) on the Formula bar.

× ✓ fx

Move the Active Cell to the Right

To complete the entry and move to the next cell in the same row, press **TAB**.

Move the Active Cell to the Next Row

To complete the entry and move the active cell to the next row, press **ENTER**. The active cell moves to the *beginning cell* in the next row (see the accompanying Note).

$1,035	$1,066	$1,129
$242	$249	$264

Change the Direction of the Active Cell

1. Click the **File** tab, click **Options**, and then click the **Advanced** option.

2. Under Editing Options, click **After Pressing Enter, Move Selection** to select it if it is not already selected.

3. Click the **Direction** down arrow, and click a direction. Down is the default.

4. Click **OK** when finished.

Move the Active Cell to Any Cell

To complete the entry and move the active cell to any cell in the worksheet, click the cell you want to become active.

 NOTE The *beginning cell* is in the same column where you first started entering data. For example, if you started entering data in cell A5 and continued through E5, pressing **TAB** between entries A5 through D5 and pressing **ENTER** in E5, the active cell would move to A6 (the first cell in the next row). If you had started entering data in cell C5, after pressing **ENTER** at the end of that row of entries, the active cell would move to C6, the cell below it.

Enter Numeric Data

Numbers are numerical data, from the simplest to the most complex. Excel provides several features to help you work more easily with numbers used to represent values in various categories, such as currency, accounting, and mathematics.

Enter Numbers

Enter numbers by simply selecting a cell and typing the numbers.

1. Click the cell in which you want to enter the numbers.
2. Type the numbers. Use decimal places, thousands separators, and other formatting as you type, or have Excel format these things for you. (See "Format Numbers" later in this chapter.)
3. Complete the entry. (See the previous section, "Complete an Entry.")

 TIP You can cause a number to be interpreted by Excel as text by typing an apostrophe (') in front of it and completing the entry. The "number" is left-aligned as text and a green triangle is displayed in the upper-left corner of the cell. When selected, an error icon displays next to the cell, indicating a number is stored as text.

G	H
	ISBN - 10
⬧	0070194351
	0070350787

Enter Numbers Using Scientific Notation

Exponents are used in scientific notation to shorten (or round off) very large or small numbers. The shorthand scientific notation display does not affect how the number is used in calculations; however, rounding provides a less precise result when moving a decimal point several orders of magnitude. (To retain precision, see the associated Tip regarding converting numbers to scientific notation.)

1. Click the cell in which you want to enter the data.
2. Type the number using three components:
   - **Base**: For example: 4, 7.56, -2.5.
   - **Scientific notation identifier**: Type the letter "e."
   - **Exponent**: The number of times 10 is multiplied by itself. Positive exponent numbers increment the base number to the right of the decimal point, negative numbers to the left. For example, scientific notation for the number 123,456,789.0 is written to two decimal places as 1.23×10^8. In Excel, you would type 1.23e8.
3. After completing the entry (see "Complete an Entry"), it will display as: 1.23E+08

 TIP You can convert a number to scientific notation from the Home tab Number group on the ribbon. Click the **Number Format** down arrow, and click **Scientific** near the bottom of the list. To set the number of decimal places, click the **Increase Decimal** or **Decrease Decimal** button at the bottom of the Number group. Also, note that the Number Format box displays the type of number format in the selected cell.

Enter Dates

If you can think of a way to enter a date, Excel can probably recognize it as such. For example, Table 5-1 shows how Excel handles different ways to make the date entry use the date of March 1, 2014 (assuming it is sometime in 2014) in a worksheet.

In cases when a year is omitted, Excel assumes the current year.

Table 5-1: Examples of Excel Date Formats

Typing This...	Displays This After Completing the Entry
3/1, 3-1, 1-mar, or 1-Mar	1-Mar
3/1/14, 3-1-14, 3/1/2014, 3-1-2014, 3-1/14, or 3-1/2014	3/1/2014
Mar 1, 14, March 1, 2014, 1-mar-14, or 1-Mar-2014	1-Mar-14

Change the Default Display of Dates

Two common date formats (long and short) are displayed by default in Excel based on settings in the Windows Region And Language (Windows 7) or Region (Windows 8) item in Control Panel, shown in Figure 5-3.

 TIP In Excel, you can determine which short date setting is currently in use by clicking a cell with a date in it and seeing what appears in the Formula bar.

f_x	12/23/2014
D	E
	23-Dec

1. In Windows 7, click **Start** and click **Control Panel**. In Windows 8, right-click in the lower-left corner of the screen and click **Control Panel**.

2. In Control Panel Category view, click the **Clock, Language, And Region** category, and then click **Region And Language** in Windows 7 or click **Region** in Windows 8.

–Or–

Figure 5-3: *You can change how Excel and other Windows programs display dates.*

In Icons view, click **Regional And Language Options** in Windows 7 or click **Region** in Windows 8.

3. On the Formats tab, click **Additional Settings**.

4. Click the **Date** tab, click the **Short Date** down arrow in the Date Formats section, and select a format. Similarly, change the long date format as necessary.

5. Click **OK** twice and close Control Panel.

 TIP To enter the current date in a cell, click the cell and press **CTRL+;** (press and hold **CTRL** and press **;**). The current date is displayed in the date format applied to the cell, the default of which is the short date.

Format Dates

You can change how a date is displayed in Excel by choosing a new format.

1. Right-click the cell that contains the date you want to change. (See "Select Cells and Ranges" later in the chapter to see how to apply formats to more than one cell at a time.)

2. Click **Format Cells** on the context menu. The Format Cells dialog box appears. Click the **Number** tab (if it isn't displayed) and then click the **Date** category, as shown in Figure 5-4.

3. Select a format from the Type list.

   –Or–

   Use custom number format codes to create a new format. To learn about number format codes, search Excel Help for the topic "Create or delete a custom number format."

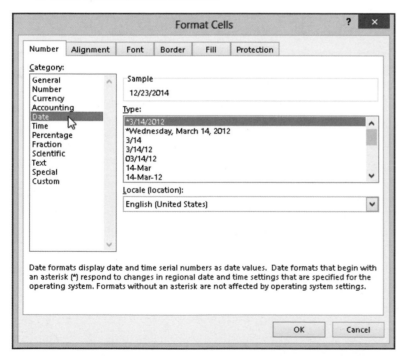

Figure 5-4: You can choose from among several ways to display dates in Excel.

4. You can see how the new date format affects your date in the Sample area. Click **OK** when finished.

Format Numbers

Numbers in a cell can be formatted in any one of several numeric categories by first selecting the cell containing the number. You can then use the tools available in the Home tab Number group or have the full range of options available to you from the Format Cells dialog box.

Display the Number Tab

Click the **dialog box launcher** in the lower-right corner of the Number group. The Format Cells dialog box appears with the Number tab displayed (shown in Figure 5-5).

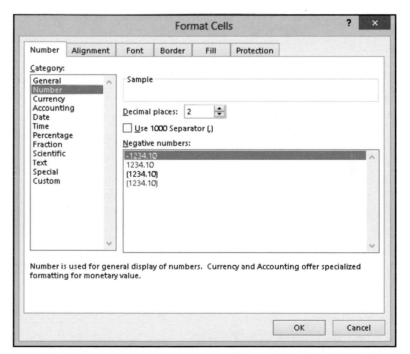

Figure 5-5: The Format Cells Number tab provides a complete set of numeric formatting categories and options.

Add or Decrease Decimal Places

1. On the Number tab of the Format Cells dialog box, choose the appropriate numeric category (Number, Currency, Accounting, Percentage, or Scientific) from the Category list box.

2. In the Decimal Places text box, enter a number or use the spinner to set the number of decimal places you want. Click **OK**.

   –Or–

   In the ribbon's Home tab Number group, click the **Increase Decimal** or **Decrease Decimal** button.

Add a Thousands Separator

On the Number tab of the Format Cells dialog box, click the **Number** category, and click **Use 1000 Separator (,)**. Click **OK**.

–Or–

In the ribbon's Home tab Number group, click the **Comma Style** button.

Add a Currency Symbol

1. On the Number tab of the Format Cells dialog box, choose the appropriate numeric category (Currency or Accounting) from the Category list box.

2. Click the down arrow opposite Symbol, choose from the Symbol drop-down list the currency symbol that you want to use, and click **OK**.

   –Or–

   Click the **Accounting Number Format** button in the Number group. (You can change the currency symbol by clicking the down arrow next to the current symbol and choosing another one.)

Convert a Decimal to a Fraction

1. On the Number tab of the Format Cells dialog box, click the **Fraction** category.

2. Click the type of fraction you want. View it in the Sample area, and change the type if needed. Click **OK**.

Convert a Number to a Percentage

1. On the Number tab of the Format Cells dialog box, click the **Percentage** category.

2. In the Decimal Places text box, enter a number or use the spinner to set the number of decimal places you want. Click **OK**.

   –Or–

   Click the **Percent Style** button **%** in the Number group.

Format ZIP Codes, Phone Numbers, and Social Security Numbers

1. On the Number tab of the Format Cells dialog box, click the **Special** category.

2. Select the type of formatting you want. Click **OK**.

> **NOTE** Formatting also can be applied to cells in advance of entering numbers (or text) so that the attributes are displayed as you complete the entry. Simply select the cells and apply the formatting. See "Select Cells and Ranges" later in the chapter for ways to select cells.

⏩ Use Times

Excel's conventions for time are as follows:

- Colons (:) are used as separators between hours, minutes, and seconds.

- AM is assumed unless you specify PM or when you enter a time from 12:00 to 12:59.

- AM and PM do not display in the cell if they are not entered.

- You specify PM by entering a space followed by "p," "P," "pm," or "PM."

QuickFacts

Understanding Excel Dates and Times

If you select a cell with a date and open the Number Format list in the Number group, you'll notice several of the formats show examples with a number around 41,000. Is this just an arbitrary number Excel has cooked up to demonstrate the example formats? Hardly. Dates and times in Excel are assigned values so that they can be used in calculations (Chapter 7 describes how to use formulas and functions). Dates are assigned a serial value starting with January 1, 1900 (serial value 1). The number you see on the Number Format list is the value of the date in the active cell (you can convert a date to its serial value by changing the format from Date to Number). For example, January 1, 2014, has a serial value of 41,640. Times are converted to the decimal equivalent of a day. For example, 4:15 P.M. is converted to 0.68. Since Excel considers dates and times as numerics, they are right-aligned in a cell. If you see what you think is a date but it is left-aligned, Excel is treating it as text, not a date, and you would receive an error message if you tried to use it in a formula.

- Seconds are not displayed in the cell if not entered.
- AM, PM, and seconds are displayed in the Formula bar of a cell that contains a time.

Enter Times

1. Select the cell in which you want to enter a time.
2. Type the hour followed by a colon.
3. Type the minutes followed by a colon.
4. Type the seconds, if needed.
5. Type a space and <u>PM</u>, if needed.
6. Complete the entry.

 TIP To enter the current time in a cell, click the cell and press **CTRL+SHIFT+:** (press and hold **CTRL** and **SHIFT**, and press **:**). The current time in the form h:mm AM/PM is displayed.

Change the Default Display of Times

By default, times are displayed in Excel based on settings configured in the Windows Region And Language feature of Control Panel. To change the default settings:

1. In Windows 7, click **Start** and click **Control Panel**. In Windows 8, right-click in the lower-left corner of the screen and click **Control Panel**.

2. In Category view, click the **Clock, Language, And Region** category, and then click **Region And Language** in Windows 7 or click **Region** in Windows 8.

   –Or–

   In Icons view, click **Region And Language** in Windows 7 or click **Region** in Windows 8.

3. On the Formats tab, click the **Short Time** and/or **Long Time** down arrows, and select the formats you want.

4. Click **OK** and close Control Panel.

 CAUTION Changing the *system* date/time formats in the Region And Language area of Control Panel changes the date and time formats used by all Windows programs. Dates and times previously entered in Excel may change to the new setting unless they were formatted using the features in Excel's Format Cells dialog box.

Format Times

You can change how a time is displayed in Excel by choosing a new format.

1. Select the cell that contains the time you want to change. (See "Select Cells and Ranges" later in the chapter for instructions on how to apply formats to more than one cell at a time.)

2. Click the **dialog box launcher** in the Home tab Number group. The Format Cells dialog box appears with the Number tab displaying the Custom category.

3. Under Type, select a format.

    –Or–

    Use custom number format codes to create a new format. To learn about number format codes, search Excel Help for the topic "Create or delete a custom number format."

4. You can see how the new time format will affect your time in the Sample area. Click **OK** when finished.

▷▷ Add Data Quickly

Excel provides several features that help you quickly add more data to existing data with a minimum of keystrokes.

Use AutoComplete

Excel will complete an entry for you after you type the first few characters of data that appears in a previous entry in the same column. Simply press **ENTER** to accept the completed entry. To turn off this feature if you find it bothersome:

1. Click the **File** tab, click **Options**, and click the **Advanced** option.

2. Under Editing Options, click **Enable AutoComplete For Cell Values** to remove the check mark.

Fill Data into Adjoining Cells

1. Select the cell that contains the data you want to copy into adjoining cells.

2. Point to the fill handle in the lower-right corner of the cell. The pointer turns into a cross.

3. Drag the handle in the direction in which you want to extend the data until you've reached the last cell in the range you want to fill.

4. Open the smart tag by clicking it, and select fill options.

    –Or–

    Select the cell containing the data that you want to fill in, along with the contiguous cells to be filled (see "Select Cells and Ranges" later in the chapter). In the Home tab Editing group, click the **Fill** button , and click the direction of the fill.

Continue a Series of Data

Data can be *logically* extended into one or more adjoining cells. For example, 1 and 2 extend to 3, 4...; Tuesday extends to Wednesday, Thursday...; January extends to February, March...; and 2012 and 2013 extend to 2014, 2015....

1. Select the cell or cells that contain a partial series. (See "Select Cells and Ranges" later in the chapter for more information on selecting more than one cell.)

2. Point to the fill handle in the lower-right corner of the last cell. The pointer turns into a cross.

3. Drag the handle in the direction in which you want to extend the series until you've reached the last cell in the range to complete the series.

4. To copy the partial series into the adjoining cells instead of extending the series, drag the fill handle to cover as many occurrences of the copy you want to make, click the smart tag, and click **Copy Cells** (see Figure 5-6).

TIP Excel 2013 has a new type of fill called Flash Fill that helps separate cells. For example, if you have a series of addresses where the city, state, and ZIP are all in one cell, and every one of these cells has all three elements, you can split these addresses into three cells by adding three columns next to the one that has the addresses (adding columns is described in Chapter 6). In the first row of the first new column, type the name of the city that appears in the cell to the left, press **ENTER**, begin to type the second city, and Excel will fill in all the cities listed on the left. Press **ENTER** again to accept the column of cities. Repeat this for the states and again for the ZIPs.

	A	B
1		
2	Seattle, WA 98115	Seattle
3	Kirkland, WA 98033	Kirkland
4	Greenbank, WA 98253	Greenbank
5	Bellevue, WA 98004	Bellevue
6	Freeland, WA 98249	Freeland
7	Everett, WA 98208	Everett
8	Langley, WA 98260	Langley

	A	B	C	D
1				
2	Seattle, WA 98115	Seattle	WA	98115
3	Kirkland, WA 98033	Kirkland	WA	98033
4	Greenbank, WA 98253	Greenbank	WA	98253
5	Bellevue, WA 98004	Bellevue	WA	98004
6	Freeland, WA 98249	Freeland	WA	98249
7	Everett, WA 98208	Everett	WA	98208
8	Langley, WA 98260	Langley	WA	98260

Remove the Fill Handle

To hide the fill handle and disable AutoFill:

1. Click the **File** tab, click **Options**, and click the **Advanced** option.

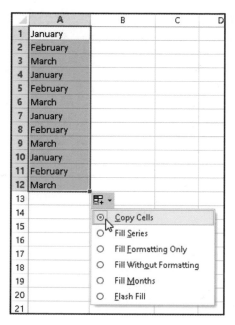

Figure 5-6: You can copy a series (January, February, and March, in this case) by using the smart tag that appears after dragging the fill handle.

2. Under Editing Options, click **Enable Fill Handle And Cell Drag And Drop** to remove the check mark.

Enter Data from a List

Previously entered data in a column can be selected from a list and entered with a click.

1. Right-click the cell at the bottom of a column of data.

2. Select **Pick From Drop-Down List** from the context menu, and then click the data you want to enter in the cell.

TIP You can fill data into the active cell from the cell above it or to its left by clicking **CTRL+D** or **CTRL+R**, respectively.

EDIT DATA

The data-intensive nature of Excel necessitates easy ways to change, copy, or remove data already entered on a worksheet. In addition, Excel has facilities to help you find and replace data and check the spelling.

▶▶ Edit Cell Data

You have several choices of how to edit data, depending on whether you want to replace all the contents of a cell or just part of the contents, and whether you want to do it in the cell or in the Formula bar.

Edit Cell Contents

To edit data entered in a cell:

- Double-click the text in the cell where you want to begin editing. An insertion point is placed in the cell. Type the new data, use the mouse to select characters to be overwritten or deleted, or use keyboard shortcuts. Complete the entry when finished editing. (See "Complete an Entry" earlier in the chapter.)

  –Or–

- Select the cell to edit, and then in the Formula bar click the cell's contents where you want to make changes. Type the new data, use the mouse to select characters to overwrite or delete, or use keyboard shortcuts. Click **Enter** on the Formula bar or press **ENTER** to complete the entry.

  –Or–

- Select the cell to edit, and press **F2**. Edit in the cell using the mouse or keyboard shortcuts. Complete the entry.

Replace All Cell Contents

Click the cell and type new data. The original data is deleted and replaced by your new characters.

Cancel Cell Editing

Before you complete a cell entry, you can revert to your original data by pressing **ESC** or clicking **Cancel** on the Formula bar.

▶▶ Remove Cell Contents

You can easily delete cell contents, move them to other cells, or clear selective attributes of a cell.

> **TIP** To undo a data-removal action, even if you have performed several actions since removing the data, click **Undo** on the Quick Access toolbar next to the File tab (or press **CTRL+Z**) for the most recent action. For earlier actions, continue clicking **Undo** to work your way back; or click the down arrow next to the button, and choose the action from the drop-down list.
>
>

Delete Data

Remove all contents (but not formatting) from a cell by selecting the cell and pressing **DELETE**. You can delete the contents of more than one cell by selecting the cells or the cell range and pressing **DELETE**. (See "Select Cells and Ranges" later in the chapter for more information on selecting various configurations.)

> **CAUTION** If you use the Delete button in the Home tab Cells group, you delete the selected cells' contents *and* the cells themselves from the worksheet. See Chapter 6 for more information on deleting cells.

Move Data

Cell contents can be removed from one location and placed in another location of equal size. Select the cell or range you want to move. Then:

- Place the pointer on any edge of the selection, except the lower-right corner where the fill handle resides, until it turns into a cross with arrowhead tips. Drag the cell or range to the new location.

	A	B	C	D	E
1	January	$ 1,476.82			
2	February	$ 2,512.57			
3	March	$ 1,199.21			
4	April	$ 2,292.74			
5					
6			D3:E6		
7					

–Or–

- On the Home tab Clipboard group, click **Cut**. Select the new location, and click **Paste** in the Clipboard group. (See "Copy and Paste Data" later in this chapter for more information on pasting options.)

Remove Selected Cell Contents

A cell can contain several components, including:

- **Formats** Consisting of number formats, conditional formats (formats that display if certain conditions apply), and borders
- **Contents** Consisting of formulas and data
- **Comments** Consisting of notes you attach to a cell
- **Hyperlinks** Consisting of links to other ranges on the current worksheet, other worksheets in the current workbook, other workbooks or other files, and web pages in websites

1. Choose which cell components you want to clear by selecting the cell or cells.
2. On the Home tab Editing group, click the **Clear** button, and click the applicable item from the menu. (Clicking **Clear Contents** performs the same action as pressing **DELETE**.)

▶▶ Select Cells and Ranges

The key to many actions in Excel is the ability to select cells in various configurations and use them to perform calculations. You can select a single cell, nonadjacent cells, and adjacent cells (or *ranges*).

Select a Single Cell

Select a cell by clicking it, or move to a cell by using the arrow keys or by completing an entry in a cell above or to the left of it.

Select Nonadjacent Cells

Select a cell and then press **CTRL** while clicking the other cells you want to select. The selected cells remain highlighted.

$8,598	$9,104
$1,290	$1,256
$1,066	$1,129

Select a Range of Adjacent Cells

Select a cell and drag over the additional cells you want to include in the range.

–Or–

Select the first cell in the range, press and hold **SHIFT**, and click the last cell in the range.

Select All Cells on a Worksheet

Click the **Select All** button in the upper-left corner of the worksheet, or press **CTRL+A**.

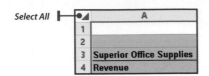

Select a Row or Column

Click a row (number) heading or column (letter) heading.

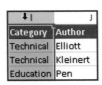

Select Adjacent Rows or Columns

Drag down the row headings or across the column headings.

Select Nonadjacent Rows or Columns

Select a row or column heading, and then press **CTRL** while clicking other row or column headings you want to select.

Resize an Adjacent Selection

Press **SHIFT** and click the cell you want to be at the end of the selection.

Select a Combination of Cells

By dragging, combined with clicking while pressing **CTRL** or **SHIFT**, you can include single cells, rows, columns, and ranges all in one selection. Figure 5-7 shows one example. The selections in Figure 5-7 are achieved by clicking a single cell, clicking a column or row heading to select a column or row respectively, and dragging a range of cells.

> **TIP** To select larger numbers of adjacent cells, rows, or columns, click the first item in the group, and then press **SHIFT** while clicking the last item in the group.

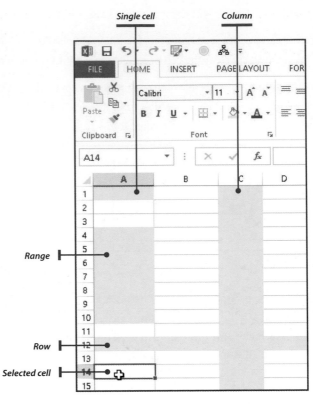

Figure 5-7: You can include a single cell, a row, a column, and a range all in one selection.

▷▷ Copy and Paste Data

Data you've already entered on a worksheet (or in other programs) can be copied to the same or other worksheets, or even to other Windows applications. You first *copy* the data to the Windows Clipboard, where it is temporarily stored. After selecting a destination for the data, you *paste* it into the cell or cells. You can copy all the data in a cell or only part of it. You can paste it on your worksheet one time, in one location, or at different locations several times. (The copied data remains on the Clipboard until you replace it with another copy action. See the related

Tip for cut actions.) While many computer users are familiar with a basic copy, Excel's paste feature lets you selectively paste attributes of the data and even shows you a preview of how the pasted information will look in its new location.

 TIP Another way to send information to the Clipboard is to *cut* the data. When you cut data ✂ Cut , like a copy action, the data is placed on the Clipboard and replaces any existing data already there. However, when you cut data, it is removed from its original location (it's essentially moved), unlike copying, where the data is retained at its original location.

Copy Data

1. Select the cell or cells that contain the data you want to copy; or double-click a cell and select the characters you want to copy.

2. In the Home tab Clipboard group, click the **Copy** down arrow, and click **Copy** (to copy data as letters and characters), or click **Copy As Picture** to choose a picture format of the material (see Chapter 12 for more information on working with pictures and graphics).

–Or–

Press **CTRL+C** (to copy as letters and characters).

In either case, the selected data is copied to the Clipboard and the border around the cells displays a flashing dotted line.

Paste Data

Once data is placed on the Windows Clipboard through a *copy* action, you can selectively include or omit formulas, values, formatting, comments, arithmetic operations, and other cell properties *before* you paste or move data. (See Chapter 7 for information on formulas, values,

and arithmetic operations.) You can preview several variations of a paste by choosing from several tools, either on the ribbon or from a dialog box. Even after you perform a paste, you can easily change your mind by selecting and previewing paste options from a smart tag.

1. Select the location (a cell or range) for the cut or copied data.

2. On the Home tab Clipboard group, click the **Paste** down arrow. A menu of several pasting tools appears, each as an icon.

–Or–

Right-click the selected cell or range, and on the context menu, view a few tools under Paste Options, or even more tools by pointing to Paste Special.

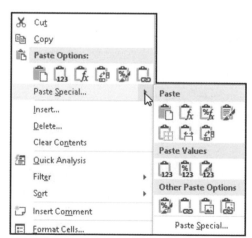

3. Point to each tool to see a short description of the pasting characteristic(s) it supports. As you point to an icon, the cell or range you had selected will show how the pasting characteristic affects the data, as shown in Figure 5-8.

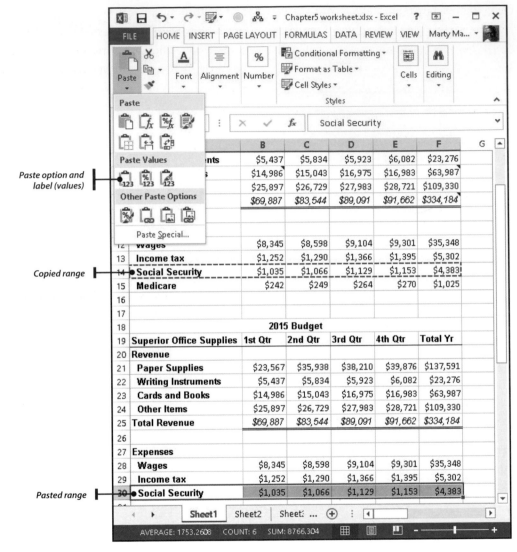

Paste option and label (values)

Copied range

Pasted range

Figure 5-8: *You can preview how each tool will show your pasted data.*

4. Click the tool you want to use to perform the paste. If you want a different pasting tool, click the smart tag 📋 (Ctrl) ▾ that appears next to the pasted cell or range and select another option.

5. Repeat steps 1 through 4 to paste the copied data to other locations. Press **ESC** when finished to remove the flashing border around the source cells.

6. Alternatively, you can choose options from a list in a dialog box without previewing the effects. After selecting the destination cell or cells to where you want the data copied or moved, in the Clipboard group, click the **Paste** down arrow, and click **Paste Special**; or right-click the destination cells, and click **Paste Special**. The Paste Special dialog box appears, as shown in Figure 5-9.

7. Select the paste options you want in the copied or moved cells, and click **OK**.

CAUTION If you paste data into a cell that contains existing data, that existing data will be replaced with the pasted data. To avoid losing data, insert blank cells, rows, and columns to accommodate the data you are pasting. See Chapter 6 for more information on inserting cells, rows, and columns.

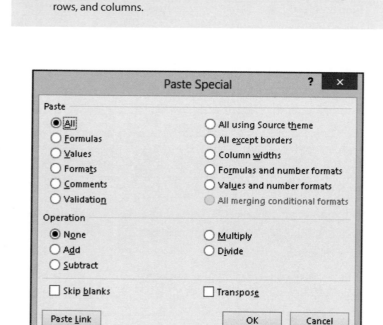

Figure 5-9: *Pasting options are listed in the Paste Special dialog box.*

Find and Replace Data

In worksheets that might span thousands of rows and columns (more than one million rows and 16,000 columns are possible), you need the ability to locate data quickly, as well as to find instances of the same data so that consistent replacements can be made.

Find Data

1. In the Home tab Editing group, click **Find & Select**, and click **Find**; or press **CTRL+F** to open the Find And Replace dialog box with the Find tab displayed.

2. Type the text or number you want to find in the Find What text box.

3. Click **Options** to view the following options to refine the search (see Figure 5-10):

   • **Format**   Opens the Find Format dialog box, where you select from several categories of number, alignment, font, border, pattern, and protection formats.

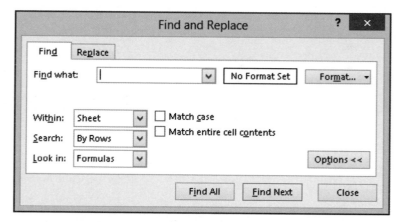

Figure 5-10: *The Find tab lets you refine your search based on several criteria.*

- **Choose Format From Cell** (from the Format drop-down list)   Lets you click a cell that contains the format you want to find.
- **Within**   Limits your search to the current worksheet or expands it to all worksheets in the workbook.
- **Search**   Lets you search to the right by rows or down by columns. You can search to the left and up by pressing **SHIFT** and clicking **Find Next**.
- **Look In**   Focuses the search to just formulas, values, or comments.
- **Match Case**   Lets you choose between uppercase or lowercase text.
- **Match Entire Cell Contents**   Searches for an exact match of the characters in the Find What text box.

4. Click **Find All** to display a table of all occurrences (shown here), or click **Find Next** to find the next singular occurrence.

Find All	Find Next	Close

Book	Sheet	Name	Cell	Value	Formula
Chapter5 worksheet.xlsx	Sheet1		I2	Technical	
Chapter5 worksheet.xlsx	Sheet1		I3	Technical	
Chapter5 worksheet.xlsx	Sheet1		I12	Technical	
Chapter5 worksheet.xlsx	Sheet1		I13	Technical	
Chapter5 worksheet.xlsx	Sheet1		I16	Technical	
Chapter5 worksheet.xlsx	Sheet1		I19	Technical	

17 cell(s) found

Replace Data

The Replace tab of the Find And Replace dialog box looks and behaves similar to the Find tab covered earlier.

1. In the Home tab Editing group, click **Find And Select**, and click **Replace**; or press **CTRL+H** to open the Find And Replace dialog box with the Replace tab displayed.

2. Enter the text or number to find in the Find What text box; enter the replacement characters in the Replace With text box. If formatting or search criteria are required, click **Options**. See "Find Data" for the options' descriptions.

3. Click **Replace All** to replace all occurrences in the worksheet, or click **Replace** to replace occurrences one at a time.

Find Specific Excel Objects

You can quickly locate key Excel objects, such as formulas and comments, without having to type any keywords. The objects you can directly search for are listed on the Find & Select drop-down menu.

1. In the Home tab Editing group, click **Find & Select**. The drop-down menu lists several categories of objects from which you can choose.

2. Click the item whose instances you want selected. The first instance is surrounded by a light-colored border, and all other instances in the worksheet are selected/highlighted (see Figure 5-11).

   –Or–

   Click **Go To Special** to open a dialog box of the same name, and select from several additional objects. Click **OK** after making your selection.

3. To remove the selection/highlight from found objects, click outside the found objects to remove the selection to turn off that feature.

 NOTE   The Go To option on the Find & Select drop-down menu lets you find cells and ranges by name or address. Using the Go To dialog box in this manner is covered in Chapter 7.

	A	B	C	D	E	F
1		Superior Office Supplies				
2		2014 Budget				
3	Superior Office Supplies	1st Qtr	2nd Qtr	3rd Qtr	4th Qtr	Total Yr
4	Revenue					
5	Paper Supplies	$23,567	$35,938	$38,210	$39,876	$137,591
6	Writing Instruments	$5,437	$5,834	$5,923	$6,082	$23,276
7	Cards and Books	$14,986	$15,043	$16,975	$16,983	$63,987
8	Other Items	$25,897	$26,729	$27,983	$28,721	$109,330
9	Total Revenue	$69,887	$83,544	$89,091	$91,662	$334,184
10						

*Figure 5-11: **Certain Excel objects, such as comments, can be located and identified with just a few clicks.***

Verify Spelling

You can check the spelling of selected cells—or the entire worksheet—using Excel's main dictionary and a custom dictionary you add words to (both dictionaries are shared with other Office programs).

 TIP If the correct spelling of a misspelled word is not shown in the Suggestions list box, edit the word in the Not In Dictionary text box, and click **Add To Dictionary** to include it in a custom dictionary that is checked in addition to the main dictionary.

1. Select the cells to check; to check the entire worksheet, select any cell.

2. In the Review tab Proofing group, click **Spelling**, or press **F7**. If the spelling checker doesn't find anything to report, you are told the spelling check is complete. Otherwise, the Spelling dialog box appears, as shown in Figure 5-12.

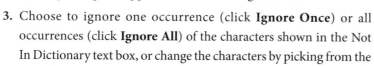

3. Choose to ignore one occurrence (click **Ignore Once**) or all occurrences (click **Ignore All**) of the characters shown in the Not In Dictionary text box, or change the characters by picking from the Suggestions list and clicking one of the Change options.

4. Click **AutoCorrect** if you want to automatically replace words in the future. (See "Modify Automatic Corrections," next, for more information on using AutoCorrect.)

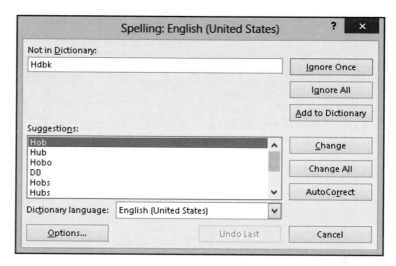

*Figure 5-12: **The Spelling dialog box provides several options to handle misspelled or uncommon words.***

5. Click **Options** to change language or custom dictionaries and set other spelling criteria.

Modify Automatic Corrections

Excel automatically corrects common data entry mistakes as you type, replacing characters and words you choose with other choices. You can control how this is done.

1. Click the **File** tab, click **Options**, click the **Proofing** option, and click **AutoCorrect Options**. The AutoCorrect dialog box appears, as shown in Figure 5-13. As appropriate, do one or more of the following:

   - Choose the type of automatic corrections you do or do not want from the options at the top of the dialog box.

   - Click **Exceptions** to set capitalization exceptions.

   - Click **Replace Text As You Type** to turn off automatic text replacement (turned on by default).

![AutoCorrect: English (United States) dialog box. Tabs: AutoCorrect, AutoFormat As You Type, Actions, Math AutoCorrect. Checkboxes: Show AutoCorrect Options buttons; Correct TWo INitial CApitals; Capitalize first letter of sentences; Capitalize names of days; Correct accidental use of cAPS LOCK key; Replace text as you type. Exceptions button. Replace/With table showing (c) ©, (e) €, (r) ®, (tm) ™, ..., with Add and Delete buttons, OK and Cancel.]

Figure 5-13: AutoCorrect provides several automatic settings and lets you add words and characters that are replaced with alternatives.

- Add new words or characters to the Replace and With lists, and click **Add**; or select a current item in the list, edit it, and click **Replace**.

- Delete replacement text by selecting the item in the Replace and With lists and clicking **Delete**.

2. Click **OK** when you are done.

▷▷ Edit Workbooks in the Excel Web App

As described in Chapter 1, with a Windows Live account, you can upload files to Microsoft's SkyDrive location in order to keep them in the "cloud" so that you, or others, can access them at any time or place from a browser. Besides simply storing files there, using the integrated Microsoft Excel Web App, you can also view, edit, and download workbooks saved in the Excel 2007, 2010, and 2013 default .xlsx file format without necessarily

having a version of Excel installed on your device. (You can view workbooks saved in the earlier .xls file format and once they are converted to .xlsx format, you can edit them.) The editing capabilities in the Excel Web App are limited to the more basic features of Excel, such as those described in this chapter, as well as minor formatting actions (described in Chapter 6) and working with tables. In fact, if the workbook contains more advanced features, such as shapes or a watch window, you cannot edit it (although you can view and download it). However, for those cases where your edits are predominately data-centric, SkyDrive and the Excel Web App provide you a great opportunity to access your information from anywhere with only a browser and Internet connection.

To use a workbook in the Excel Web App:

1. Open the SkyDrive folder that contains the workbook you want to view or edit (see Chapter 1 for information on logging on to SkyDrive).

2. Click the file you want to open. The workbook opens in a screen that appears similar to the Excel 2013 user interface but lacks certain features, including the tools located on the missing ribbon tabs and some of the options found on a standard File tab.

3. After performing editing using the tools on the available ribbon tabs, click the **File** tab and click **Save As**. (There is no option to save it in SkyDrive because the Excel Web App automatically saves the file in the same folder as the original.) You can save a copy of the file with a different name in the same location as the original, or download and save and/or open it on your computer in Excel.

4. When finished, click **Sign Out** in the upper-right corner of the Excel Web App to securely leave your work.

Chapter 6

Formatting a Worksheet in Excel

Arguably, the primary purpose of a worksheet is to provide a grid to calculate numbers, generally regarded as a rather boring display of numeric data. Excel provides you with the tools to adjust and rearrange the row-and-column grid to meet your needs, but it goes much further to bring emphasis, coordinated colors, and other features that let you add *presentation* to your data.

In this chapter you will learn how to add and delete cells, rows, and columns, and how to change their appearance, both manually and by having Excel do it for you. You will see how to change the appearance of text, how to use themes and styles for a more consistent look, and how to add comments to a cell to better explain important points. Techniques to better display workbooks and change worksheets are also covered.

WORK WITH CELLS, ROWS, AND COLUMNS

Getting a worksheet to look the way you want will probably involve adding and removing cells, rows, and/or columns to appropriately separate your data and remove unwanted space. You might also want to adjust the size and type of cell borders and add comments to provide ancillary information about the contents of a cell. This section covers these features and more.

> **NOTE** Don't ever worry about running out of rows or columns in a worksheet. You can have up to 1,048,576 rows and 16,384 columns in each Excel worksheet. As a bit of tourist information, the last cell address in a worksheet is XFD1048576.

⟫ Adjust Row Height

You can change the height of a row manually or by changing cell contents.

Change the Height Using a Mouse

1. Select one or more rows (they can be adjacent or nonadjacent; see Chapter 5 for selection options).

2. Point at the bottom border of a selected row heading until the pointer changes to a cross with up and down arrowheads.

3. Drag the border up or down to the row height you want (as you are dragging, the row height is shown in *points*—there are 72 points to an inch—and in pixels).

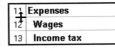

Change the Height by Entering a Value

1. Select the rows you want to adjust.

2. In the Home tab Cells group, click **Format**, and under Cell Size, click **Row Height**; or right-click a cell in the selected rows, and click **Row Height**. The Row Height dialog box appears.

3. Type a new height in points (1 inch = 72 points), and click **OK**. The cell height changes, but the size of the cell contents stays the same.

Change Row Height by Changing Cell Contents

1. Select one or more cells, rows, or characters that you want to change in height.

2. Change the cell contents. Examples of the various ways to do this include:

- **Changing font size** In the Home tab Font group, click the **Font Size** down arrow, and click a size from the drop-down list. You can drag up and down the list of font sizes and see the impact of each on the worksheet before selecting one, as shown in Figure 6-1. However, if you have already manually changed the row height, changing the font size of a cell's contents will not automatically change the row height.

- **Placing characters on two or more lines within a cell** Place the insertion point at the end of a line or where you want the line to break, and press **ALT+ENTER**.

- **Inserting graphics or drawing objects** See Chapter 12 for information on working with graphics.

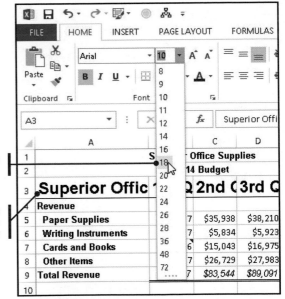

Figure 6-1: **You can preview the effects of changing row heights by increasing or decreasing the font size in selected cells.**

When a selected object changes size or a new object is inserted, if its height becomes larger than the original row height, the height of all cells in the row(s) will be increased. The size of the other cell's contents, however, stays the same.

Change Row Height to Fit the Size of Cell Contents

Excel automatically adjusts row height to accommodate the largest object or text size added to a row. If you subsequently remove larger objects or text and need to resize the row height to fit the remaining objects, you can do so using AutoFit.

- Double-click the bottom border of the row heading for a row or selected rows.

  –Or–

- Select the cell or rows you want to size. In the Home tab Cells group, click **Format** and click **AutoFit Row Height**.

The row heights(s) will adjust to fit the highest content.

▷▷ Adjust Column Width

As with changing row height, you can change the width of a column manually or by changing cell contents.

Change the Width Using a Mouse

1. Select one or more columns (columns can be adjacent or nonadjacent; see Chapter 5 for selection options).

2. Point at the right border of a selected column heading until the pointer changes to a cross with left and right arrowheads.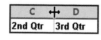

3. Drag the border to the left or right to the width you want.

 NOTE You cannot change the width of a single cell without changing the width of all cells in the column.

Change the Width by Entering a Value

1. Select the columns you want to adjust.

2. In the Home tab Cells group, click **Format** and click **Column Width**; or right-click the cell, and click **Column Width**. The Column Width dialog box appears.

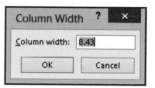

3. Type a new width, and click **OK**. The cell width changes, but the size of the cell contents stays the same.

 TIP The default column width for a worksheet is determined by the average number of characters in the default font that will fit in the column (not in points, as with row height). For example, the default Calibri 11-pt. font provides a standard column width of 8.43 characters. If you want to change the default column width, in the Home tab Cells group, click **Format** and click **Default Width**. Type a width and click **OK**. Columns at the original standard width will change to reflect the new value.

Change Column Width to Fit the Size of Cell Contents

- Double-click the right border of the column header for the column or selected columns.

  –Or–

- Select the cell or columns you want to size. In the Home tab Cells group, click **Format** and click **AutoFit Column Width**.

The column width(s) will adjust to fit the longest entry.

▷▷ Hide and Unhide Rows and Columns

Hiding rows and columns provides a means to temporarily remove rows or columns from view without deleting them or their contents.

Hide Rows and Columns

1. Select the rows or columns to be hidden.

2. In the Home tab Cells group, click **Format**, click **Hide & Unhide**, and click **Hide Rows** or **Hide Columns**; or right-click the selection, and click **Hide**.

   –Or–

   Drag the bottom border of the row header of the rows to be hidden *up*, or drag the right border of the column header of the columns to be hidden to the *left*.

The row numbers or column letters of the hidden cells are omitted, as shown in Figure 6-2. (You can also tell cells are hidden by the small space in the row or column headers between the hidden rows or columns.)

A small space between rows and columns identifies hidden rows and columns

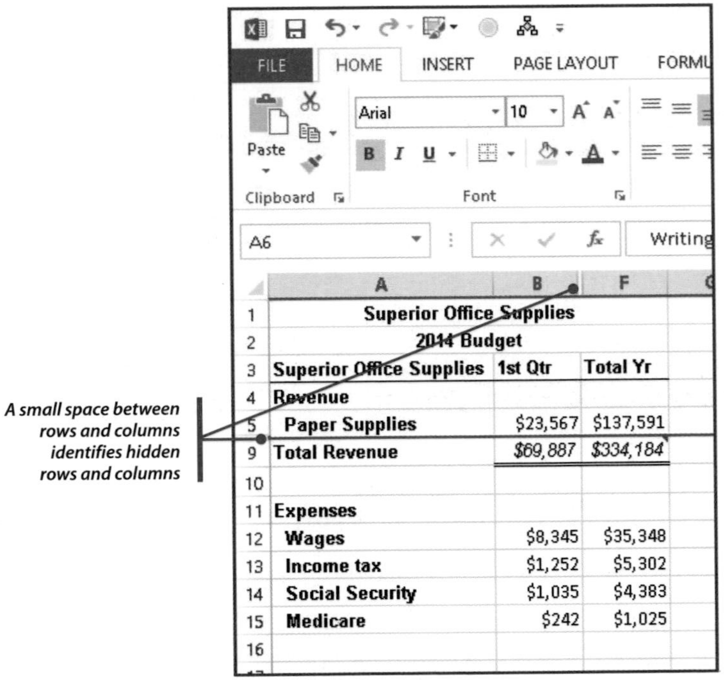

Figure 6-2: Rows 6, 7, and 8 and columns C, D, and E are hidden in this worksheet.

Unhide Rows or Columns

1. Drag across the row or column headings on both sides of the hidden rows or columns.

2. In the Home tab Cells group, click **Format**, click **Hide & Unhide**, and click **Unhide Rows** or **Unhide Columns**.

   –Or–

   Right-click the selection and click **Unhide**.

> **TIP** If you hide one or more rows or columns beginning with column A or row 1, it does not look like you can drag across the rows or columns on both sides of the hidden rows or columns to unhide them. However, you can by selecting the row or column to the right or below the hidden row or column and dragging the selection into the heading. Then when you click **Unhide** from the context menu or **Unhide Rows** or **Unhide Columns** from the Format menu, the hidden object will appear. If you don't do this, you won't be able to recover the hidden row or column.

▷▷ Add and Remove Rows, Columns, and Cells

You can insert or delete rows one at a time or select adjacent and nonadjacent rows to perform these actions on them together. (See Chapter 5 for information on selecting rows, columns, and cells.)

Add a Single Row

1. Select the row below where you want the new row.

2. In the Home tab Cells group, click the **Insert** down arrow, and click **Insert Sheet Rows**; or right-click a cell in the selected row, and click **Insert**.

Add Multiple Adjacent Rows

1. Select the number of rows you want immediately below the row where you want the new rows.

2. In the Home tab Cells group, click the **Insert** down arrow, and click **Insert Sheet Rows**; or right-click a cell in the selected rows, and click **Insert**.

Add Rows to Multiple Nonadjacent Rows

1. Select the number of rows you want immediately below the first row where you want the new rows.

2. Hold down the CTRL key while selecting the number of rows you want immediately below any other rows.

3. In the Home tab Cells group, click the **Insert** down arrow, and click **Insert Sheet Rows**; or right-click any selection, and click **Insert**.

Add a Single Column

1. Select the column to the right of where you want the new column.

2. In the Home tab Cells group, click the **Insert** down arrow, and click **Insert Sheet Columns**; or right-click a cell in the selected column, and click **Insert**.

Add Multiple Adjacent Columns

1. Select the number of columns you want immediately to the right of the column where you want the new columns.

2. In the Home tab Cells group, click the **Insert** down arrow, and click **Insert Sheet Columns**; or right-click a cell in the selected columns, and click **Insert**.

Add Columns to Multiple Nonadjacent Columns

1. Select the columns you want immediately to the right of the first column where you want the new columns.

2. Hold down the CTRL key while selecting the columns you want immediately to the right of any other columns.

3. In the Home tab Cells group, click the **Insert** down arrow, and click **Insert Sheet Columns**; or right-click any selection, and click **Insert**.

Add Cells

1. Select the cells adjacent to where you want to insert the new cells.

2. In the Home tab Cells group, click the **Insert** down arrow, and click **Insert Cells**; or right-click the cell, and click **Insert**.

3. In the Insert dialog box, choose the direction to shift the existing cells to make room for the new cells. Click **OK**.

Remove Cells, Rows, and Columns

1. Select the single or adjacent items (cells, rows, or columns) you wish to remove. If you want to remove nonadjacent items, hold down the CTRL key while clicking them.

2. In the Home tab Cells group, click the **Delete** down arrow, and click the command applicable to what you want to remove; or right-click the selection, and click **Delete**.

3. When deleting selected cells, the Delete dialog box appears. Choose from which direction to fill in the removed cells, and click **OK**.

Merge Cell

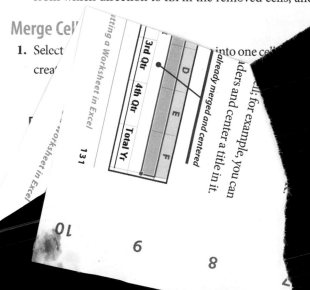

131

2. In the Home tab Alignment group, click the **Merge & Center** down arrow. (If all you want to do is merge and center, click the button.)

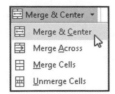

3. Click the applicable tool from the drop-down list.

⏩ Change Cell Borders

Borders provide a quick and effective way to emphasize and segregate data on a worksheet. You can create borders by choosing from samples or by setting them up in a dialog box. Use the method that suits you best.

Pick a Border

1. Select the cell, range, row, or column whose border you want to modify.

2. In the Home tab Font group, click the **Border** down arrow, and select the border style you want. (The style you choose remains as the available border style on the button.)

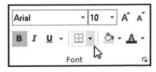

..e a border, select the cell(s), click the **Border** down arrow,
..**Border**.

..**You Change Them**

..lumn that you want to modify with

..**der** down arrow, and

Preview Borders B..

3. To remov.. and click No B..

1. Select the cell, .. a border.

2. In the .. cli.. order.

In the Home tab Font group, click the **dialog box launcher**; or right-click the selection, and click **Format Cells**. Click the **Border** tab in the Format Cells dialog box.

In either case, the Format Cells dialog box appears with the Border tab displayed, as shown in Figure 6-3.

3. In the Border area in the center of the dialog box, you will see a preview of the selected cells. Use the other tools in the dialog box to set up your borders.

- **Presets buttons**   Set broad border parameters by selecting to have no border, an outline border, or an inside "grid" border (can also be changed manually in the Border area).

- **Line area**   Select a border style and color (see "Change Themed Colors" later in the chapter for information on color options).

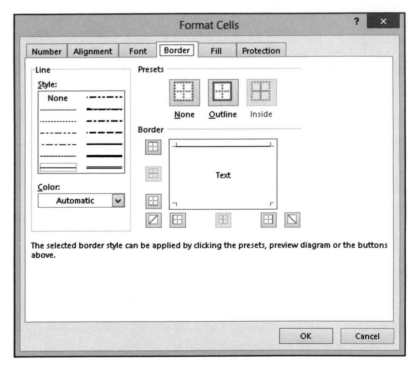

*Figure 6-3: **You can build and preview borders for selected cells in the Border tab.***

- **Border buttons** Choose where you want a border (click once to add the border; click twice to remove it).
- **Preview box** You can add borders directly by clicking in the Preview area where you want the border. The border selected in the Style box is added.

4. Click **OK** to apply the borders.

Draw Borders

1. In the Home tab Font group, click the **Border** down arrow, and under Draw Borders, select the line color and style of border you want.

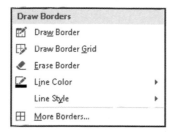

2. From the Border menu, click **Draw Border** to draw an outer border.
   –Or–
   Click **Draw Border Grid** to include interior borders.

3. Use the pencil mouse pointer to drag over the cells you want to have a border, or click a cell side to add just that border.

$8,598	$9,104	$9,301
$1,290	$1,366	$1,395

4. If you want to change a drawn border, click **Erase Border** and drag over a border to remove it.

5. When you are finished, press ESC to turn off the border drawing feature.

▷▷ Add a Comment

A comment acts as a "notepad" for cells, providing a place on the worksheet for explanatory text that can be hidden until needed.

1. Select the cell where you want the comment.

2. In the Review tab Comments group, click **New Comment**; or right-click the cell, and click **Insert Comment**. In either case, a text box labeled with your user name is attached to the cell.

 TIP To change the user name that appears in a comment, click the **File** tab, click **Options**, and click the **General** option. Under Personalize Your Copy Of Microsoft Office, edit the name in the User Name text box, and click **OK**.

3. Type your comment and click anywhere on the worksheet to close the comment. An indicator icon (red triangle) in the upper-right corner of the cell shows that a comment is attached.

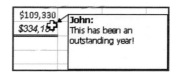

View Comments

You can view an individual comment, view comments in sequence, or view all comments on a worksheet.

- To view any comment, point to or select a cell that displays an indicator icon (red triangle) in its upper-right corner. The comment stays displayed as long as your mouse pointer remains in the cell.

- To view comments in sequence, in the Review tab Comments group, click **Next**. The next comment in the worksheet, moving left to right and down the rows, displays until you click another cell, press ESC, or click **Next** again to go to the next comment. Click **Previous** in the Comments group to reverse the search direction.

- To keep the comment displayed while doing other work, select the cell that contains the comment. In the Review tab Comments group, click **Show/Hide Comment**; or right-click the cell, and click **Show/Hide Comments**. (Click either command to hide the comment.)

- To view all comments in a worksheet and keep the comments displayed while doing other work, in the Review tab Comments group, click **Show All Comments**. (Click the command a second time to hide all comments.)

 TIP The default behavior for comments is to show the indicator icon (red triangle) and display the comment text when the mouse pointer is hovered over a cell containing a comment. You can also choose to always show the comment text and indicators or to not show the indicators and text. Click the **File** tab, click **Options**, and click the **Advanced** option. In the Display area, under For Cells With Comments, Show, select the behavior you want, and click **OK**.

> For cells with comments, show:
> ○ No comments or indicators
> ● Indicators only, and comments on hover
> ○ Comments and indicators

Edit a Comment

1. Select a cell that displays an indicator icon (red triangle) in its upper-right corner.

2. In the Review tab Comments group, click **Edit Comment**; or right-click the cell, and click **Edit Comment**.

3. Edit the text, including the user name if appropriate. Click anywhere in the worksheet when finished.

Delete a Comment

1. Select the cell or cells that contain the comments you want to delete.

2. In the Review tab Comments group, click **Delete**; or right-click the cell, and click **Delete Comment**.

 TIP You can also delete comments by selectively clearing them from a cell. In the Home tab Editing group, click **Clear** [Clear▾] and then click **Clear Comments** from the drop-down menu.

Move and Resize a Comment

Display the comment (see "Edit a Comment" for steps to open a comment for editing).

- To **resize**, point to one of the corner or mid-border sizing handles. When the pointer becomes a double arrow–headed line, drag the handle in the direction in which you want to increase or decrease the comment's size.

- To **move**, point at the border surrounding the comment. When the pointer becomes a cross with arrowhead tips, drag the comment to where you want it.

NOTE Moving a comment only moves the editing text box's position in relationship to its parent cell—it does not move the comment to other cells. The new location of moved comments only appears when editing the comment or when you display all comments in the worksheet; otherwise, when either the cell is selected or the mouse hovers over the cell, it appears in its default position.

Copy a Comment

1. Select the cell that contains the comment you want to copy (only the comment will be added to a new cell, not any other cell contents).

2. In the Home tab Clipboard group, click **Copy**; or right-click the cell, and click **Copy**; or press **CTRL+C**. The cell is surrounded by a flashing border.

3. Select the cells to which you want the comment copied. Then, in the Clipboard group, click the **Paste** down arrow, and click **Paste Special**. In the Paste Special dialog box, under Paste, click **Comments**, and then click **OK**.

4. Repeat step 3 to paste the comment into other cells. When finished, press **ESC** to remove the flashing border.

Format Comments

You can apply several formatting techniques to comments, including changing text, borders, and color. These and other attributes are changed using the Format Comment dialog box, available after a comment is opened for editing (see "Edit a Comment" earlier in this chapter).

Change the Appearance of Comment Text

1. To change the formatting of existing text, select the text first. If you do not select existing text, only new text you type will show the changes after you make them.

2. Right-click the interior of the comment, and click **Format Comment**. Make and preview the changes you want in the Font tab, and click **OK**. Alternatively, in the Home tab Font group, click the applicable control to change the font, size, and styling (see "Change Fonts" later in this chapter).

Change a Comment's Color and Border

1. Right-click the border of the comment, and click **Format Comment**.

2. In the Format Comment dialog box, click the **Colors And Lines** tab.

3. Click the **Fill Color** down arrow to open the gallery. Click the new color you want (see "Change Themed Colors" later in the chapter for information on color options).

4. In the Line area, change the attributes that control the comment's border. Click **OK** when finished.

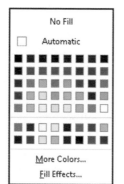

APPLY FORMATTING

Formatting gives life to a worksheet, transforming a rather dull collection of text and numbers into pleasing colors, shades, and variations in size and effects that bring attention to points you are trying to emphasize.

You can apply or create *themes* (consistent use of color, fonts, and graphic effects) to give your worksheets a coordinated appearance. If you want more control, you can apply *styles* (consistent formatting parameters applicable to specific worksheet objects) and *direct formatting* (use of ribbon buttons and dialog boxes) to cells and text. (See the "Understanding Excel Formatting" QuickFacts for more information on these formatting types.) In addition, you can transfer formatting attributes from one cell to others.

 QuickFacts

Understanding Excel Formatting

There are a plethora of ways you can change the appearance of text and worksheet elements. Without having a sense of the "method behind the madness," it's easy to become confused and frustrated when attempting to enhance your work. Excel (as well as other Office programs such as Microsoft Word and Microsoft PowerPoint) operates on a hierarchy of formatting assistance. The higher a formatting feature is on the stack, the broader and more automatic are its effects; the lower a formatting feature is on the stack, the more user intervention is required, although you will have more control over the granularity of any given feature.

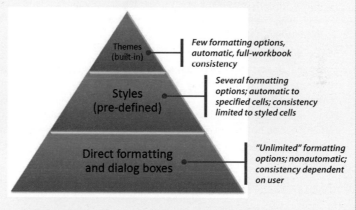

- **Themes** are at the top of the formatting heap. Themes provide an efficiently lazy way to apply professionally designed color, font, and graphic elements to a workbook. Each theme (with names like Office,

(continued)

Organic, and Celestial) includes 12 colors (4 text colors, 6 accent colors, and 2 hyperlink colors), along with 6 shades of each primary theme color. Separate collections of theme fonts are available for headings and the body text (the default workbook theme is Office, which is where the Calibri font comes from that you see in new workbooks). When you switch themes, all theme-affected elements are changed. You can modify existing themes and save them, creating your own theme.

- **Styles** occupy the middle tier of Excel formatting. Styles apply consistent formatting to directed Excel components, such as cells, tables, charts, and PivotTables. Styles, similar to themes, can be modified and saved for your own design needs. Both themes and styles are supported by several galleries of their respective formatting options, and provide a live preview by hovering your mouse pointer over each choice. Certain attributes of a style are *themed*, meaning they are consistent with the current theme and change accordingly.

- **Direct formatting** is the feature most of us have used to get the look we want, found in buttons on the ribbon and formatting dialog boxes divided into several tabs of options. Direct formatting provides the greatest control and access to formatting features, but even though Excel now provides live previews for many options, most still require you to accept the change, view the result in the workbook, and then repeat the process several times to get the result you want (and then start all over when moving, for example, from formatting a table to formatting a chart).

So how do you best put this hierarchy to work? Start at the top by applying a theme. If its formatting works for you, you're done! If you need more customization, try simply changing to a different theme. Need more options? Try applying a style to one of the style-affected components. Finally, if you need total control, use a component's formatting dialog box and ribbon buttons to make detailed changes. When you're all done, save all your changes as a new theme that you can apply to new workbooks, and also to your Word documents and PowerPoint presentations.

 ## Apply Themes

Themes are the most hands-off way to add a coordinated look and feel to a worksheet. Built-in themes control the formatting of themed elements, such as the color of table headers and rows and the font used in chart text.

In addition, you can change themes and modify themed elements (colors, fonts, and graphic effects).

TIP To quickly determine the theme currently in effect, click the **Page Layout** tab, and point to the **Themes** button in the Themes group. The tooltip displays the current theme (similarly, point to the **Fonts** button to see the current theme fonts in use).

Change the Current Theme

By default, Excel applies the Office theme to new workbooks. You can easily view the effects from the other built-in themes and change to the one you prefer.

1. In the Page Layout tab Themes group, click **Themes**. A gallery of the available themes (built-in, custom, and a selection from those available from Office Online) is displayed, as shown in Figure 6-4.

2. Point to each theme and see how colors, fonts, and graphics change in themed elements. The best way to view changes is to create a table and associated chart, and with it displayed, point to each theme in the gallery and see how the table and chart look (see Figure 6-4).

3. Click the theme you want, and save your workbook.

Change Themed Colors

Each theme comes with 12 primary colors (see the "Understanding Excel Formatting" QuickFacts) affecting text, accents, and hyperlinks.

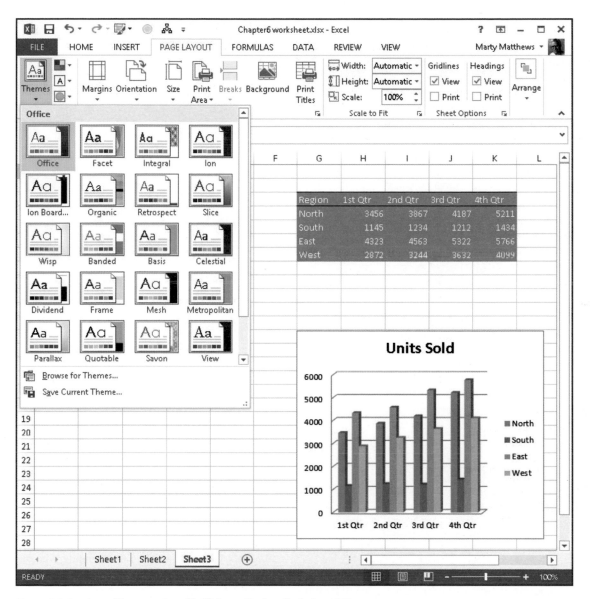

Figure 6-4: *Excel provides a number of built-in, professionally designed themes.*

You can choose a theme with different colors or modify each constituent color.

1. In the Page Layout tab Themes group, click **Colors**. The drop-down list displays the Custom (if you're already created one) and Office themes and 8 of the 12 colors associated with each theme.

2. At the bottom of the list, click **Customize Colors**. The Create New Theme Colors dialog box displays each constituent theme color and a sample displaying the current selections (see Figure 6-5).

3. Click the theme color you want to change. A gallery of colors displays and provides the following three options from which you select a new color:

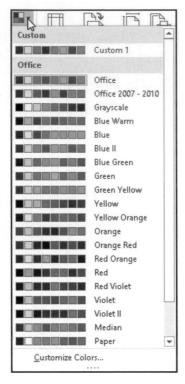

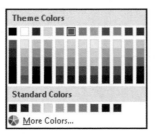

- **Theme Colors** displays a matrix of the 12 primary colors in the current theme and 6 shades associated with each. Click a color and see the change in the Sample area of the Create New Theme Colors dialog box.

- **Standard Colors** displays the 10 standard colors in the color spectrum (red through violet). Click the color you want.

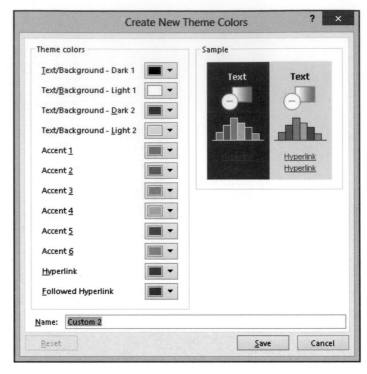

Figure 6-5: *Each theme color can be modified from an essentially infinite number of choices.*

- **More Colors** opens the Colors dialog box, shown in Figure 6-6, where you can select a custom color by clicking a color and using a slider to change its shading, or by selecting a color model and entering specific color values. In addition, you can click the **Standard** tab and select from a hexagonal array of Web-friendly colors.

4. Click **OK** to close the Colors dialog box and return to the Create New Theme Colors dialog box.

5. Repeat step 3 for any other theme color you want to change. If you get a bit far afield in your color changes, don't panic. Click **Reset** in the bottom-left corner of the Create New Theme Colors dialog box to return to the default theme colors.

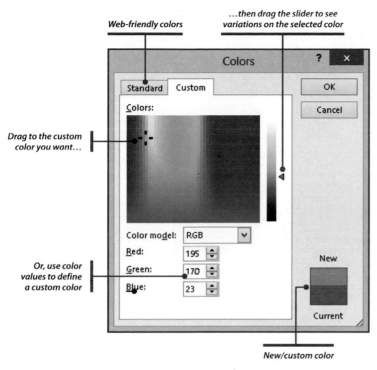

Web-friendly colors

...then drag the slider to see variations on the selected color

Drag to the custom color you want...

Or, use color values to define a custom color

New/custom color

Figure 6-6: The Colors dialog box offers the greatest control of custom color selection, as well as a collection of standard Web-friendly colors.

6. Type a new name for the color combination you've selected, and click **Save**. Custom colors are available for selection at the top of the Theme Colors drop-down list (as shown earlier following step 1).

 TIP To change a custom color or font, right-click the custom color or font in the respective theme Colors or Fonts drop-down list, and click **Edit**. Either Edit dialog box (Colors or Fonts) provides the same options as the Create New Theme Colors (or Fonts) dialog box you used to create the custom scheme.

Change Themed Fonts

Each theme includes two fonts. The *body* font is used for general text entry (the Calibri font in the default Office theme is the body font).

A *heading* font is also included and used in a few cell styles (see "Use Cell Styles" later in this chapter).

 NOTE The heading font used in Excel is primarily designed to allow consistency with Word and PowerPoint, where it is used more broadly.

1. In the Page Layout tab Themes group, click **Fonts**. The drop-down list, shown in Figure 6-7, displays theme font combinations (heading and body). The current theme font combination is highlighted.

2. Point to each combination to see how the fonts will appear on your worksheet.

 TIP Even on a blank worksheet, you can see how new theme font combinations will affect a worksheet—the column and row headings change to reflect the selected body font.

3. Click the combination you want, in which case you are finished, or click **Customize Fonts** at the bottom of the drop-down list and proceed to step 4 (see Figure 6-7).

4. In the Create New Theme Fonts dialog box, click either or both the **Heading Font** and **Body Font** down arrows to select new fonts. View the new combination in the Sample area.

5. Type a new name for the font combination you've selected, and click **Save**. Custom fonts are available for selection at the top of the theme Fonts drop-down list.

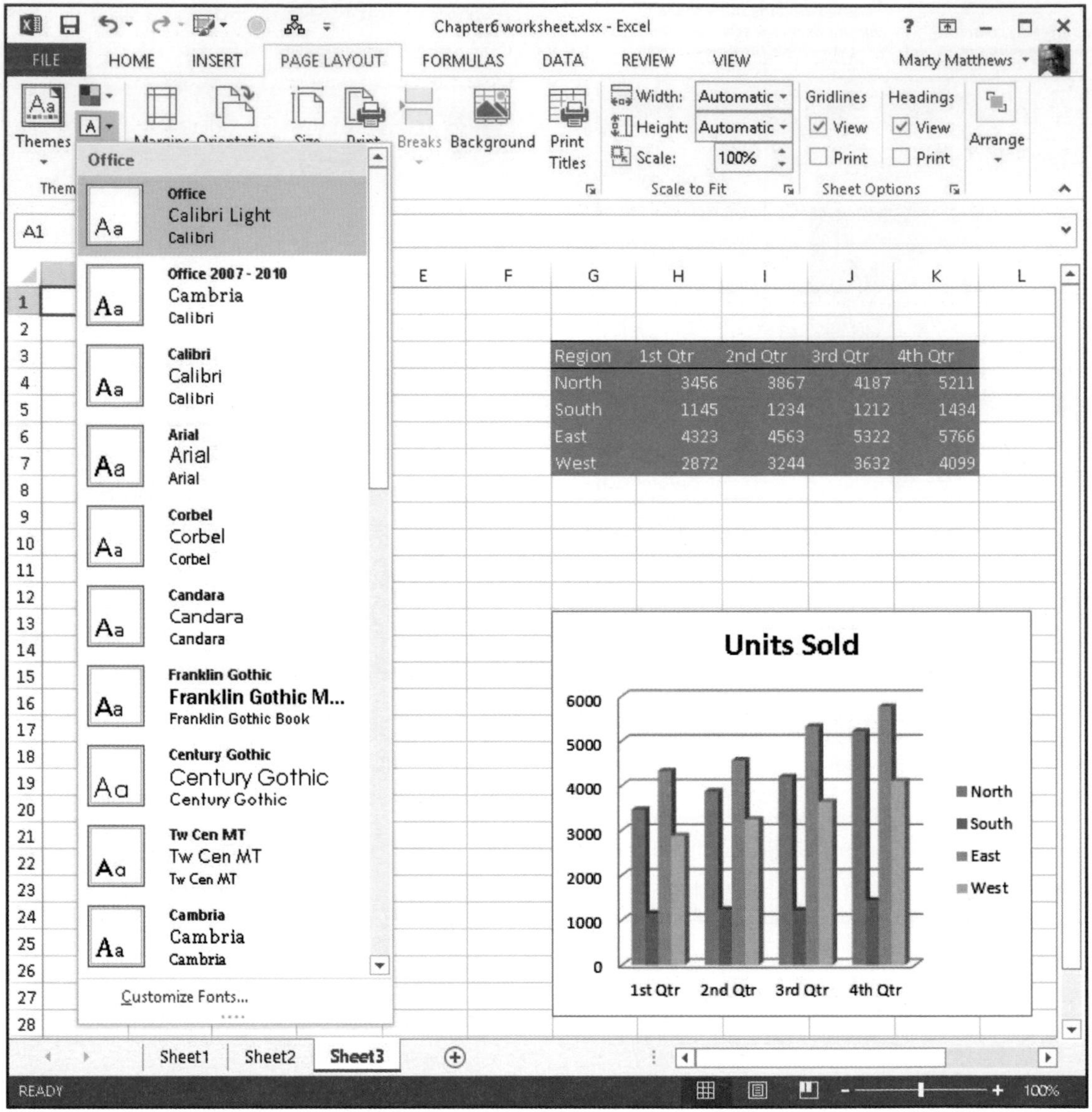

Figure 6-7: *You can see how different theme body and heading font combinations affect your worksheet simply by pointing to them.*

Change Themed Graphic Effects

Shapes, illustrations, pictures, and charts include graphic effects that are controlled by themes. Themed graphics are modulated in terms of their lines (borders), fills, and effects (such as shadowed, raised, and shaded). For example, some themes simply change an inserted rectangle's fill color, while other themes affect the color, the weight of its border, and whether it has a 3-D appearance.

1. In the Page Layout tab Themes group, click **Effects**. The drop-down list displays a gallery of effects. The current effect is highlighted.

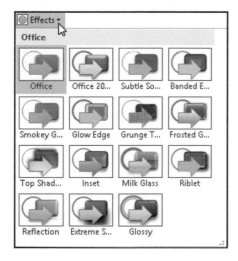

2. Point to each effect to see how it changes your worksheet, assuming you have a theme-based graphic or other element inserted on the worksheet.

3. Click the effect you want.

Create Custom Themes

Changes you make to a built-in theme (or to a previously created custom theme) can be saved as a custom theme and reused in other Office 2013 documents.

1. Make color, font, and effects changes to the current theme (see "Apply Themes" earlier in this chapter).

2. In the Page Layout tab Themes group, click **Themes** and click **Save Current Theme**. The Save Current Theme dialog box appears with the custom Office Document Themes folder displayed, as shown in Figure 6-8.

3. Name the file and click **Save** to store the theme in the Document Themes folder.

   –Or–

   Name the file and browse to the folder where you want to store it. Click **Save** when finished.

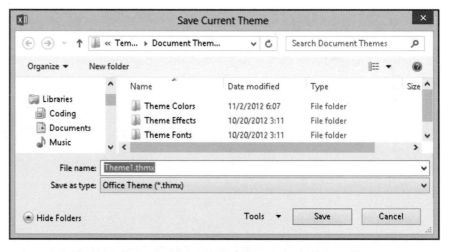

Figure 6-8: **Custom themes are saved as individual files, along with custom theme colors, effects, and fonts.**

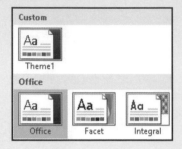

Search for Themes

You can quickly find individual theme files and themed documents, and apply them to your workbook, either as individual theme files or from other Office 2013 files that have themes applied to them.

1. In the Page Layout tab Themes group, click **Themes** and click **Browse For Themes** at the bottom of the gallery.

2. In the Choose Theme Or Themed Document dialog box, browse to the folder where the themes or themed documents are located. Only those documents will display. (*Themed documents* are Office 2013 files that contain a theme, such as Word files, Excel workbooks, PowerPoint presentations, and their respective templates.)

3. If you are only looking for theme files (.thmx), click **Office Themes And Themed Documents**, and click **Office Themes (.thmx)**.

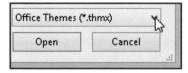

4. Select the Office document whose theme you want to apply or the theme file you want to apply, and click **Open**.

Use Cell Styles

Cell styles, which also can be applied to charts and tables, allow you to apply consistent formatting to specific cells, and let you make changes to styled cells with a few mouse clicks instead of changing each cell individually. Excel provides dozens of predefined styles, categorized by use. One category, themed cell styles, has the additional advantage of being fully integrated with the current theme. Colors associated with a theme change will automatically carry over to themed cell styles, preserving the coordinated appearance of your worksheet. Of course, you can modify any applied style and save the changes to create your own custom style.

Apply a Style

1. Select the cells you want to format with a style.

2. In the Home tab Styles group, click **Cell Styles**. A gallery of cell styles is displayed, as shown in Figure 6-9.

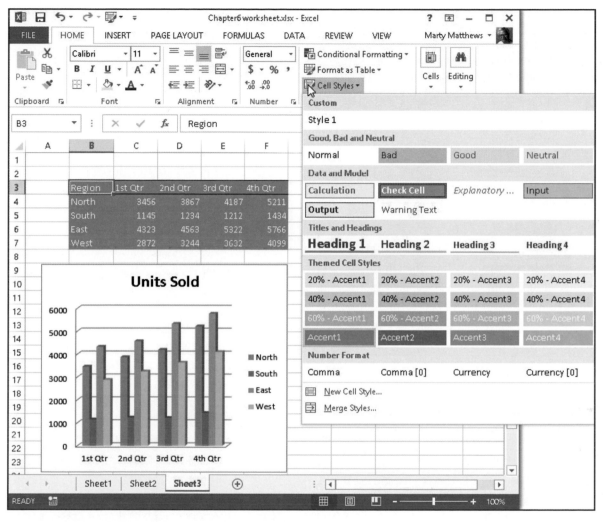

Figure 6-9: *Excel's styles provide a broad swatch of cell styling possibilities.*

3. Point to several styles in the gallery to see how each style affects your selected cells.

4. Click the style that best suits your needs. The style formatting is applied to your selected cells.

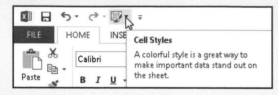

TIP You can avoid going back and forth between the Page Layout and Home tabs to apply themes and styles by placing the respective galleries on the Quick Access toolbar, as shown next. Right-click a gallery icon, and click **Add To Quick Access Toolbar**; or right-click anywhere in the open gallery, and click **Add Gallery To Quick Access Toolbar**.

Create a Custom Style

You can create your own style by starting with a predefined style and making changes, or you can start from scratch and apply all formatting directly, using the formatting tools on the ribbon or in a formatting dialog box. In either case, you can save your changes as a custom style and apply it from the Cell Styles gallery.

1. Use one or a combination of the following techniques to format at least one cell as you want:

   - Apply a predefined style to the cell(s) you want to customize.

   - Use the formatting tools in the ribbon (Home tab Font, Alignment, and Number groups).

   - Right-click a cell to be styled, click **Format Cells**, and use the six tabs in the Format Cells dialog box to create the styling format you want. Click **OK** when finished.

> **NOTE** Direct formatting using the ribbon and the Format Cells dialog box is discussed in other sections of this chapter.

2. In the Home tab Styles group, click **Cell Styles** and click **New Cell Style** at the bottom of the gallery.

3. In the Style dialog box, type a name for your style, and review the six areas of affected style formatting. If necessary, click **Format**, make formatting adjustments in the Format Cells dialog box, and click **OK** to apply formatting changes.

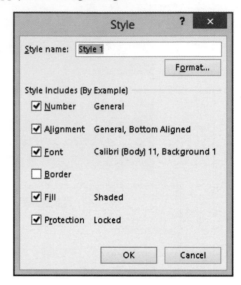

4. Click **OK** in the Style dialog box to create the style. The new custom style will be displayed in the Custom area at the top of the Cell Styles gallery.

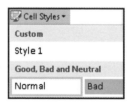

> **TIP** To quickly create a style based on an existing style, right-click the existing style in the styles gallery, and click **Duplicate**. In the Style dialog box, type a name for the new style, make any formatting changes by clicking **Format**, and click **OK** twice.

Change a Cell Style

1. In the Home tab Styles group, click **Cell Styles**.

2. Right-click a style (custom or predefined) in the gallery, and click **Modify**.

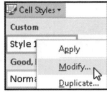

3. In the Style dialog box, click **Format** and make any formatting adjustments in the Format Cells dialog box. Click **OK** to apply the formatting changes.

4. Click **OK** in the Style dialog box to save changes to the style.

Remove a Cell Style

You can remove a style's formatting applied to selected cells, or you can completely remove the cell style from Excel (and concurrently remove all style formatting from affected cells).

- To remove style formatting from cells, select the cells, click **Cell Styles** in the Home tab Styles group, and click the **Normal** style.

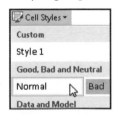

- To permanently remove a style, click **Cell Styles** in the Styles group, right-click the cell style you want removed, and click **Delete**.

Add Cell Styles from Other Workbooks

1. Open both the workbook whose styles you want to add and the workbook where you want the styles to be added.

2. In the View tab Window group, click **Switch Windows** and click the workbook to which you want the styles added, making it the active workbook.

3. In the Home tab Styles group, click **Cell Styles** and, below the gallery, click **Merge Styles**.

4. In the Merge Styles dialog box, click the workbook from which you want to add styles. Click **OK**.

▶▶ Change Fonts

Each *font* is composed of a *typeface*, such as Calibri; a *style*, such as italic; and a size. Other characteristics, such as color and super-/subscripting, further distinguish text. Excel also provides several underlining options that are useful in accounting applications.

1. On a worksheet, select either of the following:

   - Cells to apply font changes to all characters

   - Text and numbers to apply font changes to

2. Use one of the following techniques to access font tools and options:

   - On the ribbon, click the **Home** tab, and click the appropriate Font group tools (see Figure 6-10).

   - Double-click or right-click a cell or selection, and use the font tools available on the mini toolbar (you might need to move the cursor over the faded toolbar to see it more clearly).

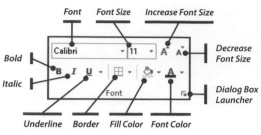

Figure 6-10: **Font group tools apply formatting to text.**

- Click the Font group **dialog box launcher** (located in the lower-right corner of group).

- Right-click a cell or selection, click **Format Cells**, and then click the **Font** tab.

3. In the latter two cases, the Format Cells dialog box appears with the Font tab displayed, as shown in Figure 6-11. Make and preview changes, and click **OK** when finished.

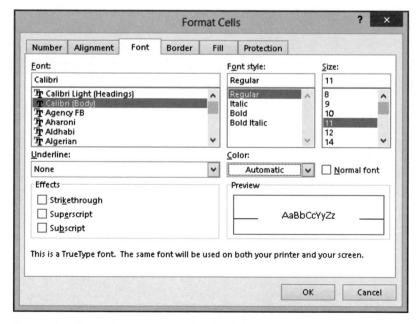

Figure 6-11: **Change the appearance of text by changing its font and other characteristics.**

TIP When selected, the Normal Font check box on the Font tab of the Format Cells dialog box (see Figure 6-11) resets font attributes to the defaults defined in the Normal template. The Normal template is an ever-present component of Excel (if you delete it, Excel will re-create another) that defines startup values in the absence of any other template.

⯈⯈ Change Alignment and Orientation

You can modify how characters appear within a cell by changing their alignment, orientation, and "compactness."

1. Select the cells whose contents you want to change.

2. Use one of the following techniques to access font tools and options:

- On the ribbon, click the **Home** tab, and click the appropriate Alignment group tools (see Figure 6-12).

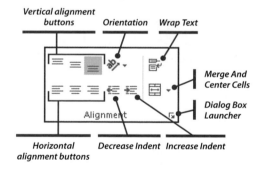

Figure 6-12: **Alignment group tools allow you to reposition text.**

- Click the Alignment group **dialog box launcher**.

- Right-click a cell or selection, click **Format Cells**, and then click the **Alignment** tab.

3. In the latter two cases, the Format Cells dialog box appears with the Alignment tab displayed, as shown in Figure 6-13. The specific features of the Alignment tab are described in Table 6-1.

4. Click **OK** when you are finished.

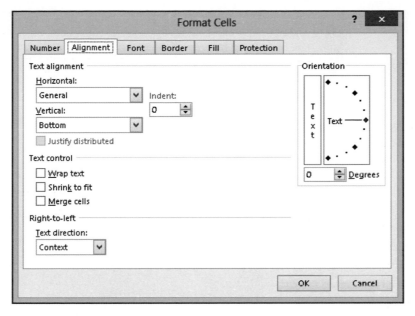

Figure 6-13: ***The Alignment tab provides detailed text-alignment options.***

Table 6-1: Text-Alignment Options in Excel

Feature	Option	Description
Text Alignment, Horizontal	General	Right-aligns numbers, left-aligns text, and centers error values; Excel default setting
	Left (Indent)	Left-aligns characters with optional indentation spinner
	Center	Centers characters in the cell
	Right (Indent)	Right-aligns characters with optional indentation spinner
	Fill	Fills cell with recurrences of content
	Justify	Justifies the text in a cell so that, to the degree possible, both the left and right ends are vertically aligned
	Center Across Selection	Centers text across one or more cells; used to center titles across several columns
	Distributed (Indent)	Stretches cell contents across cell width by adding space between words, with optional indentation spinner
Text Alignment, Vertical	Top	Places the text at the top of the cell

(continued)

Table 6-1: Text-Alignment Options in Excel *(continued)*

Feature	Option	Description
	Center	Places the text in the center of the cell
	Bottom	Places the text at the bottom of the cell; Excel default setting
	Justify	Evenly distributes text between the top and bottom of a cell to fill it by adding space between lines
	Distributed	Vertically arranges characters equally within the cell (behaves the same as Justify)
Orientation		Angles text in a cell by dragging the red diamond up or down or by using the Degrees spinner
Text Control	Wrap Text	Moves text that extends beyond the cell's width to the line below
	Shrink To Fit	Reduces character size so that cell contents fit within cell width (cannot be used with Wrap Text)
	Merge Cells	Creates one cell from contiguous cells, "increasing" the width of a cell without changing the width of the column(s)
Right To Left, Text Direction	Context	Text entry flows according to keyboard language in use
	Left To Right	Text entry flows from the left as in Western countries
	Right To Left	Text entry flows from the right as in many Middle Eastern and East Asian countries

⟩⟩ Add a Background

You can add color and shading to selected cells to provide a solid background. You can also add preset patterns, either alone or in conjunction with a solid background, for even more effect.

 TIP You can quickly add solid color and shading to selected cells from the Fill Color button in the Font group (see Figure 6-10). Click the button to apply the displayed color, or open a gallery by clicking the down arrow next to the button (see "Change Themed Colors" earlier in this chapter for information on the various gallery color options). The last color or shade selected remains on the Fill Color button until changed.

1. Select the cell, range, row, or column that you want to modify with a background.

2. In the Home tab Alignment group, click the **dialog box launcher**.

   –Or–

   Right-click the selection and click **Format Cells**.

   In either case, the Format Cells dialog box appears.

3. Click the **Fill** tab (see Figure 6-14), and choose colored and/or patterned fills.

Use Solid-Colored Backgrounds

1. In the Fill tab, click one of the color options in the Background Color area (see "Change Themed Colors" earlier in this chapter for information on the various color options).

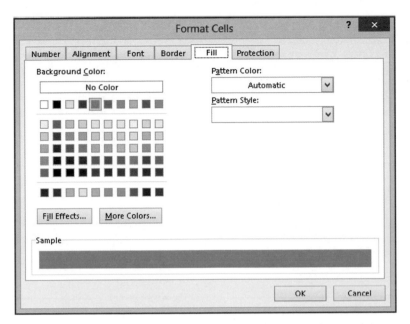

Figure 6-14: *Use the Fill tab to apply colored or patterned backgrounds to cells.*

–Or–

Click **Fill Effects** to apply blended fills, as shown in Figure 6-15. Preview your selections in the Sample area, and click **OK**.

2. Preview your selections in the larger Sample area at the bottom of the Fill tab, and click **OK** when finished.

Use Patterned Backgrounds

1. In the Fill tab, click the **Pattern Style** down arrow to display a gallery of patterns. Click the design you want, and see it enlarged in the Sample area at the bottom of the Fill tab.

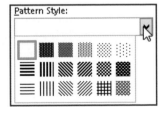

2. If you want to colorize the pattern, click the **Pattern Color** down arrow to display the color gallery (see "Change Themed Colors" earlier in this chapter for information on the various color options), and select one of the color options.

Select two colors to blend...

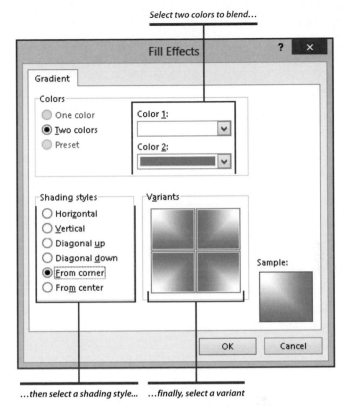

...then select a shading style...   ...finally, select a variant

Figure 6-15: *You can add pizzazz to cell fills using gradient effects.*

NOTE If you choose Automatic for the pattern color in the Format Cells Fill tab, the pattern is applied to the background color, but if you pick both a background color and a pattern color, the colors are merged.

3. Click **OK** when finished to close the Format Cells dialog box.

Copy Formatting

You can manually copy formatting from one cell to other cells using the Format Painter, as well as when you are inserting cells.

Use the Format Painter

 CAUTION When the Format Painter is turned on by double-clicking it, every time you select an object on the worksheet, formatting will be applied to it. For this reason, be sure to turn off the Format Painter immediately after you are done copying formats.

1. Select the cell whose formatting you want to copy.

2. In the Home tab Clipboard group, click the **Format Painter** button once if you only want to apply the formatting one time.

   –Or–

   Double-click the **Format Painter** button to keep it turned on for repeated use.

3. Select the cells where you want the formatting applied.

4. If you single-clicked the Format Painter before applying it to your selection, it will turn off after you apply it to your first selection; if you double-clicked the button, you may select other cells to continue copying the formatting.

5. Double-click the **Format Painter** to turn it off, or press ESC.

 TIP You can also copy formatting by using Paste Special, the Paste Options smart tag, and previewing paste options before you complete the change (see Chapter 5).

Attach Formatting to Inserted Cells, Rows, and Columns

Click the **Insert Options** smart tag (the paintbrush icon that appears after an insert), and choose from which direction you want the formatting applied, or choose to clear the formatting.

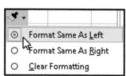

ARRANGE AND ORGANIZE WORKSHEETS

Excel provides several features to help you work with and view worksheets. You can retain headers at the top of the worksheet window as you scroll through hundreds of rows, split a worksheet, and view worksheets from several workbooks. In addition, there are several techniques you can use to add, remove, copy, and organize worksheets.

▷▷ Lock Rows and Columns

You can lock (or *freeze*) rows and columns in place so that they remain visible as you scroll. Typically, row and column headers are locked in larger worksheets, where you are scrolling through large numbers of rows or columns. You can quickly lock the first row and/or first column in a worksheet, or you can select the rows or columns to freeze.

 NOTE Freezing panes is not the same as freezing data. In an external data range, you can prevent the data from being refreshed, thereby freezing it.

Lock Rows

- In the View tab Window group, click **Freeze Panes** and click **Freeze Top Row**. The top row (typically, your header row) remains in place as you scroll down.

  –Or–

- Select the row below the rows you want to lock, click **Freeze Panes**, and click **Freeze Panes**. A thin border displays on the bottom of the locked row, as shown in Figure 6-16. All rows above the locked row remain in place as you scroll down.

Lock Columns

- In the View tab Window group, click **Freeze Panes** and click **Freeze First Column**. The leftmost column (typically, your header column) remains in place as you scroll to the right.

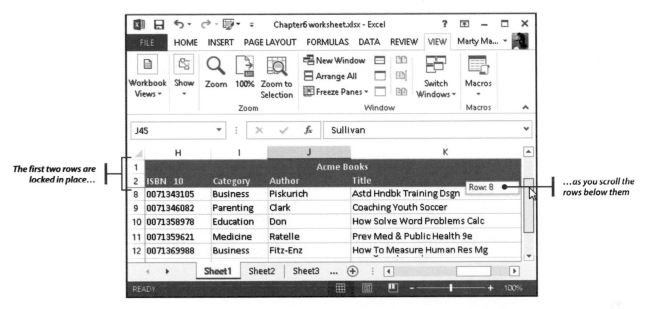

The first two rows are locked in place...

...as you scroll the rows below them

Figure 6-16: **You can lock rows in place and scroll through only those rows below the frozen rows.**

–Or–

- Select the column to the right of the columns you want to lock, click **Freeze Panes**, and click **Freeze Panes**. A thin border displays on the right side of the locked column. All columns to the left of the locked column remain in place as you scroll to the right.

Lock Rows and Columns Together

1. Select the cell that is below and to the right of the range you want to lock.

2. In the View tab Window group, click **Freeze Panes** and click **Freeze Panes**. A thin border displays below the locked rows and to the right of the locked columns. The range will remain in place as you scroll down or to the right.

Two locked columns

Seven locked rows

Unlock Rows and Columns

In the View tab Window group, click **Freeze Panes** and click **Unfreeze Panes**.

▶▶ Split a Worksheet

You can divide a worksheet into two independent panes of the same data, as shown in Figure 6-17.

1. To split the worksheet horizontally, select the row below where you want the split, then, in the View tab Window group, click **Split**.

–Or–

To split the worksheet vertically, select the column to the right of where you want the split, then, in the View tab Window group, click **Split**.

In either case, a split bar is displayed either across or down the worksheet.

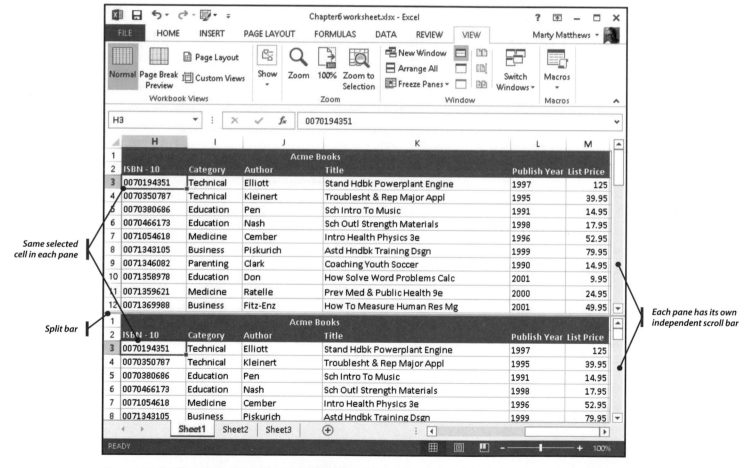

Figure 6-17: **A split worksheet provides two independent views of the same worksheet.**

2. Use the scroll bars to view other data within each pane.

3. Remove the split bar by double-clicking it.

 NOTE Any changes you make in one pane are recorded simultaneously in the other—they are really the same worksheet.

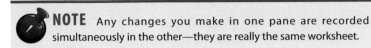 Work with Worksheets

Excel provides several tools you can use to modify the number and identification of worksheets in a workbook.

Add a Worksheet

Right-click the worksheet tab to the right of where you want the new worksheet, click **Insert**, and click **OK**.

–Or–

On the worksheet bar, click **New Sheet**. A new worksheet is added to the right of the active tab.

Delete a Worksheet

Right-click the worksheet tab of the worksheet you want to delete, and click **Delete**.

Move or Copy a Worksheet

You can move or copy worksheets within a workbook or between open workbooks by dragging a worksheet's tab. (See "View Worksheets from

Multiple Workbooks" later in the chapter for steps to arrange multiple open workbooks to facilitate dragging objects between them.)

- To move a worksheet, drag the worksheet tab to the position on the worksheet bar where you want it to appear.

- To copy a worksheet, press and hold CTRL, and drag the worksheet tab to the position on the worksheet bar where you want it to appear.

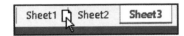

Rename a Worksheet

1. Right-click the worksheet tab of the worksheet you want to rename, and click **Rename**.

   –Or–

   Double-click the worksheet tab.

2. Type a new worksheet name and then either press ENTER or click anywhere on the grid.

Color a Worksheet Tab

1. Right-click the worksheet tab of the worksheet you want to color, and click **Tab Color**.

2. Select a color from the gallery (see "Change Themed Colors" earlier in this chapter for information on using the color gallery).

Change the Default Number of Worksheets in a Workbook

1. Click the **File** tab, click **Options**, and click the **General** option.

2. Under When Creating New Workbooks, click the **Include This Many Sheets** spinner to change the number of worksheets you want.

3. Click **OK** when finished.

Move Through Multiple Worksheets

Click the navigation buttons on the left end of the worksheet bar.

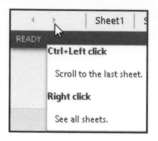

When clicked, the arrows allow you to scroll through the sheets one per click. You can also use the options shown in the previous illustration, or, if they are not displayed, you can click the three horizontal dots that appear to go to the first or last sheet. Finally, you can adjust the horizontal scroll bar by dragging the three vertical dots to give more/less territory to the worksheet bar.

▷▷ View Worksheets from Multiple Workbooks

You can arrange several Excel worksheets from multiple workbooks on your screen so that you can view them all. This arrangement makes it easy to copy data, formulas, and formatting among several worksheets.

1. Open the workbooks that contain the worksheets you want to view.

2. In the View tab Window group, click **Arrange All**. The Arrange Windows dialog box appears.

3. Select an arrangement and click **OK**.

4. To change the arrangement, simply close the worksheets you do not want to view by selecting a worksheet to close and clicking the ✕ in its upper-right corner. Return a worksheet to full view in the Excel window by double-clicking its title bar.

▷▷ Compare Workbooks

Excel provides a few tools that allow easy comparison of two workbooks.

1. Open the workbooks you want to compare.

2. In the View tab Window group, click **View Side By Side** . If you have only two workbooks open, they will appear next to one another. See the following Tip to change how two workbooks are displayed.

When you select View Side By Side, both workbook windows will scroll at the same rate. To turn off this feature, click **Synchronous Scrolling** in the Window group.

> **TIP** To change how two workbooks are displayed for side-by-side comparison (horizontally or vertically), use the Arrange Windows dialog box described in the section "View Worksheets from Multiple Workbooks."

Chapter 7

Using Formulas and Functions

Excel lets you easily perform powerful calculations using formulas and functions. Formulas are mathematical statements that follow a set of rules and use a specific syntax. In this chapter you will learn how to reference cells used in formulas, how to give cells names so that they are easily input, how to use conditional formatting to identify cells that satisfy criteria you specify, and how to build formulas. Functions—ready-made formulas that you can use to get quick results for specific applications, such as figuring out loan payments—are also covered. Finally, you will learn about several tools Excel provides to find and correct errors in formulas and functions.

REFERENCE CELLS

Formulas typically make use of data already entered in worksheets and need a scheme to locate, or *reference*, that data. Shortcuts are used to help you recall addresses as well as a *syntax*, or set of rules, to communicate to Excel how you want cells used.

 TIP To view formulas instead of cell values (see Figure 7-1), in the Formulas tab Formula Auditing group, click **Show Formulas** . Click the button a second time to return to a value display.

Understanding Cell Referencing Types

There are three basic methods and one extended method for referencing cells used in formulas that adhere to the Excel default "A1" cell reference scheme used in this book.

- **Relative references** in formulas move with cells as cells are copied or moved around a worksheet. This is the most flexible and common way to use cell references, and is the Excel default (for example, the cell in the first row and first column of a sheet is referenced as A1 in the Name box and Formula bar). For example, if you sum a list of revenue items for the first quarter, =SUM(B5:B8), and then copy and paste that summary cell to the summary cells for the other three quarters, Excel will deduce that you want the totals for the other quarters to be =SUM(C5:C8), =SUM(D5:D8), and =SUM(E5:E8). Figure 7-1 shows how this appears on the worksheet.

- **Absolute references** do not change cell addresses when you copy or move formulas. Absolute references are displayed in the worksheet and Formula bar with the dollar sign preceding the reference—for example, A1.

- **Mixed references** include one relative and one absolute cell reference. Such references are displayed in the worksheet and Formula bar with a dollar sign preceding the absolute reference but no dollar sign before the relative reference. For example, $A1 indicates absolute column, relative row; A$1 indicates relative column, absolute row.

- **External (or 3-D) references** are an extended form of relative, absolute, and mixed cell references. They are used when referencing cells from other worksheets or workbooks. Such a reference might look like this in the worksheet and Formula bar: [*workbook name*]*worksheet name*!A1.

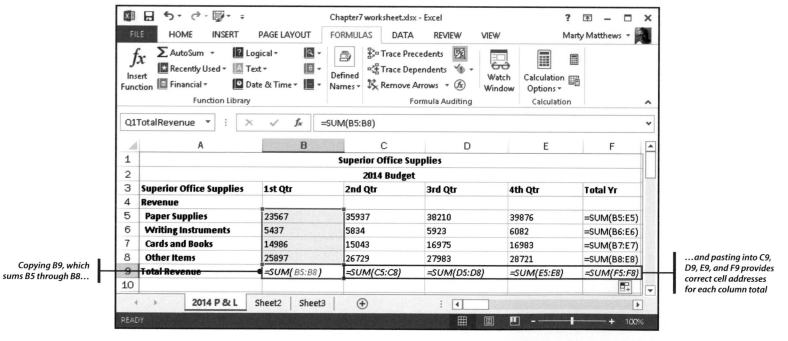

Copying B9, which sums B5 through B8…

…and pasting into C9, D9, E9, and F9 provides correct cell addresses for each column total

Figure 7-1: **Using relative references, Excel logically assumes cell addresses in copied formulas.**

Change Cell References

To change cell referencing:

1. Select the cell that contains the formula reference you want to change.

2. In the Formula bar, select the cell address, and press **F4** to switch the cell referencing, starting from a relative reference to the following in this order:

   - Absolute (A1)

   - Mixed (relative column, absolute row) (A$1)

   - Mixed (absolute column, relative row) ($A1)

   - Relative (A1)

   –Or–

   Edit the cell address by entering or removing the dollar symbol ($) in front of row and/or column identifiers.

 TIP Absolute cell references are typically used when you want to copy the values of cells and are not interested in applying their formulas to other cells, such as in a summary or report where the relative references would be meaningless. Although you can apply absolute reference syntax to each cell reference, a faster way is to right-click the destination cell. Under Paste Options, click the **Values** option. See "Copy Formulas" later in the chapter for more information on copying and pasting formulas.

 # Change to R1C1 References

You can change the A1 cell referencing scheme used by Excel to an older style that identifies both rows and columns numerically, starting in the upper-left corner of the worksheet, rows first, and adds a leading *R* and *C* for clarification. For example, cell B4 in R1C1 reference style is R4C2.

1. Click the **File** tab, click **Options**, and click the **Formulas** option.

2. Under Working With Formulas, click the **R1C1 Reference Style** check box.

3. Click **OK** when finished.

Working with formulas
☑ R1C1 reference style ⓘ
☑ Formula AutoComplete ⓘ

Use Cell Reference Operators

Cell reference operators (colons, commas, and spaces used in an address, such as E5:E10 E16:E17,E12) provide the syntax for referencing cell ranges, unions, and intersections.

Reference a Range

A *range* defines a block of cells.

Type a colon (:) between the upper-leftmost cell and the lower-rightmost cell (for example, B5:C8).

B5	▾ : ✕ ✓ *fx*	=SUM(B5:C8)

	A	B	C
5	**Paper Supplies**	$23,567	$35,937
6	**Writing Instruments**	$5,437	$5,834
7	**Cards and Books**	$14,986	$15,043
8	**Other Items**	$25,897	$26,729

Reference a Union

A *union* joins multiple cell references.

Type a comma (,) between separate cell references (for example, B5,B7,C6).

B7	▾ : ✕ ✓ *fx*	=SUM(B5,C6,B7)

	A	B	C
5	**Paper Supplies**	$23,567	$35,937
6	**Writing Instruments**	$5,437	$5,834
7	**Cards and Books**	$14,986	$15,043

Reference an Intersection

An *intersection* is the overlapping, or common, cells in two ranges.

Type a space (press the **SPACEBAR**) between two range-cell references (for example, B5:B8 B7:C8). B7 and B8 are the common cells.

| B7 | ▼ | : | × | ✓ | *fx* | =SUM(B5:B8 B7:C8) |

	A	B	C
5	**Paper Supplies**	$23,567	$35,937
6	**Writing Instruments**	$5,437	$5,834
7	**Cards and Books**	$14,986	$15,043
8	**Other Items**	$25,897	$26,729

 ## Name Cells

You can name a cell (MonthTotal, for example) or a range to refer to physical cell addresses, and then use the names when referencing the cell in formulas and functions. Names are more descriptive, easier to remember, and often quicker to enter than A1-style cell references. You can name a cell directly on the worksheet, use a dialog box and provide amplifying information, or use column or row names.

Name a Cell or Range Directly

1. Select the cells you want to reference.

2. Click the **Name** box to the left of the Formula bar.

> **TIP** If a cell or range name is longer than what can be displayed in the Name box, increase the width of the Name box by dragging the three dots to the right of the Name box to the right.

3. Type a name (see the accompanying Caution for naming rules), and press **ENTER**. (See "Use the Name Manager" for ways to modify cell names.)

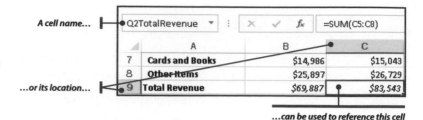

A cell name... [Q2TotalRevenue] ... =SUM(C5:C8)

	A	B	C
7	**Cards and Books**	$14,986	$15,043
8	Other Items	$25,897	$26,729
9	**Total Revenue**	*$69,887*	*$83,543*

...or its location...

...can be used to reference this cell

> **CAUTION** Cell names need to adhere to a set of rules. Names are case-sensitive, and no spaces are allowed in a cell name, although multiple words can be joined by an underscore or period. Also, names must start with a letter, underscore (_), or backslash (\).

Name a Cell or Range in a Dialog Box

1. Select the cell(s) you want to reference.

2. In the Formulas tab Defined Names group, click **Define Name**.

   –Or–

   Right-click the selection and click **Define Name**.

   In either case, the New Name dialog box appears, shown in Figure 7-2.

3. Type a name for the cell or range (see the preceding Caution for naming rules).

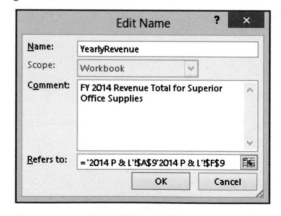

Figure 7-2: **You can easily name cells and add descriptive information.**

4. Click the **Scope** down arrow, and select whether the name applies to the entire workbook or to one of its worksheets.

5. If desired, type a comment that more fully explains the meaning of the named cells. Comments can be upwards of 1,000 characters and will appear as a tooltip when the name is used in formulas and functions.

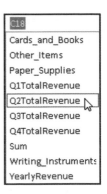

6. If you want to modify the cell or cells to be named, click the **Refers To** text box, and type the reference (starting with the equal [=] sign) or reselect the cells from the worksheet.

7. Click **OK** when finished.

Go to a Named Cell

Named cells are quickly found and selected for you.

Click the **Name** box down arrow to open the drop-down list, and click the named cell or range you want to go to.

–Or–

In the Home tab Editing group, click **Find & Select** and click **Go To**. In the Go To dialog box, double-click the named cell or range you want to go to.

Use the Name Manager

Excel provides several related tools and a Name Manager to help you manage and organize your named cells. To open the Name Manager, in the Formulas tab Defined Names group, click **Name Manager**. The Name Manager window opens, as shown in Figure 7-3, listing all named cells in the workbook.

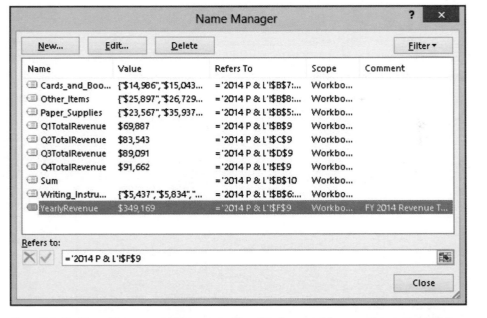

Figure 7-3: **The Name Manager provides a central location for organizing, creating, and modifying named cells.**

Change Cell Names

1. Select the name of the cell reference whose parameters you want to change, and click **Edit**.

2. In the Edit Name dialog box, type a new name, add or change the comment, and/or modify the cell reference (you cannot change the scope—that is, whether the reference applies to a particular worksheet or globally within the workbook). Click **OK** when finished.

Delete Named Cells

1. Select the name of the cell reference that you want to delete (to select more than one cell name to delete, hold down the **CTRL** key while clicking noncontiguous names in the list; or select the first name in a contiguous range, and hold down **SHIFT** while clicking the last name in the range).

2. Click **Delete** and click **OK** to confirm the deletion.

Sort and Filter Named Cells

If you have several named cells in a workbook, you can easily view only the ones you are interested in.

1. To sort named cells, click a column heading to change the sort order from ascending (numerals first 0–9, then A–Z) to descending (Z–A, numerals last 9–0). Click the heading a second time to return to the original order.

   –Or–

   To see only specific categories of named cells, click **Filter** and click the category of named cells you want to see. Only named cells that belong in the category you select will appear in the list of cell names.

2. To return a filtered list to a complete list of named cells, click **Filter** and click **Clear Filter**.

View More Data

The default width of the Name Manager and its columns might not readily display longer cell names, references, or comments.

- To increase a column width, drag the right border of the column heading to the right as far as you need.

- To increase the width of the window, drag either the window's right or left border to the left or right, respectively.

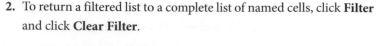

TIP To quickly open the Name Manager, press **CTRL+F3** or add the Name Manager icon to the Quick Access toolbar. (Chapter 1 describes how to add tools to the Quick Access toolbar.)

BUILD FORMULAS

Formulas are mathematical equations that combine *values* and *cell references* with *operators* to calculate a result. Values are actual numbers or logical values, such as True and False, or the contents of cells that contain numbers or logical values. Cell references point to cells whose values are to be used, for example, E5:E10, E12, and MonthlyTot. Operators, such as + (add), > (greater than), and ^ (use an exponent), tell Excel what type of calculation to perform or logical comparison to apply. Prebuilt formulas, or *functions*, that return a value also can be used in formulas. (Functions are described later in this chapter.)

⏩ Create a Formula

You create formulas by either entering or referencing values. The character that tells Excel to perform a calculation is the equal sign (=), and it must precede any combination of values, cell references, and operators.

Excel formulas are calculated from left to right according to an ordered hierarchy of operators. For example, exponents precede multiplication and division, which precede addition and subtraction. You can alter the calculation order (and results) by using parentheses; Excel performs the calculation within the innermost parentheses first. For example, =12+48/24 returns 14 (48 is divided by 24, resulting in 2; then 12 is added to 2). Using parentheses, =(12+48)/24 returns 2.5 (12 is added to 48, resulting in 60; then 60 is divided by 24).

 TIP A good way to remember the standard order of mathematical operations is by the acronym PEMDAS, which on one level means "Please Excuse My Dear Aunt Sally," or mathematically speaking, "Parentheses, Exponents, Multiplication, Division, Addition, Subtraction."

Enter a Simple Formula

1. Select a blank cell, and type an equal sign (=).

   –Or–

   Select a blank cell and click in the Formula bar in the blank area directly to the right of the Insert Function f_x icon. The function area expands with the addition of the Cancel ✕ and Enter ✓ icons.

   The equal sign displays both in the cell and in the Formula bar, as will the additional characters you type. The insertion point (where Excel expects you to type the next character) is placed to the right of the equal sign in either the cell or Formula bar, depending on where you typed it.

2. Type a value, such as <u>64</u>.

3. Type an operator, such as <u>+</u>.

4. Type a second value, such as <u>96</u>.

5. Complete the entry by pressing **ENTER** or clicking **Enter** on the Formula bar; or add additional values and operators, and then complete the entry. The result of your equation displays in the cell. (See Chapter 5 for other methods to complete an entry.)

🛈 **CAUTION** When creating a formula, be careful not to click any cells that you do not want referenced in the formula. After you type the equal sign, Excel interprets any selected cell as being a cell reference in the formula.

Use Cell References

The majority of formulas use the values in other cells to produce a result; that is, the cell that contains the formula may have no value of its own—it's derived from other cells whose values are manipulated by arithmetic operators. For example, the cell at the bottom of several values contains a formula using a function (SUM) that sums the values to produce a total.

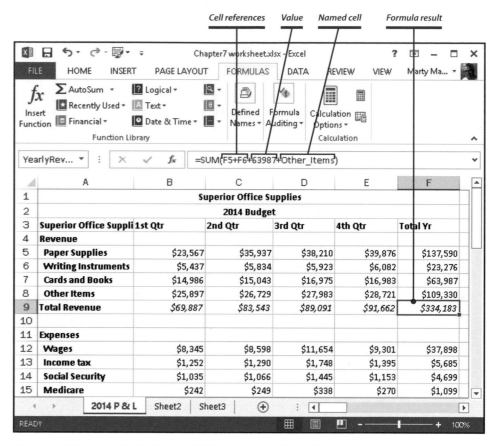

1. Select a blank cell, and type an equal sign (=). The equal sign displays in the cell and in the Formula bar.

2. Enter a cell reference in one of the following ways:

   - Type a cell reference (for example, B4) that contains the value you want.

   - Click the cell whose value you want. A blinking border surrounds the cell.

   - Select a named cell. In the Formulas tab Defined Names group, click **Use In Formula**, and click the named cell you want.

   - Type a named cell.

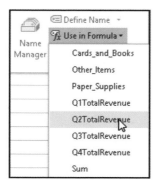

3. Type an operator.

4. Enter another cell reference or a value.

5. Complete the entry by pressing ENTER; or add additional cell references, values, and operators, and then complete the entry. The result of your formula is displayed in the cell, as shown in Figure 7-4.

Figure 7-4: *A formula with the function SUM in Excel comprises cell references, values, and named cells.*

Edit a Formula

You can easily change a formula after you have entered one.

1. Double-click the cell that contains the formula you want to change. The formula is displayed in the cell and in the Formula bar. Cell references for each cell or range are color-coded.

:	✗	✓	*fx*	=SUM(F5+F6+63987+Other_Items)			
	C	D	E	F	G	H	
	Superior Office Supplies						
	2014 Budget						
2nd Qtr		3rd Qtr	4th Qtr	Total Yr			
$35,937		$38,210	$39,876	$137,590			
$5,834		$5,923	$6,082	$23,276			
$15,043		$16,975	$16,983	$63,987			
$26,729		$27,983	$28,721	$109,330			
$83,543		$89,091	$91,662	=SUM(*F5*+*F6* +*63987*+*Other_Items*)			
				SUM(**number1**, [number2], ...)			

2. Edit the formula by:

   - Making changes directly in the cell or on the Formula bar

   - Dragging the border of a colored cell or range reference to move it to a new location

   - Dragging a corner sizing box of a colored cell or range reference to expand/contract the reference

3. Complete the entry by pressing **ENTER**.

 Use Formulas

There are several techniques you can use to get more out of working with formulas.

Replace an Entire Formula with Its Value

To replace an entire formula with its value:

1. Right-click the cell that contains the formula, and click **Copy**.

2. Right-click the cell a second time, and under Paste Options, click **Values** .

Replace a Portion of a Formula with Its Value

1. Double-click the cell that contains the formula.

2. In either the cell or the Formula bar, select the portion of the formula you want to replace with its value.

3. Press **F9** to calculate and insert the value, and press **ENTER** to complete the entry.

Cancel Entering or Editing a Formula

Press **ESC** or click **Cancel** on the Formula bar.

Delete a Formula

Select the cell that contains the formula, and press **DELETE**.

TIP If you do not see the Cancel, Enter, and Insert Function buttons in the Formula bar when editing or creating a formula, click anywhere in the Formula bar and they will be displayed.

Move Formulas

You move formulas by cutting and pasting. When you move formulas, Excel uses absolute referencing—the formula remains exactly the same as it was originally, with the same cell references. (See "Change Cell References" earlier in the chapter for more information on cell referencing.)

1. Select the cell whose formula you want to move.

2. In the Home tab Clipboard group, click **Cut**, or press **CTRL+X**.

   –Or–

   Right-click the cell whose formula you want to move, and click **Cut**.

3. Select the cell where you want to move the formula.

4. In the Home tab Clipboard group, click **Paste**, or press **CTRL+V**.

–Or–

Right-click the cell where you want to move the formula, and under Paste Options, click **Paste**.

Copy Formulas

When you copy formulas, relative referencing is applied. Therefore, cell referencing in a formula will change when you copy the formula, unless you have made a reference absolute. If you do not get the results you expect, click **Undo** on the Quick Access toolbar, and change the cell references before you copy again.

Copy Formulas into Adjacent Cells

1. Select the cell whose formula you want to copy.

2. Point at the fill handle in the lower-right corner of the cell, and drag over the cells where you want the formula copied.

| Q1TotalR... ▼ | : | × | ✓ | *fx* | =SUM(B5:B8) |

	A	B	C
4	**Revenue**		
5	**Paper Supplies**	$23,567	$35,937
6	**Writing Instruments**	$5,437	$5,834
7	**Cards and Books**	$14,986	$15,043
8	**Other Items**	$25,897	$26,729
9	**Total Revenue**	$69,887	

Copy Formulas into Nonadjacent Cells

1. Select the cell whose formula you want to copy.

2. In the Home tab Clipboard group, click **Copy** , or press **CTRL+C**.

    –Or–

    Right-click the cell you want to copy, and click **Copy**.

3. Copy formatting along with the formula by selecting the destination cell. Then, in the Home tab Clipboard group, click **Paste** and then click the **Paste** icon.

    –Or–

Copy just the formula by selecting the destination cell. Then, in the Home tab Clipboard group, click the **Paste** down arrow, and click the **Formulas** icon.

Recalculate Formulas

By default, Excel automatically recalculates formulas affected by changes to a value, to the formula itself, or to a changed named cell. You also can recalculate more frequently using the tips presented in Table 7-1.

Table 7-1: Formula Recalculations in Excel

To Calculate...	In...	Press...
Formulas, and formulas dependent on them, that have changed since the last calculation	All open workbooks	F9
Formulas, and formulas dependent on them, that have changed since the last calculation	The active worksheet	SHIFT+F9
All formulas, regardless of any changes since the last calculation	All open workbooks	CTRL+ALT+F9
All formulas, regardless of any changes since the last calculation, after rechecking dependent formulas	All open workbooks	CTRL+SHIFT+ALT+F9

To turn off automatic calculation and select other calculation options:

1. In the Formulas tab Calculation group, click **Calculation Options**.

2. In the drop-down menu, click **Manual**. You can also force an immediate calculation by clicking **Calculate Now** to recalculate the workbook or clicking **Calculate Sheet** to recalculate the active worksheet.

Use External References in Formulas

You can *link* data using cell references to worksheets and workbooks other than the one you are currently working in. For example, if you are building a departmental budget, you could link to each division's budget workbook and have any changes made to formulas in those workbooks be applied automatically to your total budget workbook. Changes made to the *external* references in the *source* workbooks are automatically updated in the *destination* workbook when the destination workbook is opened or when the source workbooks are changed and the destination workbook is open.

 TIP It is a good practice to save and close the source workbook before saving the destination workbook.

Create External Reference Links

1. Open both the source and destination workbooks in your computer.

2. Arrange the workbooks so that they are all displayed. For example, in the View tab Window group, click **Arrange All**, click **Tiled**, and click **OK**. (See Chapter 5 for more information on arranging workbooks in the Excel window.)

3. In the destination worksheet, create the formula or open an existing formula.

4. Place the insertion point in the formula where you want the external reference.

5. In the source workbook, click the cell whose cell reference you want. The external reference is added to the formula, as shown in Figure 7-5.

6. Press **ENTER** to complete the entry.

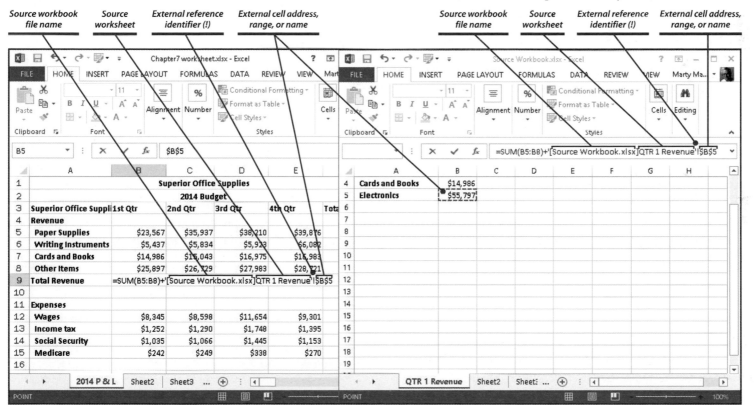

Figure 7-5: **An external reference in a formula comprises several components.**

Update and Manage External References

You can control how external references are updated, check on their status, and break or change the link.

1. Open the destination workbook.

2. In the Data tab Connections group, click **Edit Links** . The Edit Links dialog box appears, as shown in Figure 7-6.

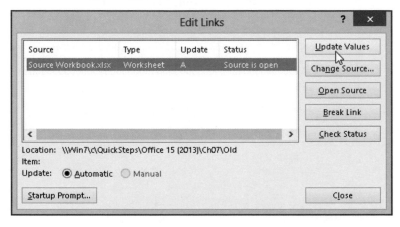

*Figure 7-6: **You can update and manage links in the Edit Links dialog box.***

3. Select a link and then use the command buttons on the right side of the dialog box to perform the action you want.

> **CAUTION** If you break an external reference link in the Edit Links dialog box, all formulas using external references are converted to values. Broken links cannot be undone except by reestablishing the links.

4. Click **Close** when finished.

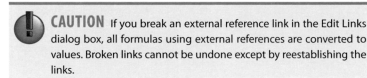 Add a Symbolic Formula

Another way to add a formula, though it won't work as one, is to use the Equation Editor, an Office-wide tool. This will allow you to display the characters of a complex formula without actually performing the calculation. To install the Equation Editor (it is not part of an Express Office installation):

1. Click **Start**, click **Control Panel**, and then under Programs, click **Uninstall A Program**. Select your version of Office, and click **Change**.

2. In the Change Your Installation Of Microsoft Office dialog box, click **Add Or Remove Features**, and click **Continue**. Click the plus sign (+) next to Office Tools, and click the **Equation Editor** down arrow.

3. Click **Run From My Computer**, and click **Continue**.

4. To use the Equation Editor, restart Excel, select where you want the equation placed, and then in the Insert tab Symbols group, click **Equation**.

Update Links

When you open a destination workbook with external links to source workbooks, you are potentially introducing a security risk to your computer by allowing data from other sources into your system. By default, automatic updating is disabled and the user opening a destination workbook needs to provide permission to enable the links (unless the source workbooks are open on the same computer as the destination workbook). If you are unsure of the origination of the source workbooks when updating links in a destination workbook, open the Edit Links dialog box to view the files involved in the links. See how in the recent section "Update and Manage External References."

> **NOTE** Just as there can be a myriad of combinations of links and referencing in your workbooks from source files on your own computer to lose on networks, there are also several permutations of security warnings you may see, depending on your specific circumstance. To try and describe each situation and show its result would take a chapter in and of itself and not really provide much value. Suffice it to say that when you see security warnings, read them carefully, and just be cognizant of what you are accepting.

 **QuickFacts**

Understanding the Trust Center

Microsoft Office 2013 recognizes the need to provide enhanced file security against the world of viruses and other malicious code that can compromise your data and impair your computer. To provide a unified approach in applying security settings for all Office 2013 programs installed on your system, Office 2013 includes a *Trust Center* to help you manage your security settings. It also provides information on privacy and general computer security (see Figure 7-7). The Trust Center security settings window organizes security settings in 12 categories. Taking a "better safe than sorry" approach, Microsoft errs on the side of caution by limiting any automatic updates or actions without user approval. You can change these defaults to allow more or less intervention. Security settings in the Trust Center are applicable to all workbooks and "trump" the automatic link updating behavior set for individual workbooks. To allow automatic link updating for individual workbooks, you must first enable automatic link updates in the Trust Center.

To open the Trust Center, click the **File** tab, click **Options**, click the **Trust Center** option, and then click **Trust Center Settings**.

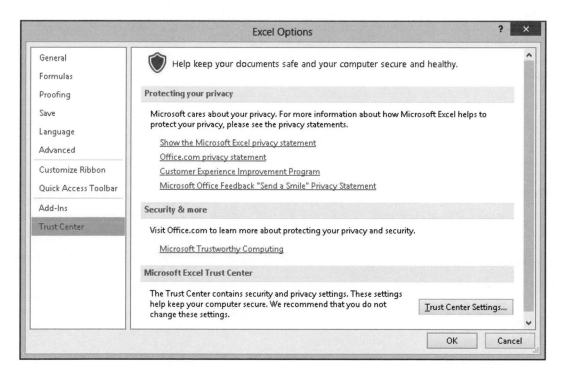

Figure 7-7: **The Trust Center provides a focal point for accessing privacy and security information and settings for Office 2013 programs.**

1. Open the destination workbook. A message box, shown in Figure 7-8, opens to tell you that updating links will use new data from the source files and warns you that this could be unsafe. Click **Update**, assuming you trust the source file; click **Don't Update** if you do not.

Figure 7-8: *To protect you from erroneous or malicious data, Office asks if you want to update external links.*

2. When you open the source file, which also has a link to an external workbook, unless default settings have been changed, a Security Warning message displays below the ribbon notifying you that automatic link updating is disabled. Click **Enable Content** to allow updates to occur.

3. For additional protection, if your source workbook is located in a network location (that is, not on the same computer as your destination workbook), a second warning is displayed. Assuming you trust the source data, click **Yes**. The links will be updated.

Change Automatic Link Updating for All Workbooks

You can change how links are updated in the Trust Center security settings window.

1. Click the **File** tab, click **Options**, and click the **Trust Center** option. In the Trust Center window, click **Trust Center Settings**.

2. In the Trust Center security settings window, click the **External Content** category, shown in Figure 7-9.

3. In the Security Settings For Workbook Links area, select the automatic link updating behavior you want, and click **OK** twice.

Change Automatic Link Updating for Individual Workbooks

You can choose to not display the security alert in a destination workbook prompting users to update links. You can also choose to update links, or not, without user intervention.

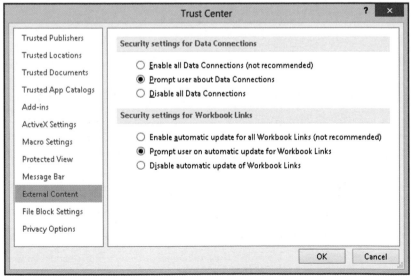

Figure 7-9: *The Trust Center allows you to set the degree to which you trust the links among your workbooks.*

NOTE Before you can allow automatic link updating in an individual workbook, you must enable it in the Trust Center for all workbooks. See how in the preceding section "Change Automatic Link Updating for All Workbooks."

1. Open the destination workbook whose security alert behavior you want to change.

2. In the Data tab Connections group, click **Edit Links**, and click **Startup Prompt**.

3. In the Startup Prompt dialog box, select the behavior you want, click **OK**, and click **Close**. The next time the workbook is opened, the new behavior will be enabled.

Format Conditionally

Excel 2013 continues to improve the ease and capabilities with which data can be identified in a worksheet based on rules you select. Rules are organized into several types that allow you to easily format cells that compare values against each other; meet specific values, dates, or other criteria; match top and bottom percentile values you choose; match values above or below an average; or identify unique or duplicate values. If no pre-existing rule accommodates your needs, you can use a formula to set up criteria that cells must match. The number of conditional format scenarios that can be applied to a cell is only limited by your system's memory.

Compare Cells

You can highlight the comparative values of selected cells by using one of three formatting styles:

- **Data bars** display in each cell colored bars whose length is proportional to their value as compared to the other values in the selection.

5	Paper Supplies	$23,567
6	Writing Instruments	$5,437
7	Cards and Books	$14,986
8	Other Items	$25,897

- **Color scales** blend two or three colors (such as a green-yellow-red traffic light metaphor) to differentiate among high to low values.

5	Paper Supplies	$23,567
6	Writing Instruments	$5,437
7	Cards and Books	$14,986
8	Other Items	$25,897

- **Icon sets** use from three to five similar icons (such as the red and black circles used in *Consumer Reports*) to differentiate among high to low values.

5	Paper Supplies	⬤	$23,567
6	Writing Instruments	⬤	$5,437
7	Cards and Books	◯	$14,986
8	Other Items	⬤	$25,897

1. Select the cells that will be compared.

2. In the Home tab Styles group, click **Conditional Formatting** and click the style for which you want to see a submenu of options.

3. Point to each option to see a live preview of its effect on your selected data, as shown in Figure 7-10. Click the option you want to use, or proceed to step 4 to see more options.

 NOTE If your selected cells don't change as you point to different style options, Live Preview has been turned off. To turn on Live Preview, click the **File** tab, click **Options**, and click the **General** option. Under User Interface Options, select **Enable Live Preview**, and click **OK**.

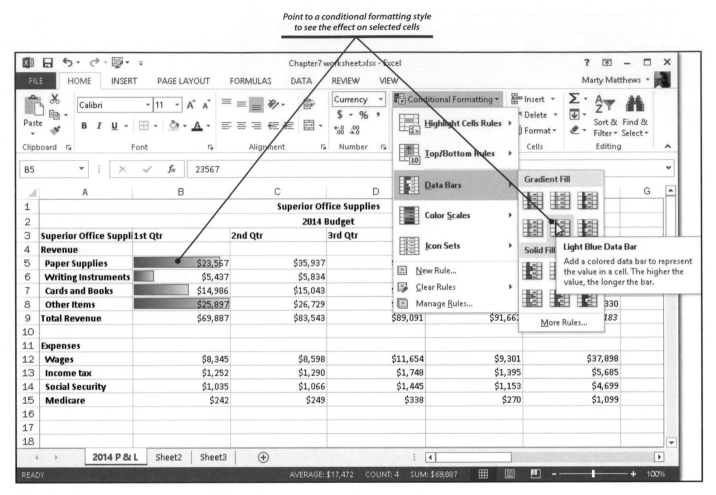

Point to a conditional formatting style to see the effect on selected cells

Figure 7-10: *You can see a live preview of each formatting style on your data before selecting one.*

4. For more choices of each style, click **More Rules** at the bottom of each of their respective submenus.

5. In the New Formatting Rule dialog box, under Edit The Rule Description, you can change from one style to another and,

depending on the style, change colors, change the values attributed to an icon or color, and make other customizations (see Figure 7-11). Click **OK** when finished.

New Formatting Rule

Select a Rule Type:

- ► Format all cells based on their values
- ► Format only cells that contain
- ► Format only top or bottom ranked values
- ► Format only values that are above or below average
- ► Format only unique or duplicate values
- ► Use a formula to determine which cells to format

Edit the Rule Description:

Format all cells based on their values:

Format Style: [Icon Sets ▼]   [Reverse Icon Order]

Icon Style: [●○○ ▼]   ☐ Show Icon Only

Display each icon according to these rules:

Icon			Value		Type	
● ▼	when value is	[>= ▼]	67	📊	Percent ▼	
○ ▼	when < 67 and	[>= ▼]	33	📊	Percent ▼	
● ▼	when < 33					

[OK]   [Cancel]

*Figure 7-11: **Each style has a set of customizations (or rules) that apply to how data is visually identified.***

TIP When changing values in dialog boxes for conditional formatting, as in the New Formatting Rule dialog box (and when setting up functions, described later in this chapter), you can type a value or formula in the associated text box, or you can select a cell that contains the value or formula you want and have it entered for you. When selecting a cell, click the **Collapse Dialog** 📊 button to shrink the dialog box so that you can see more of the worksheet. Click **Expand Dialog** to return to the full-size dialog box.

Value

[>= ▼]   [67]   📊

New Formatting Rule   ?   ☒

[67]   📊

Format Cells That Match Values or Conditions

Excel provides several pre-existing rules that let you easily format cells that meet established criteria.

1. Select the cells that will be formatted if they meet conditions you select.

2. In the Home tab Styles group, click **Conditional Formatting** and click **Highlight Cell Rules** to view a submenu of rules that compare values to conditions.

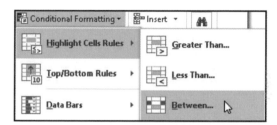

–Or–

Click **Conditional Formatting** and click **Top/Bottom Rules** to view a submenu that lets you select cells based on top/bottom ranking or whether they're above or below the average of the selected cells.

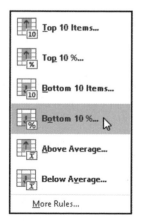

3. In either case, click the option you want to use, or for more choices, click **More Rules** at the bottom of each of the respective submenus.

4. In the New Formatting Rule dialog box, under Edit The Rule Description, you can change criteria and the formatting you want applied (see Chapter 6 for more information on using the Format Cells dialog box that opens when you click the Format button). Click **OK** when finished.

Manage Conditional Formatting Rules

Using the Conditional Formatting Rules Manager, you can view any conditional formatting rules in a workbook, as well as edit, delete, reorder, and create new rules.

1. In the Home tab Styles group, click **Conditional Formatting** and click **Manage Rules**. The Conditional Formatting Rules Manager appears, as shown in Figure 7-12.

2. Click the **Show Formatting Rules For** down arrow to select the scope of where you want to look for rules.

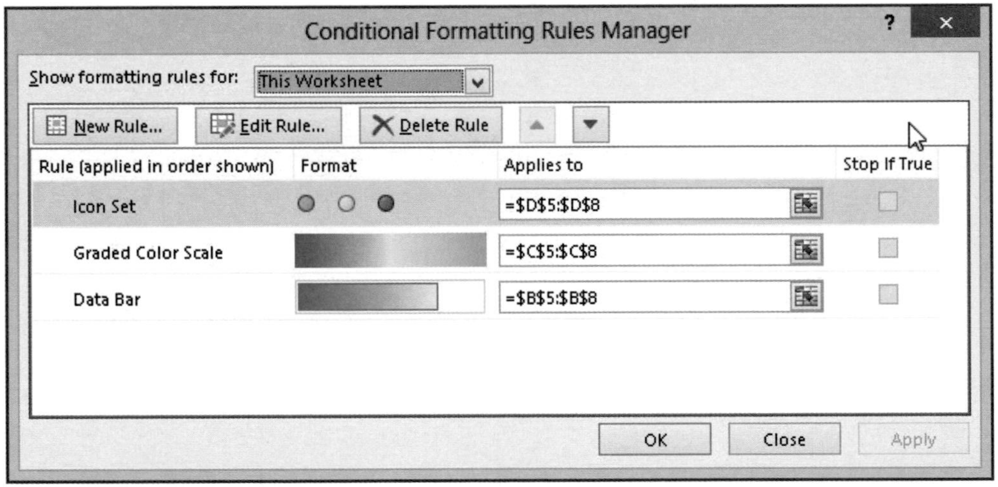

3. Select a rule and perform one or more of the following actions:

- Click **Edit Rule** to open the Edit Formatting Rule dialog box and change criteria or conditions. Click **OK** to close the Edit Formatting Rule dialog box.

- Click **Delete Rule** to remove it (alternatively, you can click **Clear Rules** on the Conditional Formatting drop-down menu to remove all rules in the selected cells or worksheet).

- Click the up and down arrows to change the order in which rules are applied (rules are applied in order from top to bottom).

- Click the **Stop If True** check box to discontinue further rules from being applied if the selected rule is satisfied as being True.

4. Click **New Rule** to open the New Formatting Rule dialog box and create a new rule. Click **OK** to close the New Formatting Rule dialog box.

5. Click **OK** when finished.

USE FUNCTIONS

Functions are prewritten formulas that you can use to perform specific tasks. They can be as simple as =PI(), which returns 3.14159265358979, the value of the constant pi; or they can be as complex as =PPMT(rate,per,nper,pv,fv,type), which returns a payment on an investment principal.

A function comprises three components:

- The **formula identifier**, the equal sign (=), is required when a function is at the beginning of the formula.

- The **function name** identifies the function, and typically is a two- to five-character uppercase abbreviation.

Figure 7-12: You can view and manage conditional formatting rules set up in a workbook.

- **Arguments** are the values acted upon by functions to derive a result. They can be numbers, cell references, constants, logical (True or False) values, or a formula. Arguments are separated by commas and enclosed in parentheses. A function can have up to 255 arguments.

Use Functions Quickly

You can view the results of several popular functions by simply selecting a range. By default, the sum, average, and count of the selected cells are shown on the right of the status bar at the bottom of the Excel window.

You can change which function results are displayed on the status bar by right-clicking it and selecting the results you want.

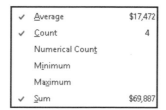

✓	A̲verage	$17,472
✓	C̲ount	4
	Numerical Coun̲t	
	Mi̲nimum	
	Ma̲ximum	
✓	S̲um	$69,887

Enter a Function

You can enter functions on a worksheet by typing or by a combination of typing and selecting cell references, as described earlier in this chapter for formulas. In addition, you can search for and choose functions from Excel's library of built-in functions.

TIP You do not need to type the closing parenthesis; Excel will add it for you when you complete the entry. However, it is good practice to include a closing parenthesis for each opening parenthesis. This is especially true if you use complex, nested functions that include other functions as arguments. (You may nest up to 64 levels!)

Type a Function

To type a function in a cell on the worksheet:

1. Select a blank cell, and type an equal sign (=). The equal sign displays in the cell and the Formula bar.

2. Start typing the function name, such as AVERAGE, MAX, or PMT. As you start typing, functions with related spellings are displayed. Click any to see a description of the function.

3. Double-click the function you want. The function name and open parenthesis are entered for you. Excel displays a tooltip showing arguments and proper syntax for the function.

4. Depending on the function, for each argument you need to do none, one, or both of the following:

   - Type the argument.
   - Select a cell reference.

5. Type a comma to separate arguments, and repeat steps 4 and 5 as necessary.

6. Type a closing parenthesis, and press **ENTER** or click **Enter** on the Formula bar (shown next) to complete the entry. A value will be returned. (If a *#code* is displayed in the cell or if a message box displays indicating you made an error, see "Find and Correct Errors" later in this chapter.)

Insert a Function

You can find the function you want using the Function Wizard or using the function category buttons on the ribbon. In either case, the wizard helps you enter arguments for the function you chose.

1. Select a blank cell. In the Formulas tab Function Library group, click the relevant function category button, and scroll to the function you want. Point to a function and wait a second to see a tooltip that describes it. When ready, click the function and skip to step 5 to view its arguments.

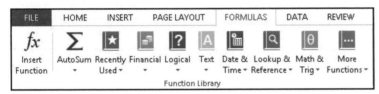

–Or–

Click **Insert Function** in the Function Library group or its button on the Formula bar 𝑓𝑥 , or press **SHIFT+F3**. The Insert Function dialog box appears, as shown in Figure 7-13.

2. Type a brief description of what you want to do in the Search For A Function text box, and click **Go**. A list of recommended functions is displayed in the Select A Function list box.

–Or–

Open the **Select A Category** drop-down list, and select a category.

3. Click the function you want from the Select A Function list box. Its arguments and syntax are shown, as well as a description of what the function returns.

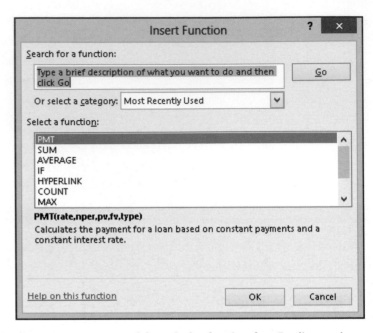

Figure 7-13: **You can search for and select functions from Excel's extensive library in the Insert Function dialog box.**

4. If you need more assistance with the function, click **Help On This Function**. A Help topic provides details on the function and an example of how it's used.

5. Click **OK** to open the Function Arguments dialog box, shown in Figure 7-14. The function's arguments are listed in order at the top of the dialog box, and the beginning of the function displays in the cell and in the Formula bar.

6. Enter values for the arguments by typing or clicking cell references. Click the **Collapse Dialog** button to shrink the dialog box so that you can see more of the worksheet. The formula on the worksheet is built as you enter each argument.

7. Click **OK** to complete the entry.

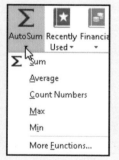

Function Arguments ? ×

PMT

Rate		▦	= number
Nper		▦	= number
Pv		▦	= number
Fv		▦	= number
Type		▦	= number

=

Calculates the payment for a loan based on constant payments and a constant interest rate.

Rate is the interest rate per period for the loan. For example, use 6%/4 for quarterly payments at 6% APR.

Formula result =

Help on this function   OK   Cancel

*Figure 7-14: **Type or click cell references to enter argument values.***

TIP Using the AutoSum technique, you can apply common functions to selected cells, such as averaging and getting a count. In either the Formulas tab Function Library group or the Home tab Editing group, click the **AutoSum** down arrow, and click the function you want; or click **More Functions** to open the Function Wizard and access the full function library.

Σ ☆ 📄
AutoSum Recently Financia
        Used ▾   ▾

Σ Sum
   Average
   Count Numbers
   Max
   Min
   More Functions...

▷ Enter a Sum in Columns or Rows Quickly

AutoSum uses the SUM function to add contiguous numbers quickly.

1. Select a blank cell below a column or to the right of a row of numbers.

---

2. In the Formulas tab Function Library group, click **AutoSum**. The cells Excel "thinks" you want to sum above or to the left of the blank cell are enclosed in a border, and the formula is displayed in the cell and in the Formula bar.

◢	A	B	C	D
1	**Superior Office Supplies**	**1st Qtr**		
2	**Revenue**			
3	Paper Supplies	$23,567		
4	Writing Instruments	$5,437		
5	Cards and Books	$14,986		
6	Other Items	$25,897		
7	Total Revenue	=SUM(B3:B6)		
8		SUM(**number1**, [number2], ...)		

3. Modify the cells to be included in the sum by dragging a corner sizing box, by editing the formula in the cell or the Formula bar, or by selecting cells.

4. Press **ENTER** or click **Enter** on the Formula bar to complete the entry. The sum of the selected cells is returned.

5. Alternatively, for an even faster sum, select a contiguous column or row of cells, and click **AutoSum**. The sum is entered in the first blank cell at either the bottom of a column of cells or to the right of a row of cells.

FIND AND CORRECT ERRORS

Excel provides several tools that help you see how your formulas and functions are constructed, recognize errors in formulas, and better locate problems.

NOTE You can perform the same actions and access the same dialog boxes from the smart tag displayed next to a selected cell containing an error as you can using the Error Checking button in the Formula Auditing group.

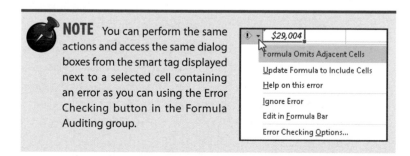

ⓘ ▾ $29,004

Formula Omits Adjacent Cells
Update Formula to Include Cells
Help on this error
Ignore Error
Edit in Formula Bar
Error Checking Options...

▷▷ Check for Errors

Excel can find errors and provide possible solutions.

1. In the Formulas tab Formula Auditing group, click **Error Checking**.

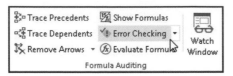

If you have an error on the worksheet, the Error Checking dialog box appears, as shown in Figure 7-15.

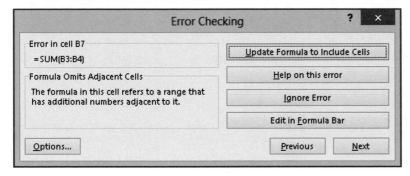

Figure 7-15: **You can manage how errors are checked and locate cells that contain errors.**

2. Use the command buttons on the right side of the dialog box to perform the indicated action. Click **Next** or **Previous** to check on other errors.

3. Click **Options** to view the Excel Options Formulas window (see Figure 7-16), where you can customize error checking.

   - **Error Checking**, **Enable Background Error Checking** lets you turn on or off error checking as you enter formulas and lets you determine the color of flagged cells that contain errors. Errors are flagged in green by default.

- **Error Checking Rules** provides several criteria that cells are checked against for possible errors.

▷▷ Trace Precedent and Dependent Cells

Precedent cells are referenced in a formula or function in another cell; that is, they provide a value to a formula or function. *Dependent* cells contain a formula or function that uses the value from another cell; that is, they depend on the value in another cell for their own value.

This interwoven relationship of cells can compound one error into many, making a visual representation of the cell dependencies a vital error-correction tool.

1. Click a cell that uses cell references and/or is itself used as a reference by another cell in its formula or function.

2. In the Formulas tab Formula Auditing group, click **Trace Precedents** to display blue arrows that point to the cell from other cells.

	A	B
1	**Superior Office Supplies**	1st Qtr
2	**Revenue**	
3	**Paper Supplies**	$23,567
4	**Writing Instruments**	$5,437
5	**Cards and Books**	$14,986
6	**Other Items**	$25,897
7	**Total Revenue**	$69,887

–Or–

Click **Trace Dependents** to display blue arrows that point to other cells.

3. Click the **Remove Arrows** down arrow, and select whether to remove precedent, dependent, or all arrows.

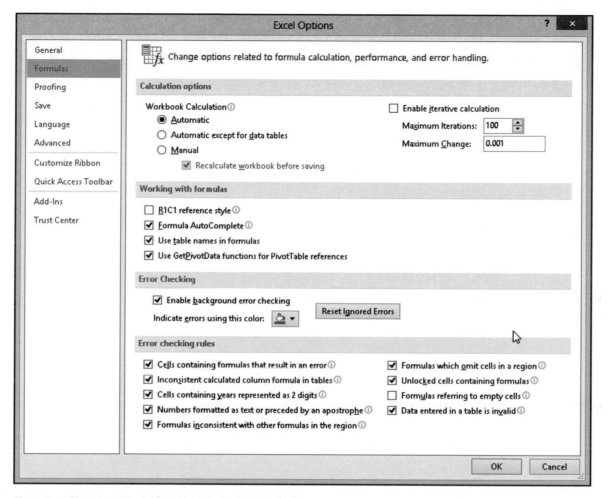

Figure 7-16: *You can customize how Excel performs error checking.*

Watch a Cell

You can follow what changes are made to a cell's value as its precedent cells' values are changed, even if the cells are not currently visible.

1. In the Formulas tab Formula Auditing group, click **Watch Window**. The Watch Window opens.

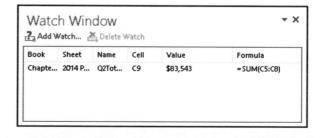

2. Click **Add Watch** to open the Add Watch dialog box.

3. Select the cell or cells you want to watch, and click **Add**. Each selected cell will be listed individually in the Watch Window. As changes are made to a precedent cell, the value of the cells "being watched" will be updated according to the recalculation options you have set. (See "Recalculate Formulas" earlier in the chapter.)

4. Close the Watch Window when you are done.

 TIP To remove a watch you have placed, in the Formulas tab Formula Auditing group, click **Watch Window**, select the watch you want to remove, and click **Delete Watch**.

▷▷ Evaluate a Formula in Pieces

You can see what value will be returned by individual cell references or expressions in the order they are placed in the formula.

1. Select the cell that contains the formula you want to evaluate.

2. In the Formulas tab Formula Auditing group, click **Evaluate Formula**. The Evaluate Formula dialog box, shown in Figure 7-17, appears.

3. Do one or more of the following:

- Click **Evaluate** to return the value of the first cell reference or expression. The cell reference or expression is underlined.

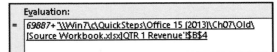

- Continue clicking **Evaluate** to return values for each of the cell references or expressions (again, underlined) to the right in the formula. Eventually, this will return the value for the cell.

- Click **Restart** to start the evaluation from the leftmost expression. (The Evaluate button changes to Restart after you have stepped through the formula.)

- Click **Step In**, if available, to view more data on the underlined cell reference.

- Click **Step Out** to return to the formula evaluation.

4. Click **Close** when finished.

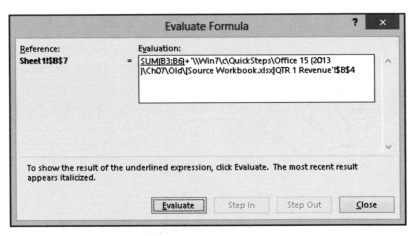

Figure 7-17: **You can dissect each expression or component of a formula to see its cell reference, its formula, and its value.**

Chapter 8

Creating a Presentation in PowerPoint

In this chapter, you are introduced to PowerPoint 2013, Microsoft Office's powerful presentation program. If you have used other versions of PowerPoint, you will find many of your favorite tools available, some of which are enhanced in the 2013 version. For instance, PowerPoint 2013 includes new features such as the ability to merge shapes, an improved alignment for layouts, an improved Presenter View, slide zoom, and navigator allowing you to see other slides while the audience only sees the current slide, and offers the choice between a widescreen- or standard-sized slide. These new features are explored in Chapters 8, 9, and 10. PowerPoint 2013 gives you a wide variety of templates, themes, and designs from which to choose. As is true with other Office programs, you can share your work on a presentation with other people in different locations.

This chapter shows you how to create a presentation from scratch, from a template, or by borrowing from an older slide show. It also shows you how to organize and manage your slides by using an outline. You will see how to use the various views within PowerPoint to work with your presentations and you will be introduced to PowerPoint's unique ribbon.

STEP INTO POWERPOINT

If you are not already acquainted with PowerPoint and its terminology, this section serves to introduce you to the important concepts and terms you need to understand to work with PowerPoint. It introduces the PowerPoint Start screen and the PowerPoint ribbon, gives you a brief look at the different views you can use when creating and managing a presentation, sends you on a guided tour of PowerPoint, and introduces you to other important concepts and tools you'll find in PowerPoint.

 NOTE Refer to Chapter 1 for instructions on how to open PowerPoint in either Windows 7 or Windows 8. Chapter 1 also explains how to add a shortcut for PowerPoint to your taskbar or Start menu so that you can quickly access your presentations.

Use the PowerPoint Start Screen

When you first open PowerPoint 2013, you'll see the Start screen, as shown in Figure 8-1. From here, you can start your presentation with one of the many listed templates or themes, search online for additional templates and themes, or base your new presentation on either a recent presentation or one you've created some time ago. You can also choose a blank template to start your presentation "from scratch." Refer to Chapter 1 for details on how to choose your beginning presentation or template.

 NOTE To bypass the Start screen when you open PowerPoint 2013, open a presentation in PowerPoint, click **File**, and then click **Options**. On the General tab, under Start Up Options, clear the **Show The Start Screen When This Application Starts** check box. Click **OK** to save your selection.

See the PowerPoint Views

Once you have an active presentation open in PowerPoint, even if it's a blank presentation, you need to understand how to see the various aspects of your slides. PowerPoint *views* are the way in which you see your slides on your computer. Each view is tailored for a specific use in assisting you to create and manage your presentation. There are four primary views and three more specialized views, as discussed next.

Use Primary PowerPoint Views

These views are available both from the View tab, Presentation Views group, and from the view icons in the task bar (see Figure 8-2):

- **Normal** Displays the currently selected slide in the main Presentation pane and displays thumbnails of all the slides in your current presentation in the Slides pane to the left, as shown in Figure 8-2. You can choose Normal view by clicking the **Normal** icon on the taskbar (located below the Presentation pane), or by clicking the **View** tab and then clicking **Normal** in the Presentation Views group.

- **Slide Sorter** Displays thumbnails of each slide in the Presentation pane, as shown in Figure 8-3. You can quickly rearrange your slides by selecting a slide and dragging it to a new location within your presentation. The currently selected slide has a colored border. To choose this view, either click the **Slide Sorter** icon on the taskbar, or click **Slide Sorter** in the View tab, Presentation Views group.

- **Reading View** Displays each slide in a full window without the ribbon, which is useful for reviewing a PowerPoint slide show presentation. This view is useful for proofing a slide with animations and transitions without going through the whole slide show in a full screen view. To use this view, click the **Reading View** icon on the taskbar, or click **Reading View** in the View tab Presentation Views group. A reduced toolbar is available on the bottom of the window.

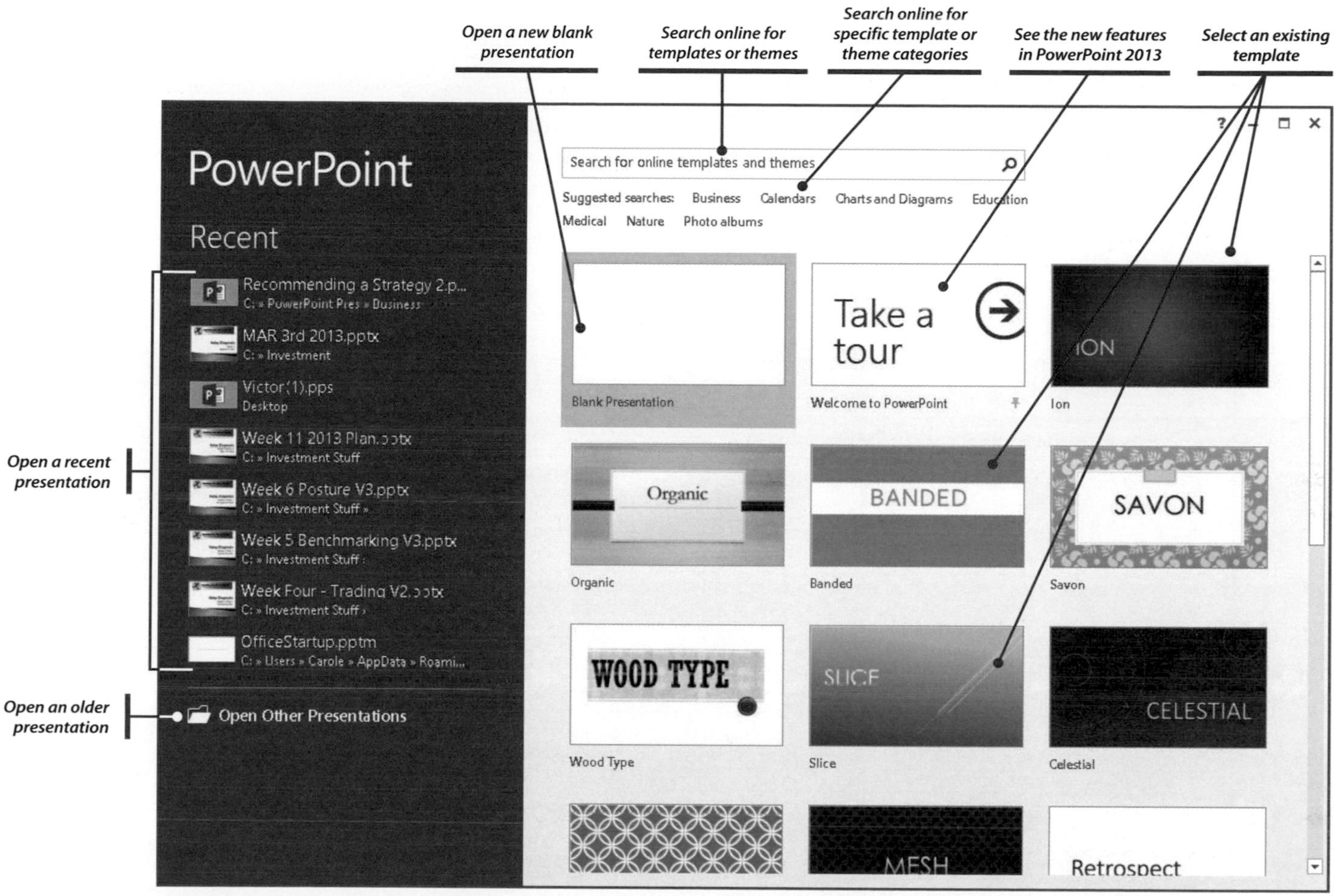

Callouts, clockwise from top:
- Open a new blank presentation
- Search online for templates or themes
- Search online for specific template or theme categories
- See the new features in PowerPoint 2013
- Select an existing template
- Open a recent presentation
- Open an older presentation

PowerPoint

Recent

Search for online templates and themes

Suggested searches: Business   Calendars   Charts and Diagrams   Education
Medical   Nature   Photo albums

Recommending a Strategy 2.p...
C: » PowerPoint Pres » Business

MAR 3rd 2013.pptx
C: » Investment

Victor(1).pps
Desktop

Week 11 2013 Plan.pptx
C: » Investment Stuff

Week 6 Posture V3.pptx
C: » Investment Stuff »

Week 5 Benchmarking V3.pptx
C: » Investment Stuff :

Week Four - Trading V2.pptx
C: » Investment Stuff »

OfficeStartup.pptm
C: » Users » Carole » AppData » Roami...

Open Other Presentations

Blank Presentation

Take a tour
Welcome to PowerPoint

Ion

Organic

BANDED
Banded

SAVON
Savon

WOOD TYPE
Wood Type

SLICE
Slice

CELESTIAL
Celestial

MESH

Retrospect

*Figure 8-1: **The Start screen for PowerPoint allows you to select a recent presentation or a template for a new one.***

- **Slide Show**   Displays the slide show, with each slide filling the screen as your audience will see it as you give your presentation. To use Slide Show view, click the **Slide Show** icon on the taskbar. In this view, you can also click the **Slide Show** tab and, in the Start Slide Show group, click where you want to start the show, from the beginning or from the current slide. Chapter 10 describes in more detail how to activate your slide show presentation.

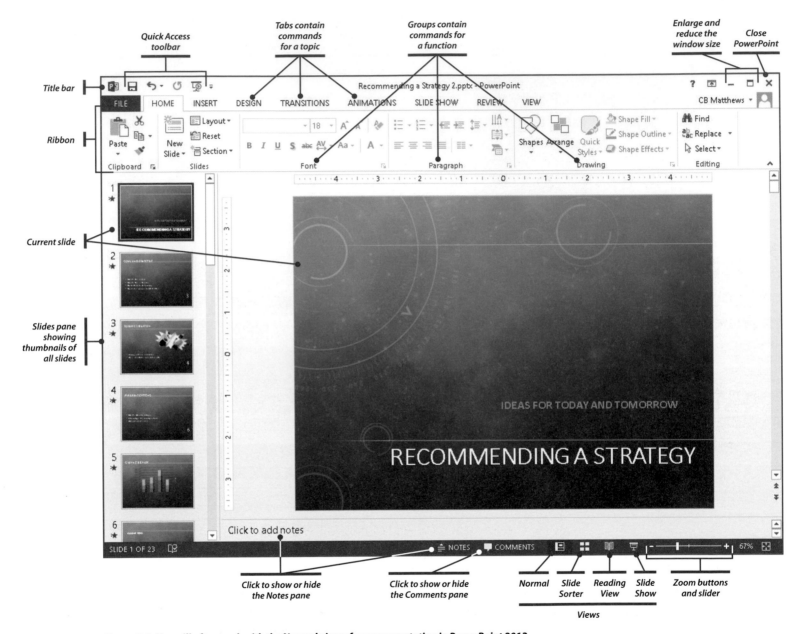

Figure 8-2: *You will often work with the Normal view of your presentation in PowerPoint 2013.*

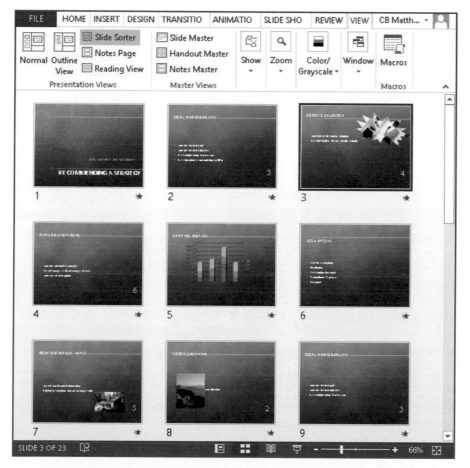

Figure 8-3: **Slide Sorter view makes it easy to organize and see your presentation as a whole.**

Use Specialized Views

There are additional views that you will most likely use: Outline View, for creating a presentation using an outline to capture key thoughts and organize the slides, Notes, for creating handouts for slide show viewers, and Comments, for creating comments for yourself or other presentation collaborators.

- **Outline View** is used to create an outline for your presentation and then fill it in, thereby creating the whole slide show with an organized approach. You can use this view both to create a presentation from a beginning outline you create and to review the text on your slides. A reduced image of the content on each slide is displayed on the left pane of your PowerPoint window. When you change something in the Outline pane, it changes the current slide in the Presentation pane. To display Outline View, click **Outline View** in the View tab Presentation Views group.

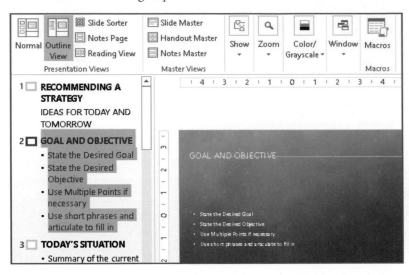

- **Notes** are viewed in two ways: as a Notes pane on the current slide displayed in Normal or Outline View and as a Notes Page where the notes are displayed beneath the slide on which they are based. The Note Page can be used as speaker notes for each slide, in printed handouts to viewers, or posted to a web page. It contains a page with the slide on top and notes on the bottom. To initially create the notes, in Normal view or Outline View, open the Notes pane to add and edit notes by clicking in the **Click To Add Notes** space beneath the slide. The Notes icon on the taskbar at the bottom of the PowerPoint window acts as a toggle to open or hide the Notes pane. To display the Notes Page as it will be printed, click **Notes Page** in the View tab Presentation Views group.

- The **Comments** view allows you to add comments about each slide for future reference. These comments are not displayed to your audience. To open the Comments pane, click **Comments** in the taskbar beneath the PowerPoint Presentation pane. Click **New** to add a comment.

Understanding PowerPoint Terminology

Slides, *views*, and *slide show* are among the many terms you will encounter in PowerPoint 2013. Each term is important as you begin to work with PowerPoint.

Understand the Basics

Slides in PowerPoint are the backbone of a PowerPoint presentation. Slides contain the content of the presentation, comparable to pages in a report. With PowerPoint slides, you can include text, pictures, animations, graphics, audio, and video components.

Master slides include predefined elements to help give your presentation a consistent look—see Chapter 10 for additional information. Master slides, which are just another kind of template, define the parts of a slide or a background that you want to be the same for a whole presentation or a group of contiguous slides. In addition to any color and design elements (such as fonts) found in themes, master slides might include unique graphics (such as a logo), a specific header or footer, and options for inserting placeholders for text and other objects while you are creating a presentation.

A group of slides makes up a PowerPoint *presentation*, which can be shown on many types of devices, such as a computer, a projector, or a widescreen TV, or on the Internet. You can print your slides (along with notes) as handouts so that your audience can follow along as you give your presentation.

Views are different displays of PowerPoint slides, enabling you to see each slide individually (Normal view), groups of slides (Slide Sorter), outlines of the presentation (Outline View), and the presentation in action (Slide Show)—what you are creating. In addition, you can makes notes for your audience (Notes Page) and quickly preview your slide show (Reading View). As you create and manage your slides, you'll find yourself using all of these views.

Understand Working Definitions

Themes in PowerPoint lend presentations color and design coordination. A theme defines a set of colors, special effects, and fonts that complete a look. A number of themes are available in a ribbon gallery in PowerPoint, and you can download additional choices from Microsoft's online templates (http://office.microsoft.com/en-us/templates/). Chapter 9 explains how themes can be changed and customized to give you almost unlimited variations in how your presentation looks.

Templates are not the same as themes. Templates contain themes, but also include specific layout suggestions on where to place elements (text or art, for instance). See Chapter 1 for more information on templates.

Layouts, an example of which is shown in Figure 8-4, define where the objects of a slide (such as the text, spreadsheets, diagrams, pictures, headings and footers, and so on) will be placed and formatted. Objects are positioned on a slide by using placeholders that identify the specific object being inserted (a text placeholder versus a chart placeholder, for instance). PowerPoint has defined several standard layouts that you can choose from when you insert a new slide. When you insert a new slide into a given theme, the slide takes on the colors and design elements of the theme, with the chosen layout attribute's placeholder positioning.

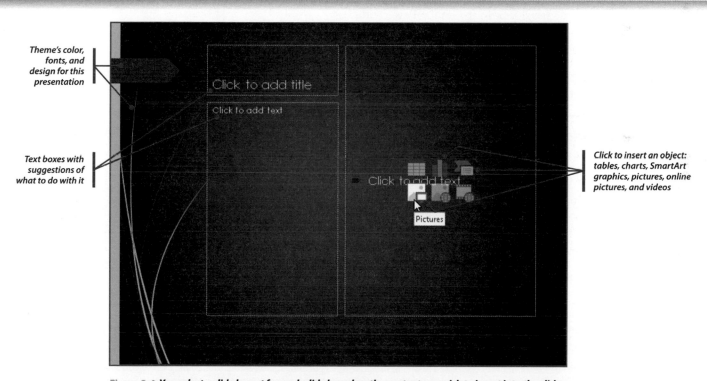

Theme's color, fonts, and design for this presentation

Text boxes with suggestions of what to do with it

Click to insert an object: tables, charts, SmartArt graphics, pictures, online pictures, and videos

Figure 8-4: *You select a slide layout for each slide based on the content you wish to insert into the slide.*

▶▶ Take the PowerPoint Tour

When you first open PowerPoint, as shown earlier in Figure 8-1, among the many templates displayed is a useful one named Welcome to PowerPoint, the icon for which shows the text "Take a Tour." To learn more about PowerPoint 2013:

1. Double-click the **Take a Tour** icon to open the presentation in the PowerPoint window.

2. Press the **F5** key on your keyboard to view the presentation in Slide Show view. If you are using a touch screen, tap the **Touch Keyboard** button on the taskbar and press the **FN** key to show the function keys.

3. Press the **SPACEBAR** on your keyboard to move through the presentation. The final slide has a link to the online PowerPoint Getting Started Center. If your computer is connected to the Internet, click the link to view the many tips and ideas from Microsoft for working with PowerPoint 2013.

4. Close the browser window by clicking the **X** button in the upper-right corner to return to your tour presentation.

5. To close the tour, press **ESCAPE**, or right-click the screen and click **End Show** to return to the PowerPoint Tour slides.

6. Click the **File** tab to open the File menu. From here, you can choose **New** to create a new presentation or **Open** to work with an existing presentation.

▶▶ Use PowerPoint Ribbon Tabs

The primary way you access the tools and commands in PowerPoint, as is true with all Office programs, is via the ribbon tabs. Each tab contains all the commands related to a particular topic associated with creating a PowerPoint presentation. The commands on each tab are then organized into groups, with each group relating to a function, such as working with text or illustrations. A partial view of the PowerPoint ribbon is shown next, with the View tab selected.

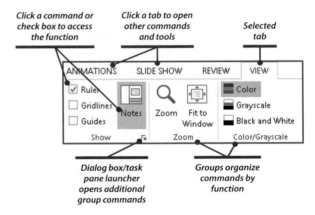

There are nine tabs in the starting PowerPoint window. But when you select an object on a slide, other tabs will appear with commands specifically for working with the selected object, as shown in Figure 8-5.

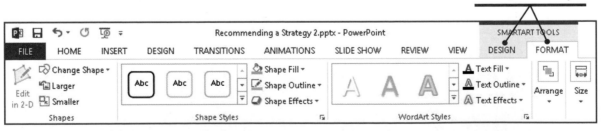

Figure 8-5: **Tabs organize the tools you need to create and manage your slides. Contextual tabs display when you select an appropriate object.**

As you begin to use the tabs, you'll learn what they do. Here is a brief overview of the main tabs:

- **File** Commands for working with the PowerPoint files and program preferences.

- **Home** Commands for typical text editing and drawing functions.

- **Insert** Commands for adding a new object to the slide, such as a table, picture, shape, chart, hyperlink, or other object. This is also where you work with headers, footers, and WordArt in text.

- **Design** Commands for assigning themes to a presentation or customizing slide backgrounds.

- **Transitions** Commands for creating movement and sound for transitioning from one slide to another.

- **Animations** Commands for adding action and sound to a single slide.

- **Slide Show** Commands for controlling the actual slide show.

- **Review** Commands for performing functions such as text proofing, translating languages, adding comments, and comparing slide shows.

- **View** Commands for controlling such functions as views, master slides, zoom, and the window with one or more slide shows.

As previously mentioned, when you click a particular object in the slide, you will also see contextual tabs for working with that object. Figure 8-5 shows an example of the SmartArt Tools contextual tab and Format and Design subtabs, when a SmartArt object is selected. Here are some examples of contextual tabs:

- **SmartArt Tools, Format and Design** contain commands specifically for working with SmartArt objects. The Format subtab allows you to edit shapes and choose shape styles and WordArt styles in text. The Design subtab allows you to create graphics, modify layouts, and apply SmartArt styles.

- **Drawing Tools, Format** appears when you are working with a shape. It allows you to insert and apply drawings embellished with shape styles and WordArt. You can manage layers of drawn objects

and control dimensions. This subtab can also display when a chart or graph is selected.

- **Table Tools, Design and Layout** are displayed when a chart or table is displayed and selected. The Design subtab allows you to apply tables styles, column banding, and WordArt styles, and to create unique tables with drawing tools and art. The Layout subtab allows you to work with table columns, rows, and cells to manage margins, cell dimensions, and alignment. Chart Tools, Design and Format may also be displayed to work with chart designs and formatting of chart elements.

- **Picture Tools, Format** appears when you are working with an image such as a picture or clip art. It allows you to apply artistic effects and styles to pictures. You can apply borders to the images, special effects (such as shadow or bevels), and manage layers of pictures. You can control dimensions.

You will learn more about the commands and tools contained in each of these tabs as you learn how to create PowerPoint presentations in this chapter and the next two chapters.

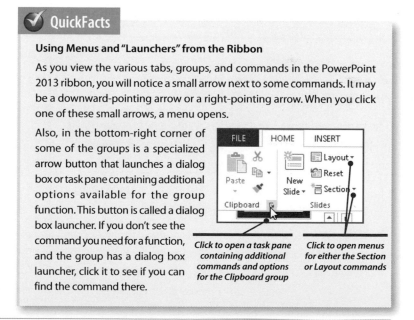

✓ QuickFacts

Using Menus and "Launchers" from the Ribbon

As you view the various tabs, groups, and commands in the PowerPoint 2013 ribbon, you will notice a small arrow next to some commands. It may be a downward-pointing arrow or a right-pointing arrow. When you click one of these small arrows, a menu opens.

Also, in the bottom-right corner of some of the groups is a specialized arrow button that launches a dialog box or task pane containing additional options available for the group function. This button is called a dialog box launcher. If you don't see the command you need for a function, and the group has a dialog box launcher, click it to see if you can find the command there.

Click to open a task pane containing additional commands and options for the Clipboard group

Click to open menus for either the Section or Layout commands

CREATE A PRESENTATION

There are three ways to begin creating your presentation:

- Use an existing presentation that has already been formatted with themes and layouts, and then modify it
- Use a template that defines the theme and layout of a slide
- Start from scratch, creating your own template with its themes and layouts in the process

In other words, sometimes you may find that one of your previous presentations has what you need, so you can simply borrow slides or design elements from past successful efforts. Other times, you'll find what you need in the prepackaged themes and templates that are designed with specific presentation types in mind (for instance, an academic or business presentation or a presentation fashioned for *your* industry). You might also encounter a situation where nothing you have in your presentation library or that is offered by PowerPoint can fill your particular requirements. In that case, you can create your own template from scratch or with Office-wide themes and the styling assistance of PowerPoint.

▷▷ Create a Presentation from Another Presentation

The easiest and most direct way to create a new presentation is to start with an existing one. To copy a presentation, rename it, and then modify it according to your needs, follow these steps:

1. Open PowerPoint by any of the methods discussed in Chapter 1. You'll see the screen shown earlier in Figure 8-1.

2. If the presentation you want is not available in the Recent list, click **Open Other Presentations** from the Start screen. (If you have disabled the Start screen, click the **File** tab

and then click **Open**.) If it is listed under Recent, just click it and go to Step 3.

- The resulting page defaults to Recent Presentations. If you do not see the presentation with which you want to work, click either **Computer** or **SkyDrive**, depending on where you expect to find your presentation.

- You'll see a list of Recent Folders. If you do not find the folder containing your presentation, click **Browse**.

- The Open dialog box will open, where you can search your computer (or SkyDrive) for your presentation. An example is shown in Figure 8-6. Follow the path to the presentation and click **Open**.

- When you see the presentation you want to modify, double-click its name, or click **Open** in the dialog box.

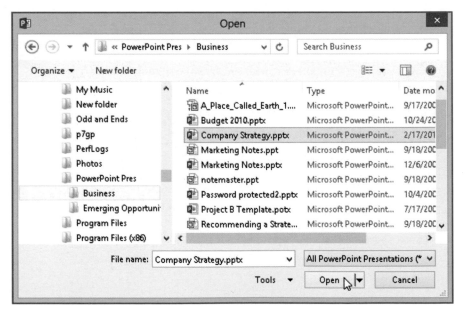

Figure 8-6: Use this window to find and open the presentation you want to use as a model for a new presentation.

3. Modify the presentation by replacing the theme; highlighting text and replacing it with your own; deleting unnecessary slides; inserting new slides; inserting your own graphics, charts, and art; and rearranging the slides according to your needs (Chapters 9 and 10 describe how to do these actions). See Figure 8-7 for an example of an existing presentation that can easily be updated for another presentation.

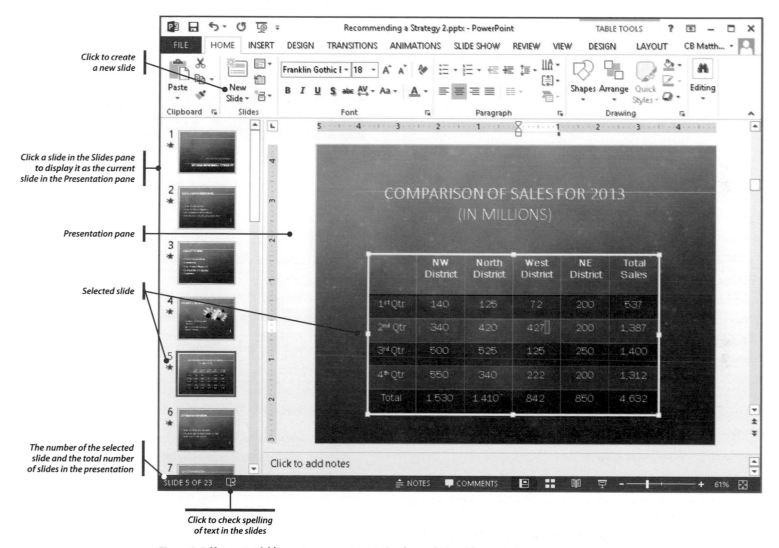

Figure 8-7: *You can quickly create a new presentation by working with an existing one.*

4. Click the **File** tab, and click **Save As**. Select a location in which to save your presentation, or click **Browse**. The Save As dialog box appears.

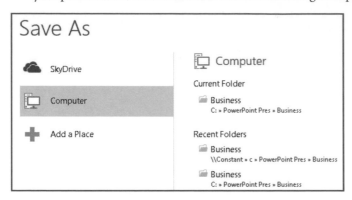

5. Rename your presentation by typing over the **File Name** text box name. Then verify it will be saved as the **Save As Type** PowerPoint Presentation (.pptx) option, and click **Save**.

Create a Presentation Using a Template

PowerPoint 2013 offers many preset templates with a variety of themes to give your presentation a unified and professional look. Remember, templates and themes are not the same: themes provide background color and design, predefined fonts, and other elements that hold a presentation together. Templates also organize themes into layouts, which you can change. Once you have defined your template, it is a simple task to insert additional slides with the appropriate layout for the data you wish to present. You can select a template from the list available in the opening New screen or search for a predefined template or theme online. To use one of PowerPoint's preset templates:

1. Click the **File** tab, and click **New**.

2. Select the template you want to use by clicking its thumbnail. A preview will be displayed.

TIP You may scan the templates by clicking a beginning thumbnail to display a preview of it. Then click the **Next** and **Previous** arrows to go from one template to the next. When you find one you like, click **Create**.

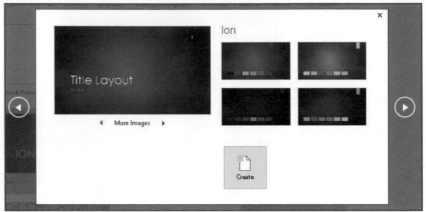

3. Click **Create** to use this template. The single Title Slide will be created. At this point you can either begin to add additional slides and content to an actual presentation (see "Add Content to a Slide") or create a template for a new presentation (see "Create a Custom Template").

Search Online for Templates

PowerPoint 2013 uses your Internet connection to give you access to thousands of predesigned themes and templates. You can choose from several suggested categories on which to search.

1. On the New screen (click **File** and then **New**), click a category in the Suggested Searches, or type your desired category in the Search box and press **ENTER**. Another New page will open listing the templates in that category, as shown in Figure 8-8.

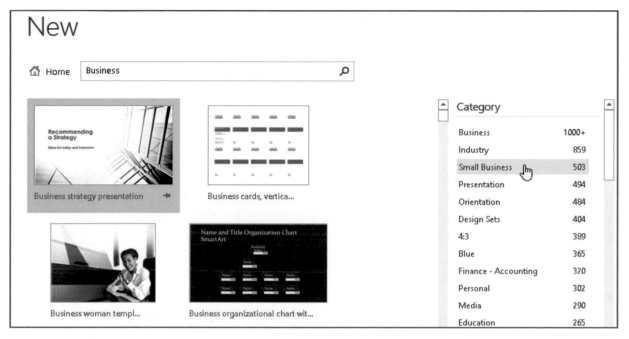

Figure 8-8: Searching online provides thousands of possibilities for finding the exact template and theme you want.

2. Browse through the Category list to narrow your selection. The thumbnails on the left will change to reflect your Category selection.

3. Click the thumbnail you want to select. You can either click **Create** to create your initial title slide, or click the **Next** and **Previous** arrows to scan additional templates in the Category list.

Create a Custom Template

If you have looked for a template but haven't found one you like, or if you are creating a new slide show and you want it to have a unique look, you may want to create a custom template rather than use an existing one (although you may use an existing one as a starting point).

A template, as you've learned, is one or more slides with attributes of the color themes, design elements, and standard layouts you want to have available to presentations without recreating a "look" for each slide.

A key point about a template is that it contains information that you want to use on a whole presentation or a group of slides—characteristics they share, such as color, a logo, or formatting. For instance, a company may have its own templates for certain types of projects. To use a custom template again when you start creating a presentation, you must save your modified slides as a template rather than as a document. Then, you can simply add content and data unique to a slide without being concerned about maintaining a common look from slide to slide.

Here is an overview of how to create a custom PowerPoint template:

1. Find your beginning template, as described in "Create a Presentation Using a Template." Click the **File** tab, and click **New**. You can create a new template in two ways. You can open an existing template and modify it based on your requirements, or you can create one

from scratch. Double-click a template's thumbnail or the **Blank Presentation** thumbnail to see the basic slide layout. You may then change your selection according to your needs.

2. Modify your template with the characteristics you want your slides to share:

- Click the **Design** tab. In the Themes group, click the **More** down arrow, to select themes or design elements (color, fonts, effects, or background styles) for the template. As you mouse over an option, you can see it reflected in the template slide. If you've used a sample template, you may use this method to change it. (See "Apply Themes to Slides.")

- Click the **Insert** tab and insert any objects you want to have on all pages, such as a logo graphic, your name in WordArt, or a "confidential" or "copyright" footer.

- Click the **Home** tab. In the Slides group, click the **New Slide** down arrow for a list of possible layouts, and then select the layouts you expect to find in the presentation. (See "Choose a Slide Layout.")

3. When you have a template that carries the attributes you want the presentation to have, save the modified document as a template as follows:

a. Click the **File** tab, click **Save As**, and click **Browse** to open the Save As dialog box.

b. In the File Name box, type a name for the new template.

c. In the Save As Type drop-down list box, click **PowerPoint Template (.potx)**.

d. Click **Save**.

The template is now available in the Custom Office Templates subfolder located in the My Documents folder.

Create a Presentation from Scratch

To create a presentation from scratch, you'll need an idea of which slides you want in the presentation and the order in which you want to present them. Using an outline to help define the content and order of the slides can be helpful. Check out "Outline a Presentation" later in this chapter if you prefer to develop your presentation content using an outline.

When you create a presentation from scratch, you begin with blank slides and add layouts, color schemes, fonts, graphics and charts, other design elements, and text.

1. Click the **File** tab, and click **New**. The New Start Screen appears.

2. Click **Blank Presentation**; a Title Slide will be created.

3. Click the **Design** tab, and select a theme from the Themes group. In the Variants group, click the **More** down arrow to check the color, fonts, and background color to vary the look of your presentation.

4. Click and type over "Click To Add Title" to enter the title of your presentation. If you want to add a subtitle, click and type over "Click To Add Subtitle."

5. When you are satisfied with that slide, click **New Slide** in the Home tab Slides group. Typically, when you click the New Slide button, the next slide contains the Title and Content layout. If you want a different layout, click the **New Slide** down arrow to choose another layout from a list of layout choices. (See "Choose a Slide Layout.")

6. Click the **Insert** tab, and click the relevant buttons to add text and other content to your slides. (See "Add Content to a Slide.")

7. Repeat steps 5 and 6 for as many slides as you have in your presentation.

8. Save the presentation. Click the **File** tab, and click **Save As**. Enter a name and click **Save**.

COMPLETE YOUR LOOK AND CONTENT

To finish your presentation, you must insert slide layouts where you need them, add themes to make your presentation come alive, and then add the defining content to your slides—text, art and graphics, tables, and transitions and animations.

Choose a Slide Layout

You will find that you need to add slide layouts to new or existing slide shows. You also add slide layouts to templates you are creating. When you add a new slide layout, you are shown a list of possibilities in the current theme. Figure 8-9 shows an example. Choose the slide with the layout that most closely matches the content you are going to create. To choose the right layout, you can either use a menu of layouts or duplicate the layout of existing slides.

Use a Menu to Select Layouts

1. Click the **Home** tab and then click the **New Slide** down arrow (not just the button) in the Slide group. You will see a list of possible layouts for your slide, as you can see in Figure 8-9. You can click a layout from the list. Choose a layout that you want; possibilities include, among others, Title Slide, Section Header, Picture with Caption, and even Blank.

2. Alternatively, you can select an option below the slides list to duplicate existing slides, create slides from an outline, or reuse existing slides from another slide show.

> **NOTE** You can also insert a slide layout onto an existing slide, preferably a blank one. Right-click the slide in a blank area of the slide (not on top of another object) and click **Layout**. A context menu of layout options is displayed. Click the one you want. (To create a new, blank slide, click between two slides in the Slides pane and press **CTRL+M**).

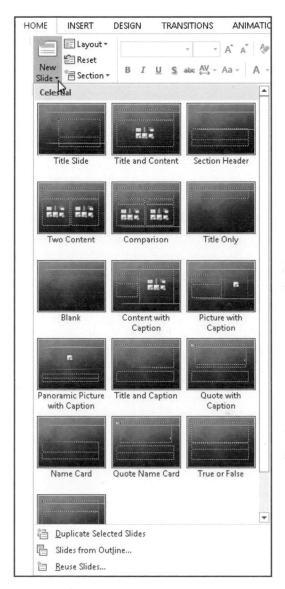

Figure 8-9: **PowerPoint 2013 gives you several layout options from which to base a new slide.**

Use Existing Slides for Layouts

If you are adding a layout slide to an existing slide or a new one after you have inserted several layouts:

1. Click a slide in the Slides pane containing a similar layout to that which you need.

2. Click the **New Slide** button (not the down arrow) and a duplicate, blank layout slide will be inserted.

3. Note: If you are creating a new presentation from a blank template, your first slide by default will be the Title Slide. It is inserted when you create the new blank presentation. The next slide after the Title Slide for a blank presentation, inserted when you click the **New Slide** button (not the down arrow), will be a Title and Content layout. Thereafter, by clicking the **New Slide** button you can either add layouts by duplicating the previous Title and Content layouts, or click the **New Slide** down arrow to add a layout from the Layout menu.

Apply Themes to Slides

Themes add color and design to slides, as we have seen. Applying a theme to a slide is easy. You just select a theme from a list and it will be applied to all slides in the presentation, unless you specify differently (you can have different themes in a presentation).

Apply a Theme to All or Selected Slides

If you want to apply the theme to only some of the slides in your presentation, select the slides to which you want to apply the theme by pressing CTRL while you click the thumbnails in the Slides tab or in the Slide Sorter view. If you want the theme to apply to all of the slides or to matching slides (slides with the same theme), don't select any of the slides.

1. Click the **Design** tab and right-click the desired theme thumbnail in either the Themes group or the Variants group.

2. From the context menu, you have these choices:

- Click **Apply To Selected Slides** to apply the theme to only the selected slides.

- Click **Apply To All Slides** to apply the theme to all slides in the presentation.

- Click **Apply To Matching Slides** to apply the theme to slides with the same theme.

Set a Default Theme to Apply to All Future Presentations

When you set a theme as a default, future presentations will be created using that theme. You can, of course, change the theme. But it is a good way to remember which theme you used, especially if several people are collaborating on the slides. First, find the thumbnail of the theme you want to use as the default:

1. Click the **Design** tab, click the **More** down arrow in the Themes group, and right-click the theme thumbnail you want.

2. Click **Set As Default Theme**.

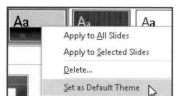

Add Content to a Slide

There are many elements available to help you present the points you are making in the presentation. You can add text, photos, charts, graphs, or add or change color schemes, and more. These elements add interest, emphasis, and detail to the data.

Work with Text

Text can be added to placeholders, text boxes, and some shapes. Your template will use a default font, but you can change that easily. Chapter 10 deals with text in detail. To add text, click inside of a text box, a shape (one that accepts text), or a placeholder and begin to type. To replace text, select it and then type over it. To delete text, select it and press DELETE. (See Chapter 9 for additional information on using text.)

There are three ways you can access text tools:

- To add or modify text attributes, first select the text that you want to edit. (You can find details on how to select text in Chapter 2.) A mini toolbar will appear that you can use for simple character and paragraph changes. The mini toolbar (along with a context menu) is also displayed when you simply right-click a word or phrase. (Clicking the mini toolbar removes the context menu.)

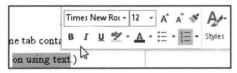

- Click the **Home** tab, and click any of the Font or Paragraph group buttons. These tabs are the primary ways you work with text.

- Click the **Font dialog box launcher**, as shown next, to display a Font dialog box that contains additional commands, as you can see in Figure 8-10.

Add or Change Color Schemes

When planning your new presentation, consider which color schemes you might want to use. Are there company colors that you want to use? Are there specific colors you do *not* want to use? You will primarily use Themes (found in the Design tab, Themes group) to change colors schemes. You can vary themes by choosing options in the Variant group, or by clicking the Variant group **More** down arrow to access Colors, Fonts, Effects, and Background Styles menus, as shown next. See "Apply Themes to Slides" in this chapter for more information.

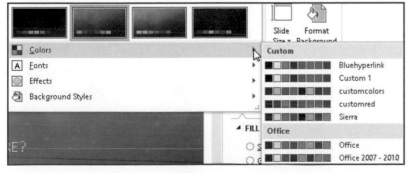

*Figure 8-10: **The Font dialog box contains additional text commands not found in the ribbon's Font group.***

Insert Art and Graphics

To include images or other graphics on your slide:

1. Click the **Insert** tab and, in either the Images group or Illustrations group, click the button for the photo, art, or graphic object you want to insert. Depending on which button you click, a menu or dialog box will be displayed where you can find and click the image or illustration you seek.

2. The Images group allows you to choose:

   - Pictures from files on your computer

- Online pictures to download (remember that most pictures found online contain copyrights)
- Pictures from photo albums on your computer
- Screenshots from your computer

3. From the Illustrations group, you can enter:
   - Shapes contained within PowerPoint 2013
   - SmartArt that is included with PowerPoint 2013
   - Charts that you can create in your slide

4. After the object has been inserted, drag it to where you want it placed on your slide, and resize it as needed.

   –Or–

   Create and insert your own drawing using shapes in the Home tab Drawing group.

 NOTE If you have used earlier versions of PowerPoint, you may be familiar with WordArt. To access WordArt in PowerPoint 2013, click the **Insert** tab and you will see WordArt in the Text group.

Insert a Table

Insert a table to present your data in an organized manner. You can insert three types of tables: a PowerPoint-created table, a table that you draw, or a table from Excel. Click the **Insert** tab, click the **Table** down arrow in the Tables group, and select your choice:

- Drag your mouse pointer over the squares to select the number of rows and columns you want your table to have and then click.

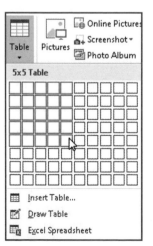

- Click **Insert Table** to access a dialog box in which you can define the number of rows and columns.
- Click **Draw Table** for drawing tools so that you can draw your own table.
- Click **Excel Spreadsheet** to import a table from an existing spreadsheet in Excel.

OUTLINE A PRESENTATION

If you are creating a large presentation, it is often easier to use an outline to organize your thoughts and visually see the slides as you create them, rather than creating individual slides from scratch. Figure 8-11 shows an example.

To outline a presentation in PowerPoint 2013, click the **View** tab and click **Outline View** in the Presentation Views group. Now, begin typing, either into the Outline page, or in the current slide in the Presentation pane, the text that will appear on your slides. The following sections explain how to create, manipulate, modify, and print an outline.

 TIP For more typing room in Outline View, expand the Outline pane by dragging its inside edge into the Presentation pane.

Create an Outline

You can create an outline from scratch or by inserting text from other sources, such as a Word document. You create an outline by indenting subtopics under topics. When you create a subtopic, or indent it under the one above it, you *demote* the point, or make it a lower-level topic than the previous topic. It is contained within the higher-level topic. When you remove an indent, you *promote* the point, making it a new topic. It becomes a higher-level topic and may contain its own subtopics. See "Use the Outlining Commands" later in this chapter for further information.

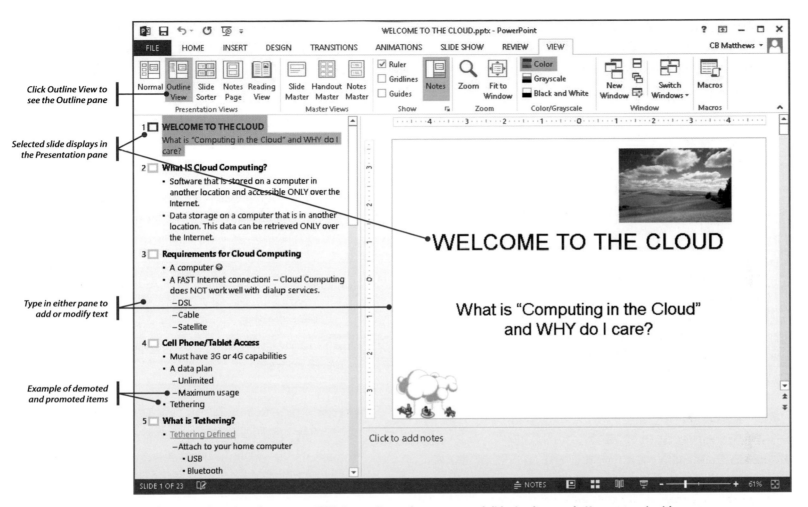

Figure 8-11: *Outline View allows you to "fill in" an outline and see your actual slide simultaneously. You can type in either pane.*

Understanding the Outlining Feature

PowerPoint's outlining feature is not only an organizational tool but also a quick way to create a cohesive and logical path for your presentation. As you type the outline, you are creating the actual slides in a presentation. This is an alternative way to create a presentation from scratch. If you like to outline your presentation prior to jumping in and creating complete slides, you'll like this way of building your presentation. The outline should contain the following:

- The main points you want to make. These will become the titles of the slides.

- Subsidiary points that support the main points. These will become the bulleted content of each slide.

Your main and subsidiary points are essential to the presentation. Although not essential at this point, certain secondary considerations are beneficial in flushing out your main points and the "feel" of your presentation. For example, you should consider questions such as these: Which graphics do you want to use on each slide? Do you have charts or graphs that tell the story? Will photos take up part of the slide? Will you have a logo or other mandated identification on the chart? The more you think these questions through initially, the more smoothly your presentation will flow. Answering these questions will help you design a great presentation.

Create an Outline from Scratch

To create a fresh outline, just type your text into the Outline pane. Selection is important. Select the slide's icon to do something to the slide itself (such as to move it or copy its contents); select a line item to affect the line only.

1. Open a new or existing presentation and display the Outline pane—click **Outline View** in the View tab Presentation Views group.

2. In the Outline pane, click to the right of the Outline slide icon to place the insertion point where you want to start typing, as shown in Figure 8-12, where the insertion point is positioned next to the icon for the first slide.

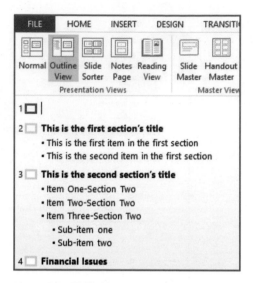

Figure 8-12: **Place your mouse pointer to the right of the Outline slide icon to start typing at the insertion point.**

3. On the first slide, type the title (the first slide is typically the title of your presentation).

4. Use a combination of the following techniques to build your outline:

- Press **ENTER** to insert a new slide after typing the title only. Thereafter, pressing **ENTER** advances to a new line.

- Press **CTRL+ENTER** to insert a new slide after typing text following the title. Pressing **CTRL+ENTER** after the title advances to the next line.

- Right-click a slide and select **New Slide** to insert a new slide immediately following the current one.

- To demote a line item (indent it to the right), place the insertion point at the start of the line and press **TAB**, or right-click the line and select **Demote** (see Figure 8-13), or click **Increase List Level** in the Home tab Paragraph group.

- To promote a line item (indent it to the left), place the insertion point on the beginning of the line and press **SHIFT+TAB**, or right-click the line and select **Promote** (see Figure 8-13), or click **Decrease List Level** ⇐ in the Home tab Paragraph group.

- If you promote the last line of a slide, it becomes the title of a new slide. If you demote the title of a slide, it becomes a subitem in the previous slide.

- To move a slide up or down in the Outline pane, either click and drag the slide's icon to where you want the slide to appear in the outline or right-click the slide's text and select **Move Up** or **Move Down** until the slide is positioned properly

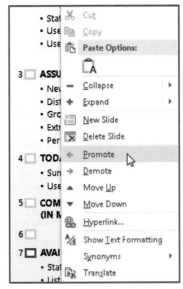

Figure 8-13: *The context menu in Outline View is useful for completing your outline.*

- To move a line item up or down in the slide, select the line item to be moved and then either drag the line to where you want it positioned or right-click the line and select **Move Up** or **Move Down**.

- Click a slide and press **DELETE** to remove it from the presentation.

5. Continue typing and promoting or demoting line items to move text into headings and bulleted points until the presentation is outlined.

Insert an Outline from Other Sources

You can create slides from an outline you have previously created in another document. Depending on the format of the text, the formatting retained and used by PowerPoint will differ.

- A **Microsoft Word (.doc or .docx)** outline will use paragraph breaks to mark the start of a new slide. Each paragraph will become a slide title. However, if the document is formatted with headings, Heading 1 will become the title of the slide, Heading 2

will be the second level, Heading 3 the third level, and so on, as shown in Figure 8-14.

- A **Rich Text Format (.rtf)** outline will adopt the styles of the current presentation. PowerPoint will use paragraph separations to start a new slide. The text can be edited only in the Presentation pane.

To insert an outline from another source:

1. In the Home tab Slides group, click the **New Slide** down arrow and, at the bottom of the menu, click **Slides From Outline**.

2. In the Insert Outline dialog box, find the location and name of the outline to be used, select it, and click **Insert**. The outline will fill the slides, as shown in Figure 8-14.

▷▷ Use the Outlining Commands

Although some of the buttons available on the ribbon work well with the outlining function, you can display commands specifically for use with the Outline View.

1. Select the slide or line of text in the Outline pane.

2. Right-click to open the context menu. Select one of the commands, which are described in the following sections. You can see these in Figure 8-13.

Promote or Demote Outline Text

- Click **Promote** to move the selected text in a slide up one level (that is, indent it to the left).

- Click **Demote** to move the selected text in a slide down one level (that is, indent it to the right).

Move Outline Text Up or Down

- Click **Move Up** to move the selected text of a slide up one line or up one slide (if you select the slide's icon).

- Click **Move Down** to move the selected text of a slide down one line or down on slide (if you select the slide's icon).

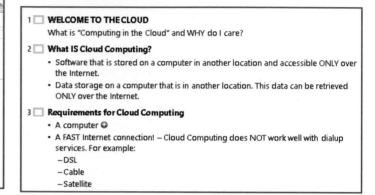

Figure 8-14: *Inserting an outline into a presentation from a Word document retains the heading-level formatting to separate slides and bulleted items.*

Collapse or Expand a Slide

- Click **Collapse** to open the submenu, and click **Collapse** to hide the detail beneath the title of a selected slide or click **Collapse All** to hide all the detail lines in the outline.

- Click **Expand** to open the submenu, and click **Expand** to show the detail beneath a title of a selected slide or click **Expand All** to show all the detail lines in the outline.

Preview and Print the Outline

To preview an outline and then print it:

1. Right-click anywhere in the outline in Outline View. Click **Expand**, and then click **Expand All** in the submenu to expand the outline so that all detail is showing.

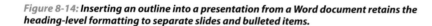

2. Click the **File** tab, and click **Print**.

3. Under Settings, click the second drop-down list box, and click **Outline**.

4. Click **Print** to print the outline.

Chapter 9

Working with Slides

Getting around in a presentation and being able to manipulate slides easily is a critical skill when using PowerPoint. In this chapter you will learn how to work with presentations at the slide level, including how to navigate through the slides in various views of PowerPoint; insert, delete, rearrange, and copy slides; change a presentation's basic components of themes, fonts, and colors; and use SmartArt to spiff up presentations. You'll also learn about hyperlinks and footers in PowerPoint. Finally, you'll learn how to use transitions and animations.

NAVIGATE AND MANIPULATE SLIDES

Each PowerPoint presentation consists of individual slides. You may modify an individual slide or make changes to all of the slides at the same time. This section addresses how to insert and delete slides, display slides in a variety of ways, and move and duplicate slides.

⏩ Navigate from Slide to Slide

To move between the slides, you can use the Slides pane in Normal view or the Outline pane in Outline View to select and move to the slide you want to display in the Presentation pane. To access the various views, click the **View** tab and make your choice in the Presentation Views group, as shown in Figure 9-1. See Chapter 8 for additional information on using views.

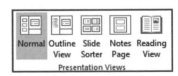

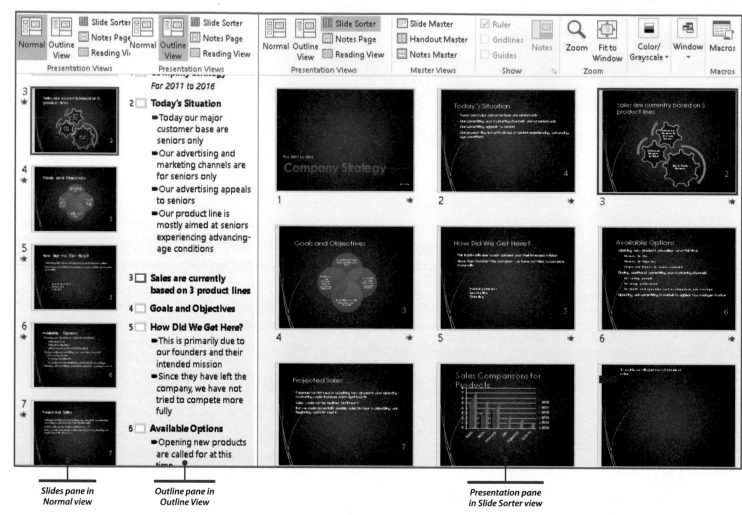

Slides pane in Normal view · *Outline pane in Outline View* · *Presentation pane in Slide Sorter view*

*Figure 9-1: **You can easily navigate in PowerPoint by using the various views.***

NOTE You can also use the taskbar at the bottom of the PowerPoint window to change views (except to Outline View).

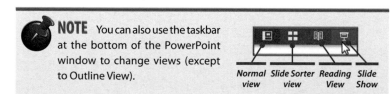

Normal view · *Slide Sorter view* · *Reading View* · *Slide Show*

- In Normal view, click the thumbnail of the slide you want from the Slides pane. To move between the slides, use the vertical scroll bar.

- In Outline View, click the icon of the slide you want from the Outline pane. Use the vertical scroll bar to move up or down to locate the slide you want.

- In Slide Sorter view, click the vertical scroll bar to move to the next screen of thumbnails. Click a slide to select it.

Insert a Slide

You can insert new slides in various ways in PowerPoint. You can also insert slides from other presentations.

Insert a New Slide

You can insert a new blank slide from several places in PowerPoint. The most common ways are

- From either the Home tab or the Insert tab, click **New Slide** in the Slides group.
- In the Outline tab, when entering bulleted text, press **CTRL+ENTER**.
- In Normal, Outline, or Slide Sorter view, right-click the slide immediately preceding the location where you want the new slide, and click **New Slide**.

Insert a Slide from Another File

To insert a slide duplicated from another presentation, you must find and display the slides from the source presentation, and then select the slide or slides that you want to copy into your destination presentation.

1. Open the destination presentation. In the Slides pane, click the slide positioned immediately before the one to be inserted.
2. In the Home tab Slides group, click the **New Slide** down arrow. From the drop-down menu, click **Reuse Slides** (at the bottom of the menu). The Reuse Slides task pane displays to the right.
3. Click the **Browse** down arrow to find the source file containing the slide or slides to be copied. Click **Browse File**. When you find the source file, select the file and click **Open**. Thumbnails of the

presentation will appear in the Reuse Slides task pane, as illustrated in Figure 9-2.

4. To insert one or more slides from the source presentation into the destination presentation, you must work back and forth between the Slides pane (destination) and the Reuse Slides task pane (source).

- Scroll through the thumbnail images in the Reuse Slides task pane, and click the one to be inserted into the Slides pane. It will be inserted when you click it. Alternatively, you can right-click a thumbnail in the Reuse Slides task pane and click **Insert Slide** on the context menu.
- To insert all the slides in the Reuse Slides task pane, right-click a thumbnail and click **Insert All Slides** on the context menu (seen in Figure 9-2).

- To apply the formatting of the source slides to those in the destination Slides pane, right-click any slide and choose **Apply Theme To All Slides** to copy the formatting to all of them, or choose **Apply Theme To Selected Slides** to copy the format only to previously selected destination slides.
- Normally the reused slides will take on the format of the destination presentation. To retain the formatting of the source reuse slides as you copy them, click the **Keep Source Formatting** check box at the bottom of the Reuse Slides task pane.

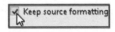

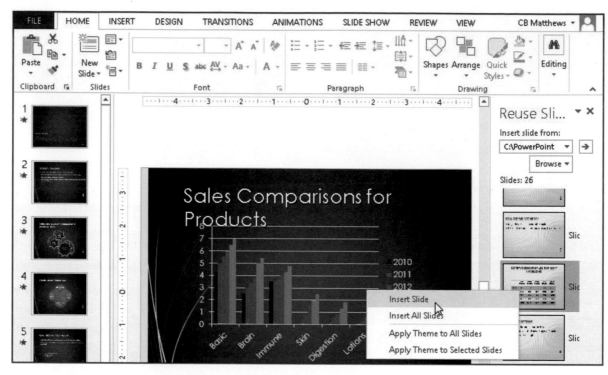

Figure 9-2: *The Reuse Slides task pane allows you to find another presentation and copy one or more slides from it into your current presentation.*

5. After you have inserted all the slides you want to include in the destination presentation, click **Close** in the upper-right corner of the Reuse Slides task pane.

 TIP Before closing the task pane, you can browse for other files and insert slides from them.

Display Multiple Presentations at Once

Opening and displaying two or more presentations opens many possibilities for dragging one slide from one presentation to another, copying color or formatting from one slide or presentation to another, and for comparing the presentations or slides side by side.

1. Click the **File** tab, click **Open**, and complete the sequence of locating and opening the presentations.

2. Click the **View** tab, and from the Window group, choose one of the following views:

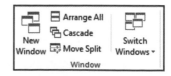

- **New Window** opens your current presentation in a new window.

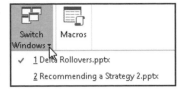

- **Switch Windows** lists open presentations so you can switch between them.

- **Cascade** opens all windows in an "offset-stacked" view.

- **Arrange All** tiles all open windows.

TIP **Move Split** allows you to use arrow keys to move the split between the Slides pane and the Notes pane. See "Work with Notes" in Chapter 10 to learn more about Notes in PowerPoint. Another way to perform a move split action is to place the pointer over the border between the Slides pane and the Notes pane and drag the two-headed arrow icon up or down to increase or decrease a pane, respectively.

3. Click the **Arrange All** button to display each presentation window side by side, as shown in Figure 9-3.

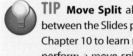

TIP To enlarge one of the presentations so that it occupies the whole window again, click its **Maximize** button.

Duplicate One or More Slides

You can copy or duplicate one or more slides using the Duplicate Slide/ Slides command.

From Normal view, in the Slides pane, select the slide you want to copy. To copy multiple thumbnails, press CTRL while you click the slides to select them. For contiguous slides, you can press SHIFT and click the first and last slide in the range. (In Normal view, the active slide is the one that is displayed in the Presentation pane.)

- To duplicate a single slide or multiple selected slides, right-click the slide or slides, and click **Duplicate Slide** from the context menu.

–Or–

- To duplicate multiple selected slides, click the **New Slide** down arrow (on the Home tab), and click **Duplicate Selected Slides** from the bottom of the menu. This also works for a single slide.

Move or Copy Slides

You can move or copy your slides most easily from Normal, Outline, or Slide Sorter view.

- To copy a slide, right-click the slide to be copied, and click **Copy** on the context menu. Right-click the slide preceding where you want the new slide to go, and select the paste option you want: **Use Destination Theme**, **Keep Source Formatting**, or **Picture**. (For more information about the Paste options in PowerPoint 2013, see "Reviewing the Paste Options" QuickFacts.) In Normal view or Slide Sorter view, you can click between slides to place the insertion point there to mark the location where the slide will be pasted.

- To move a slide, click the slide icon or thumbnail to be moved, and drag it to the new location.

CAUTION When you copy and paste a slide, the insertion point determines where the new slide will be positioned. It's possible to insert a slide into the middle of another one, splitting its contents unintentionally. Make certain you place the insertion point precisely where you want the new slide to go. When you drag the slide, a position in the slide pane will open as you drag over the space. Drop it into the correct slot.

NOTE If you have more than one design theme applied to a presentation, the first one will be copied; if you haven't opened the presentation recently, you will be asked if you want the remaining themes to be made available.

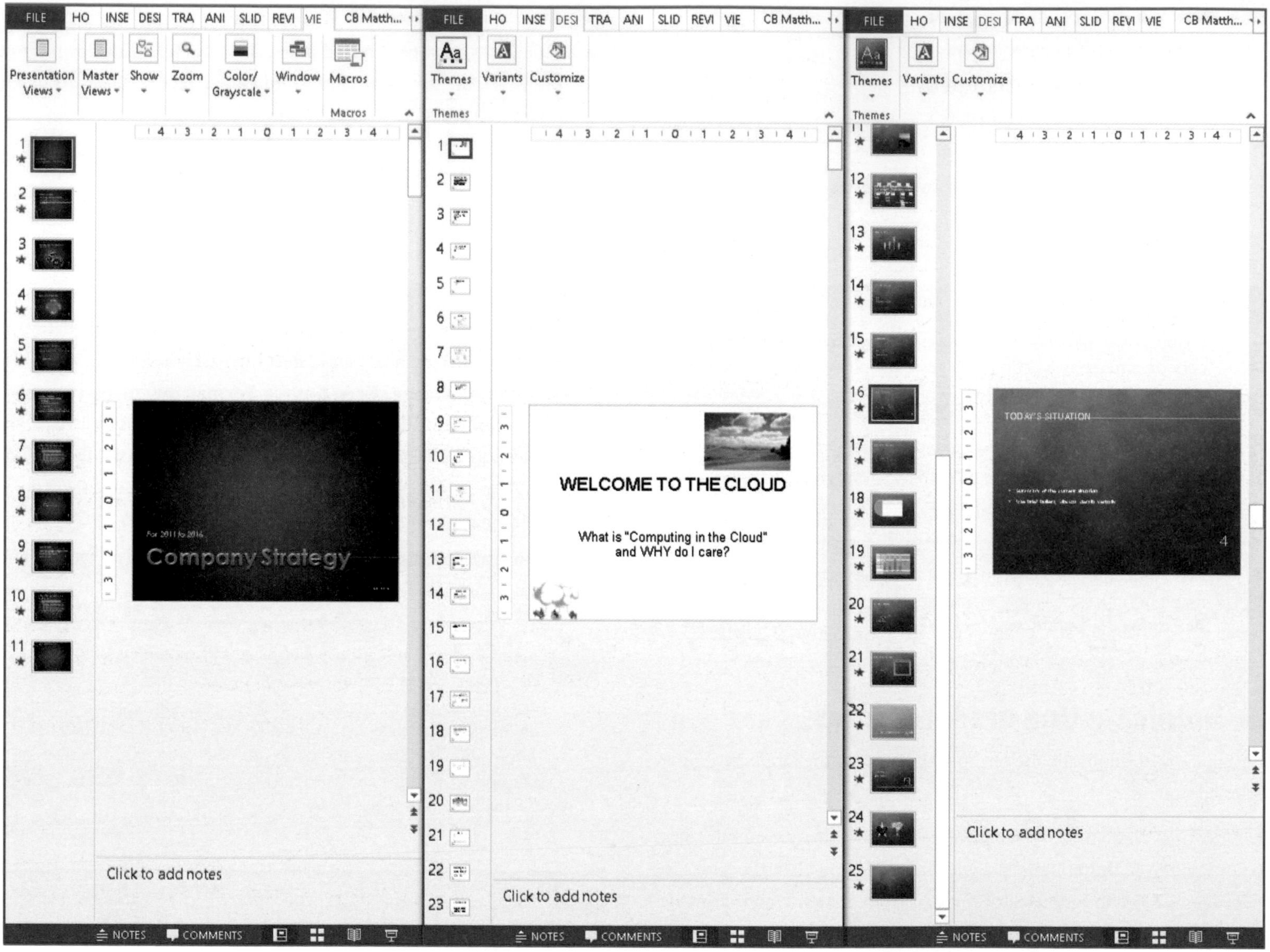

Figure 9-3: See each presentation window separately by using the Arrange All command.

Reviewing the Paste Options

In PowerPoint 2013, you have several options when pasting from one location to another:

- **Use Destination Theme**   The theme of the slide into which you are pasting will be applied to the object. The slide will "adopt" its new theme.

- **Keep Source Formatting**   The formatting of the object you copied will be kept, even when the destination formatting is different.

- **Picture**   The object you are moving into the new slide will be pasted as a picture instead of the text or other format from which you copied the object.

- **Keep Text Only**   The text will be moved without any of the other formatting of the object.

Copy a Design Using Browse

To copy just the design (and not the content) of a presentation, use the Browse feature of the Design Themes feature.

1. In Normal view, open the presentation to which you will apply the design of another presentation.

2. Click the **Design** tab, click the Themes group **More** down arrow and click **Browse For Themes**.

3. In the Choose Theme Or Themed Document dialog box that appears, find the document or presentation containing the theme you want to copy and click it.

4. Click **Apply**, and the theme will be copied to the original presentation.

Use Zoom

You can zoom in on or zoom out of a slide, which enables you to work at a very detailed level or back off to see the total slide, respectively.

- To control the zoom with a specific percentage, click the **View** tab, and click the **Zoom** button in the Zoom group. When the Zoom dialog box appears, shown next, click the radio button corresponding to the percentage you want displayed. Another option is to type a number in the Percent text box or click the up and down arrows in the **Percent** spinner. A smaller percentage will reduce the image; a larger percentage will increase it. Click **OK** when finished.

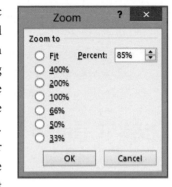

- To make the slide fit in the window, click the **View** tab, and then click the **Fit To Window** button in the Zoom group. The image will be reduced or increased in size to fit in the Presentation pane. If you are not in the View tab, a quicker way to do this is by clicking the **Fit Slide To Current Window** button on the right end of the taskbar.

- To increase or decrease the zoom effect with a slider, drag the **Zoom** slider on the right end of the status bar, or click the **Zoom In** (+) or **Zoom Out** (–) button on either side of the slider to zoom in or out in smaller increments. The percentage of the zoom shows to the right of the slider.

Use a Keyboard with Slides

If you are more comfortable using the keyboard than a mouse pointer, you have the following commands, and more. Some of the commands use a combination of pointer and keyboard commands, such as Copy. These are your options:

- To start a new presentation, press CTRL+N.

- To insert a new slide, press CTRL+M.

- To remove a slide, use the arrow keys to select the thumbnail you want (or click a thumbnail to select it), and press **DELETE** or press **CTRL+X**.

- To copy a slide, use the arrow keys to select the thumbnail you want (or click a thumbnail to select it), and press **CTRL+C**. Select the slide prior to the one you want to insert, and press **CTRL+V**.

CHANGE THE LOOK AND FEEL OF SLIDES

At some point or another, you will want to change the look and feel of slides in a presentation. Perhaps you will be using slides created from another presentation and will want the new presentation to be unique. Or maybe you'll need to tweak only a few components of the presentation. As this section describes, you can change the theme and variants (color, fonts, and special effects) of a presentation.

 Change a Theme

As you have seen in Chapter 8, you can select a built-in (or PowerPoint standard) theme for your slides. You can change these themes to fit your own presentation requirements. You can change a theme for a single slide or the whole presentation by altering the fonts, color, and design elements.

Change the Color of a Theme

You can change any single color element within a presentation or all of them. When you change the colors, the font styles and design elements remain the same.

1. With your presentation open, click the **Design** tab.

QuickFacts

Using Variants of Themes

As discussed in Chapter 8, you may choose to customize any of the predesigned themes within PowerPoint. While each theme's design contains colors, fonts, and other effects that complement your original choice, you may change any of the components on a single slide, on a group of slides, or on all slides in the presentation.

- Each theme consists of a set of four colors for text and background, six colors for accents, and two colors for hyperlinks.

- Each theme includes two fonts. The *body* font is used for general text entry, and the *heading* font is used for headings. The default font used in PowerPoint for a new presentation without a theme is Calibri for both headings and body text.

- Shapes, illustrations, pictures, and charts include graphic effects that are controlled by themes. Themed graphics are modulated in terms of their lines (borders), fills, and effects (such as shadowed, raised, and shaded). For example, some themes simply change an inserted rectangle's fill color, while other themes affect the color, the weight of its border, and whether it has a 3-D appearance.

- Background styles include gradients or solid fills. You can also use a picture, texture, or even a pattern as a background for one or more slides.

2. If you want to change the theme colors on only some of the slides, select those slides now. Use **CTRL**+click to select noncontiguous slides or use **SHIFT**+click to select contiguous slides.

3. Click the **More** down arrow in the Variants group, and choose **Colors**. The menu of color combinations will be displayed, as shown in Figure 9-4.

4. Run the pointer over the rows of color combinations to see which appeals to you.

5. When you find the one you want, right-click the row and click **Apply To All Slides** to change the colors throughout the whole presentation, or click **Apply To Selected Slides** to change just the slides you have chosen.

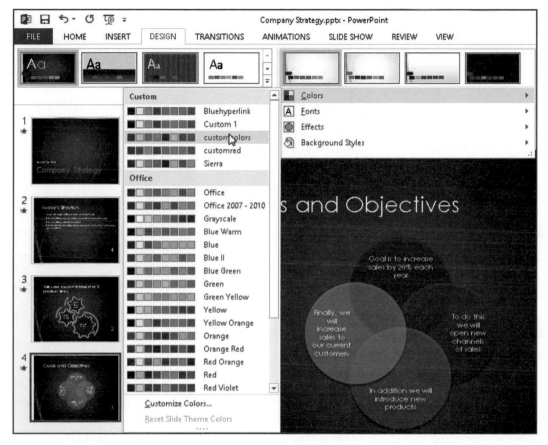

Figure 9-4: *The menu of color combinations offers alternatives for your theme colors.*

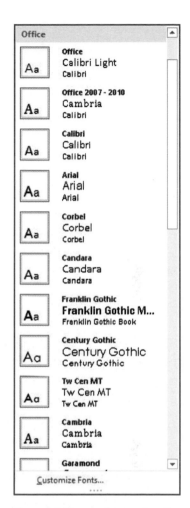

Figure 9-5: *You can choose a heading font or a body font from the fonts available in your Windows system.*

Change Theme Fonts

Once a theme is assigned to slides, the fonts may be different, but you can change them.

1. Click the **Design** tab.

2. Click the **More** down arrow in the Variants group, and click **Fonts**. The drop-down list displays a list of theme fonts, as shown in Figure 9-5.

3. Point to each font combination to see how the fonts appear on your presentation.

4. Click the font name combination on which you decide. If you click a font name combination, the font will replace both the body and heading fonts on all slides.

TIP You may have to drag your text placeholder to the right or left to see the effects of the fonts as you pass your pointer over them.

Create a New Theme Font

You may also decide that you want a unique set of fonts for your presentation. You can create a custom font set that is available in the list of fonts for your current and future presentations.

1. In the Design tab Variants group, click the **More** down arrow, and then click **Fonts**.

2. Click **Customize Fonts** at the bottom of the drop-down list.

3. In the Create New Theme Fonts dialog box, click the **Heading Font** and **Body Font** down arrow in turn to select a new fonts combination. View the new combination in the Sample area.

4. Type a new name for the font combination you've selected, and click **Save**. The name defaults to Custom 1 if you don't enter a new name. The newly created custom fonts are then available for selection at the top of the Variants group's Fonts drop-down list.

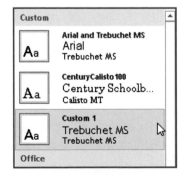

Change Themed Effects

You can change the appearance of any of the graphic objects you've inserted into your presentation, such as a chart, a SmartArt graphic, or a graphic shape.

1. Select the graphic object you wish to enhance with a modified effect.

2. In the Design tab Variants group, click the **More** down arrow. From the list that appears, click **Effects**. The drop-down list displays a gallery of effects combinations. If you have previously chosen effects for your presentation, the current effects combination is highlighted.

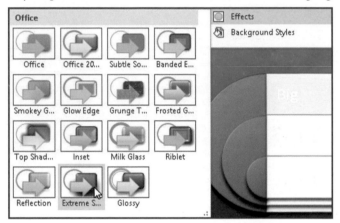

3. Point to each combination to see how the effects appear on your selected object, assuming you have a graphic or chart inserted on the slide (see Chapter 12 for information on inserting charts, graphics, and shapes).

4. Click the effects combination you want.

Change Background Styles

PowerPoint 2013 offers a number of ways you can change the background of a chosen theme.

1. In the Design tab Variants group, click the **More** down arrow. From the list that appears, click **Background Styles**. The drop-down list displays a gallery of background styles.

2. Click **Format Background** to open the Format Background pane. Choose the type of fill you want for your slides.

- **Solid Fill** fills the entire slide with the color you select in the **Color** drop-down box.

- Move the **Transparency** slider (or type a number in the corresponding text box, or click the spinner) to adjust how light or dark the chosen color will be (100% is totally transparent).

- **Gradient Fill** gives you several tools with which you can change how the color you choose fills the background, as shown in Figure 9-6.

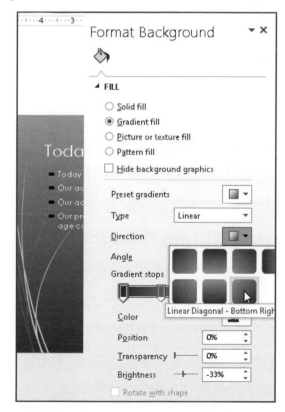

Figure 9-6: *Use background options to add interest to your slides.*

- **Picture Or Texture Fill** allows you to select a picture from a file on your computer, from the Clipboard, or from an online location, as shown in Figure 9-7.

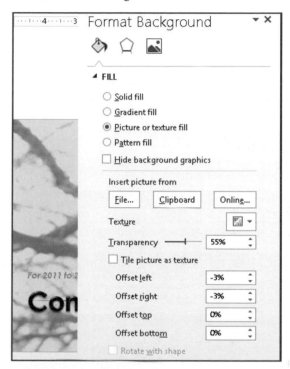

Figure 9-7: *You can choose pictures from several locations to use as backgrounds for your slides, altering the transparency according to your needs.*

- Click **Texture** (as shown in Figure 9-8) to choose from a number of textures. You can also set the transparency of your textures (or other elements) by moving the Transparency slider.

- **Pattern Fill** allows you to use a pattern as a background fill. You can choose from several Pattern options. Figure 9-9 shows some examples.

3. To hide background graphics, click the **Hide Background Graphics** check box.

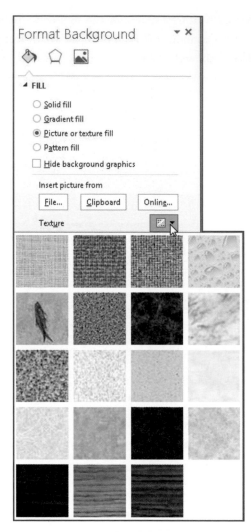

Figure 9-8: *Textures can be useful as backgrounds on your slides.*

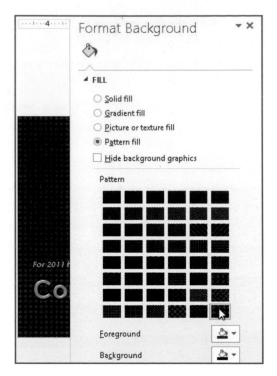

Figure 9-9: *Patterns can be used both in the foreground and background of your slides.*

Create a Custom Theme

You can create a new theme, save it, and use it in your presentations. You create a custom theme by selecting a group of text, background, accent, and hyperlink colors and giving the group a name. To save changes to a theme, in the Themes group, click the **More** down arrow, and click **Save Current Theme** after you have made changes to the background, color, font, and/or effects in the current theme. Give this new theme a name in the Save Custom Theme dialog box. Your altered theme is saved as a custom theme.

4. To have your settings apply to all slides in the presentation, click **Apply To All**. Otherwise, the settings will apply to just the current slide.

5. To erase your formatting settings and start over, click **Reset Background**.

Change Theme Colors

To customize the color scheme:

1. In the Design tab Variants group, click the **More** down arrow, and click **Colors**.

2. At the bottom of the menu of colors, click **Customize Colors**. The Create New Theme Colors dialog box will appear, as shown in Figure 9-10.

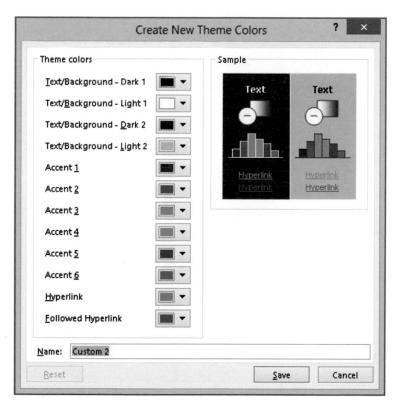

Figure 9-10: *The Create New Theme Colors dialog box allows you to create new theme colors to use in presentations.*

3. To select a color for one of the color groups, click the down arrow for the Text/Background, Accent, and/or Hyperlink group, and click the color you want to test. It will be displayed in the Sample pane.

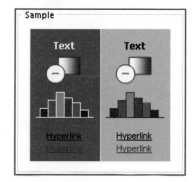

4. Go through each set of colors that you want to change.

5. When you find a group of colors that you like, type a name in the Name text box, and click **Save**.

> **TIP** To restore the original colors in the Create New Theme Colors dialog box Sample pane and start over, click **Reset**.

Use Custom Colors

Using a similar technique to creating your own themes, you can create your own unique color mix for text, background, accents, and hyperlinks. Here is how you work with custom colors:

1. Select the slides to be affected with the new colors, whether all of them or a selected few.

2. In the Design tab Variants group, click the **More** down arrow, and click **Colors**. At the bottom of the rows of color combinations, click **Customize Colors** to open the Create New Theme Colors dialog box (see Figure 9-10).

3. Click the theme color group that you want to work with. The Theme Colors submenu will be displayed. Click **More Colors**.

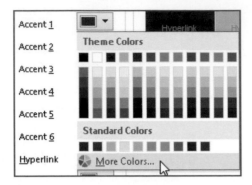

4. In the Colors dialog box that opens, you have two options:

   • Click the **Standard** tab to see the dialog box shown in Figure 9-11. Click the color unit you want to see it displayed in the New preview pane. When you want to see it in the Sample pane, click **OK**.

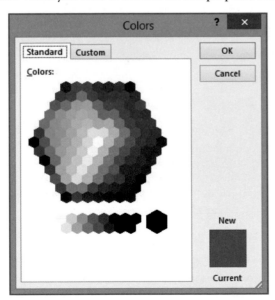

Figure 9-11: You can change the color precisely by clicking the specific color shade you want.

• Click the **Custom** tab to see the dialog box shown in Figure 9-12. Click somewhere on the color rainbow to get the approximate color. Then drag the slider to the right to get precisely the color you want. You will see it displayed in the New preview pane.

–Or–

• In the Custom tab you can also click the **Red**, **Green**, or **Blue** spinners (or enter values into the text boxes) to get the precise color mix you want. RGB (Red, Green, Blue color standard) is the default setting in the Color Model drop-down list box, but you can also select HSL (Hue, Saturation, and Luminosity color standard). When you are finished, click **OK**.

5. When you get the colors you want, type a name in the Name text box, and click **Save** to create a custom theme color.

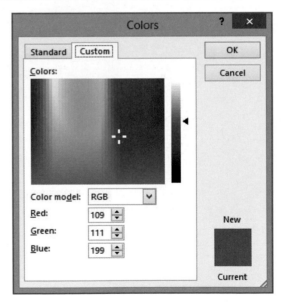

Figure 9-12: You can create unique colors by "mixing" the combination of red, green, and blue.

Copy Attributes with the Format Painter

The Format Painter can be used to copy all attributes (such as fonts, alignment, bullet styles, and color) from one slide to another as well as from one presentation to another.

1. Display the source slides in the Normal view's Slides pane or in Slide Sorter view.

2. Find and click the source slide containing the color to be copied.

3. Click the **Home** tab. Click **Format Painter** in the Clipboard group once to copy the source format to one slide. If you want to use the source slide to reformat several slides, double-click **Format Painter** to turn it on until you click it again (or press **ESC**) to turn it off.

4. Find the destination slide, in the same or a different presentation, and click it to receive the new attributes.

5. If you are copying the source attributes to multiple slides, continue to find the destination slides and click them.

6. When you are finished, click **Format Painter** or press **ESC** to turn it off.

> **TIP** If you want to copy the formatting of more than one text selection, double-click **Format Painter** to turn it on. You can then copy multiple text selections, one after the other. To turn it off, click **Format Painter** again or press **ESC**.

 ## Work with Hyperlinks

Inserting hyperlinks in a presentation allows you to link to other files or presentations, to a website, to an e-mail address, or to another slide within the current presentation.

 > **NOTE** Hyperlinks work only in the Slide Show view.

Insert a Hyperlink

To insert a hyperlink in your presentation:

1. On your slide, select the text that you want to contain the hyperlink.

2. In the Insert tab Links group, click **Hyperlink**.

3. In the Insert Hyperlink dialog box, find the destination for the link.

   - If the destination is within the presentation outline itself, click **Place In This Document**, and click the slide, as shown in Figure 9-13.

   - If the destination is on an existing document or web page, click **Existing File Or Web Page**, and follow the prompts to the destination.

   - If you need to create a new document for the hyperlink to point to, click **Create New Document**, and proceed as prompted.

   - If you want to place a hyperlink to an e-mail address, click **E-mail Address**.

4. Click **OK**.

> **TIP** To change the color of a hyperlink, refer to "Change Theme Colors" earlier in this chapter. In the Create New Theme Colors dialog box (shown in Figure 9-10), select the Hyperlink or Followed Hyperlink set and choose a color as described. Save the new color set.

Remove a Hyperlink

To remove a hyperlink from text or an object:

1. Right-click the text or object containing the hyperlink.

2. Select **Remove Hyperlink** from the context menu.

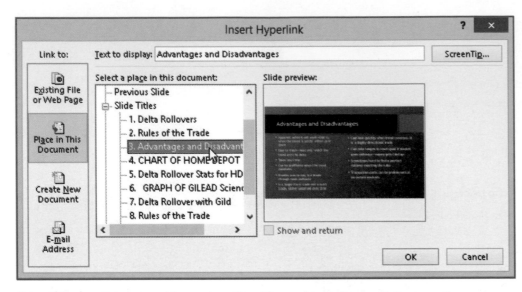

Figure 9-13: *Hyperlinks can provide a means to "jump" from one part of a presentation to another.*

3. In the Header And Footer dialog box, click the **Slide** tab (if it's not already displayed).

4. Select the **Footer** check box.

5. In the Footer text box, type the text for the footer.

6. If you do not want the footer to be displayed on the title slide, click the **Don't Show On Title Slide** check box.

7. When you have finished making your selections, described next, click **Apply** to apply the footer to selected slides only, or click **Apply To All** to apply the footer to all slides.

Use Footers on Slides

Footers can be useful for displaying company information for the presentation, such as a copyright or confidential notices. (Headers are available for notes and handouts only.) To work with any aspect of footers, you need to display the Header And Footer dialog box (shown in Figure 9-14). To display this dialog box and create a footer, follow these steps:

1. If you want only some of the slides to have this footer, select those slides. If you want to apply the footer to all slides, you don't need to select them.

2. In the Insert tab Text group, click **Header & Footer**.

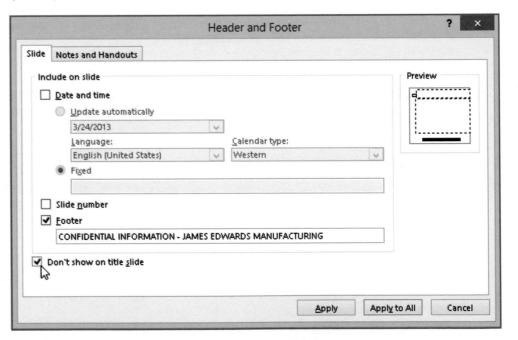

Figure 9-14: *You can add footers to selected slides or to the whole presentation.*

Display Time or Date

To display the time or date in your footer, open the Header And Footer dialog box, as described previously, and then click the **Date And Time** check box.

- To apply a time or date that reflects the actual time or date, click **Update Automatically**. From the drop-down list box, click the date only, time only, or time and date format you prefer.

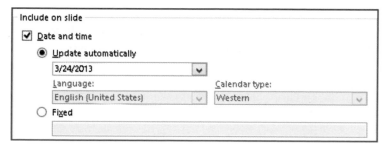

- To apply a fixed time or date, or other text, click **Fixed**. In the Fixed text box, type the text that will always appear in the footer.

 TIP To display slide numbers on the slides, in the Header and Footer dialog box, click the **Slide Number** check box.

Remove Footers

To remove footers, in the Header And Footer dialog box:

1. Clear the Date And Time, Slide Number, and Footer check boxes.
2. To remove the footer for selected slides, click **Apply**.

   –Or–

   To remove the footer for all slides, click **Apply To All**.

WORK WITH TEXT

Entering and manipulating text is a major part of building a presentation. Text is not only titles and bulleted lists. It is also captions on a picture or a legend or labels on a chart. Text can be inside a shape or curved around it on the outside. Text communicates in a thousand ways. Here is how you work with text in PowerPoint.

Use a Text Layout

When you create a new blank slide, you must choose whether to use an existing layout that Microsoft provides or to create your own layout. See "Choose a Slide Layout" in Chapter 8 for more details.

1. In Normal view, click the slide immediately preceding the one you want to insert.
2. Click the **Home** tab, and click the **New Slide** down arrow.
3. Look at the placement of text, titles, and content in the various layouts.
4. Click the layout you want. To create your own layout, click the **Blank** layout
5. Click within the title or text placeholders to begin entering text.

Insert a New Text Box

Office programs, including PowerPoint, use text placeholders to contain text. Text placeholders are text boxes that contain text and other objects. Text boxes can be moved or rotated. As discussed in the previous section and in Chapter 8, text boxes are already included in the various layouts provided by Microsoft (other than the Blank layout), but you can also insert new text boxes. Even when you use a predefined layout that Microsoft provides, you will find times when you want to insert a new text box.

1. Display the slide within which you will place the text box.
2. In the Insert tab Text group, click **Text Box**. The pointer first turns into a line pointer.
3. Place the pointer where you want to locate the text box, click and hold until the pointer morphs into a crosshair shape, and then drag the pointer to create a new text box. Don't worry about where the

9

box is located; you can drag it to a precise location later. When you release the pointer, the insertion point within the text box indicates that you can begin to type text.

4. Type the text you want.

5. When you are finished, click outside the text box.

 NOTE The border of a placeholder indicates what you can do with the placeholder. If the border is dashed, the text area is selected and you can enter or edit text. If the border is solid, the placeholder itself is selected and can be moved or manipulated. You can change the solid border to dashed by moving the pointer inside and clicking the text, or by clicking outside the text box and then clicking the text to select it again.

✅ QuickFacts

Changing Font Attributes

You can change font attributes for text as follows:

- On one slide only, by changing the text directly on an individual text character
- On only one type of slide, by changing a slide layout
- Throughout all slides, by changing the font or character in the master slide (see "Edit a Slide Master" in Chapter 10)

The following font commands are found in the Font group of the Home tab. (When you select text, a mini toolbar appears with additional commands available. See "Use the Mini Toolbar" in Chapter 1.) Hover your mouse over each item in the Font group, shown in Figure 9-15, to see the command's name. Select the text that is to receive the formatting, and then use the commands to change text attributes.

- **Font** Changes the font typeface.
- **Font Size** Changes the point size of fonts.
- **Increase Font Size** Increases the point size in increments.
- **Decrease Font Size** Decreases the point size in increments.

- **Clear All Formatting** Removes all formatting from a selection and retains only plain text.
- **Bold** Applies boldface to selected text.
- **Italic** Applies italics to selected text.
- **Underline** Applies an underline to selected text.
- **Text Shadow** Applies a shadow effect to selected text.
- **Strikethrough** Applies a strikethrough to selected text.
- **Change Character Spacing** Increases or decreases the space between the characters of a word. Choose Very Tight, Tight, Normal, Loose, Very Loose, or More Spacing—where you can set specific points between characters and set *kerning*, a more sophisticated method of setting the space between characters.
- **Change Case** Changes the case of a word between several alternatives: Sentence Case, lowercase, UPPERCASE, Capitalize Each Word, and tOGGLE cASE.
- **Font Color** Changes the color of the font.
- **Font dialog box launcher** Opens a dialog box in which you can make character changes.

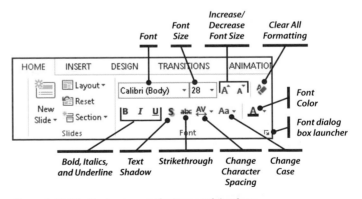

Figure 9-15: The Font group on the Home tab is where you'll access most of the character attributes you need when working with text.

Change Regular Text to WordArt Styles

You can change the text to WordArt styles. When you double-click a text or title placeholder, the Drawing Tools Format tab, where WordArt styles are found, becomes available, but it is not activated until you click the tab. So when you want to access a tool from the Drawing Tools Format tab, you first need to click the tab.

1. Select the text to be converted to WordArt.

2. In the Drawing Tools, Format tab, click the **WordArt Quick Styles** button in the WordArt Styles group. You will see a gallery of the WordArt styles that can be applied to selected placeholders or text.

3. Click the WordArt Style you want.

 # Work with Text Boxes

You work with text and text boxes by typing text into a text box, moving or copying the text box, resizing the text box, positioning the text box, deleting it, rotating it, filling it with color, and more.

 TIP As you type and the text reaches the edges of the text box, the words will wrap around to the next line, causing the text box to expand vertically so that the text fits. You can then drag the sizing handles to the shape you want. Drag left or right to change the width of the text box. Drag up or down to change the height of the text box.

Enter Text into a Text Box

To enter text into a text box, simply click inside the text box; the insertion point will appear in the text box, indicating that you can now type text. Begin to type.

Move a Text Box

To move a text box, you drag the border of the placeholder.

1. Click the text within a text box to display the text box outline.

2. Place the pointer over the border of the text box and between the handles. The pointer will become a four-headed arrow.

3. Click and drag the text box to where you want to place it, and release the mouse button.

Resize a Placeholder

To resize a placeholder, you drag the sizing handles of the text box.

1. Click the text to display the text box border.

2. Place the pointer on the border over a sizing handle so that it becomes a two-headed arrow.

3. Drag the sizing handle in the direction you want the text box expanded or reduced. As you drag, the pointer will morph into a crosshair.

Delete a Text Box

To delete a text box:

1. Click the text within the text box to display the border.

2. Click the border of the text box again to select the text box, not the text (the insertion point will disappear and the border will be solid).

3. Press **DELETE**.

Copy a Text Box

To copy a text box with its contents and drag it to another part of the slide:

1. Click the text within the text box.

2. Place the pointer on the border of the text box (not over the handles), where it becomes a four-headed arrow.

3. Drag the text box while pressing **CTRL**.

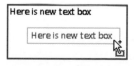

Rotate a Text Box

When you first insert a text box (or click it to select it), a green rotate handle appears above it, allowing you to rotate the box in a circle.

1. Place the pointer over the rotate handle.

2. Drag it in the direction in which you want to rotate the text box.

3. Click outside the text box to "set" the rotation.

> **TIP** To rotate a text box or object that doesn't have a rotate handle, select the text box, and click the **Drawing Tools Format** tab. Click the **Rotate** down arrow in the Arrange group. As you point at the various options in the context menu, you'll see the effects of the selected object. To see a dialog box so you can enter more precise measurements, click **More Rotation Options**.

Position a Text Box Precisely

To set the position of a text box precisely on a slide:

1. Click the text box to select it. A Drawing Tools Format tab will appear.

2. Click the **Format** tab, and in the Arrange group, click **Rotate** and then click **More Rotation Options**. The Format Shape task pane appears with the Size option selected.

3. Click the **Size & Properties** icon and then click the **Position** option.

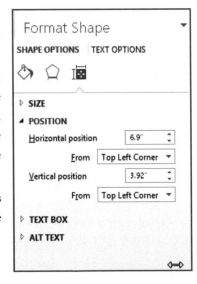

4. Click the **Horizontal Position** or **Vertical Position** spinner to enter the exact measurements, in inches, of the text box. Click the drop-down list boxes to select the originating location of the text box between the upper-left corner and the center.

5. Click **Close**.

Change the Fill Color in a Text Box

To change the background color of a text box, you use the Drawing Tools Format Shape dialog box.

1. Right-click the text box, and click **Format Shape** from the context menu. The Format Shape task pane appears.

2. Click the **Fill & Line** icon [icon], click **Fill**, and then select the type of fill you want to see. A group of options will appear, depending on your choice.

3. Click the **Preset Gradients**, **Color**, or another drop-down list box to select a color. Set other attributes as you wish, as illustrated in Figure 9-16.

4. When finished, click **Close**.

> **TIP** If none of the colors is exactly right, click the **Color** down arrow, click **More Colors**, and click the **Custom** tab. Click a color unit to select it. In the preview box, you can see the new color compared to the current color. Click **OK** and then click **Close**.

Set Paragraph and Tab Settings

To change the default paragraph spacing and tab settings, you can use the Paragraph dialog box, as shown in Figure 9-17.

1. Click the paragraph text that you want to change in a placeholder or text box. Click the **Home** tab, and click the **dialog box launcher** in the lower-right corner of the Paragraph group.

–Or–

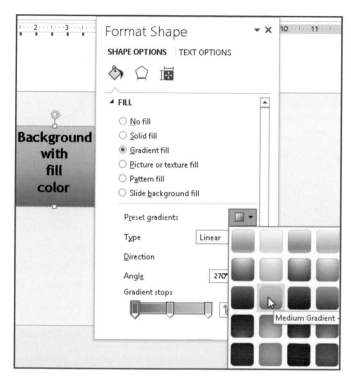

Figure 9-16: *You have several options for changing the background of your text box.*

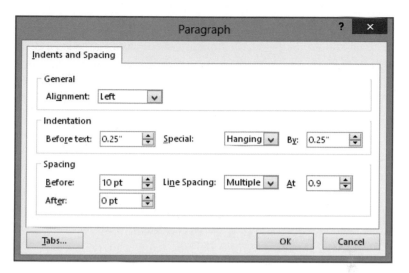

Figure 9-17: *The Paragraph dialog box allows you to change paragraph and tab settings.*

Right-click the paragraph text that you want to change in a placeholder or text box, and click **Paragraph** from the context menu. The Paragraph dialog box appears.

2. Configure the settings as required.

- **Set the general positioning**. Click the **Alignment** down arrow, and then click Left, Centered, Right, Justified, or Distributed (which forces even short lines to be justified to the end of the line), depending on how you want the text aligned.

- **Set the indentation**. Click the **Before Text** spinner to set the spacing before the text begins on a first line; click the **Special** down arrow to allow for hanging indents, an indented first line, or no indents.

- **Set the spacing**. Click the **Before** spinner to set spacing before the line starts (in points); click the **Line Spacing** down arrow, and click Single, Double, 1.5, Exactly (where you set the exact spacing in points in the At box), or Multiple (where you enter the number of lines to space in the At box).

- **Set tabs**. Click the **Tabs** button to set tabs precisely in the Tabs dialog box. Click the **Tab Stop Position** spinner to set the tab stop, and then click **Set**. Repeat as needed. Click **OK**.

3. Click **OK**.

 Use Lists

Lists allow you to put order into your presentation, and make text easier to read and comprehend. Lists can be either numbered or bulleted. You can choose the shapes of bullets, change the style of numbering, and use SmartArt (see "Spiff Up Your Presentation with SmartArt") for your lists.

Create a Numbered List or Bulleted List

You can choose the type of list option either before you enter text in the text box or afterward. After you click in the text box, you have the following options for creating a bulleted list or numbered list:

- **Create a bulleted list before you begin typing your list items** Click in a text box. Then before typing, in the Home tab Paragraph group, click the **Bullets** icon. A small bullet appears at your insertion point. Type your first list item and then press ENTER. The next line begins with a bullet. Type your second list item, press ENTER, type your third list item ... and so on until your list is complete. If you need to enter nonbulleted text after the last bullet item, press ENTER, press BACKSPACE to remove the bullet, and begin typing.

> **TIP** If you want a different type of bullet, click the down arrow rather than the Bullets icon itself. Then click the icon you'd prefer to use as a bullet.

- **Create a bulleted list after you begin typing your list items** When you are finished typing your list, or at any point in the creation of the list, select all the list text and click the **Bullets** icon in the Paragraph group. The group is redisplayed with a bullet preceding each item in the list, as shown next. If you want to continue the list, click the end of the last bullet item, press ENTER, and a new bullet will appear on the next line. If you need to enter nonbulleted text after the bulleted list, press ENTER, press BACKSPACE to remove the bullet, and begin typing.

Bulleted List
- First item
- Second item
- Third item
- Fourth item

- **Create a numbered list before you begin typing your list items** Click in a text box. Then before typing, in the Home tab Paragraph group, click the **Numbering** icon. The first number will appear at your insertion point. Type your first list item and then

press ENTER. The next line begins with the next number. Type your second list item, press ENTER, type your third list item ... and so on until your list is complete. If you need to enter unnumbered text after the last numbered item, press ENTER, press BACKSPACE to remove the number, and begin typing.

> **TIP** If you want a different type of numbering system, such as Roman numerals or alphabetic letters, click the down arrow rather than the icon itself. Then click the numbering system you'd prefer to use for your numbered list.

- **Create a numbered list after you begin typing your list items** When you are finished typing your list, or at any point in the creation of the list, select all the list text and click the **Numbering** icon in the Paragraph group. The group is redisplayed with a numbered sequence, as shown next. If you want to continue the list, click the end of the last numbered item, press ENTER, and a new number will appear on the next line. If you need to enter unnumbered text after the numbered list, press ENTER, press BACKSPACE to remove the number, and begin typing.

Numbered List
1. First item
2. Second item
3. Third item
4. Fourth item

Change Bullet Shapes or Numbered Lists Appearance

To change bullet shapes, see the "Change the Master Slide Bullet Style," "Use a Picture as a Bullet," and "Change the Appearance of a Numbered List" sections in Chapter 10.

⤵ Use the Font Dialog Box

To set multiple font and character attributes at once or to set the standard for a slide, using the Font dialog box is easier than using individual buttons. (See the "Changing Font Attributes" QuickFacts earlier in this chapter.)

1. Select the text to be changed.

2. Click the **Home** tab, and click the **dialog box launcher** in the lower-right corner of the Font group. The Font dialog box will appear, as shown in Figure 9-18.

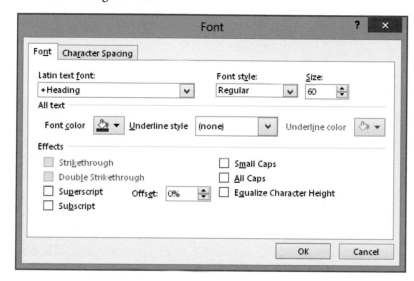

Figure 9-18: *Using the Font dialog box, you can change all occurrences of certain fonts within selected text.*

3. Click the **Latin Text Font** down arrow, and select the type of text (Heading or Body) or font name. This establishes how the selected text will be changed.

4. Choose the options you want, such as font style, size, color, and effects, and click **OK**.

 **Align Text**

PowerPoint 2013 lets you align text in several ways: horizontally on a line, vertically on a page, or distributed horizontally or vertically. This section describes how to use these text-alignment techniques.

Align Text on a Line

You align text by centering it (placing text in the center of the horizontal margins), left-justifying it, right-justifying it, or justifying it (where the

Moving or Copying Text

There are at least four ways you can move text (the option to copy text rather than move it, where applicable, is shown in parentheses):

● **Use keypresses** Select the text you want to move, and press **CTRL+X** (**CTRL+C**) to "cut" (copy) the text to the Clipboard. Position your insertion point where you want to insert the text, and press **CTRL+V** to paste your text at the new location.

● **Use the ribbon** Select the text you want to move, and click **Cut** (**Copy**) in the Clipboard group of the Home tab. Click where you want to locate the text, and click **Paste** in the Clipboard group.

● **Use the context menu** With your right-mouse key held down, select the text you want to move, and click **Cut** (**Copy**) from the context menu. Place your insertion point in the new location for the text, right-click to open the context menu, and click one of the **Paste** options.

● **Use drag and drop** Select the text you want to move. Click the selected text and drag it to the new location. When the insertion point is in the correct location, release the pointer. You can use this technique to move text within the same text box, to another text box, or to other slides. However, you can move text to other slides only in Outline View.

left and right edges are equal). All four options are available in the Home tab Paragraph group.

1. Select the text to be aligned, and click the **Home** tab.

2. From the Paragraph group, choose one of these options:

● To left-align text, click the **Align Left** button.

● To right-align text, click the **Align Right** button.

● To justify text, click the **Justify** button.

● To center text, click the **Center** button.

Align Text Vertically in a Placeholder

To align text with the top, middle, or bottom of a text box or placeholder, click the **Align Text** button in the Home tab Paragraph group, and click your choice in the menu. Click **More Options** at the bottom of the menu to open a Format Shape task pane with a Text Options tab to precisely specify measurements.

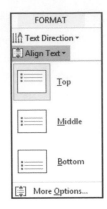

Align Text to the Slide

You can align a placeholder or text box horizontally or vertically on a slide—that is, the spacing on the top and bottom will be equal or the spacing from the left and right edges of the slide will be distributed evenly.

1. Click the placeholder or text box to select it.

2. From the Drawing Tools Format tab, click the **Align** button in the Arrange group. A menu will appear.

3. Click one of these options:

   - Click **Distribute Horizontally** to align the object horizontally on the slide.

   - Click **Distribute Vertically** to align the object vertically on the slide.

Turn Off AutoFit

AutoFit is used to force text to fit within a text box. It often resizes text to make it fit, which you may not want it to do. AutoFit is turned on by default. To turn it off:

1. Click the **File** tab, click **Options**, and then click **Proofing**.

2. Under AutoCorrect Options, click **AutoCorrect Options**. The AutoCorrect dialog box appears.

3. Click the **AutoFormat As You Type** tab.

4. Under the Apply As You Type section, choose these options:

   - To remove the AutoFit feature for titles, clear the **AutoFit Title Text To Placeholder** check box.

   - To remove the AutoFit feature for body text, clear the **AutoFit Body Text To Placeholder** check box.

5. Click **OK** twice.

⟫ Spiff Up Your Presentation with SmartArt

SmartArt adds professional-looking graphics to your lists, charts, and graphic representations. Figure 9-19 shows all the graphic possibilities: lists, processes, cycles, hierarchies, relationships, matrixes, pyramids, and pictures. For instance, if you want to portray an organizational chart, the Hierarchy category would be the most likely place to look for options. If you are describing a circular relationship, where one process leads to the next, the Cycle category would be your best option. How you use SmartArt really depends on the type of information you're trying to explain in your presentation. The examples in this section explain how to work with cycles, but all the SmartArt options are similar in how you use them.

Use SmartArt for New Lists

To make a list artistic and professional looking, you can choose some of the SmartArt options offered by PowerPoint 2013. These dramatically change the look and feel of lists. To apply these options:

1. Click the slide on which you want to use the SmartArt.

2. In the Insert tab Illustrations group, click **Smart Art**.

3. In the Choose A SmartArt Graphic dialog box, shown in Figure 9-19, choose one of the categories of graphics on the left.

4. To see any of the graphics in the middle pane displayed in the Preview pane on the right, with a description below it, click the graphic.

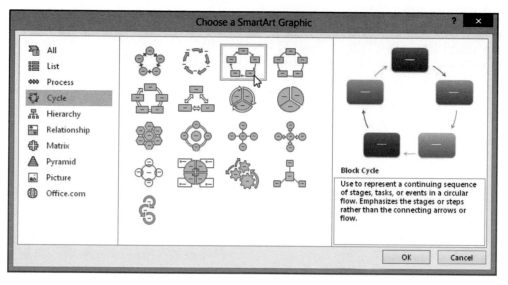

*Figure 9-19: **There are many types of SmartArt graphics available for your use.***

5. When you find a graphic you want to try out in your slide, click **OK**, and you will see the SmartArt effect on the slide plus a text box enabling you to enter the text into the list, as displayed in Figure 9-20.

6. The SmartArt Tools appear on the selected slide.

7. Type your text into the text box, and it appears in the SmartArt object. You may type either directly into the text box or in the text area to the left of the graphic.

8. Drag the shape to resize it.

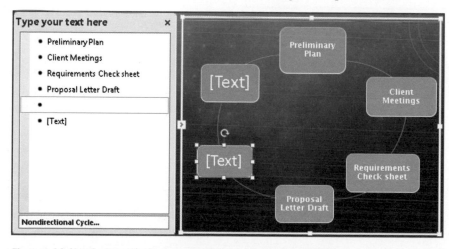

*Figure 9-20: **Use the SmartArt tools to create dramatic lists on your slides.***

TIP To hide or show the text area to the left of the SmartArt object, click the small arrow to the left of the selected object.

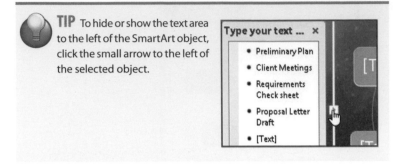

Use SmartArt on Existing Lists

To use SmartArt on an existing list:

1. Select the list you want to convert.

2. Right-click the selected area and choose **Convert To Smart Art**.

3. Mouse over the SmartArt options and then click the one you want to use, as shown in Figure 9-21.

4. After you have made all of your changes, click outside the text box to save your changes.

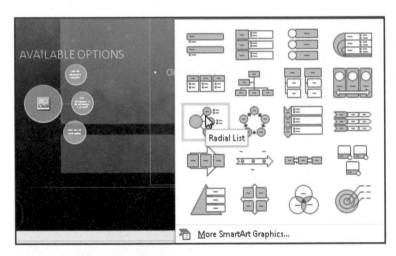

Figure 9-21: SmartArt effects can make your existing lists look more professional.

Use the SmartArt Design Tab Tools

When you click a SmartArt object, the SmartArt Tools tabs appear. The Design tab, shown in Figure 9-22, allows you to make changes to graphics, layouts, and SmartArt styles, and allows you to reset or convert SmartArt to and from normal text.

The Create Graphic group allows you to do the following:

- Add an additional shape or a bullet in your list. You may choose to have the shape (or bullet) added either before or after the current position of your mouse pointer.

- Click **Text Pane** to toggle the display of the text pane in your list.

- Demote or promote selected items on your list.

- Switch the flow of your list (if it is in a circular pattern) from right to left or from left to right.

- Move chosen list items up or down in the list.

Use the Layouts group to change your SmartArt design. (What you see in the Layouts and SmartArt Styles groups depends on the SmartArt option you're using.) The Layouts group allows you to change the layout of your list to another SmartArt option within the same category (from one type of organizational chart to another, for instance).

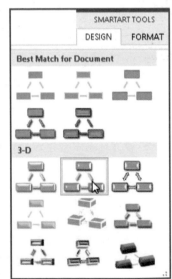

From the SmartArt Styles group, you can change the colors and style of your SmartArt. It offers enhanced effects, such as embossing, 3-D, and rotations.

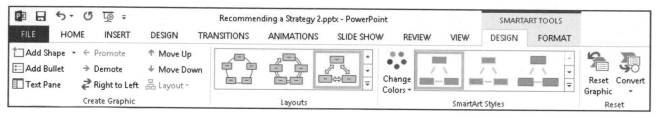

Figure 9-22: *Use the SmartArt Design tab to modify your SmartArt selections.*

You can use the Reset group to do the following:

- Reset your existing SmartArt to its original colors and shapes
- Convert your SmartArt to text or shapes

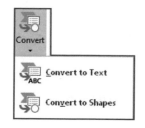

Use the SmartArt Format Tab Tools

The SmartArt Tools Format tab is used to modify the shape or color of the individual elements in your SmartArt object, or its text. Figure 9-23 shows the SmartArt Tools Format tab, which has the following groups:

- **Shapes** Enables you to make a shape larger or smaller by increments, change the shape to something else, or edit it in 2-D (only some SmartArt objects allow this).

- **Shape Styles** Enables you to change the shape to something different, but in the same category. For instance, you can make a rectangle have sharp corners or rounded corners, make it squarer in shape or oblong, fill it with any of various colors, or give it borders.

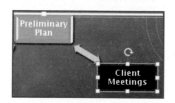

- **WordArt Styles** Enables you to make text more artistic, make it more colorful, give it an outline, fill it with pictures, gradient color, or textures, or give it special effects such as shadows, glows, bevels, or more.

- **Arrange** Enables you to select elements in the SmartArt object and rearrange them, rotate them, align them, or combine them so that they can be formatted as a group instead of individually.

- **Size** Enables you to precisely change the size of elements within the SmartArt object.

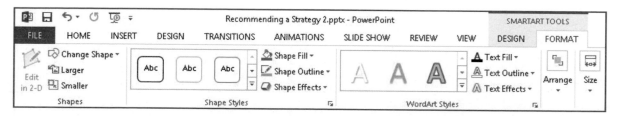

Figure 9-23: *The SmartArt Tools Format tab allows you to change elements of the SmartArt object, such as a shape or text color.*

USE TRANSITIONS AND ANIMATIONS

Today, with the tools and features available in PowerPoint, there's no excuse for delivering a presentation that is a static and undramatic listing of facts on slides that abruptly turn on and off one at a time. Instead, through the use of transitions, your slides should drift in, fly in, fade in, or appear in any of a number of other interesting ways. And, through animations, you can display the contents of your slides in colorful and surprising ways, such as by adding lines one at a time, having lines or other objects fly in from any direction, or grow and shrink for emphasis and attention-getting techniques. No longer must audiences endure the boring and staid presentations of the past; transitions and animations now add life to them.

⟫ Work with Transitions

Transitions work with the effects between slides. When you advance from one slide to the next, you can create special visual and sound effects. You can initiate the slide transition either by a mouse click or via timing. Before you give a presentation, you'll need to choose whether you want to control the slide movement yourself or make it a timed slide show.

The transition effect occurs when you exit one slide and enter another. You set the transition on the second slide, the entry one. So, for example, if your transition is from slide 4 to 5, place the transition effect in slide 5.

1. Click the slide that will receive the transition effect, and click the **Transitions** tab.

2. In the **Transition To This Slide** group, click the **More** down arrow. A list of all transitions opens, as shown in Figure 9-24.

3. Click an effect to see how it is manifested in your slide show. If you don't like the effect, you can easily change it to another one. You then have these options:

- Click **Effect Options** to see how the transition you have chosen can be altered. The options on this menu will differ depending on the transition. In this instance, the Clock transition can have the effect by Clockwise, Counterclockwise, or Wedge (sweeps down from "noon" in both directions).

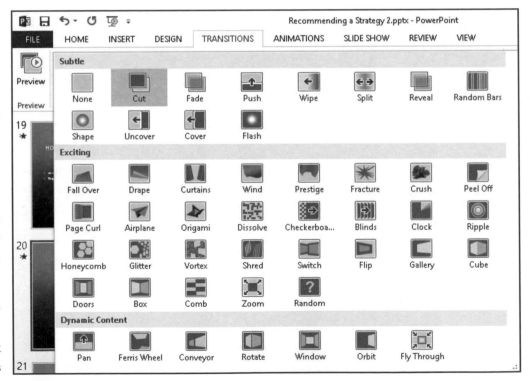

Figure 9-24: Transition effects between slides add interest and predictability to your presentation.

- Choose whether the transition will have a sound effect as well as a visual one. In the Timing group, click the **Sound** drop-down list box and choose a sound. Click **Preview** to listen to it. Repeat this process until you find one you like.

- Click the **Duration** spinner to set how long the transition takes. You'll want to experiment with this—if it's too short, it can be jarring to the audience, and if it's too slow, the audience will go to sleep.

- Click **Apply To All** if you want the transition, visual and sound, to be applied to all slides in the presentation.

- If you want the slide to advance at your prompting, check the **On Mouse Click** check box. You would choose this if you intend to explain each slide as it is displayed in your presentation.

- If you want the slides to advance according to a preset time, check the **After** check box and then click the spinner to set the time. You would choose this for a "canned" presentation to be shown without a presenter, for instance.

4. Click **Preview** to see the total transition.

NOTE You'll need to edit your transitions and animations. Use the Slide Show icon in the taskbar at the bottom of the window to see how the transitions and animations flow from slide to slide. Click the beginning slide from which to start, and then click **Slide Show**. Is the timing right? Are the sounds and actions in sync? Is it pleasing to the eye and ear?

Add Animations to Your Slides

Animations are used to give your slides life and action. They add movement and "color" to content. You can use animations to move from one line item on your slide to the next. Perhaps you want to talk about item two before displaying item three. Animation allows you to do this. You can emphasize items with color or movement when you want them to display.

To animate items on a slide, you use the Animations tab, shown in Figure 9-25, to select the item, select the animation, and then move to the next item, continuing until you have added animations to all items that you want to be animated in the slide. To do this, you'll need to have some idea of the impact you're trying to make. For instance, do you want lines on your presentation to fly in from the top, one at a time, when you click your mouse? The animations you choose usually should be mostly the same from slide to slide, so that that your presentation is consistent and the animation doesn't distract your audience from the message.

Here is how you add animation to your slides:

1. Click the slide that is going to receive the animation, and click the **Animations** tab.

2. Click **Animation Pane** in the Advanced Animation group to open the Animation Pane, shown in Figure 9-26, so that you can see what happens as you add and remove animations.

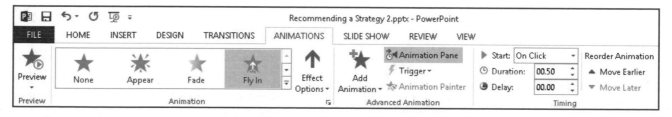

Figure 9-25: *On the Animations tab, select animations to make your slides come alive with motion and sound.*

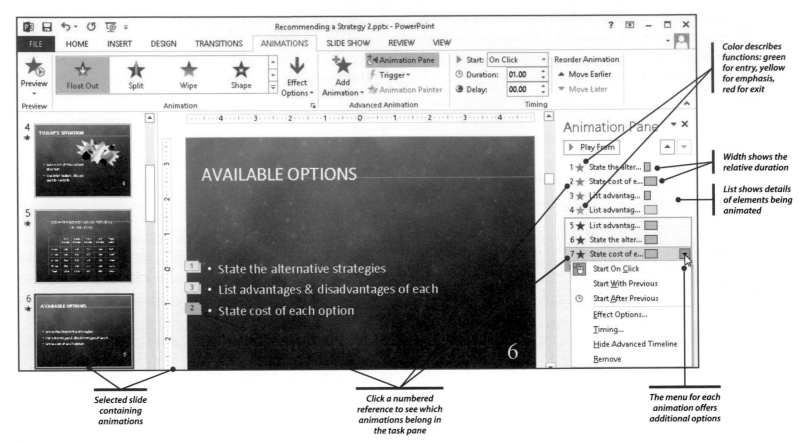

Figure 9-26: *You can see your animations listed on the slide and in the Animation Pane.*

3. Select the element to receive the animation. It could be one line on a page or several lines. It could be a picture or a graph.

4. In the Animation group, click an animation effect. You'll see it activate. Click **Preview** in the Preview group to repeat it. You'll have these options:

   - Click the **Effect Options** down arrow in the Animation group to see options for the item being animated. The options will differ depending on which animation you have chosen. For example,

the options might enable you to specify from which direction the effect will originate.

   - Click the **dialog box launcher** in the lower-right corner of the Animation group to see the effects and timing in one place. The Effect tab allows you to select a sound, dim the item being animated after its display (to deemphasize it), add animation to text (by word, letter, or all at once), and more. The Timing tab, shown next, allows you to identify how the animation will start (On Click, for instance), whether it should be delayed before animating, how long it should last, whether it should be repeated, and whether it should be rewound when done playing.

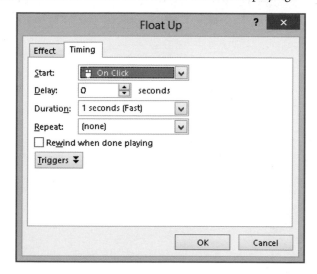

- In the Timing group, click the **Start** down arrow to choose how the animation will be initiated: by click of the mouse, at the same time as the previous animation, or after the previous animation.
- Click the **Duration** spinner to change for how long the animation should last.
- Click the **Delay** spinner and choose a time period if you want the animation to be delayed before displaying. You might do this when two animations overlap, for instance.

5. If you want to add another animation, click **Add Animation** in the Advanced Animation group and repeat the previous steps.

6. To move animations in the Animation Pane, select the item and then click **Move Earlier** or **Move Later** in the Timing group.

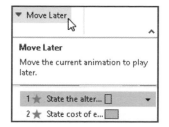

7. Click **Preview** in the Preview group to see the effects on the slide.

TIP If you have developed an animation that you like, you can copy it to another slide or to multiple slides by using the Animation Painter, which is similar to the Format Painter on the Home tab. First, select the item containing the animation you'd like to copy, click the **Animation Painter** in the Advanced Animation group, and then click the item to which you want to apply the animation. To apply it to multiple items, double-click the **Animation Painter**. To remove the effects, click **Animation Painter** again.

QuickSteps to...

- Edit a Slide Master or Layout Master
- Perform Additional Slide Master Tasks
- Understand the Slide Master Ribbon
- Work with the Notes Master
- Change the Handout Master
- Display the Notes Pane
- Preview Speaker Notes
- Use Headers and Footers on Notes and Handouts
- Print Notes and Handouts
- Share in a Variety of Ways
- Export Your Presentation
- Set Controls for Two Monitors
- Set Up Your Slide Show
- Use a Presenter View Slide Show
- Start the Slide Show
- Set Up an Automated Slide Show
- Record Narrations and Timings
- Rehearse Your Timing

Chapter 10

Polishing and Publishing Your Presentations

This chapter covers important features, such as slide masters and other elements, that help you to create and deliver a more consistent and effective presentation. To begin, you'll see how slide masters allow you to make changes to your presentation that are reflected on each slide or on only those you select. Then, you'll learn how to share and publish the final product. Finally, you'll learn how to set up and deliver your presentation either as a standalone slide show on a kiosk, or as a presenter using dual monitors to project slides and control the timing and display of the slides. You'll learn how to create and use speaker Notes and to create handouts.

WORK WITH MASTER SLIDES

Working with master slides gives you an opportunity to change a presentation globally. PowerPoint gives you a set of master slides for slides, notes, and handouts.

The term, *master slides* and *masters*, are catch-all terms applying to all slide masters and layout slides, notes and handout masters. The term *slide master* refers to one specific master, as described next. You access all of the masters from the View tab in the Master Views group. The master views have their own ribbon tabs containing the

1 2 3 4 5 6 7 8 9 10

tools you'll need to work with the master slides. You'll learn more about this in the following topics.

- **Slide masters** Control the formatting of slides of a presentation. In a set of slide masters you have one slide master, which is the top slide in the Slides pane and several slide layouts (described next). When you refer to "slide master" you are talking about this top-most slide. Most global changes you make to a presentation are made to the slide master since edits to it appear on all slides in the presentation (unless you have a presentation with more than one theme applied to it—then you have multiple sets of master slides). You access the slide master and its layouts from the View tab, the Slide Master option in the Master Views group.

- **Layout masters** (or just layout slides) are attached to a slide master and are used to change elements on a layout, such as the type of placeholders. When you make changes to a layout slide, all slides created with that layout will have the formatting and content as defined in the layout master. The title slide, for example, has a layout slide for unique positioning of page components, formatting, headings, and design elements. Layout slides are available when you view slide masters.

- **Notes master** Controls the global aspects of notes, such as the formatting defaults and any graphics, such as a logo. You access the notes master from the View tab, Notes Master in the Master Views group.

- **Handout master** Controls the global formatting defaults and placeholders for handouts. You access the handout master from the Views tab, Handout Master in the Master Views group.

The notes and handout masters are not automatically created—you create them manually if you want to use global attributes for them.

When you initially create a presentation, you select a template on which the formatting and design will be based. The specific formatting of the slide master comes from that template, but you can change the slide master without changing the original template. This is one way that you can customize your presentation even after using a suggested template to get started. For instance, you can apply a different theme to the master slide, adding a new set of master slides but without changing the original template. You can change the fonts, colors, and placeholders of the master slides. You can save a presentation with its modified master slides as a custom template. You'll see how to edit your presentation using master slides in the following topics.

 NOTE The best time to set up master slides is at the beginning of your development of the presentation, before you have applied themes and fonts, color, etc. Otherwise, you'll have to make some of the global changes individually to pre-existing layout slides. When you modify layout slides after actual presentation slides have been created, the changes in the master slide or layout slides will not overwrite existing content. Instead a new set of master slides is created. When you add a new slide in Normal view, you have a choice of which set of masters to use.

⏩ Edit a Slide Master or Layout Master

You have seen how in a set of master slides there is one slide master that sets the standards for all slides in the presentation. It is the first slide in the Slides pane. Editing a slide master changes all the slides to which it applies. Attached to the master slide is a set of associated layout slides, about ten of them, which, by default, carry the slide master's theme and other formatting. Each layout slide is specific to a type of layout that might be part of the presentation. For example, perhaps you will have one particular layout for all slides containing graphs. Another example for a specific type of layout is the title layout master. A layout slide usually carries the same color, design elements, and formatting as the theme assigned to a slide master. You can change particular layouts to be different from the slide master.

1. In the View tab Master Views group, click **Slide Master**. The slide master is displayed, as shown in Figure 10-1.

2. You have these options for changing slide masters and layout slides as described in the following topics, particularly "Understand the Slide Master Ribbon" topics later in this chapter.

- For the slide master, determine which placeholders will be in each slide in the presentation, such as titles, dates, slide numbers, footers, and text, seen in Figure 10-1.

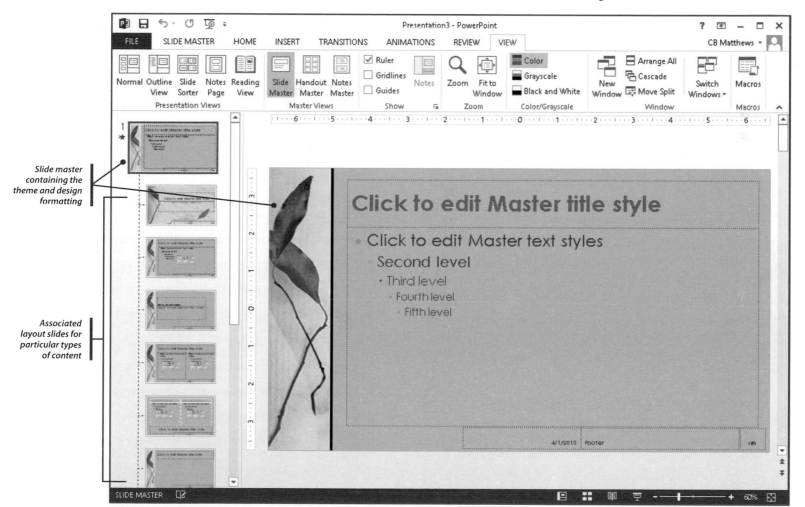

Figure 10-1: *The masters for a new presentation contain a slide master and several layout slides. This example is based on a new, blank presentation.*

- For the slide master or layout slides, determine the font and font size for the headings, subtitles, and list text (such as numbered or bulleted steps), and change colors or effects. Change background colors and styles.

- For layout slides, add or change placeholders found in a layout, such as text, pictures, charts, tables, SmartArt, media, or online images.

- For layout slides, hide titles or footers that are displayed by default.

Change the Master Slide Font Style

To change the overall font style of your slide master:

1. In the master slide, click the placeholder for the text you want to change, or select the actual heading or body text.

2. In the Home tab Font group, choose the attribute you want to modify—for example, click **Font** and choose the one you want to modify the font face. See the "Changing Font Attributes" QuickFacts in Chapter 9 for more information.

 NOTE If you want to change the attributes of text on only one type of slide, you change a layout slide; if you want to change attributes throughout all slides, you change the font or format in the slide master. The font commands are found in the Font group of the Home tab. (When you select text, a mini toolbar appears with additional commands available.) See the "Changing Font Attributes" QuickFacts in Chapter 9.

Change the Master Slide Bullet Style

To change the bullet style on your master slides:

1. Select the bullet style you wish to change—select the line it is on.

2. In the Home tab Paragraph group, click the **Bullets** down arrow to open the list of styles.

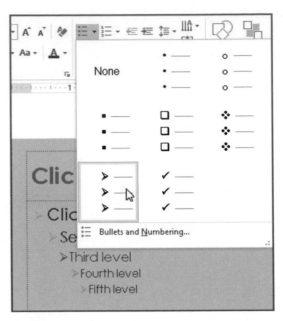

Figure 10-2: You can quickly select a new bullet style for your master slides.

3. Point at each bullet type to see the results in the background master slide, as shown in Figure 10-2.

4. Click the style you want, and it will be applied to the master slide.

Use a Picture as a Bullet

To insert a picture that serves as a bullet:

1. Select the level of bullet for which you want to use the picture.

2. In the Home tab Paragraph group, click the **Bullets** down arrow, and then click **Bullets And Numbering** at the bottom of the list to open the Bullets And Numbering dialog box.

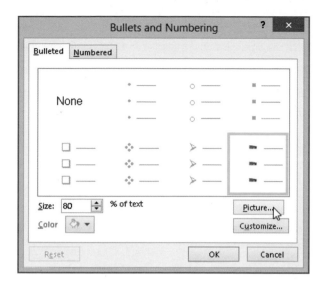

3. On the Bulleted tab, click the **Picture** button. PowerPoint uses your Internet connection to open the Insert Pictures dialog box, shown in Figure 10-3.

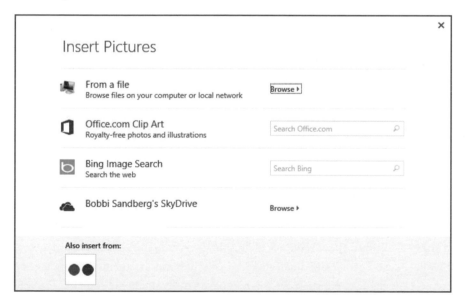

4. Choose the location of the picture and select the picture you want to use:

 - Choose **From A File** and click **Browse** if the picture is on your computer.
 - Choose **Office.com Clip Art** and click **Search Office.com** to find an image on the Microsoft website.
 - Choose **Bing Image Search** to use the Bing search engine to search the Web for images.
 - Choose **Sky Drive** and click **Browse** to find images you have stored online in your SkyDrive folder.
 - Choose **Also Insert From** (the two round circles) to view the photos you've stored on Flickr.com and connect them with your Outlook account.

5. When you have located the picture you want to use as the bullet, select it and click **Insert**.

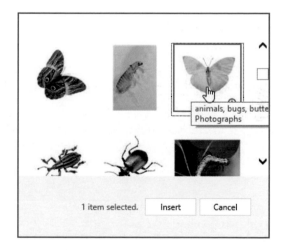

6. Your choice appears as the bullet for the level you selected in step 1.

Figure 10-3: For your bullets, you can insert pictures from your computer or from the Internet.

Change the Appearance of a Numbered List

You can change the appearance of numbers in a numbered list in your layout slide as well. To do so:

1. From within a layout slide, select the numbered list you want to change.

2. In the Home tab Paragraph group, click the **Numbering** down arrow. If you have previously chosen a numbering style, that style will be selected. You can point at each item in the list to see the results in the background layout slide. If you don't find a style you like, skip to Step 4.

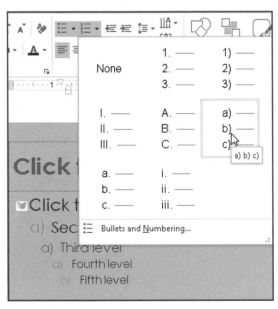

3. Click the style you want to use.

4. If the Numbering menu does not contain a style you want, click **Bullets And Numbering** at the bottom of the list to choose a size or color that is not on the list. The Bullets And Numbering dialog box appears.

5. Click the **Numbered** tab.

   - Click the **Size** spinner to increase or decrease the size of your font.
   - Click the **Start At** spinner to reset the beginning number.
   - Click the **Color** down arrow to select a new color for the set of numbers.

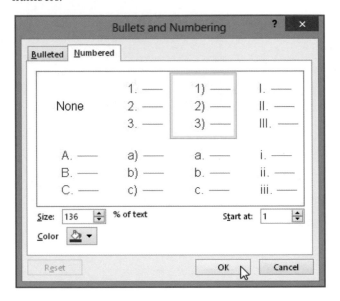

6. Click **OK** to close the dialog box.

▷▷ Perform Additional Slide Master Tasks

You can duplicate masters, create layouts that vary from the other layouts, retain a master slide with a presentation, or create multiple new title and slide masters.

Duplicate a Slide Master

If you'd like a second set of slide masters containing your standard theme, you can create duplicates. You can then modify them with updates or changes. For example, you may have a different theme you'd like to apply to part of the presentation while retaining the other standards of the slides master. To duplicate a slide master:

1. In the View tab Master Views group, click **Slide Master**.

2. Right-click the thumbnail of the slide master or layout slide that you want to duplicate. The options on the context menu will vary, depending on the type of master you select.

   - For a slide master, click **Duplicate Slide Master**. The slide master and the set of layout slides it includes will be duplicated.

   - For a layout master, click **Duplicate Layout**. Only the layout master will be duplicated.

In either case, one or more new slides is added.

Create a Title Master

To make the format of your title layout slide different from the format of the rest of your slides, create a title master to contain its unique formatting or design elements.

1. In the View tab Master Views group, click **Slide Master**, and click the layout thumbnail immediately beneath the slide master in the Slides pane. This is normally the title layout master.

2. Select the default text in the title placeholder, and type your title. Enter a subtitle if necessary. Note that changing the content of the text box, such as typing in a title in the layout slide, will not appear in your actual title slide when you switch back to Normal view—only the formatting applied to it is changed.

3. Format the text as needed using the tools discussed in Chapters 8 and 9, such as the Drawing Tools Format tab.

4. Insert a logo or other graphic by clicking the **Insert** tab and clicking the type of graphic you want. Follow the prompts to find what you want. Refer to Chapter 8 or 12 for information on how to do this.

Retain a Slide Master

To retain a slide master within the presentation, even if it is not being used, use the Preserve Master button. You might want to do this if you intend to use the presentation again in the future when the slide master will be used. This option is unavailable for layout slides.

1. With the Slide Master tab active, right-click the slide master to be retained.

2. From the context menu, click **Preserve Master** to retain the selected master—keep it with the presentation. You will see a pushpin icon to the left of the master.

Create Multiple Slide and Title Masters

Multiple slide masters and their associated sets of layout masters are used in a presentation to create different looks in layout or formatting for different sections of the presentation.

 TIP When you apply a new theme to a presentation, slide masters are automatically created.

To create additional new slide masters:

1. In the View tab Master Views group, click **Slide Master**.

2. Right-click any slide master or layout slide, and click **Insert Slide Master**. A new slide master and its associated layout masters will be inserted following the set of original slide masters.

3. Make any changes to the new masters as needed.

4. Click the **Slide Master** tab, and then click **Close Master View** in the Close group to close the Slide Master view.

Understand the Slide Master Ribbon

As explained in "Manage Slide Appearance" earlier in this chapter, each theme comes with its own set of master slides. When you work with slide masters, the Slide Master tab appears with its accompanying ribbon, as shown in Figure 10-4. Each group in the tab has special tools that apply

- **Rename** enables you to rename a selected slide that you have modified so that you can find and use it easily again.

- **Preserve** makes sure that the slide master is not removed from the presentation even if it is never used. This option is not available for layout masters.

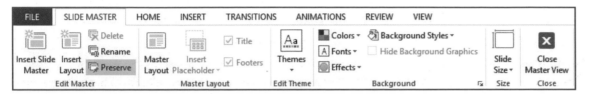

Figure 10-4: The Slide Master tab has six groups for use with slide masters.

just to slide masters. When you are finished working with the Slide Master tab's groups, click **Close Master View** to close the tab.

Manipulate Master Slides

The first group in the Slide Master tab, the Edit Master group, allows you to work with the slides themselves. It includes the following buttons:

- **Insert Slide Master** inserts a set of masters, including a slide master and its associated layout slides. If you insert a slide master without first selecting a theme, it will be a blank set, without a theme. If you use the Edit Theme button, a new set of slides will be inserted with the selected theme.

- **Insert Layout** inserts one layout master immediately following the selected slide. Click this button if you need to add another layout for the content of your slides.

- **Delete** removes a set of slide masters from the group. You cannot delete the last one—your presentation always has at least one set of slide masters.

Hide or Show a Master Layout Placeholder

The Master Layout group contains buttons with which you can edit the layout of your slide master, the first slide in the set of your master slides.

1. Click the slide master, the first slide of a group, to open the Master Layout dialog box. By default, all of the listed placeholders are available in your master slide.

2. Clear the check boxes for any of the placeholders you do not want to use with this theme in this presentation.

3. Click **OK** to close the dialog box when you have completed your choices.

Insert a Master Layout Placeholder

When you have selected any slide other than the first slide master in the Slides pane in the Slide Master tab, the Insert Placeholder button becomes available. Use it to add placeholders in slides that you want to contain specific types of content, such as pictures, charts, or media. To use this button:

1. Choose one of the layout slides in the Slides pane.

2. Click the **Insert Placeholder** down-arrow to open the list of content choices. Choose the placeholder you want. Your pointer will change to a crosshair so that you can draw the size of placeholder you want.

3. To draw the placeholder in the slide, click and drag in the area where you want to place the content until the placeholder is the proper size.

The placeholder that is now in the layout slide will be available when you create a regular slide based on this layout slide, so that you can click the icon, such as the Chart icon, to insert a chart in the slide show.

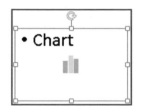

Hide or Show a Title or Footer

1. Click a layout slide.

2. In the Slide Master tab Master Layout group, check the **Title** check box if you want to show the title, or clear the check box if you want to hide the title.

3. Check the **Footers** check box if you want to show the footers, or clear the check box if you want to hide the footers.

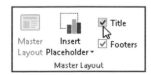

Edit Master Themes

This option is not as much about changing a current master theme as creating new master slides containing a theme. When you choose this option, a new set of master slides is inserted with the theme you've chosen. You can also browse for themes or save a theme under a new name.

- In the Slide Master tab, click **Themes** in the Edit Theme group. Select a theme. A set of master slides will be inserted using the selected theme.

- To save a custom theme, in the Slide Master tab, click **Themes** in the Edit Theme group, and select **Save Current Theme**. In the Save Current dialog box, enter a custom name, and click **Save**. The new theme will be saved and displayed in the Themes list under Custom.

Edit a Master's Color, Fonts, and Effects

The Slide Master tab Background group of commands allows you to change your theme. From this group you can change colors, fonts, effects, and background in any theme.

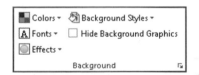

1. Click the master slide to change the color, fonts, effects, or background for all of its associated layout slides. Click a layout slide to change them for just the one type of layout slide.

- To change the color of a theme and its coordinated fonts, click **Colors** and mouse over the options to see the results. Select the color you want on all slides. (This does not change the color for a single slide, regardless of what is selected.)

- To change the fonts, click **Fonts** and mouse over the options until you find a font you like. Click it and the font will be changed on all slides. (This does not work for a single slide, regardless of what is selected.)

- Click **Effects** and mouse over the options. You can only see the results of effects if you have graphics, shapes, or SmartArt on a slide master or layout slide. When you find an effect you like, click it and the SmartArt graphics for all slides will be changed.

- Click **Background Styles** and mouse over the possibilities. Select the one you like. The background of all slides will change if a master slide is selected, or just the background of an individual layout slide if that is selected.

- Click the **Hide Background Graphic** check box to hide the background graphic included in the theme you have chosen—this is only available for individual layout master slides.

2. You can also click the **task pane** launcher in the lower-right corner of the Background group to display the Format Background task pane, shown in Figure 10-5. This allows you to change the slide background with additional fills, gradients, patterns, or colors. This changes formatting in a single slide unless you click **Apply To All**.

Set Slide Size for the Monitor

In the Slide Master tab, the Size group contains only one button, Slide Size, with which you can set your slide size based on the size of the monitor on which the presentation will be shown. When you click **Slide Size**, the default choices are Standard and Widescreen.

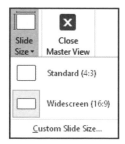

To set a specific slide size for your presentation, click **Custom Screen Size** to open the Slide Size dialog box. Here you can set not only the

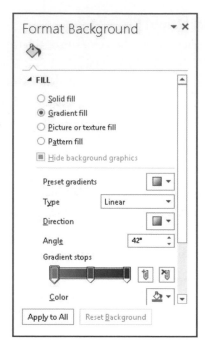

Figure 10-5: The Format Background task pane offers additional ways you can perfect the background of your master slides.

size for slides, notes, handouts, and outlines, but also the orientation, Portrait or Landscape.

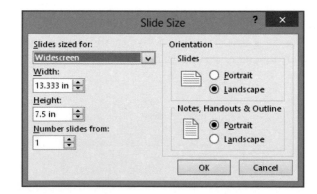

Work with the Notes Master

If you plan to use your notes as handouts for your presentation, you will want them to be consistent in formatting and appearance. To make global changes to all notes in a presentation, use the notes master. You can add a logo or other graphics, change the positioning of page components, change formats, and add headings and text design elements for all notes. Figure 10-6 shows the Notes Master tab with its ribbon. The Edit Theme, Background, and Close groups are used in the same way as the similar groups in the Slide Master ribbon, discussed in the previous section of this chapter, so this section describes only the Page Setup and Placeholders groups.

Figure 10-6: Use the Notes Master tab to globally change such note features as headers, footers, logos, or graphics; note text formatting; and placement of note elements.

1. To access the notes master tools, click the **View** tab, and then click **Notes Master** in the Master Views group. The notes master itself, shown in Figure 10-7, contains the current formatting for your speaker notes.

2. To adjust the zoom so that you can see the notes area better, click the **View** tab, and click **Zoom**. In the Zoom dialog box, choose the magnification and click **OK**.

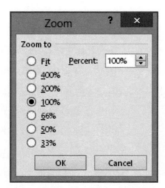

TIP You can also use the Zoom slider in the taskbar to magnify your notes area.

Set Orientation for Notes

You can choose whether your notes will be normal size or wider—that is, portrait or landscape.

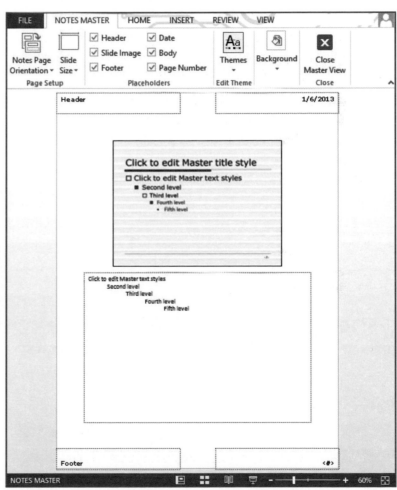

Figure 10-7: Use the notes master to customize your speaker notes.

10

Click the **Notes Master** tab, and click the **Notes Page Orientation** down arrow in the Page Setup group.

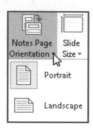

- Click **Portrait** to select a standard size Notes Page.
- Click **Landscape** to select a wider size Notes Page.

Set Placeholders in the Notes Master

In the Notes Master tab Placeholders group, you have the option of setting six placeholders in your notes master. By default, all six are chosen. To remove any placeholder from your notes master, simply clear the check box. When you remove the check mark, the item disappears from the notes master.

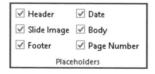

▷▷ Change the Handout Master

Handouts display thumbnails of the slides on a printed page. You can have one, two, three, four, six, or nine slides per page. To prepare your handouts for printing with titles and other formatting, use the handout master.

1. In the View tab Master Views group, click **Handout Master**. The handout master will be displayed, as shown in Figure 10-8.

2. In the Handout Master tab Page Setup group, click **Slides Per Page** to set the number of slides to be displayed in the handout: one, two, three, four, six, or nine. If you click **Slide Outline**, you can set page attributes of a printed handout of your slide outline (the handout for the slide outline does not contain slide thumbnails, but the content of the outline of the slides).

3. Make changes to the handout master as needed. In the Page Setup group:
   - Click **Handout Orientation** to give the handout a portrait or landscape orientation.
   - Click **Slide Size** to set the size of the slides in this presentation to standard or widescreen, or to a custom size.

4. In the Placeholders group:
   - Click the **Header**, **Date**, **Footer**, or **Page Number** check box to remove the check mark if you do not want the corresponding element to appear on the handouts. They all are checked by default. If you choose to retain headers and footers, enter the text in the appropriate text boxes.
   - To format the date, click in the date text box, click the **Insert** tab, and in the Text group, click **Date & Time**. Choose a format and click **OK**. Return to the Handout Master tab.

5. Click **Themes** in the Edit Themes group to make changes to the current theme (or themes).

6. Use the Background group to:
   - Select a style for the background
   - Hide the background graphics by clicking the **Hide Background Graphics** check box

7. To close the handout master, click **Close Master View** in the Close group.

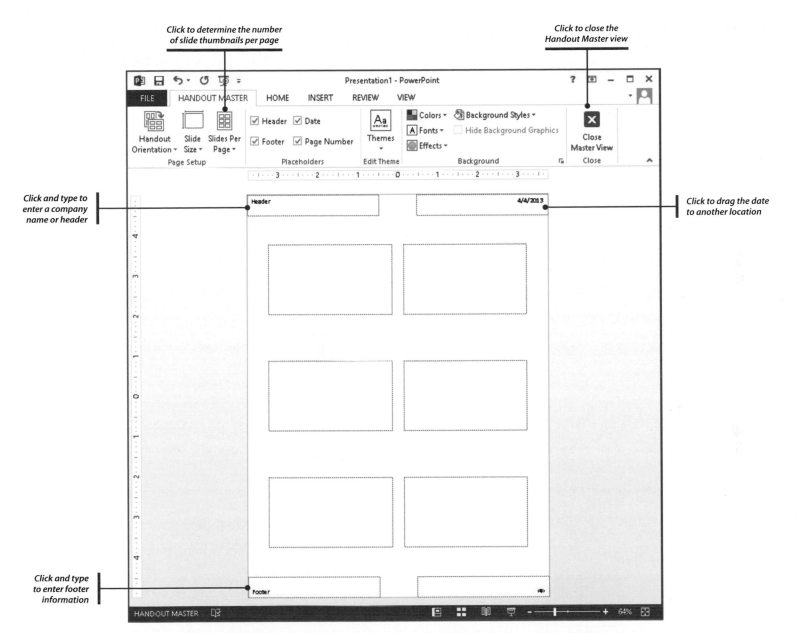

Click to determine the number of slide thumbnails per page

Click to close the Handout Master view

Click and type to enter a company name or header

Click to drag the date to another location

Click and type to enter footer information

Figure 10-8: *The Handout Master tab allows you to hide or show placeholders, vary the number of slides and orientation displayed in the handout, and edit themes and backgrounds as needed.*

WORK WITH NOTES

You can use the Notes feature in PowerPoint to create speaker notes to aid you during a presentation. As previously described, you can also create distributable handouts from these notes so that your audience can follow the presentation easily. The notes do not appear on the slides during a slide show presentation; they are visible only to the presenter.

> **TIP** If you use more of the Notes pane than is available, PowerPoint may reduce the font size and line spacing so that the text will fit, or it may insert a vertical scroll bar. The action depends on your settings in the AutoCorrect dialog box. To configure these settings, choose the **File** tab and then click **Options**. Click **Proofing**, and then click the **AutoCorrect Options** button to open the AutoCorrect dialog box. In the AutoFormat As You Type tab, beneath Apply As You Type, clear the **AutoFit Title Text To Placeholder** and **AutoFit Body Text To Placeholder** check boxes to remove the automatic resizing of the text in the title and text box placeholders.

> Apply as you type
> ☑ Automatic bulleted and numbered lists
> ☑ AutoFit title text to placeholder
> ☑ AutoFit body text to placeholder

 ## Display the Notes Pane

The Notes pane, which allows you to create speaker notes (or handouts), is by default shown below the Presentation pane. You can switch the Notes pane on and off using either of two toggles:

- In the View tab, Presentation Views group, click **Normal**. Then click **Notes** in the Show group.
- Click **Notes** on the taskbar.

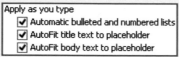

Then, just type in the Notes pane. You can format the notes text in the same ways as you format normal text.

> **TIP** To change the background of one or all notes, in the View tab Presentation Views group, click **Notes Page**. Right-click the **Notes** text box, and click **Format Shape** in the context menu. Click the **Fill** option, click the **Solid Fill** option in the Fill area, and click the **Color** button to choose your color.

Create a Note in the Notes Page

1. In the View tab Presentation Views group, click **Notes Page**. The Notes Page opens, an example of which is shown in Figure 10-9.

2. Click in the **Click To Add Text** placeholder and start typing your notes.

3. To move to another slide, click the scroll bar above the scroll box (the scroll bar and box are on the right of the window) to move to previous slides or click the scroll bar below the scroll box to move to following slides.

Each slide has its own Notes Page. To add or change attributes or text to all notes in a presentation, make changes to the notes master. (See "Work with the Notes Master" earlier in this chapter for more information about master slides.)

> **TIP** Text on Notes Pages can be edited and formatted like any other text.

Size Your Notes Page Text Box

When working in the Notes text box, you can size the text box by using the sizing handles.

1. Click inside the text box to turn on the sizing handles, as shown in Figure 10-9.

2. Click and drag any of the sizing handles to change the text box to the size you want it to be.

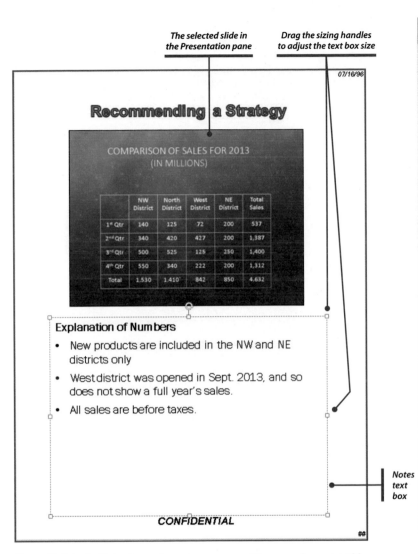

Figure 10-9: In the Notes Page view, you can expand the area where you add
your notes by dragging the sizing handles of the Notes text box.

TIP You can also magnify the Notes Page and the size of the Notes
text box with the Zoom command. Click the **View** tab, and in the
Zoom group, click **Zoom**. Choose the zoom magnification you want,
and click **OK**. Or, you can use the Zoom slider in the taskbar.

Understanding PowerPoint Images and Illustrations

PowerPoint 2013 includes many ways to enhance your slides. The Insert tab
has two groups, Images and Illustrations, that allow you to add graphics
and art to your Note Pages.

The Images group includes the following:

- **Pictures**   This tool allows you to insert both clip art and pictures from
  your computer or from any other computer to which your computer
  is connected.

- **Online Pictures**   Use this tool to access clip art from the Office.com
  website or to search the Internet for an image. While copyright laws
  apply to most images on the Internet, you can safely use clip art from
  the Office.com website.

- **Screenshot**   This tool allows you to quickly "take a picture" of any
  window, or part of a window (using the Screen Clipping option), that
  is currently open on your desktop.

- **Photo Album**   With this tool you can create or access a photo
  album on your computer or any computer to which your computer
  is connected. This album becomes a new PowerPoint presentation.

Options in the Illustrations group are

- **Shapes**   This tool helps you insert a shape in your slide, slide master,
  or Notes Page. You can then customize the color, outline, and effects
  of the shape.

- **SmartArt**   SmartArt is a series of graphics that help you present lists
  (or blocks) of information in a graphic format. These graphics work
  in much the way bulleted lists work in a word processing document.

- **Chart**   With this tool, you can insert a bar chart, line chart, or columnar
  chart (or any of several other chart types) into slides, slide masters, or
  your notes.

Add an Object to Your Notes Page

You can add an object, such as a picture, graph, chart, or organizational
chart, to your notes.

1. Open your slide in Notes Page view.

2. Click in the Notes text box in the spot where you want to insert
   the object.

3. Click the **Insert** tab, as shown in Figure 10-10. In either the Images group or the Illustrations group, click the button of the object you want to insert (see the "Understanding PowerPoint Images and Illustrations" QuickFacts for information on each object).

4. Resize the image, if needed, and drag the object to where you want it on the page.

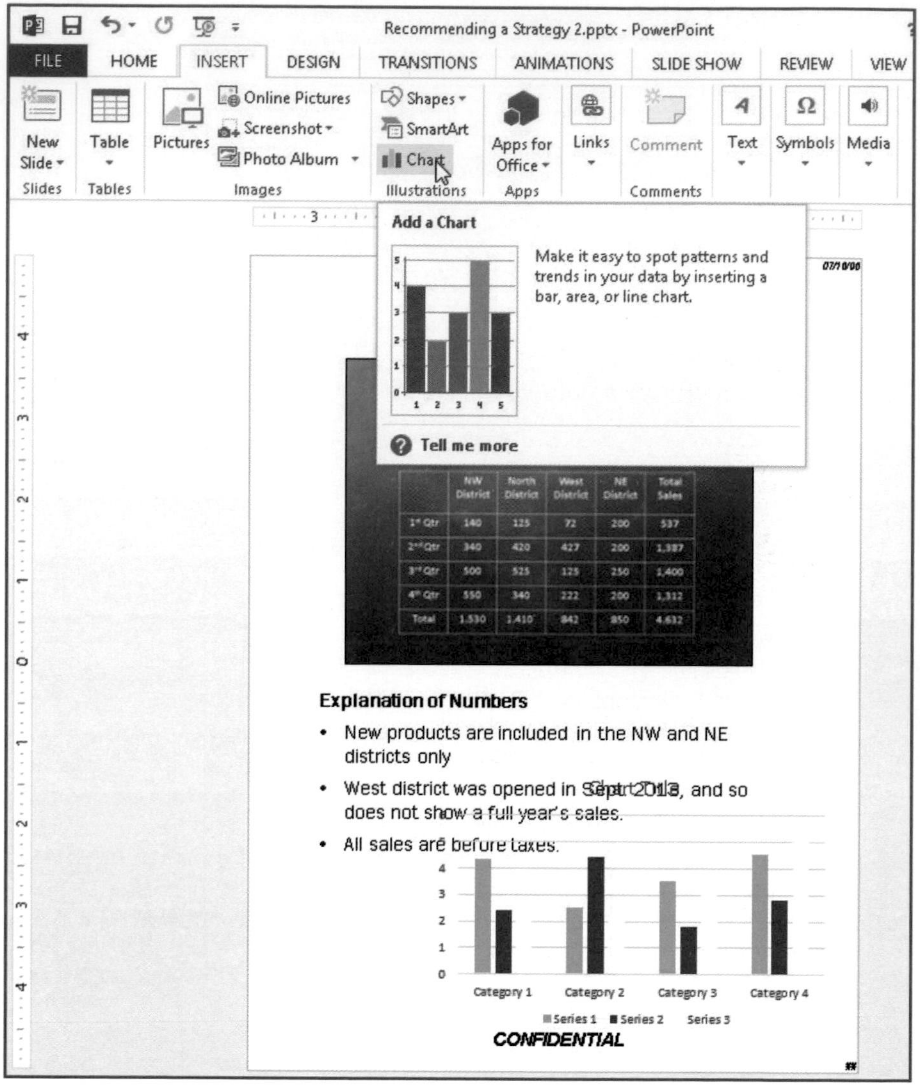

⏩ Preview Speaker Notes

If you want to proof your notes before you print them, you can preview them on the Print page. This allows you to see them as they will look when printed.

1. Click the **File** tab and click **Print**. The Print page appears.

2. Under Settings, click the second drop-down list box and, under Print Layout, click **Notes Pages**. You will see the preview of the Notes Page, as the notes will be printed, in the right pane, shown in Figure 10-11.

3. Scroll through the pages by using either the scroll bar on the right or the **Next Page** and **Previous Page** arrows at the bottom of the pane.

4. Click **Print** to print slides with notes (see the upcoming section "Print Notes and Handouts"), or click **Back** (the left-facing arrow in the top-left corner) to return to the Notes Page.

⏩ Use Headers and Footers on Notes and Handouts

Figure 10-10: *Add images or illustrations to your notes from the Insert tab.*

Many presenters distribute handouts of their presentation for their audience to use as a reference. In PowerPoint you can print your presentation in the form of paper handouts with one, two, three, four, six, or nine slides on a page. If you wish to do so, you can include headers and footers on both your Notes Pages and any handouts you prepare for your audience. To put headers and/or footers on notes and handouts:

1. In the View tab Presentation Views group, click **Notes Page**.

2. Click the **Insert** tab, and in the Text group, click **Header & Footer**. (If you can't see it, your screen is too small.) The Header And Footer dialog box appears.

3. Click the **Notes And Handouts** tab, shown in Figure 10-12.

4. Check the corresponding check box for the items you want to include on each page.

   - To include a date and time in the header, check the **Date And Time** check box, and choose between **Update Automatically**, for a time/date that updates according to the current date, or **Fixed**, for a time/date or other text that remains the same each time the presentation is printed.

   - Check the **Page Number** check box to print a page number on the note or handout page. Clear the check box to suppress the page number.

   - Check the **Header** check box, click in the text box, and type the header text for notes and handouts. Clear the check box to suppress the header.

   - Check the **Footer** check box, click in the text box, and type footer text. Clear the check box to suppress the footer.

5. Click **Apply To All** if you want to include the information on all Notes Pages and handouts.

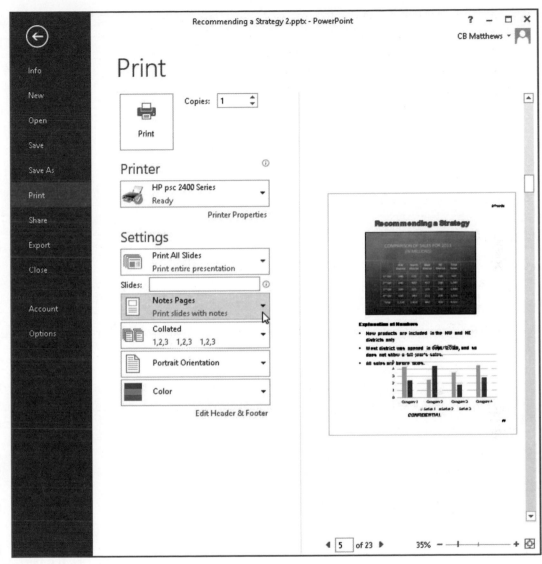

Figure 10-11: The Print page's setting for Notes Pages displays a preview of the speaker notes with the accompanying slide.

10

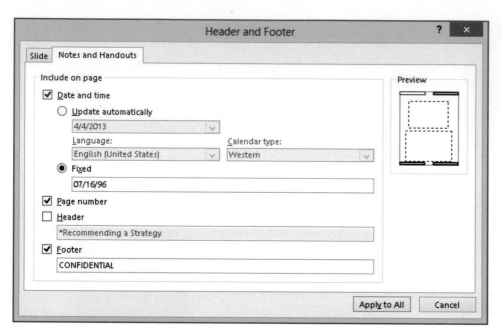

Figure 10-12: The Header And Footer dialog box is where you can establish a header and/or footer for all your slides.

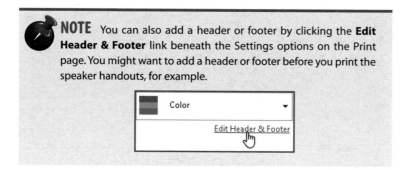

NOTE You can also add a header or footer by clicking the **Edit Header & Footer** link beneath the Settings options on the Print page. You might want to add a header or footer before you print the speaker handouts, for example.

▷▷ Print Notes and Handouts

You can print both speaker notes and handouts in much the same way.

Print Speaker Notes

To print your notes:

1. Click the **File** tab, and click **Print**. The Print page appears, as shown earlier in Figure 10-11.

2. Under Settings, click the first drop-down list box, and click **Print All Slides**, **Print Selection**, **Print Current Slide**, or **Custom Range** (to enter the slide numbers for specific slides or slide ranges in the Slides text box).

3. Under Settings, click the second drop-down list box, and click **Notes Pages**, shown next. You have these options:

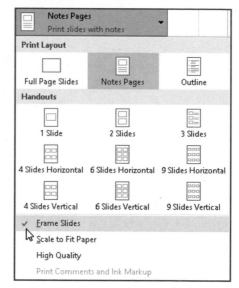

- Click **Collated** to collate the notes.
- Click the **Portrait Orientation** drop-down menu (the fourth beneath Settings) to choose between **Portrait** (tall) or **Landscape** (wide).
- Click the **Color** drop-down menu, and choose **Color**, **Grayscale**, or **Pure Black And White**.

- Click **Edit Header & Footer** to open the Header And Footer dialog box. After you make your selections (described earlier in the section "Use Headers and Footers on Notes and Handouts"), click **Apply To All** to close the dialog box and return to the Print page.

- At the top of the Print page, click the **Copies** spinner to set the number of copies to print.

4. Click **Print** to print your speaker notes.

Print Handouts

Before you print your handouts, you can choose how many thumbnail slides will be displayed on each page. Figure 10-13 shows an example in which each of the four pages of the printed handout will contain six thumbnail slides.

Figure 10-13: You can choose the number of thumbnail slides displayed on each page of your printed handout.

1. Click the **File** tab, and click **Print** to display the Print page.

2. Under Settings, click the second drop-down list box. In the Handouts section, click the number of thumbnail slides to be displayed in the handouts.

3. Click the **Copies** spinner to set the number of copies, and make any other adjustments as needed.

4. Click **Print** to print.

TIP To add or remove borders that are placed around the handout thumbnail slides, on the Print page, open the second drop-down menu under Settings. Click the **Frame Slides** check box to add or clear the check mark. The border will be added when a check mark is present.

SHARE YOUR PRESENTATION

If you want to share your presentation online or by e-mail, PowerPoint 2013 offers several methods. The File page contains two categories of sharing tools found: Share and Export. The Share category provides ways you can share your presentation by saving it to an online location and sharing the link by e-mail or a social network, such as Facebook. You can control the slide show yourself at a designated time, or invite viewers to look at it on their own time. Export, on the other hand, converts the presentation to a different form, such as a PDF/XPS document, a video, a packaged version for a CD, using handouts, or providing a menu of file types from which you can choose. The following topics lead you through these various methods of sharing.

Share in a Variety of Ways

You may share your presentation in several ways. To access your options, click **File** and choose **Share** to open the Share page, shown in Figure 10-14.

10

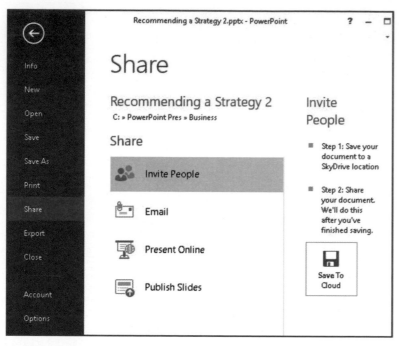

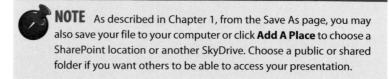

3. On the right side of the Save As page, choose the location to which you want to save the presentation file. You may choose a location from the Recent Folders list or click **Browse**. In either case, the Save As dialog box opens, shown in Figure 10-15, and browse to the location. In order to share your presentation, the folder will need to be public, or shared with the people you'll invite to view the presentation.

> **NOTE** As described in Chapter 1, from the Save As page, you may also save your file to your computer or click **Add A Place** to choose a SharePoint location or another SkyDrive. Choose a public or shared folder if you want others to be able to access your presentation.

4. Click **Save** to save the file. The page shown in Figure 10-16 will be displayed.

5. Click in the **Invite People** text box and type the names or e-mail addresses of the people you want to invite to view your presentation. You have these options:

- Click the **Address Book** icon to the right of the name to select names from your computer address book. Separate the names of multiple people by inserting semicolons between the names.

- Click the **Can Edit** down arrow to select whether an individual can edit the presentation or just view it.

Figure 10-14: Share your presentation in several ways with PowerPoint 2013.

Invite Viewers to See Your Presentation

On the Share page, the Invite People option enables you to save your presentation online so that you can invite people to view it online.

1. Select **Invite People**.

2. Click **Save To Cloud**. (This assumes you have already created a SkyDrive account. If you have not created one, follow the directions in the section "Get SkyDrive for Your Files" in Chapter 1.) On the left side of the Save As page, click the **SkyDrive** destination.

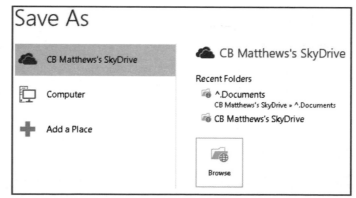

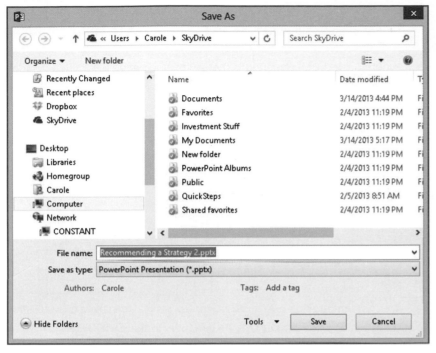

Figure 10-15: Saving a presentation to your SkyDrive folder is as easy as saving to a folder on your computer.

Figure 10-16: After you have saved the file to a shared location, you'll have additional options for how you can share your presentation.

- Click the message text box and type a message you want to send as part of your invitation.

- Click the **Require User To Sign In Before Accessing Document** if you want to protect this presentation from casual viewers.

6. Click **Share** to send mail with the people you have invited.

7. At this point, your presentation has been saved and you have invited people to view your presentation. The following topics discuss how you might want to share with your invited persons.

Share via E-mail

To send your presentation by e-mail, click **Email** in the Share page, shown in Figure 10-17. You have the following alternatives for sharing your presentation (or a link to it) via e-mail:

- **Send As Attachment** Each recipient receives a copy of the presentation as an attachment.

- **Send A Link** Each recipient receives a link to the presentation. This option keeps the e-mail size small, and everyone views the same, latest copy of the presentation. This is available only if you have saved your presentation to a shared location, such as SkyDrive.

Click the e-mail option you want. An e-mail will be sent with either a link address pointing to it, or an attachment to an e-mail. If it is sent as a link, the recipient will simply click the link to access the presentation online. If the presentation is sent as an attachment, the invited persons can open the presentation and view it accordingly.

Share with a Link or Post to Social Networks

After you have saved your presentation to SkyDrive (or Office 365 SharePoint), additional options are available on the Share page, as shown earlier in Figure 10-16. You may share your presentation by creating a link, posting a link to one or more social networks, e-mailing a link or attachment (as described earlier), or using Microsoft's Office Presentation Service (as described in the next section).

- Click the **Get A Sharing Link** option to create a link to your presentation posted online by clicking **Create Link**. You can then copy the link and paste it into an e-mail to invite others to view your presentation. This is a good way to share with larger groups of people. It is not a secure way to show the presentation, so don't do it this way if you are concerned about privacy. When you are finished sharing the presentation, right-click the **Shared Links** icon, and click **Disable Link** to remove the link from being accessible.

- If your Microsoft account is connected to social networks, click **Post To Social Networks** to make your presentation available to that network. If your account is not connected and you would like it to be, click **Click Here To Connect Social Networks**. You will be led through the connecting process.

Present Online

In this scenario, after you create a presentation, you can send invitations (with a link) to people you'd like to show it to online, in real time, via Microsoft's Office Presentation Service. You may want to set various options, as described in the Note at the end of this section. You need a Microsoft account to do present online (See "Use a Presenter View

Figure 10-17: Use e-mail in several different ways to distribute your presentation.

- **Send As PDF** Each recipient receives the file as a PDF attachment.
- **Send As XPS** Each recipient receives the file as an XPS attachment.

NOTE Both of the preceding options preserve all the formatting of your presentation and make changing its content difficult. See "Create a PDF/XPS Document" later in the chapter for instructions on saving your presentation as a PDF or XPS file.

- **Send As Internet Fax** Each recipient receives the file as an Internet fax. You don't need a fax machine, but you must have a fax service provider. The recipients receive the Internet fax in their e-mail Inbox.

Slide Show," later in the chapter, for additional information on how to use that environment.)

1. You have two ways you can access the Present Online feature:

- On the Share page, click the **Present Online** option in the left pane. Click the **Enable Remote Viewers To Download The Presentation** check box to allow your viewers to download the presentation to their own computers. Then click the **Present Online** icon in the right pane. After a minute, you'll see a link.

- In the Slide Show tab Start Slide Show group, click **Present Online.** Click the **Enable Remote Viewers To Download The Presentation** check box to allow your viewers to download the presentation to their own computers. Then click **Connect**. After a minute, you'll see the link.

2. Click **Copy Link** to copy and paste the link into an e-mail you've created for this occasion, or click **Send In Email** to have PowerPoint create an e-mail containing the link for you to send to selected persons.

3. In the e-mail form, you'll need to fill in the To addresses, tell viewers what the presentation is about, and specify the exact time at which you'll be presenting it. Click **Send**.

4. Upon receiving the e-mail, at the designated time, your viewers will need to cut and paste the link in a browser. When they go to the link, they will see an empty page, waiting for the presentation to begin.

5. At the designated time, click **Start Presentation** in the Present Online dialog box. The full-screen slide show will begin, and you can either lead viewers through it click by click, or let it run automatically if it is set up to do so. Right-click the screen and click **Show Reviewer View** to use the tools in Presenter View. Your viewers will see the slide show as you are presenting it, and will be able to download it if you have checked the **Enable Remote Viewers To Download The Presentation** check box.

6. When you are ready to end the slide show, right-click the screen and click **End Show**. Or, in the Present Online tab Present Online group, click **End Online Presentation**.

NOTE While you are in Present Online view, after getting the link but before starting the presentation, a Present Online ribbon is available. You can test your presentation from this and set certain parameters. For example, you can choose whether to use Presenter View or to share notes with viewers (you'll need One Note notes for this). You can also send invitations from here and end your online presentation. When you are finished with this mode, be sure to click **Close Present Online** in the Present Online group to restore the ribbon to its normal status.

10

Publish Your Slides

If you are connected to a slide library or SharePoint site that allows you to share files and folders, you can publish your slides for everyone to review or edit.

1. Click **File**, and then click **Share**. On the Share page, click **Publish Slides**. The right pane displays further information. Click **Publish Slides**.

2. Select the slides you want to include by clicking the check box to the left of each slide you want to publish, as shown in Figure 10-18. To choose all of the slides, click the **Select All** button. (If you need to start over, click the **Clear All** button.)

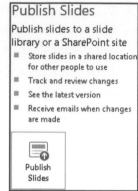

Publish Slides

Publish slides to a slide library or a SharePoint site

- Store slides in a shared location for other people to use
- Track and review changes
- See the latest version
- Receive emails when changes are made

Publish
Slides

3. If you have a large presentation and want to see only slides that will be published, click the **Show Only Selected Slides** check box.

4. Click the **Browse** button to choose the network to which you want to publish your slides.

5. When you have completed your choices, click **Publish**.

6. If you change your mind about publishing your slides, click the **Cancel** button.

You can now give other viewers the link to your shared file so that they can access and edit the published presentation.

▷▷ Export Your Presentation

PowerPoint 2013 offers several ways in which you can "package" your presentation for easy export:

- Create a PDF or XPS document
- Create a video
- Make a package presentation on a CD that can be viewed on nearly every computer
- Create handouts
- Change your presentation's file type

One reason you might want to do this is to protect your presentation from being changed by others. Converting it to another form, such as a PDF or XPS, or .ppsx file type, makes it harder for others to edit your work. To access these options, click **File** and then click **Export** to open the Export page, shown in Figure 10-19.

Create a PDF/XPS Document

On the Export page, click **Create PDF/XPS** to save your presentation as a PDF or XPS document. This option retains your original presentation file and creates a copy as a PDF or XPS—it is good if you want to save the formatting and content of your presentation and send it via e-mail, for instance. Even if

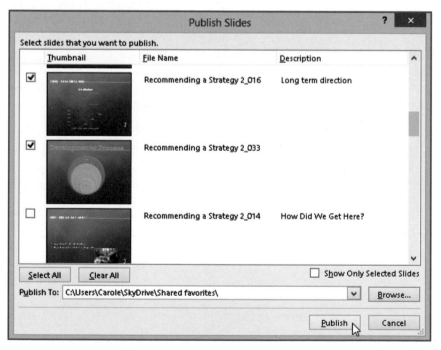

Figure 10-18: You may make your slides available for others to edit or view.

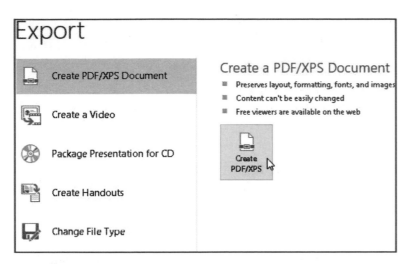

Figure 10-19: The Export page provides several options for exporting your presentation.

your recipients do not have the programs for viewing these documents, there are many free viewers for both file types available on the Internet.

Create a Video of Your Presentation

You can create a video of your presentation and then burn it to a DVD, e-mail it, or upload it to the Internet, perhaps to share it via YouTube. Incidentally, a viewer does not need PowerPoint to view these videos. This is an easy way to distribute a slide show.

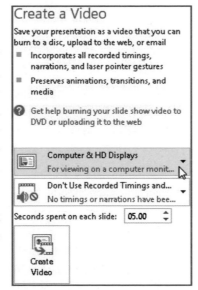

1. Open the presentation. Click **File** and **Export** to open the Export page.

2. Click **Create A Video**.

3. Click the **Computer & HD Displays** down arrow (the first drop-down list box) to select the type of display you want.

   - Choose **Computer & HD Displays** to create a video with high resolution. It will be large in file size because of the increase in quality.

   - Choose **Internet & DVD** to create a video with average quality and moderate file size.

   - Choose **Portable Devices** to create a very small-sized file of lower quality.

4. If you have included narration or set timings for any of your slides (see "Record Narrations and Timings," later in the chapter), click the **Don't Use Recorded Timings And Narrations** down arrow (the second drop-down list box) to set those options.

   - Click **Don't Use Recorded Timings And Narrations** if your presentation has no set timings or narrations. It will use the default 5 seconds per slide for display time—you can change this.

   - Click **Use Recorded Timings And Narrations** if you have those recorded on your presentation.

   - Click **Record Timings And Narrations** to stop what you're doing and record right now. You'll see a dialog box that allows you to select whether to record slide and animation timings or record narrations and laser pointers (if you have a microphone connected).

   - Click **Preview Timings And Narrations** to go through the presentation and view it in action so that you can judge how the timings work in the actual presentation.

5. Click the **Seconds Spent On Each Slide** spinner to set the time spent on each slide, if you want something different from the default of 5 seconds.

6. Click **Create Video** to open a Save As dialog box to save your file in a video .mp4 format. The File Name will default to the presentation name, and the Save As Type to .mp4. Select and type over these if you want something different.

7. Select the file location and click **Save**. If you have a large presentation, this may take a lot of time, perhaps hours. You may want to wait to do this overnight.

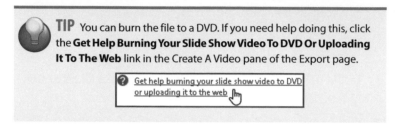

TIP You can burn the file to a DVD. If you need help doing this, click the **Get Help Burning Your Slide Show Video To DVD Or Uploading It To The Web** link in the Create A Video pane of the Export page.

Package Your Presentation for a CD

The Package Presentation For CD option on the Export page helps you to package your entire presentation into a show that you can save onto a CD or into a folder for later distribution.

1. Click **File**, and then click **Export**. On the Export page, click **Package Presentation For CD** to open the Package For CD dialog box, shown in Figure 10-20.

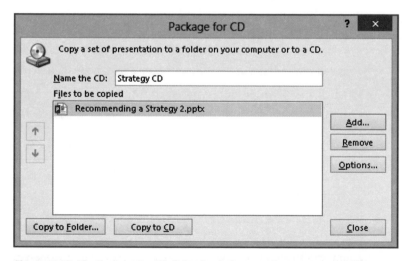

Figure 10-20: The Package For CD dialog box helps you save your presentation to either a folder or a CD.

2. Type a name for your presentation in the **Name The CD** text box.

3. If you want to include additional presentations on this CD, click **Add** to open the Add Files dialog box. (Presentations are played in the order listed in the Package For CD dialog box.) If you add a presentation by mistake, select it and click **Remove** to delete it from the Files To Be Copied list.

4. Click **Options** to open the Options dialog box.

- Check the **Linked Files** and/or **Embedded TrueType Fonts** check boxes to include those items in your presentation.

- If you want to require a password to either view or modify your presentation, type the password in the appropriate box.

- Check the **Inspect Presentation For Inappropriate Or Private Information** check box if you would like to run that inspection.

5. Click **OK** to close the Options dialog box and return to the Package For CD dialog box.

6. If you want to save your packaged presentation to a folder, perhaps to distribute later, click the **Copy To Folder** button. Change the default name and location if appropriate (click **Browse** to find the folder you want). If you have opted to include linked files, you will see a warning message that linked files should be from a trusted source. If you trust your files, click **Yes** to continue.

- If you opted to have the file inspected, the Document Inspector dialog box will appear. After you have completed the inspection, click **Close**.

- When the operation is complete, your packaged presentation will be saved by default to the My Documents folder in a subfolder named after your default filename, unless you have changed it.

  —Or—

  To copy to a CD, click the **Copy To CD** button and follow the onscreen directions. If you have opted to include linked files, you will see a warning message that linked files should be from a trusted source. If you trust your files, click **Yes** to continue. When the package is done copying to the CD, the drive will eject so you can put the newly created CD into a holder.

7. Click **Close** to close the Package For CD dialog box.

 TIP If you have multiple presentations on a CD, they will play in the order they are copied onto the CD.

Create Handouts as a Word Document

From the Export page, use the Create Handouts option to save both your slides and notes as a Microsoft Word document.

1. Click **File**, and then click **Export**. Click **Create Handouts** on the Export page.

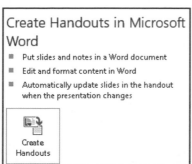

2. Click **Create Handouts** in the right pane to open the Send To Microsoft Word dialog box, shown in Figure 10-21.

3. Choose your page layout option from the options.

4. Click **Paste** to simply paste your slides into your Word document, or click **Paste Link** to ensure that any changes you make to your presentation in PowerPoint will be reflected in this Word document.

5. Click **OK** to close the dialog box. A Word document will open with the handouts included. Be sure to save it.

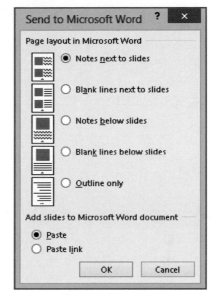

Figure 10-21: You can send your presentation to a Microsoft Word document on your computer or a network with which you are connected.

Change the File Type

When you export a file, you can change the file type. You might do this, for instance, to save the file to an earlier version of PowerPoint, so that others who don't have PowerPoint 2013 can view it more easily. Or you might want to save the file as a template, so that you can create other slide shows using it as a beginning point. You can also make each slide into an image that can be viewed as an image on the Internet, for instance.

1. Click **File**, and then click **Export**. Click **Change File Type** on the Export page, as shown in Figure 10-22. A list of Change File Type options is displayed as follows:

   - Under **Presentation File Types**, select a PowerPoint file type: .pptx for a presentation that can be edited; .ppt for an earlier

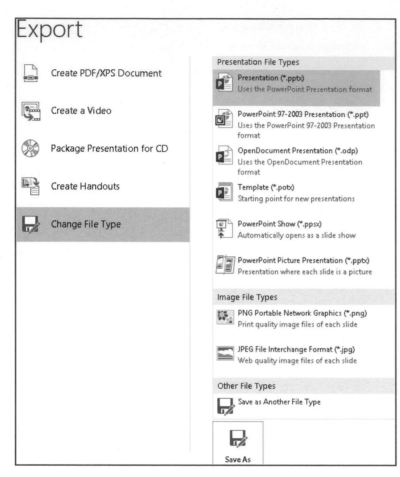

each slide, or select **JPEG** to create a web-quality (.jpg) image of each slide.

- Under **Other File Types**, select **Save As Another File Type** to change to a file type not listed here. There are many others available in the Save As dialog box, Save As Type drop-down list.

File name:	Recommending a Strategy 2.pptx
Save as type:	PowerPoint Presentation (*.pptx)
	PowerPoint Presentation (*.pptx)
Authors:	PowerPoint Macro-Enabled Presentation (*.pptm)
	PowerPoint 97-2003 Presentation (*.ppt)
	PDF (*.pdf)
e Folders	XPS Document (*.xps)
	PowerPoint Template (*.potx)
	PowerPoint Macro-Enabled Template (*.potm)
	PowerPoint 97-2003 Template (*.pot)
COMPARISON OF S.	Office Theme (*.thmx)
(IN MILLI	PowerPoint Show (*.ppsx)
	PowerPoint Macro-Enabled Show (*.ppsm)
Mid North Clerks Clerks	PowerPoint 97-2003 Show (*.pps)

2. Double-click your **Change File Type** option. In the Save As dialog box that displays, verify the Save As address, the File Name, and the Save as Type. Then click **Save**.

PRESENT A SLIDE SHOW

If you plan to present your slide show to an audience, you first need to make some preparations. You must "set up" your slide show, which means you must determine what kind of a presentation it will be and how you will manage it. For instance, you'll need to identify which slides to use and decide whether you'll use a pen or a laser pointer.

▷ Set Controls for Two Monitors

You must set your monitor display settings if you want to use a second monitor during your presentation. For instance, in Presenter View, an environment for presenting a slide show explained later, you control the slide show from a laptop (usually) and display it on a secondary monitor or projector. Only you can see the controls on the primary monitor,

Figure 10-22: Use the Export page to change your presentation's file type.

version of PowerPoint; .odp for an OpenDocument format (used by Google Docs, for example—to save it this way, the presentation must first be saved as a .pptx file); .potx for a PowerPoint template; .ppsx for a PowerPoint slide show (cannot be edited, just viewed as a presentation); or .pptx, where each slide is an image.

- In the **Image File Types** section, select **PNG** to create a print-quality Portable Network Graphics (.png) formatted image of

Understanding Equipment Setup for Presenting with Dual Monitors

If you'll be using dual monitors for the presentation (where one monitor or projector is used for the audience and a second, usually a laptop, is used for the presenter), you'll need to understand how to hook up your laptop to the secondary device.

- To use a laptop computer as the control device for a projector or monitor, you must have the presentation and all linked files on the laptop or have a CD/DVD in the disc drive.

- In addition, you must connect the laptop to the projector or other monitor.

- If you are going to be using sound, you might also need to connect an audio cable from your laptop to the projector or separate speakers if your laptop does not have the capacity you need.

- You may also need to connect a cable from the laptop to the projector to use a wireless mouse.

- Finally, you may need to activate the video-out port on the laptop—that is to set the controls for two monitors.

To connect the laptop to other devices, read the documentation for your laptop.

and the audience only sees the presentation on the secondary monitor. The two displays need to "see" each other and have their resolution and volume fine-tuned.

To set display controls:

1. As described in "Understanding Equipment Setup for Presenting with Dual Monitors QuickFacts," connect the cables from the projector or monitor to the laptop, and connect the audio cables from the speakers to the laptop (consult your laptop documentation).

2. Use the keys appropriate for your computer (for example, **FN+F8** for a Dell computer or **FN+F4** for an HP computer) to synchronize the laptop to the monitor or projector so that both the computer and the monitor display the same image—the screen of the laptop.

3. To set the controls on your laptop computer running Microsoft Windows 7 or 8, right-click the **Desktop** and click **Personalize**.

4. Click **Display**, and then click **Change Display Settings** on the left. The Screen Resolution window shown in Figure 10-23 displays. If your setup is correct, you should see two monitor icons or images. Microsoft displays the recommended settings.

   - If your secondary monitor is not shown, click **Detect**. If it still does not show up, check the wiring to make sure it is connected correctly.

   - If you are not sure which computer is primary (the controlling one) and which is secondary, click **Identify** and a large number 1 and 2 will display on each computer's screen, showing you which is which.

   - Click each of the two monitor images in the dialog box to verify that the settings are correct for each. As you click each, the setting for that monitor will be displayed.

   - Click the **Resolution** down arrow and drag the slider to the resolution if you know that the recommended setting is incorrect. Otherwise, leave it as is.

5. With the Secondary Monitor selected, click the **Multiply Displays** down arrow and choose one of these options:

   - **Extend These Displays** Causes the display to be extended to the second monitor. Use this if you plan to use the Presenter View mode and manually manipulate the slide show. If you plan to use the full-screen slide show on both monitors, do not choose this option.

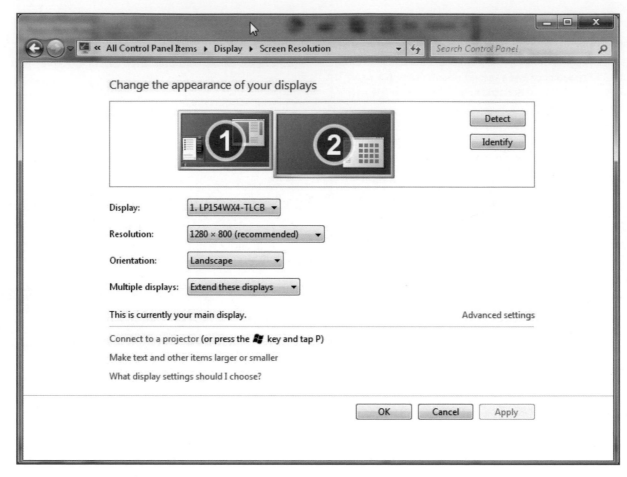

Figure 10-23: You'll need to set up the monitor Display function to use two monitors in your presentation.

- **Duplicate These Displays** Causes the image on the Primary Monitor to be echoed in the Secondary Monitor. Choose this option if you are setting up an automatic slide show, such as in a kiosk.

- **Show Desktop Only On 1 (or Only On 2)** Displays your Desktop on the selected monitor. Use this for a single-monitor display, such as for an individual to watch the standalone presentation.

6. Click **OK** to close the dialog box.

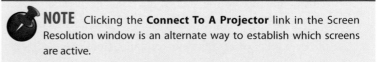 **NOTE** Clicking the **Connect To A Projector** link in the Screen Resolution window is an alternate way to establish which screens are active.

10

Choosing a Presentation Format

Which format you should choose for delivering your presentation depends, of course, on the purpose of the presentation and the intended audience. There are basically three types of slide shows:

● **Looped slide show** This type of slide show, which runs by itself, is useful for a trade show, a kiosk, or any other scenario where you want a full-screen presentation to run automatically, repeatedly, and with no presenter. Viewers who are watching the presentation have limited or no ability to manipulate the delivery of the presentation. This choice is best for delivering your presentation to a large, non-captive audience that will be strolling by and may choose to watch briefly or watch the full slide show.

● **Presenter View** This type of slide show is useful when you want to manually control the delivery of your presentation to an audience, whether it's a full auditorium of listeners or a small group such as a classroom, a meeting, or a family gathering. Presenter View offers a structured way of controlling the slide show. The audience sees the full-screen slide show on a secondary monitor. On the primary monitor (usually a laptop), you see "presenter view" with a smaller-sized slide show, tools to use during the slide show, thumbnails of the slides, and speaker notes.

● **Browsed by an individual** This is an automatic slide show with limited control given to the audience. The slide show is displayed in a computer window, not necessarily full screen, while an individual simply watches it.

In all three cases, you must set up the controls to display appropriately, and you must prepare the slide show.

Set Up Your Slide Show

Setting up your slide show includes determining what kind of slide show you want to give and how you want to present it. You need to determine whether you will manually control the slide advancement or have it occur automatically, and which slides you want to display in the slide show.

Establish Slide Show Controls

You establish the slide show controls in the Set Up Show dialog box, shown in Figure 10-24.

1. Click the **Slide Show** tab, and click **Set Up Slide Show** in the Set Up group.

2. You have these choices:

   ● Under Show Type, determine the type of presentation and how it will be run:

      ● Click **Presented By A Speaker (Full Screen)** to display a full-screen slide show that will have a speaker controlling the slide display.

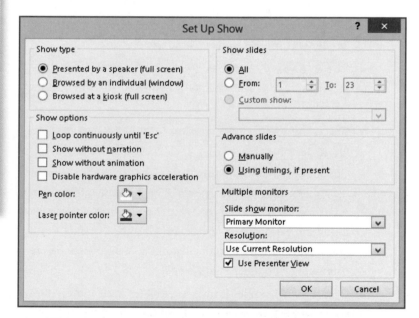

Figure 10-24: The Set Up Show dialog box controls essential information about the slide show.

- Click **Browsed By An Individual (Window)** if the slide show will be run by the viewer.

- Click **Browsed At A Kiosk (Full Screen)** if the slide show is to run automatically with no intervention by the viewer.

- Under **Show Slides**, determine which slides will be displayed:

  - **All**, the default setting for a slide show, shows all slides in the presentation.

  - To show a range of slides, click the **From** and **To** spinners to set the range.

  - To show slides selected for a custom show, check the **Custom Show** check box, and click the name of the custom show you want from the drop-down list. (Note that you first must create a custom show for it to be available here. Click **Custom Slide Show** in the Start Slide Show group to begin.)

- Under **Show Options** you have these choices:

  - Check **Loop Continuously Until 'Esc'** to cause the presentation to repeat until ESC is pressed. This can be used for a trade show, for instance.

  - Check **Show Without Narration** to suppress the narration during the slide show.

  - Check **Show Without Animation** to hide any animation in the presentation. This can speed up the slide show and make it easier to control. You do not have to click the mouse repeatedly to initiate various animations and advance the slide show, nor do you have to wait for the animations to occur before continuing with the presentation.

  - Do not check **Disable Hardware Graphics Acceleration** since you want the presentation to be as fast as it can be.

- If you will be using a pen to mark up the slide show, click the **Pen Color** down arrow and pick a color.

- If you will be using a laser pointer to help guide your viewers through the presentation, click the **Laser Pointer Color** down arrow and choose a color.

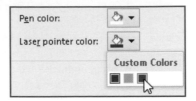

- Under **Advance Slides**, designate whether you will manually advance slides (**Manually**) or use timings already set on the slides (**Using Timings, If Present**).

- Refer to the next section, "Use a Presenter View Slide Show," for what to do with the Multiple Monitors area of the dialog box.

3. When you are done with the Set Up Show dialog box, click **OK** to close it.

 CAUTION If you have set any animations to occur, they may also be included in the timings. For instance, if you have the automatic timing set for 10 seconds and also have a heading that will be displayed, the slide will be displayed first, the heading will be displayed after 10 seconds, and the next slide will appear 10 seconds after that. If the animation does not advance the way you expect, look in your animation settings to see if the start of the animation is set for "on click," requiring you to click the mouse to start the animation.

Use a Presenter View Slide Show

Presenter View offers a structured way of controlling the slide show. The full-screen slide show is displayed on the secondary monitor, and a smaller-sized window for working with the slide show, the primary monitor, contains tools, thumbnails of the slides, and speaker (Figure 10-25 shows an example).

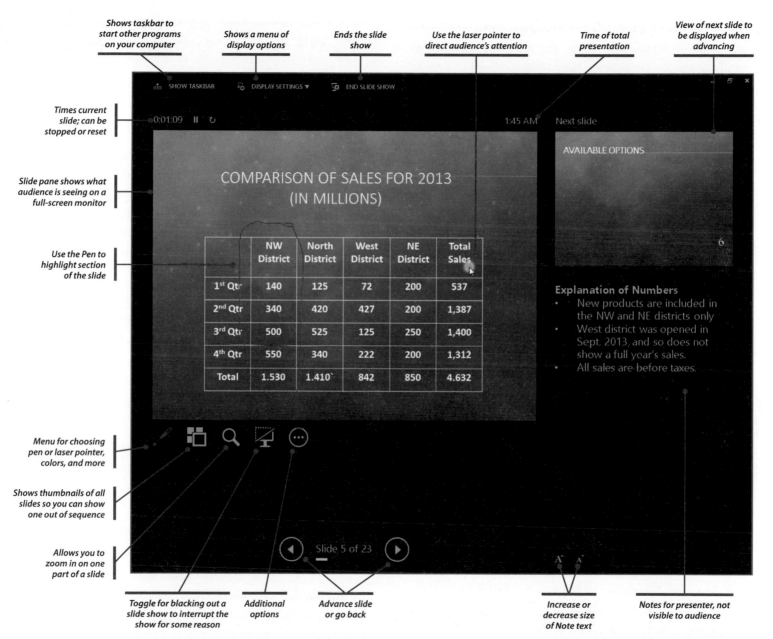

Shows taskbar to start other programs on your computer

Shows a menu of display options

Ends the slide show

Use the laser pointer to direct audience's attention

Time of total presentation

View of next slide to be displayed when advancing

Times current slide; can be stopped or reset

Slide pane shows what audience is seeing on a full-screen monitor

Use the Pen to highlight section of the slide

Menu for choosing pen or laser pointer, colors, and more

Shows thumbnails of all slides so you can show one out of sequence

Allows you to zoom in on one part of a slide

Toggle for blacking out a slide show to interrupt the show for some reason

Additional options

Advance slide or go back

Increase or decrease size of Note text

Notes for presenter, not visible to audience

SHOW TASKBAR   DISPLAY SETTINGS ▼   END SLIDE SHOW

@0:01:09 ‖ ↺   1:45 AM   Next slide

AVAILABLE OPTIONS

COMPARISON OF SALES FOR 2013 (IN MILLIONS)

	NW District	North District	West District	NE District	Total Sales
1st Qtr	140	125	72	200	537
2nd Qtr	340	420	427	200	1,387
3rd Qtr	500	525	125	250	1,400
4th Qtr	550	340	222	200	1,312
Total	1.530	1.410`	842	850	4.632

6

Explanation of Numbers
- New products are included in the NW and NE districts only
- West district was opened in Sept. 2013, and so does not show a full year's sales.
- All sales are before taxes.

Slide 5 of 23

A˙ A˙

Figure 10-25: Presenter View contains a duplicate of what the audience is seeing plus notes, thumbnails of coming slides, and tools for interacting with the slides during the show.

After you have enabled the dual-monitor support, you can open your presentation to set up the slide show. The following steps take you through the slide show controls you need to set.

1. Open your presentation in PowerPoint.
2. In the Slide Show tab Set Up group, click **Set Up Slide Show**. The Set Up Show dialog box is displayed (shown earlier in Figure 10-24).
   - Under Show Type, click **Presented By A Speaker (Full Screen)**.
   - Under Advance Slides, click **Manually**.
   - Under Multiple Monitors, click the **Slide Show Monitor** down arrow, and choose between **Automatic** and (usually) **Primary Monitor**.

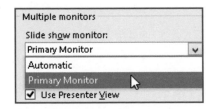

   - Check the **Use Presenter View** check box to make the Presenter View tools available to you on the primary monitor.
3. Click **OK**.

Start the Slide Show

Here are the ways you can start a slide show:

- In the Slide Show tab Start Slide Show group, click **From Beginning**.
- Click **Slide Show** in the taskbar to test the display from the current slide.
- Press **F5** to start the presentation from the beginning.
- In My Computer or Windows Explorer, find the .pptx file for the presentation and double-click it, or right-click the file name and click **Show** on the context menu.

Set Up an Automated Slide Show

As mentioned previously, a repeating, automated slide show is useful, for example, for delivering a marketing pitch at a trade show. This is usually executed with a dual-monitor system controlled from "behind the scenes" by a laptop that is managed by someone who initiates the slide show and ensures that it runs smoothly. The following steps explain your options for setting up an automated slide show (see the earlier section "Set Up Your Slide Show" for additional information).

1. In the Slide Show tab Set Up group, click **Set Up Slide Show** to open the Set Up Show dialog box (refer to Figure 10-24).
2. Click **Browsed At A Kiosk (Full Screen)**. When you choose this option, the Loop Continuously Until 'Esc' check box under Show Options is checked by default and is dimmed (unavailable to be changed).

   –Or–

   Click **Browsed By An Individual (Window)** and check **Loop Continuously Until 'Esc'** to have the slide show automatically repeat with some viewer manipulation possible.

   –Or–

   Click **Presented By A Speaker (Full Screen)** and select the **Loop to use that method of getting automatic play**.
3. Under Advance Slides, click **Using Timings, If Present**. This ensures that the slides advance by themselves without external manipulation.
4. Click **OK** to close the Set Up Show dialog box.

Record Narrations and Timings

If you are creating a presentation that will run automatically, you'll want to record your narrations of the slides and any pen, laser pointer, or highlight gestures. As you do this, the timing for each slide will be recorded. You can then edit your narration to modify the timings if need be.

To record your slide show:

1. In the Slide Show tab Set Up group, click the **Record Slide Show** down arrow (as shown next). Click **Start Recording From Beginning** to start the recording from the first slide; click **Start Recording From Current Slide** to start the recording from the currently selected slide.

 TIP If you need to start over, click **Clear** and select which timing or narration you want to remove.

2. In the Record Slide Show dialog box, choose what you want to record (you can check both boxes):

   - Check **Slide And Animation Timings** to record the timings of how long each slide and animation should be displayed.

   - Check **Narrations And Laser Pointer** to record your voice and any laser or pen gestures you'll use during the presentation. You must have a microphone to do this.

3. Click **Start Recording**. You'll see a Recording toolbar on your screen, as shown in Figure 10-26.

   - Click the **Next** arrow to advance to the next animation or slide.

   - Click **Pause Recording** to halt the recording.

   - Click **Repeat** to start recording over again, allowing you to edit what you've done.

   - You can see each slide's timing and the total time for the slide show.

4. When you are finished recording, click **Close** in the Recording toolbar.

5. When you see a message informing you of the total time and asking if you want to save it, click **Yes**. Each slide for which you've recorded timing will display according to its time when the controls described in the following topics are set.

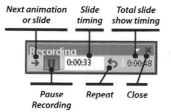

Figure 10-26: The Recording toolbar allows you to monitor and control the timings on your recording and rehearsal sessions.

Rehearse Your Timing

You can gauge the length of time it takes you to present your slide show by rehearsing it. You can experiment with the timings, either testing previously recorded narratives that you have created or using your own presenter notes as a tool to help you move through the presentation.

1. With your presentation in Normal or Slide Sorter view, click the **Slide Show** tab, and click **Rehearse Timings** in the Set Up group.

2. The presentation will begin with a full-screen slide show, with the Recording toolbar in the upper-left corner of the screen (previously shown in Figure 10-26).

3. Go through your slide show as you expect to actually present it, using the tools in the toolbar as needed to advance to the next slide, to pause the rehearsal, or to repeat and try it again.

4. When you are done, click **Close** in the Recording dialog box, and click **Yes** to record the timings and create a timed presentation. The timings will appear on the bottom of the slides in Slide Sorter view. Click **No** to discard the timings.

> **TIP** Try these tricks to speed up your presentation: reduce the screen resolution; use hardware graphics acceleration if it is available on your computer; reduce animation of individual objects and bullets or the size of animated pictures on a slide; simplify the animations you have; and avoid using background special effects, such as gradient-, textured-, or transparency-enhanced backgrounds.

QuickSteps to...

Chapter 11

Using Outlook

When someone mentions Outlook, the first thought is generally the sending and receiving of e-mail. Outlook does handle e-mail quite competently, but it also does a lot more, including managing your schedule with the Outlook Calendar. This chapter covers some of the many features of Microsoft Outlook 2013.

SET UP E-MAIL

The Internet provides a global pipeline through which e-mail flows; therefore, you need a connection that lets you tap into that pipeline. Both local and national Internet service providers (ISPs) offer e-mail with their Internet connections. At your work or business, you may have an e-mail account over a local area network (LAN) that also connects to the Internet. You can also obtain e-mail accounts on the Internet that are independent of the connection. You can access these Internet accounts (Gmail by Google, for example) from anywhere in the world. These three ways of accessing Internet e-mail—ISPs, corporate connections, and Internet e-mail—use different types of e-mail systems.

- **POP3** (Post Office Protocol 3), used by ISPs, retrieves e-mail from a dedicated mail server, and is usually combined with SMTP (Simple Mail Transfer Protocol) to send e-mail from a separate server.
- **MAPI** (Messaging Application Programming Interface) lets businesses handle e-mail on Microsoft Exchange Servers and LANs.

- **HTTP** (HyperText Transfer Protocol) transfers information from servers on the World Wide Web to browsers (that's why your browser's address line starts with "http://") and is used with Outlook .com and other Internet mail accounts.

See how to set up your Outlook account in the sections that follow.

Set Up Your Outlook Account

The first time you start Outlook on either a new computer with Office 2013 or a new installation of Office 2013, the Welcome to Outlook 2013 message appears. Proceed as follows to set up e-mail in Outlook:

1. Click **Next** to open the Outlook 2013 Account Setup dialog box.

2. Accept the default response of Yes to configure an e-mail account, and click **Next**.

3. With the default **E-mail Account** radio button selected, type your name, e-mail address, and password. Then retype the password. Click **Next**.

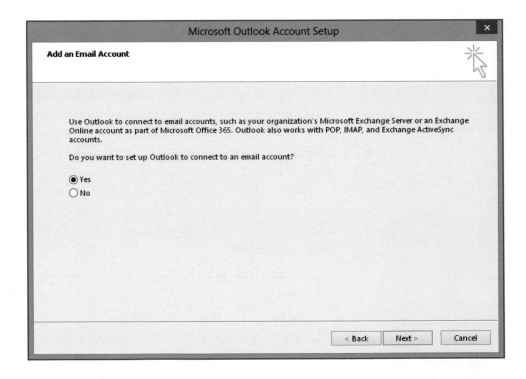

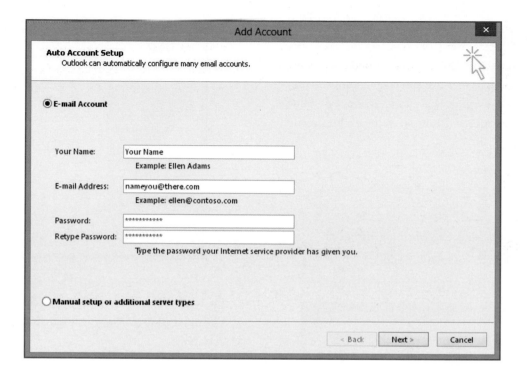

4. E-mail configuring may take several minutes. Click **Next** for both an encrypted account and one that is unencrypted. Depending on your ISP, you may have to check **Manually Configure Server Settings**, click **Next**, click **Internet E-mail**, click **Next**, enter the information provided by your Internet mail provider, and click **Next**.

5. When the configuration has finished and your account settings have tested successfully, you will see a dialog box showing the steps that were taken and the results. Click **Close** to continue.

6. Click **Finish** and your new Outlook account will open.

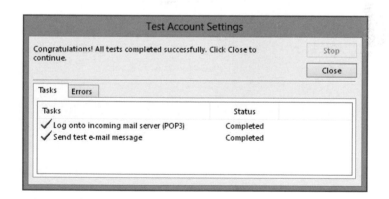

7. If you have been using another e-mail program, you may be asked if you want to make Outlook 2013 your default e-mail program. If you do (this is recommended), click **Yes**.

▷▷ Upgrade to Outlook

If you have been using Outlook 2003, 2007, or 2010, Outlook 2013 should automatically locate your previous message and contact files and move them over to Outlook 2013. You cannot have two versions of Outlook on your computer, so Outlook 2013 will uninstall your previous version and pick up your old files.

If you have been using an older version of Outlook and were not asked if you want to upgrade, you can still import your e-mail files into Outlook.

1. Start Outlook (in one of the ways described in Chapter 1).

2. Click the **File** tab and then click **Open & Export**.

3. Click **Import/Export**. The Import And Export Wizard opens.

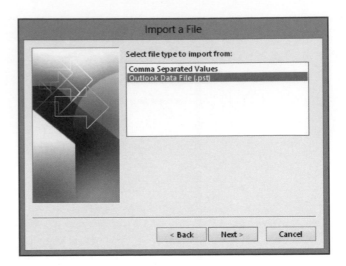

4. Click **Import From Another Program Or File**, and click **Next**.

5. In the Import A File dialog box, leave the default selection of Outlook Data File (.pst) and click **Next**.

6. In the Import Output Data File dialog box, click **Browse** to locate the data file you want to import. Select it and click **Open**. Under **Options**, choose how you want to handle duplicates, and then click **Next**.

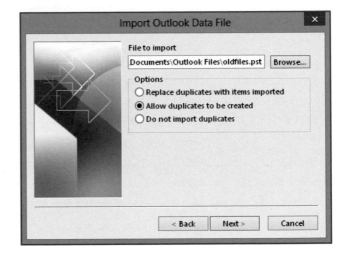

7. After you have made your choices, click **Finish**.

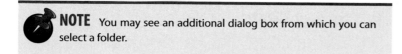

NOTE You may see an additional dialog box from which you can select a folder.

A message reports the progress as the file is being imported, after which you will see a summary upon completion.

EXPLORE OUTLOOK

The Outlook 2013 window, in keeping with the upgrades to Office 2013, uses a wide assortment of windows, toolbars, menus, the ribbon, and

special features to accomplish its functions. This chapter explores how to find and use the most common of these items. In this section, you'll explore the primary Outlook window, including the parts of the window, the ribbon, buttons in the principal groups, and the major menus.

Explore the Outlook Window

The initial view when you first start Outlook is for handling mail, as shown in Figure 11-1. It contains the primary tools for navigating and performing tasks within Outlook.

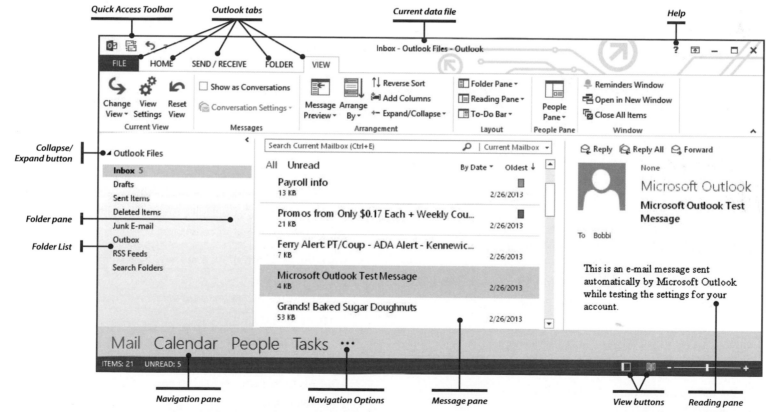

Figure 11-1: Use the default Outlook window for handling mail.

Here is a quick overview of how you use these features—most will be more fully explained in this chapter:

- **Quick Access toolbar**   Contains the most common commands you use. You can customize this toolbar so that it contains exactly the tools and commands you need all the time.

- **Outlook tabs**   Contain commands organized for a specific function. For example, the Send/Receive folder contains the commands you need to send and receive e-mail.

- **Current data file**   This is the Outlook account you are currently using.

- **Help**   Opens the Help system for Outlook.

- **Reading pane**   Contains the content for the selected message.

- **View buttons**   Contain a quick way to vary your views of the window. The Normal view contains the various panes as displayed in Figure 11-1. The Reading view replaces the Folder pane and the To-Do bar (introduced later in the chapter) with an enlarged Reading pane.

- **Message pane**   This section displays your e-mail messages.

- **Navigation Options**   Allows you to change the display of your navigation tools.

- **Navigation pane**   Lists the Outlook sections available with a simple click. This list can be tailored to display the options you choose. You may choose to display up to six options; in Figure 11-1, we have chosen to include four options, including Tasks. By default, it does not list Tasks, Journal, and Notes, but you can add them by clicking the Navigation Options ellipsis.

- **Folder List**   Lists the folders available to you.

- **Folder pane**   Contains your folders.

- **Collapse/Expand button**   Displays or hides the information within a particular folder.

 ## Change Views

You can easily change the view on the main Outlook window, depending on what you want to see. Typically, you will see the Folder pane, the Message pane, and the Reading pane. Both the Message and Reading panes relate to the mail component. You may change these by clicking another Outlook view. For example, clicking Calendar in the Navigation pane replaces the Message and Reading panes with the current calendar.

 ## Use the Navigation Pane

You choose the Outlook section with which you want to work in the Outlook Navigation pane (see Figure 11-1). You can choose to work with Mail, the Calendar, the People with whom you correspond, upcoming (or completed) Tasks, and, by clicking the Navigation Options ellipsis, Notes, and Folders.

 NOTE   In Outlook 2013, your contact list and address book are found in the People view.

Minimize and Restore the Folder Pane

If you need more room to display a message's contents, you can minimize the Folder pane or turn it off completely.

- Click the **Minimize** button at the top of the Folder pane to reduce its size. Click it again (now the Expand button) to restore the pane to its regular size.

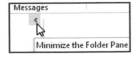

  –Or–

- In the View tab Layout group, click **Folder Pane | Minimized**. To restore the Folder pane, click **Folder Pane | Normal**.

Use Navigation Options

There are three additional options found in the Navigation Options ellipsis:

- **Notes** allows you to create a "virtual" yellow sticky note. This note can be dragged to any part of your desktop for easy access.
- **Folders** makes your Folders pane visible when you are in any view other than the Mail view.
- **Shortcuts** helps you set shortcuts to access your favorite folders.

To change the order of the views in the Navigation pane:

1. Click the **Navigation Options** ellipsis. The Navigation Options menu opens.
2. Click **Navigation Options** to open the Navigation Options dialog box. In the Display In This Order box, select a view whose order you want to change in the Navigation pane and then click the **Move Down** or **Move Up** button to change its position. Repeat this process until the views are in your preferred order.

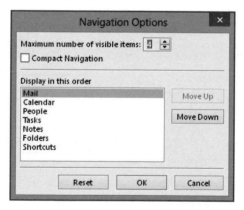

3. Click the **Maximum Number Of Visible Items** spinner if you want to change the maximum number of items number displayed in the Navigation pane.

4. To show each item as an icon instead of the word, check the **Compact Navigation** check box.

5. Click **OK** to close the Navigation Options dialog box.

RECEIVE E-MAIL

With at least one e-mail account installed in Outlook, you're ready to receive mail. If Mail view, shown in Figure 11-2, is not currently displayed, click **Mail** in the Navigation pane.

⏩ Check for E-mail

Once you are set up, it's easy to download mail. You can check for your e-mail manually or set Outlook to check automatically.

Manually Check for E-mail

1. Make sure your computer is connected to the Internet or is configured to automatically connect.
2. Click **Send/Receive All Folders** on the Quick Access toolbar (or on the Home tab) or press **F9**.

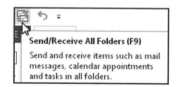

3. If the Inbox folder is not already selected in the Folder list, click it now, and watch the mail come in. If you have several e-mail accounts, each with its own *mailbox* in the Folder list, select the specific Inbox folder that you want to view from among the several mailboxes. You may need to scroll through the Folder list and first click the mailbox to see its Inbox.

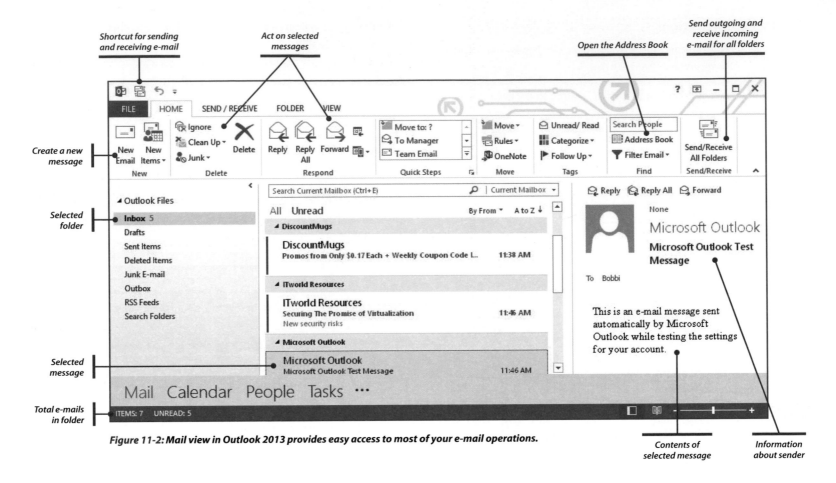

Shortcut for sending
and receiving e-mail

Act on selected
messages

Open the Address Book

Send outgoing and
receive incoming
e-mail for all folders

Create a new
message

Selected
folder

Selected
message

Total e-mails
in folder

Contents of
selected message

Information
about sender

Figure 11-2: Mail view in Outlook 2013 provides easy access to most of your e-mail operations.

Receive E-mail Automatically

You can configure Outlook to automatically check your e-mail provider's server for new e-mail on a regular basis. Outlook then gives you a brief Desktop alert if it finds new e-mail. Desktop alerts are subtle, given the way they quietly fade in and out.

1. Click the **File** tab, click **Options** and the Outlook Options window opens. From the left side of the window, click **Advanced**. The Options for Working with Outlook window opens.

2. Scroll to Send And Receive, and click **Send/Receive**. The Send/ Receive Groups dialog box appears, shown in Figure 11-3.

3. Under the Setting For Group "All Accounts" section, check **Schedule An Automatic Send/Receive Every**, type or click the spinner to enter the number of minutes to elapse between checking, and click **Close**. Click **OK** to close the Outlook Options window.

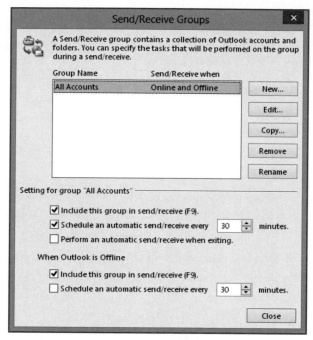

Figure 11-3: Use the Send/Receive Groups dialog box to specify how to receive e-mail messages.

Read E-mail

Besides being easy to obtain, e-mail messages are effortless to open and read. There are two ways to view the body of the message:

- Double-click the message and read it in the window that opens, as shown in Figure 11-4.

    –Or–

- Click the message and read it in the Reading pane, scrolling as needed.

Of course, you can also control which accounts you check, what kinds of e-mail you let in, and how e-mail messages are presented from the related Outlook Options windows.

Filter Junk Mail

Outlook can automatically filter out a lot of annoying spam before you ever see it, and it can set aside suspicious-looking messages in a Junk

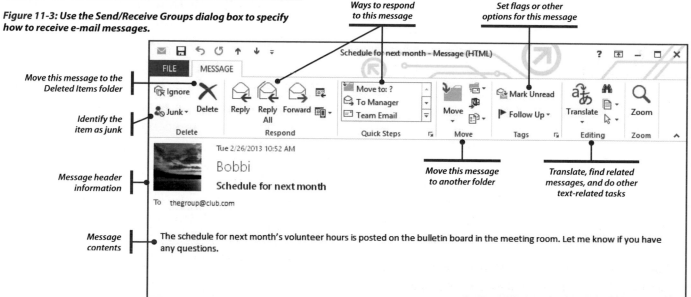

Ways to respond to this message

Set flags or other options for this message

Move this message to the Deleted Items folder

Identify the item as junk

Message header information

Message contents

Move this message to another folder

Translate, find related messages, and do other text-related tasks

Figure 11-4: The e-mail Message window contains the information and tools you need to reply to the message.

e-mail folder. It does this in two ways: by analyzing message content based on a protection level you choose, and by having you identify good and bad senders.

Outlook also prevents pictures and sounds from being downloaded into messages that contain HTML formatting. Up to now, savvy spammers have been able to design messages that only download images when you open or preview the message. They plant *Web beacons* in the messages, which tell their server that they have reached a valid address so that they can send you even more junk. Outlook blocks both the external content, as shown in Figure 11-5, and the beacon, unless you tell it to unblock it.

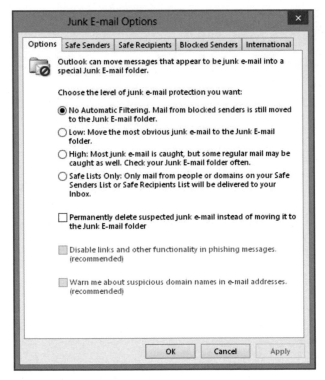

Figure 11-5: The Junk E-mail Options dialog box is where you can block image and sound files, as well as specific senders.

 NOTE One easy way to reduce the junk e-mail you get is to *avoid* replying to any suspicious message. If you reply and tell them to go away, they learn that they reached a valid address, which they will hit again and again.

Unblock Picture Downloads

By default, picture downloads are blocked to speed up the downloading of e-mail. To change that for specific items:

- For a **single opened message**, click **Click Here To Download Pictures** in the information bar at the top of the message, or right-click an individual picture and click **Download Pictures**.

- For **all mail from the source of the open message**, right-click a blocked item, point at **Junk**, and click **Never Block Sender's Domain (@example.com)**.

- For **all HTML mail** (not recommended), click **File**, click **Options**, click **Trust Center**, click **Trust Center Setting**, and clear the **Don't Download Pictures Automatically In HTML E-mail Messages Or RSS Items** check box. Click **OK** twice.

WRITE MESSAGES

Creating an e-mail message can be as simple as dispatching a note or as elaborate as designing a marketing poster. It's wise to get used to creating simple messages before attempting to make an art project of one. Without your having to impose any guidelines, however, Outlook is set to create an attractive basic e-mail message.

 NOTE The Outlook 2013 new Message window has many of the features of the Microsoft Word 2013 window and provides many of the tools available in Word.

▷▷ Create a Message

One click starts a message, and the only field you have to complete is the address of the recipient. However, at least three fields should be filled in before you send the message:

- **Recipient** One or more e-mail addresses or names in your Address Book

- **Subject** Words indicating the contents of the message (also used by the Find tool in a search)

- **Message body** Whatever you want to say to the recipient

To start a message, with Outlook open and Mail selected in the Navigation pane, click the **New Email** button in the Home tab New group. A new Message window opens, as shown in Figure 11-6.

New Email

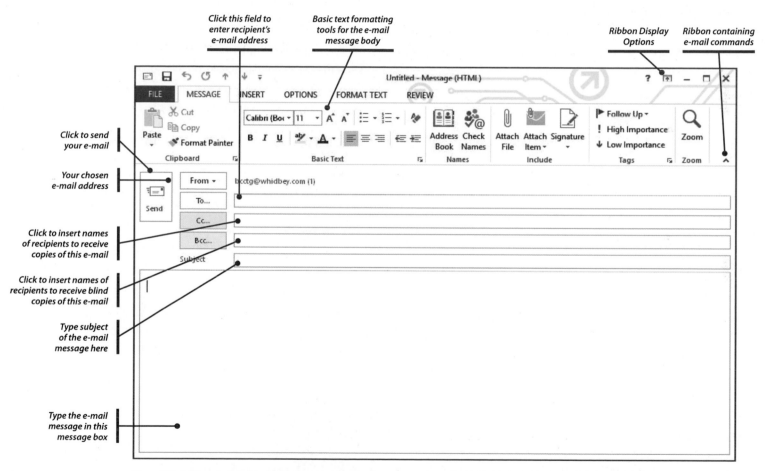

Figure 11-6: The window for creating a message contains important differences from the one in which you read them.

TIP To gain more working space, click the **Ribbon Display Options** button on the right, next to the Help icon, or double-click the active tab name. This opens a menu of options that lets you hide the ribbon/ title bar, show only tabs, or show tabs and commands.

TIP Click any of the To, Cc, or Bcc buttons to open a list of contacts.

▷ Address a Message

Addressing messages in Outlook is easy. Of course, the address itself is simple: *username@domain.extension* (such as "mary@someisp.com"). Once you have entered names in the Address Book or the Contacts workspace, as described later in the chapter, you can address your messages with almost no typing.

Type the Address

This is the most basic addressing technique. As soon as you click New Email, the cursor blinks in the To field of the Message window.

- For a **single recipient**, type the address.

- For **multiple recipients**, type each address, separating them with a semicolon (;) and a space. (You can also separate with a comma and a space. Outlook will automatically replace commas with semicolons once it recognizes the entries as e-mail addresses.)

Select a Name from the Address Book

1. Click **To**. The Select Names dialog box displays your Address Book, shown in Figure 11-7.

2. Scroll through the list, and double-click the name of the person to whom you want to send the e-mail.

3. For multiple recipients, if a comma or semicolon wasn't automatically added after a name you selected or entered, type one of those characters and a space between names or e-mail addresses.

4. Repeat steps 2 and 3 as needed until the names of all recipients are listed in the To text box. An alternate way is to hold down CTRL while you scroll manually and click all desired names. Then click **To**.

5. Click **OK**.

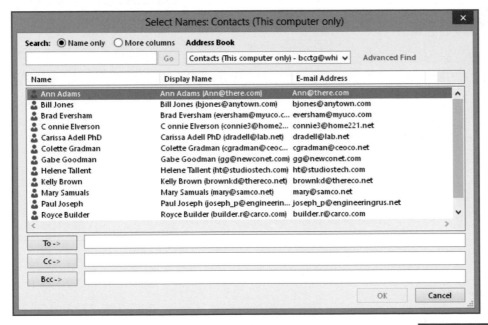

Figure 11-7: Your Outlook Address Book can become a valuable repository.

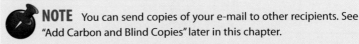

NOTE You can send copies of your e-mail to other recipients. See "Add Carbon and Blind Copies" later in this chapter.

Complete Addresses Automatically

Outlook runs AutoComplete by default. As soon as you type the first letter of an address, Outlook begins searching for matches among names and addresses you've typed in the past.

1. Begin typing a name or address in the To field in the Message window. The closest names to what you have typed will be displayed in the Name list.

2. If the name you want appears in the list, click it, or press **DOWN ARROW** (if necessary) until the name is highlighted, and then click it or press **ENTER** to accept the address. The name displays, a semicolon follows it, and the cursor blinks where the next name would appear.

3. If you wish to add another recipient, begin typing another name, and repeat the process as needed.

4. Press **TAB** to go to the next desired field.

 NOTE If you want to turn off AutoComplete, click the **File** tab, click **Options**, and click **Mail** in the left pane. Under Send Messages, clear the **Use Auto-Complete List To Suggest Names When Typing In The To, Cc, And Bcc Lines** check box. Click **OK** to close.

Send messages

Default Importance level: ⬚ Normal ▾

Default Sensitivity level: Normal ▾

☐ Mark messages as expired after this many days: 0 ⬚

☐ Always use the default account when composing new messages

☑ Commas can be used to separate multiple message recipients

☑ Automatic name checking

☑ Delete meeting requests and notifications from Inbox after responding

☑ CTRL + ENTER sends a message

☐ Use Auto-Complete List to suggest names when typing in the To, Cc, and Bcc lines

☑ Warn me when I send a message that may be missing an attachment

Enter a New Name into the Address Book from Mail View

You can quickly enter a new name into your e-mail Address Book in Outlook 2013.

1. In the Home tab Find group, click **Address Book**. The Address Book dialog box appears.

2. Click **File | New Entry**.

3. In the New Entry dialog box, select **New Contact** and click **OK** to continue.

4. Enter the information, including name, e-mail address, and so on, using the **TAB** key to move from field to field.

5. When you have entered all the information, click **Save & Close** to close the dialog box.

For another method, see "Create Contacts in People View" later in this chapter.

▷▷ Add Carbon and Blind Copies

You may never have seen a real carbon copy, but Outlook keeps the concept alive by way of this feature located just below the To field in the new Message window. Persons who receive a message with their e-mail address in the *Cc* (carbon copy) line understand that they are not the primary recipients—they got the message as an FYI (for your information), and all other recipients can see that they got it (see Figure 11-8). A *Bcc* (blind carbon copy) hides addresses entered in that line from anyone else who receives the message.

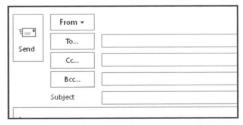

Figure 11-8: The way a message is delivered suggests different roles for the various recipients.

Include or Remove Bcc on New Messages

1. In the Message window, click the **Options** tab.

2. In the Show Fields group, click **Bcc** to toggle the Bcc field on and off.

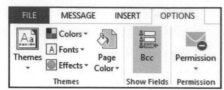

Address the Copies

Type addresses in the Cc and Bcc fields completely or with the aid of AutoComplete.

1. Click **Cc** or **Bcc** in the Message window.

2. If you have AutoComplete turned off, type the addresses. With AutoComplete turned on, begin typing a name to scroll through the names, and double-click the name(s) in the Address Book you want to be copied.

▷▷ Edit a Message

With Outlook, you can create e-mail in any of three formats, and you have the additional option of using the powerful formatting capability of Microsoft Word for composing messages. Outlook handles all three formats quite easily, but sometimes you need to consider your recipients' computer resources and Internet connections.

- **HTML** (HyperText Markup Language), the default format, lets you freely use design elements, such as colors, pictures, links, animations, sound, and movies (though good taste and the need to control the size of the message file might suggest a little discretion!).

- **Plain Text** format lies at the other extreme, eliminating embellishments so that any computer can manage the message.

- **Rich Text Format** (RTF) takes the middle ground, providing font choices—including color, boldface, italics, and underlining—basic paragraph layouts, and bullets.

With Outlook, you can edit messages you create and messages you receive (when replying to or forwarding them). Regardless which of the three formats you choose, some editing processes are always available, as shown in Table 11-1.

Using HTML or Rich Text Format provides a wide range of options for enhancing the appearance of a message. Finally, you can also create the message in another program and copy and paste it into a message body. HTML will preserve the formatting exactly, and Rich Text Format will come close.

Table 11-1: Standard Editing Operations

To		Do This	
Insert new text in the message body		Click where new text belongs, and type new text.	
Indent the start of a paragraph		Click before the first letter of the paragraph, and press **TAB**.	
Replace a	Word	Double-click the word.	Type new text.
	Line	Click to the left of the line.	
	Paragraph	Double-click to the left of the paragraph to select it. Triple-click to select all the text in the message.	
Move a	Word	Double-click the word.	Drag to a new location in the message.
	Line	Click to the left of the line.	
	Paragraph	Double-click to the left of the paragraph.	
Delete a	Word	Double-click the word.	Press **DELETE**.
	Line	Click to the left of the line.	
	Paragraph	Double-click to the left of the paragraph.	

TIP You can also edit received messages when you forward them. This can be handy if you want to forward only the final comment and eliminate the original message text, other comments, or any addresses that show on the message.

Select a Default Message Format

The type of message format being used is displayed in the title bar of the new Message window. You can set a format for an individual message, or set a default format for all messages.

Untitled - Message (HTML)

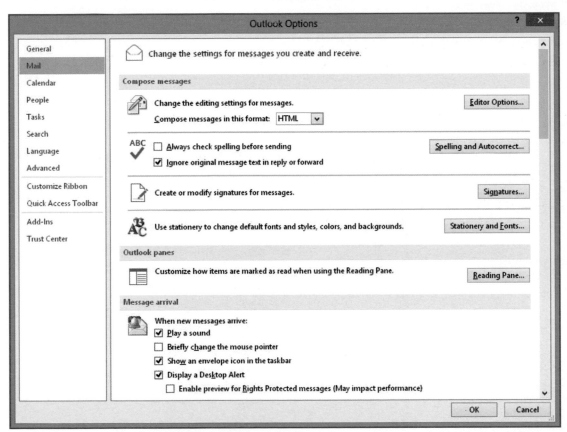

| General |
| Mail |
| Calendar |
| People |
| Tasks |
| Search |
| Language |
| Advanced |
| Customize Ribbon |
| Quick Access Toolbar |
| Add-Ins |
| Trust Center |

Outlook Options

Change the settings for messages you create and receive.

Compose messages

Change the editing settings for messages.   Editor Options...
Compose messages in this format: HTML ▾

ABC ☐ Always check spelling before sending   Spelling and Autocorrect...
✓   ✓ Ignore original message text in reply or forward

Create or modify signatures for messages.   Signatures...

ABC Use stationery to change default fonts and styles, colors, and backgrounds.   Stationery and Fonts...

Outlook panes

Customize how items are marked as read when using the Reading Pane.   Reading Pane...

Message arrival

When new messages arrive:
✓ Play a sound
☐ Briefly change the mouse pointer
✓ Show an envelope icon in the taskbar
✓ Display a Desktop Alert
   ☐ Enable preview for Rights Protected messages (May impact performance)

OK   Cancel

Figure 11-9: You can choose from a number of Outlook Mail options.

To set a default format for all e-mail:

1. In either the Outlook window or a Message window, click the **File** tab, click **Options** to open the Outlook Options window, and click **Mail** in the left pane to open the Mail options, some of which are shown in Figure 11-9.

2. Click the **Compose Messages In This Format** down arrow, and select one of the choices.

3. Click **OK** to close the Outlook Options window.

To set formatting for an individual message:

1. In the Message window, click the **Format Text** tab.

2. In the Format group, click the formatting option you want.

HTML ▾
HTML
Rich Text
Plain Text

Attach Files

Sometimes you will want to send a message that is accompanied by one or more pictures, word-processed documents, sound, or movie files. Creating attachments is like clipping newspaper stories and baby pictures to a letter. If you are editing or otherwise working on the item you want to attach, make sure that you save the latest version before you proceed. After that, click **New** to open the new Message window, and use one of the following attachment procedures.

QuickFacts

Including Hyperlinks

You can add hyperlinks (whether to an Internet site, to other locations in the current document, or to other documents) to your e-mail by typing them into the message body or by copying and pasting them. Outlook creates a live link, which it turns to a blue, underlined font when you type or paste any kind of Internet protocol (such as http:// mailto:, or www.something .com), regardless of what mail format you use.

Define a Hyperlink

In addition to typing the hyperlink address, you can use a dialog box to select the location of the link.

1. In the Message window Insert tab Links group, click **Hyperlink**.

2. In the dialog box that appears, find and select the location of the link—in an existing file, a place in a document, a web page, a new document, or an e-mail address.

3. Click **OK**.

Type Over Hyperlinks

In HTML and Rich Text Format, you can substitute different text for the actual uniform resource locator (URL) or e-mail address and still retain the link. For example, you might display a link entitled "Click here to view the photo gallery" that has an actual link of "www.someorg.com/ mygallery.html."

1. Establish the link as a hyperlink by clicking **Hyperlink** in the Insert tab Links group. Click **OK** in the dialog box, regardless of the selected location.

2. Drag within the URL hyperlink to select it. Leave at least one letter intact at each end of the link.

3. Type something different in the middle of the URL hyperlink. Erase the remaining letters of the original URL hyperlink.

Insert a File

When you attach a file to an e-mail message, you can choose whether you want to actually attach it as a file or have it entered as text into the body of the message. In some cases, you may "attach" it as a hyperlink. The attached file and its commands are identified with a paper clip icon.

1. Display the Insert File dialog box:

   - In the Insert tab Include group, click **Attach File**.

   –Or–

   - In the Message tab Include group, click **Attach File**.

2. In the Insert File dialog box, find and select the file to be attached. Then:

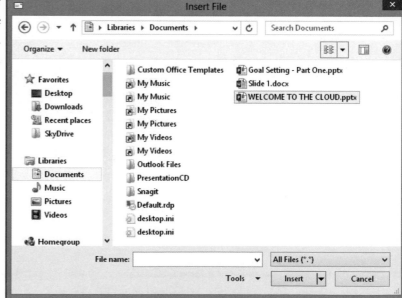

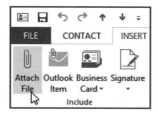

- Click the **Insert** button to insert the file as an attachment. If the e-mail format is HTML or plain text, it will be attached in a field labeled "Attached" beneath the Subject field. If the format is Rich Text Format, the file attachment will be in the body of the message.

  –Or–

- Click the **Insert** down arrow and choose **Insert As Text** to enter the file as text in the message. The file content of certain file types, such as .txt, .doc, and .eml, and the source code of others, such as HTML or HTA (HTML Application), will become part of the message. Everything else—pictures, sound, and movies—will generate nonsense characters in the message body.

3. Complete and send the e-mail message.

Embed a Picture into a Message

Though any kind of file you save on your computer or on a disk can be sent by following the previous steps, you have the added option of placing pictures (.gif, .jpg, .bmp, .tif, and so on) right into the message body.

1. Click in the message body to set the insertion point.

2. In the Insert tab Illustrations group, click **Pictures** to open the Insert Picture dialog box, as shown in Figure 11-10.

3. Select the picture file you want, and click the **Insert** down arrow. From the submenu, choose one of the following options:

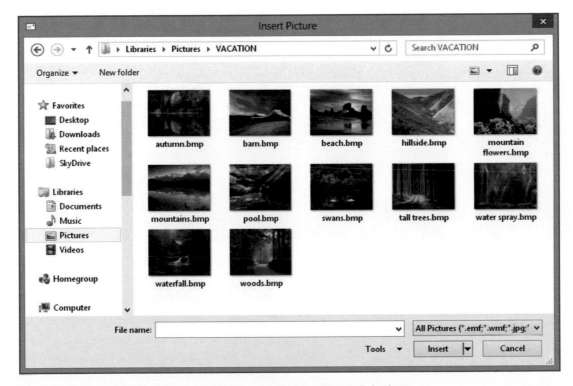

Figure 11-10: You can insert a picture or a link to it using the Insert Picture dialog box.

- Click **Insert** to embed the picture in the message. You can then drag it or size it correctly for your message or right-click and select **Format Picture** to display the Format Picture pane and edit the photo.

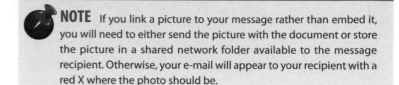

NOTE If you link a picture to your message rather than embed it, you will need to either send the picture with the document or store the picture in a shared network folder available to the message recipient. Otherwise, your e-mail will appear to your recipient with a red X where the photo should be.

- Click **Link To File** to send a link to where the file is stored. This reduces the size of the message, but requires that the recipient have access to the location where the file is stored.

- Click **Insert And Link** to both embed the photo and send a link to its location.

4. Complete and send the e-mail message.

SEND MESSAGES

No postage, no trip to the post office, no running out of envelopes. What could be better? Once a message is ready to go, you can just click a button. Outlook provides features that let you exercise more control over the process than you could ever get from the postal service, or "snail" mail.

Make sure that your message is complete and ready to send, and then click **Send** in the upper-left area of the message.

Reply to Messages

When you receive a message that you want to answer, you have several ways to initiate a reply:

- Open the message and click **Reply** in the Message tab Respond group.

  –Or–

- Right-click the message in the Folder pane, and click **Reply** in the context menu.

  –Or–

- Click the message in the Message pane, and click **Reply** in the Home tab Respond group.

Whichever way you choose, a reply Message window opens. The message will be formatted using the same format the sender used, and the subject will be "RE:" plus the original subject in the Subject line. By default, the pointer blinks in the message body above the original message and sender's address (see also "Change the Reply Layout"). Treat it like a new Message window: type a message, add attachments or links, and click **Send**.

Reply to All Recipients

If the To field in the message contains several recipients, all of whom should read your reply, Outlook makes this simple. Use any of the ways listed in the previous section, but click **Reply All** instead of Reply. The reply Message window will list all original recipients in the To and Cc fields. Send the message as usual.

 TIP Reply, Reply All, and Forward buttons are also located at the top of the Reading pane.

Change the Reply Layout

You can select from five different ways to incorporate the original message. Also, if you'd rather just insert your responses into the original text, Outlook lets you decide how to identify your remarks.

1. Click the **File** tab, click **Options**, and click **Mail** in the left pane.

2. Scroll down the Outlook Options window to the Replies And Forwards section, click the **When Replying To A Message** down arrow, and select how you want the original message included.

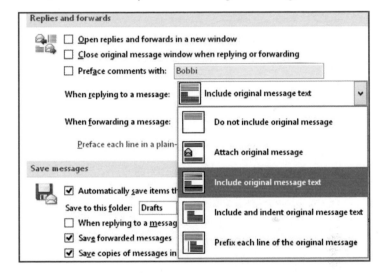

3. Check the **Preface Comments With** check box, and type the label you want.

4. Click **OK**.

Forward Messages

When you forward a message, you send an incoming message to someone else. You can send messages to new recipients, using the same techniques as with the Reply feature.

When you receive a message that you want to forward to someone else, use one of these techniques:

- Open the message and click **Forward** in the Message tab Respond group.

  –Or–

- Right-click the message in the Message pane, and select **Forward** from the context menu.

  –Or–

- Click the message in the Message pane, and click **Forward** in the Home tab Respond group.

  –Or–

- Click the message in the Message pane and click **Forward** in the Reading pane.

A forward Message window opens, with the cursor blinking in the To field and a space above the original message for you to type your own message. Once the forward Message window opens, the simplest action is to enter the recipient's (or recipients') address(es), insert attachments as needed, and send as usual.

Forward Multiple Messages

Rather than forward a bunch of messages one by one, you can bundle them and forward them in one message. In the Message pane:

1. Press **CTRL** while you click each message that you want to forward.

2. Right-click one of the messages in the group, and click **Forward**. A new mail message opens with the messages included as attachments. You may also see the attachments in the Attached box rather than in the message area.

3. Complete the message and send as usual.

HANDLE E-MAIL MESSAGES

E-mail messages have a way of building up fast. Outlook offers a few ways to help you stay organized.

Find a Message

No matter how many messages your e-mail folders contain, Outlook can help you find a specific one. You can perform instant searches for large files, related messages, or messages from a particular sender. You can further qualify the search by having Outlook search only certain folders, or by specifying content for which you're searching.

Perform Instant Searches

Click in the search text box in the Message pane of the Inbox (or whichever folder you want to search in), and type the text for which you want to search. The search will immediately display the found messages beneath the search text box.

Click the down arrow to the right of the search box to include other locations in Outlook.

To remove a search, close the search box by clicking on the X close button.

Refine Searches

In addition to the instant search found in the Message pane, you can use the Search Tools Search contextual tab to refine your searches, as shown in Figure 11-11. These tools become available when you activate an instant search.

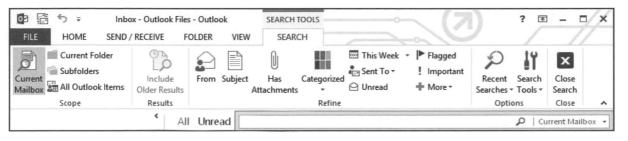

Figure 11-11: Use the Search contextual tab for more in-depth searches.

1. Begin an instant search as described in the previous section. When you click in the instant search box, the Search Tools Search contextual tab will open with the following tab groups that you can use to refine your search:

   - **Scope** Lets you choose the folders you want to include in the search.

   - **Results** Includes all older results. Including this option results in a much longer search time, depending on the number of e-mails in your folder.

   - **Refine** Lets you choose the elements you want to search on. The More drop-down list provides many more elements you can search on.

   - **Options** Lets you repeat previous searches. Click **Search Tools** to choose from the following options for more sophisticated searching:

     - **Indexing Status** Displays a message box telling you the extent to which Outlook messages have been indexed.

     - **Locations To Search** Lets you choose which of your accounts you want to search.

- **Advanced Find** Displays the Advanced Find dialog box, where you can define a search on multiple criteria with considerable detail.

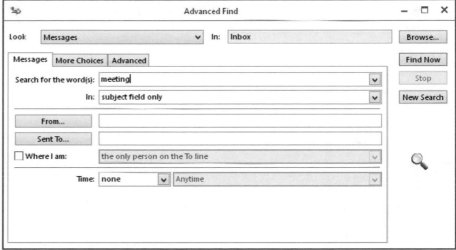

- **Search Options** Opens the Outlook Options window with the Search option selected. See the following section.

2. Make your choices from the Search tab groups. Your choices will appear in the instant search box and the results of your choices are displayed.

3. After you have reviewed the results of your search, click the X on the instant search box to close the search.

Change Search Options

You can change some of the search defaults used with instant search in the Search options of the Outlook Options window, shown in Figure 11-12.

1. Display the Search options, either as described in the previous section (in the Search tab Options group, click **Search Tools | Search Options**) or by clicking the **File** tab, clicking **Options**, and clicking **Search**.

2. In the Sources section, click the **Indexing Options** button, and then click **Modify** to select the drives and folders to be indexed so that searches can be faster. Click **OK** and then click **Close** to close both Indexing dialog boxes.

3. In the Results section, choose, as a default, whether to search just the currently selected folder, the current mailbox, or all mailboxes.

4. Click the **Include Messages From The Deleted Items Folder In Each Data File When Searching In All Items** check box if you wish to include those items in your search.

5. Clear the second, third, and/or fourth check boxes if you want to change the defaults, which are to display results as you type the search text, to limit the number of results so that the searches are faster, and to highlight the search text in results (which also allows you to change the highlight color).

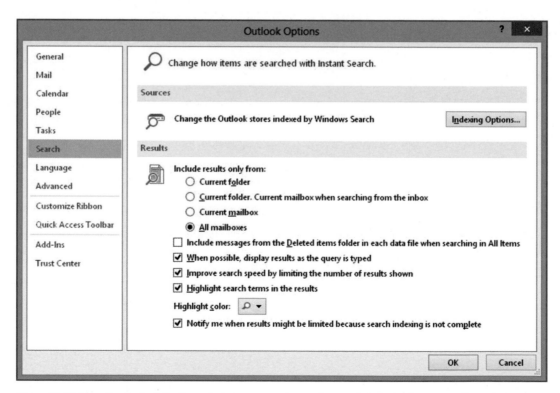

Figure 11-12: Using the Outlook Options window, you can change the search defaults that are used in an instant search.

Archiving Messages

Archiving is for people who have a hard time throwing things away. Outlook is set up on a schedule, which you can see by clicking the **File** tab, clicking **Options**, clicking **Advanced**, and, under AutoArchive, clicking the **AutoArchive Settings** button. (Alternatively, you can click the **File** tab, click **Info**, click **Cleanup Tools**, and click **Archive** to archive your items manually.)

The AutoArchive dialog box that appears allows you to turn on AutoArchive, set the time interval between archive functions, determine when to delete old messages, specify the path to the archived file, and choose other settings. Click **OK** when you are finished.

Your archived files are saved in a file structure that mirrors your Personal folders yet compresses the files and cleans up the Inbox. To open archived files, click **Expand** ▸Archives beside Archives in the Folder pane, and click a folder.

6. Clear the last check box if you don't want to receive a message when results might be limited because the indexing is incomplete for a selected file. If this message is displayed, it tells you that the indexing is still in process and that results will be incomplete.

7. Click **OK**.

⏭ Delete Messages

Outlook creates two stages for deleting messages by providing a Deleted Items folder, which holds all the items you deleted from other folders. In the first stage, you remove deleted items to a separate folder, and in the second stage, you remove the messages from your computer.

Delete Messages from the Inbox

Delete messages by opening a folder in the Folder pane and performing one of the following actions:

- Delete one message by clicking the message and clicking **Delete** in the Home tab Delete group.

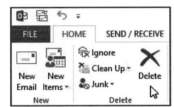

- Right-click a message and click **Delete** from the context menu.

- Delete a block of messages by clicking the first message, holding down SHIFT, clicking the last message (all the messages in between are selected as well), and clicking **Delete** in the Home tab Delete group.

- Delete multiple noncontiguous messages by pressing CTRL while clicking the messages you want to remove, and then clicking **Delete** in the Home tab Delete group.

Empty the Deleted Items Folder

1. Click the **Deleted Items** folder.

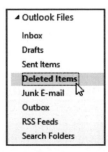

2. Perform one of the following actions:

- Right-click the **Deleted Items** folder, click **Empty Folder**, and click **Yes**.

- Press CTRL+A to select all items in the folder, click **Delete**, and click **Yes**.

- Select files to be permanently deleted (as described in the previous section), click **Delete**, and click **Yes**.

Manage Attachments

Messages that contain files, such as pictures and documents, display a paper clip icon in the second message line within the Message pane to show that there's more to see. Attachments are listed in the message itself in the Reading pane. Since computer vandals like to broadcast debilitating viruses by way of attachments, you should be sure that you are dealing with a trusted source before you open any attachments. Also, it's important to have an up-to-date antivirus program running on your system, as well as any protection provided by your ISP. Make sure you have it, and keep your virus definitions up to date. If you are running Windows 7 or Windows 8, several Internet and e-mail protections are built into them.

When a message comes in with an attachment, you can preview the attachment, open it, or save it first.

Open Attachments

You can open or view an attachment only in the Reading pane.

- Double-click the attachment to open it in your default image program (for example, Windows Photo Viewer in Windows 8).

–Or–

- Right-click the attachment and click either **Preview** or **Open**.

 NOTE If you preview an attachment, it will open in the Reading pane, where you can scroll through the document. To return to the message body, click the **Message** icon next to the attachment at the top of the message.

Save Attachments

You can save any attachment to your hard drive. To do so:

1. Right-click the attachment icon, and click **Save As**.

2. Use the Save Attachment dialog box to navigate to the desired folder.

3. Type a name in the File Name text box, and click **Save**.

 TIP To select multiple attachments in an e-mail at one time—for example, to copy or save them to the same folder—right-click one attachment and click **Select All**. Then, right-click one of the selected attachments and choose the copy or save action.

Open Saved Attachments

1. Navigate to the folder where you saved the file.

2. Double-click the file.

CREATE CONTACTS IN PEOPLE VIEW

The People view allows you to maintain information about your business and personal contacts. It is in this view that you'll find the Address Book and Outlook Contacts. Using the Address Book in Outlook replaces the address book that fits in your pocket and has spaces so tiny that you're forced to write phone numbers trailing down the margins. You no longer have to scratch out and replace entries when people move, or try to fit multiple phone numbers for a contact into a space that's too small to fit more than one.

Outlook Contacts provides a satisfying alternative, helping you keep everything straight and up to date, even information for acquaintances who don't have e-mail. If you are using Outlook on your home computer, there is little difference between the Contacts list and the Address Book. When a company uses Outlook, the Address Book often includes information about each employee and is available across the company network, while the Contact list is stored on each individual's computer rather than the company file server.

A name is all you need to save a contact. The Contact window, shown in Figure 11-13, however, also provides a flexible layout that can store an immense amount of information, which you can use later for professional and social purposes. The ribbon provides for data entry and control in five different groups:

- **Actions** provides file management commands, including Save & Close, Delete, and Save & New. For example, you can click the **Save & New** down arrow and click **Contact From The Same Company** to quickly add a new contact from the same company as the last entry you made. You can also forward the contact information to a third party.

- **Show** commands display all information about your new contact:

  - **General** displays basic information for identifying and getting in touch with the person (shown in Figure 11-13).

  - **Details** provides business and personal data.

  - **Certificates** allows you to import and maintain a contact's digital ID.

  - **All Fields** lets you quickly look up the contents of a variety of fields completed for that contact.

- **Communicate** commands give you tools to send an e-mail message to the new contact, set up a meeting, send an instant message, telephone your new contact, connect to the contact's website, assign a task to the contact, create a journal entry about the contact, or see a map based on the contact's address.

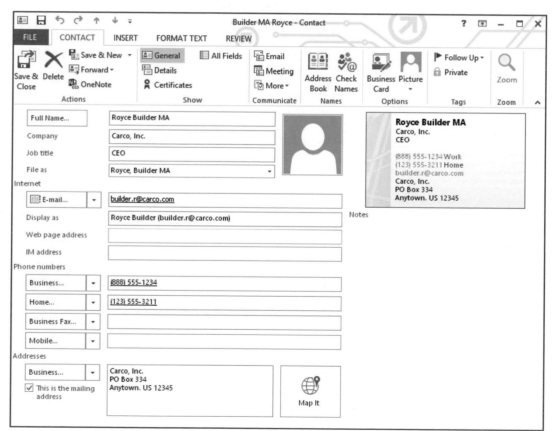

Figure 11-13: The Contact window displays fields into which you can enter information for reaching a contact in a variety of ways.

- **Names** commands let you display the entire Address Book as well as verify names and e-mail addresses to ensure you have typed the information correctly.

- **Options** commands allow you to add or modify the contact's electronic business card and add a picture to your Contact dialog box.

- **Tags** commands let you categorize your contact with any one of six categories that you can customize, create follow-up flags and reminders for this contact, and mark an item as private.

- The **Zoom** command lets you zoom in on the data in the Notes section of your contact.

▷▷ Add a New Contact

To add a new contact to Outlook 2013, you begin in an Outlook window, typically the Mail window:

1. Open Outlook and click **People** in the Navigation pane, if it is not already selected.

2. In the Home tab New group, click **New Contact**.

–Or–

Press **CTRL+N**.

–Or–

From anywhere in Outlook, press **CTRL+SHIFT+C**.

3. In the Contact window, in the Contact tab Show group, click **General**. This opens a number of fields that allow you to enter basic contact information (see Figure 11-13). Use the **TAB** key to move through the fields, or click in the desired fields.

- **Full Name** Click the button to enter separate fields for title and first, middle, and last name; or type a full name in the text box. This is all that is required to create a contact.

- **Company** Type the name of the company or organization with which the person is affiliated.

- **Job Title** Type any title that you need to remember.

- **File As** Click the down arrow beside the text box to select the combination of name and company that will dictate its place in the Contacts window. You need to enter the name and company first before you can access this information.

- **Internet** These fields allow you to enter:

  - **E-mail** Click the down arrow to select up to three e-mail addresses to be associated with the person. For each one, type an address in the text box.

  - **Display As** Press **TAB** or drag to select the default display, and, if desired, type a new name. This is the field that determines how the person's name will appear in the To field in an e-mail message.

  - **Web Page Address** Type the URL for the contact's web page.

  - **IM Address** Type the Internet mail address that the person uses for instant messaging.

- **Phone Numbers** Click the down arrow beside each button to select among 19 number types, and then click the label button to enter detailed information about it; or type the number in the text box.

- **Addresses** Click the down arrow beside the button to select among three types of addresses, and then click in the text box to enter detailed information; or type the address in the text box. If you have more than one address for a contact, check the **This Is The Mailing Address** check box to specify the address to be used for mail.

- **Notes**   Type any comments or notes in the large text box on the right side of the screen.

4. In the Contact tab Show group, click **Details** to display the Detail fields.

- **Specific Office Information**   Complete the text fields as needed, such as department, manager's name, etc.

- **Personal Information**   Type information such as the person's nickname, spouse's name, and birthday, selecting from drop-down date boxes, as appropriate.

5. In the Contact tab Show group, click **Certificates**, and click **Import** to browse for the person's digital certificate. Click a certificate in the list, and click **Properties** to review details. Click **Set As Default** to use the selected certificate by default.

6. In the Contact tab Show group, click **All Fields**, select a type of field from the drop-down list, and review the contents of the associated fields.

7. In the Contact tab Actions group, click **Save & Close** when finished. If you need to enter another contact, click **Save & New** to open a new Contact window.

 TIP   A quick way to create an e-mail message from the Contact window is to right-click the contact, select **Create**, and click **E-mail**.

Copy Contacts from E-mail

When you copy an address in the From or Cc e-mail message fields, the Contact window opens with the Full Name and E-mail address fields filled in.

1. Open an e-mail message you have received.

2. Right-click the name in the Message window, and click **Add To Outlook Contacts**. Fill in any additional information you want.

3. Click **Save & Close**. The name and e-mail address are added to your contacts.

Edit a Contact

Once you have created a contact, you can change the information as much as you want. Just open the contact and change or enter new information. The following tasks all begin with an open Contact window and end with clicking **Save & Close**.

Add or Change an Image

To add an image to your contact:

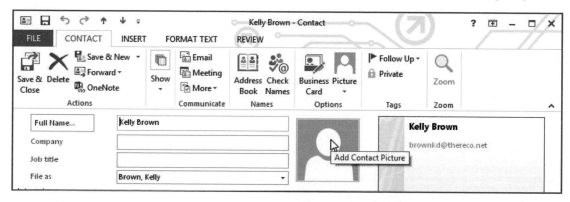

1. Click **Add Contact Picture** to open the My Pictures folder. If the image you want to use is not in the My Pictures folder, locate the folder in which the image is kept.

2. Double-click the image to select it.

To change the image:

1. Double-click the existing image to open the folder in which the original image resides.

2. Either choose another image from that folder or choose an image from a different folder and double-click your new choice.

You can also change or remove the image by clicking the **Picture** down arrow in the Options group and choosing either **Change Picture** or **Remove Picture**.

Add an Item

You can place a copy of an Outlook item (e-mail message, task, appointment, and so on) in the contact, as shown in the example in Figure 11-14.

1. Open the contact, and in the Insert tab Include group, click **Outlook Item**. The Insert Item dialog box appears.

2. Select the item you want to include with your contact. You may insert the item as:

   - Text only

   - An attachment

   - A shortcut to the item

3. When you are done, click **OK**.

▷▷ Create a Contact Group

You can group your contacts into *contact groups* (aka distribution lists), giving you an even quicker way to add multiple addresses to messages.

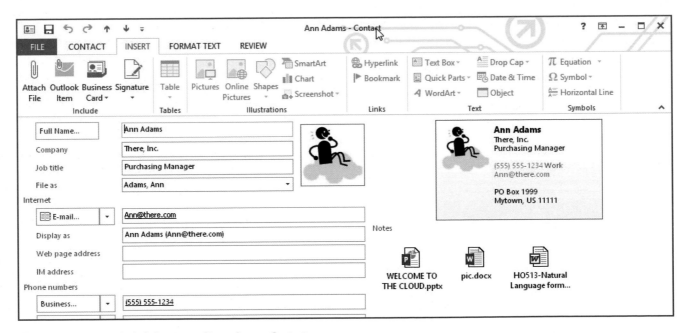

Figure 11-14: You can include images and items in your Contacts.

Use any of the preceding procedures to enter individuals in the Address Book. You can then create a group of contacts. To do so:

1. Select People from the Navigation Pane.

2. In the New group of the Home tab, click **New Contact Group** to open the Contact Group context tab.

3. In the Name field, type a name for this group of contacts.

4. In the Members group, click **Add Members**. You may choose from either your Outlook Contacts list, an Address Book, or create a new contact to add to the group.

5. To select from either your Contacts list or an Address Book, double-click on the name you want to choose and click **OK**.

6. If you choose to create a new e-mail contact, an Add New Member dialog box will appear. Enter a name and an e-mail address. If you wish to add this person to your Contacts list, click **Add to Contacts**. After you have entered the information, click **OK** to return to your new Contact Group window.

7. After you have included all the names you want to use in your Contact Group, click **Save and Close** in the Actions group.

After you have created your contact group, its name appears in your Contact list. It will have a plus sign next to it, which you can click to expand the contact list name and see the individuals in the list (you will be warned that, once expanded, you can't contract it).

When you send your e-mail message, it goes to everyone in the group.

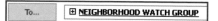

EXPLORE THE CALENDAR

The Calendar has the following unique items in its Outlook window (see Figure 11-15):

- The current date and each appointment are displayed on the calendar in Normal view.

- Your tasks appear at the bottom of each day in the Day, Work Week, and Week views.

The Calendar is designed to enable you to easily keep track of appointments, meetings, events, due dates, anniversaries, birthdays, and any other date-related happening. You can schedule several different types of activities, as shown in Table 11-2.

Table 11-2: Common Calendar Activities

Appointments	Appointments involve you only. They take time on your calendar, are less than 24 hours long, and do not require inviting others within Outlook to attend. Examples include a sales call, lunch with a buyer, or time you want to set aside to write a report.
Meetings	Meetings are appointments that require that others be invited and/or that resources be reserved. Meetings are set up using e-mail. They happen at a scheduled time, just like an appointment. You invite others via e-mail, and the meeting displays in your calendar with the location and the organizer's name.
Events	All-day events are 24 hours or longer, do not occupy time on your calendar, and appear as a banner on each day's calendar. Examples are conferences, birthdays, or your vacation. Unlike a meeting or an appointment, events that you put on your calendar do not block out time, so you can have other entries for that day display on your calendar.
Tasks	Tasks are activities that do not need specific time scheduled for them. They are your own personal tasks, even if they are part of a larger project of which you are a team member. Your tasks will display in the Day and Week views of your calendar, as well as on your To-Do bar.

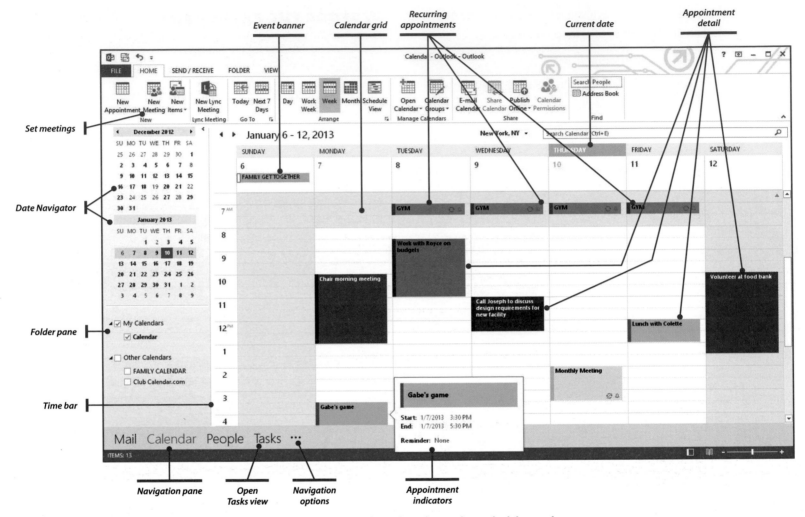

Event banner   Calendar grid   Recurring appointments   Current date   Appointment detail

Set meetings

Date Navigator

Folder pane

Time bar

Navigation pane   Open Tasks view   Navigation options   Appointment indicators

Figure 11-15: The Outlook Calendar displays your day, week, work week, month, or schedule at a glance.

▷ Create an Appointment

These steps offer a quick overview of how you set up an appointment.

1. Click **Calendar** in the Navigation pane.

   –Or–

   Press **CTRL**+2 on the keyboard.

2. Click a date on the calendar, and that day displays in Day view. If the calendar shows in Work Week, Week, or Month view, double-click any date on the calendar.

3. A new Appointment window opens, as shown in Figure 11-16.

4. After you have entered your information, click **Save & Close** to close the Appointment window.

▷ Create a New Task

1. Click **Tasks** in the Navigation pane to open the Task pane. In Outlook, a task is an item you track until it is completed. It may not have a specific timetable, but it is something you want to monitor.

2. In the Home tab New group, click **New Task** to create a new task.

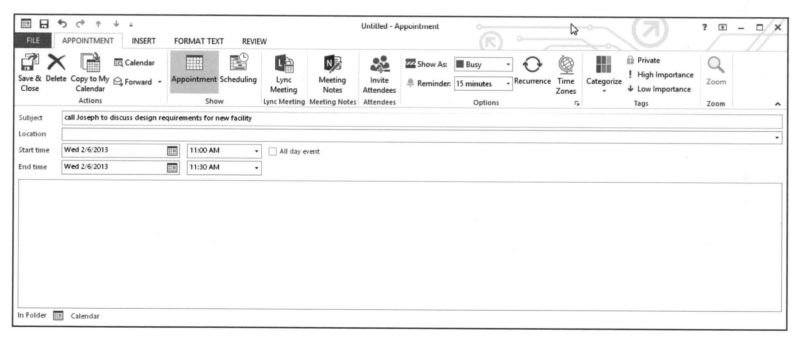

Figure 11-16: An appointment or an all-day event can be any date-related activity, such as due dates or birthdays.

3. After you have created the task, set the appropriate choices in the Task window, shown in Figure 11-17:

- Use the Start Date and Due Date fields if this task has specific date requirements.

- In the Status field, indicate the current status of this task (for example, In Progress).

- Set the priority and percentage of completion.

- Check **Reminder** to set a date and time to be reminded of this task.

4. Click **Save & Close** in the Actions group to close the Task window.

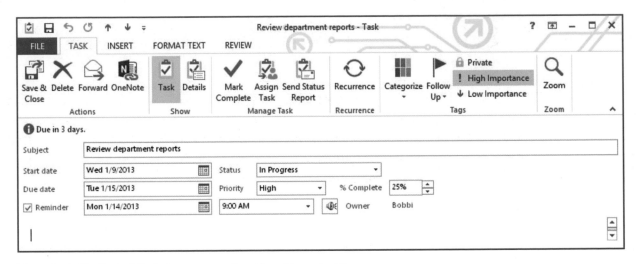

Figure 11-17: Use Outlook Tasks to ensure you do not forget important items.

Chapter 12

Printing, Using Mail Merge, and Working with Graphics

The printing capabilities provided by Office 2013 go beyond just printing a document. In this chapter you will learn how to set specific parameters with regard to what is printed. Office also includes a convenient feature called Mail Merge within Word that you can use to merge mailing lists into documents, including letters or envelopes.

Graphics is a term used to describe several forms of visual enhancements that can be added to a document. In this chapter you will learn how to insert, format, and manage graphic files (*pictures*), such as digital photos and clip art images. In addition, you will see how to embed products of other programs (*objects*) alongside your text and how to produce organizational charts and other business-oriented *diagrams*. Finally, you'll see how to capture screenshots.

PRINT DOCUMENTS

While printing documents may seem like a fairly basic function, there are several tasks associated with it that deserve attention, including setting up the default printer.

NOTE Due to the wide variety of printers available, this chapter cannot cover them all. The examples and figures in this chapter use an HP Photosmart 2400 printer. Depending on your printer model and how it's configured, you may see differences between your screen and what is shown in the figures and illustrations here.

Set a Default Printer

When you print, Office programs default to a given printer. You can choose which one that is:

1. From Windows 7, click **Start**, click **Control Panel**, and then click **Devices And Printers**. Look for the icon of the printer you want to make your default. (If you have to add it first, click **Add A Printer** and follow the prompts.)

NOTE To see defaults for a printer if you are viewing the Control Panel in Category view, you'll have to click **View Devices and Printers** under the Hardware and Sound category.

—Or—

From Windows 8 in Desktop view, right-click the very bottom-left corner of the screen and click **Control Panel**. Click **Devices And Printers** in Icons view and look for the printer you want to make the default. (If you need to add it first, click **Add A Printer** and follow the prompts.)

2. Right-click the icon for the printer you want to use as the default printer, and then click **Set As Default Printer**. A check mark is displayed next to the printer icon you have selected.

NOTE If there is a check mark next to the Printer icon, that printer is already set as the default printer.

HP psc 2400
Series

Define How a Document Is Printed

Your printer options, such as number of copies, printer to use, which pages to print, and so on, are set in the Print view. The options for printing will vary by application and also by printer.

NOTE You can also "print" to a fax and OneNote by selecting them as your printer.

Customize a Print Job

Customizing the print settings is done in the Print view, shown in Figure 12-1.

1. Click the **File** tab, and click **Print**. The Print page appears. The options available will differ, depending on the printer you have and the Office application. Those displayed in Figure 12-1 are for the HP Photosmart 2400 series printer in the Word application.

2. Click the **Printer** down arrow if more than one printer is available to you, and select the printer you want to use. Usually, the default printer is displayed automatically in the Printer list box.

3. Click the **Copies** spinner to set the number of copies to be printed.

4. Under **Settings**, select any of these options:

   - Select an option in the first drop-down list in Figure 12-1 (normally entitled Print All Pages), choosing between printing all pages, only the pages now selected, only the current page, and a custom set of pages (for instance, for a range of pages). To print custom page numbers, click in the **Pages** text box. Then to print contiguous pages, use a hyphen (for example, 1-4); to print noncontiguous pages, use commas (for example, 1, 3, 5). You can also mix them (such as 1-4, 6, 8).

   - Click the **Print One Sided** drop-down list (the second list) to choose between printing on only one side of the paper and

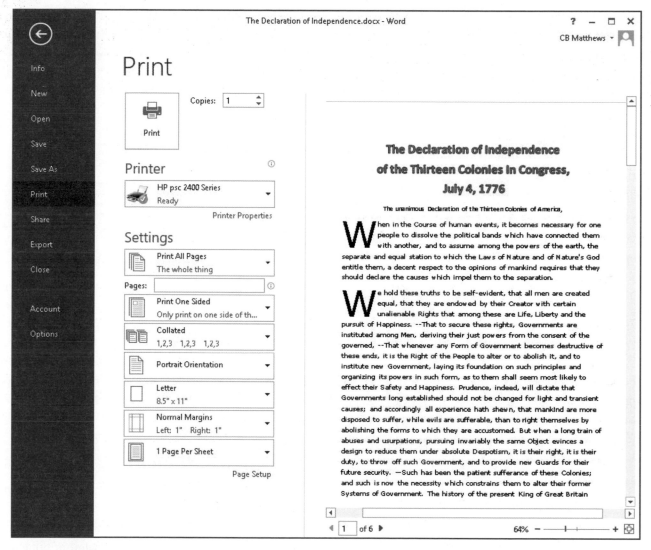

Figure 12-1: The Word Print view provides a preview of your document and many options for printing it.

printing on two sides. If you choose Manually Print On Both Sides, the printer will print every other page. When it finishes the first run, you'll need to take the paper out of the printer and reload it so that it is printed on the back of the printed page, and right-side up (so that the back page is not upside down). Depending on your printer, you may have to test a few pages first.

- If you are printing multiple copies and do not want the copies to be collated, click the **Collated** drop-down list (the third list) and click **Uncollated**. By default, multiple copies will print collated (for instance, five copies of a 20-page printed document will all be printed in order, pages 1–20, instead of five copies of page 1 being printed, then five copies of page 2, etc.)

- Click the **Portrait Orientation** drop-down list (the fourth list), and choose between Portrait Orientation and Landscape Orientation (tall vs. wide, respectively). By default, your document is printed in Portrait Orientation.

- Click the **Letter** drop-down list (the fifth list)to select the paper size. Here is where you choose between an 8-½–size letter, labels, an envelope, or a legal- or tabloid-size document, if your printer handles those sizes.

- Click the **Normal Margins** drop-down list (the sixth list) to choose the document margins you want to use. For instance, if you want to print fewer pages, you can create narrower margins; to print with more white space, create wider margins.

- Click the **1 Page Per Sheet** drop-down list (the seventh list) if you can print more than one page on a sheet of paper. This only makes sense for small-page documents. The other options can be used for proofreading or approving the layout of documents when you want to save paper.

5. Click the **Page Setup** link beneath the Settings options to set more precise margins, page size, or layout settings.

6. Click the **Printer Properties** link beneath the Printer drop-down list to set other properties for your printer. These options will differ for each printer, and will duplicate many of the options set in the main Print view.

7. When you have selected all the options you want and are ready to print your document, click **Print**. Your document is printed.

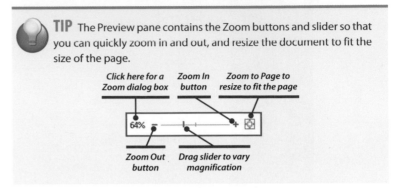

TIP The Preview pane contains the Zoom buttons and slider so that you can quickly zoom in and out, and resize the document to fit the size of the page.

Preview Your Document in Read Mode

Before you print your document, you may want to preview it in Read Mode, without the ribbon or the vertical scroll bars present, as shown in Figure 12-2. To display it, click the **View** tab, and then click **Read Mode** in the Views group. As shown in the figure, you can set certain options to vary the appearance of the page. You can move from one page to another by clicking the right- and left-pointing arrows. When you are finished, click the **View** menu and click **Edit Document** to return to the regular window.

▷▷ Print a Document

If you're in a hurry, or if you don't care about changing margins, then printing a document can be as easy as clicking a **Print** icon on the Quick Access toolbar. By default, that icon isn't on that toolbar, but you can add it (see Chapter 1). To set specific options before printing your document, you need to use the Print page.

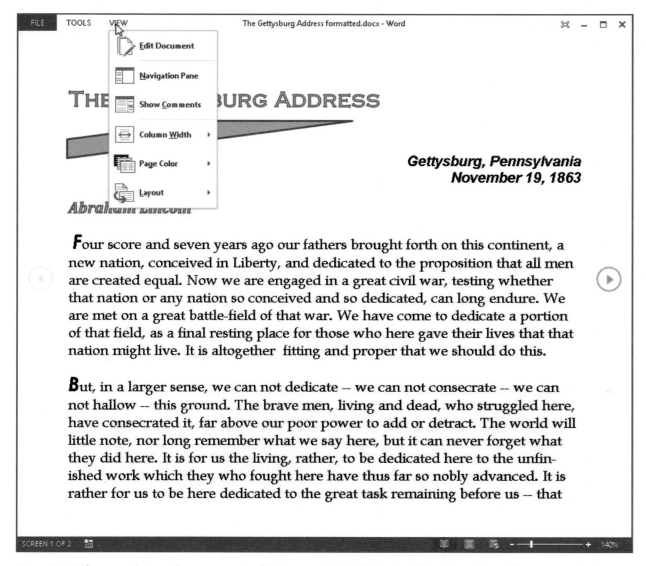

Figure 12-2: *Before you print your document, use Read Mode to preview it without the ribbon or vertical scroll bars present (as shown here in Word).*

MERGE LISTS WITH LETTERS AND ENVELOPES

The *Mail Merge* feature allows you to combine a mailing list with a document to send the same thing to a number of people. You can merge a mailing list to letters, e-mail messages, envelopes, and labels. A mail merge combines two kinds of documents: the *main document*, which is the text of the document—for example, the body of a letter—and the *data source*, which is the information that changes with each copy of the document—for example, the individual names and addresses of the people who will be receiving the letter.

 NOTE Word also allows you to take a list other than a mailing list, such as a parts list, and merge it with a document to create a catalog or directory.

The main document has two parts: static text and merge fields. *Static text* is text that does not change—for example, the body of a letter. *Merge fields* are placeholders that indicate where information from the list or data source goes. For example, in a form letter, "Dear" is static text, and <<First Name>> <<Last Name>> are merge fields. When the main document and the data source are combined, the result is "Dear John Doe," "Dear Jane Smith," and so on.

The following sections show you how to create a main document, create a data source, and then merge them together. You can also start out with an existing main document, an existing data source, or both and just use the parts of the wizard that you want to use.

 TIP You cannot use the Mail Merge feature unless a document is open, although it can be a blank document.

Perform a Mail Merge Using the Wizard

You can compose the static text in a document first and then insert the merge fields, or you can compose the static text and insert the merge fields as you go. You cannot insert merge fields into a main document until you have created the data source and associated it with your main document.

The mail merge process consists of the following six steps, which are described in the following sections:

1. Select a document type (letter, envelope, labels, for instance).
2. Identify the starting document, which may be blank to start with.
3. Select recipients (the data source), which can be an existing or new name list you will create now.
4. Finalize the main document, adding merge fields.
5. Preview the merge.
6. Complete the merge.

Select the Type and Identify the Document

To begin the mail-merge process:

1. In Word, open the document you want to use as your primary document, or open a new document.
2. In the Mailings tab Start Mail Merge group, click **Start Mail Merge**, and then click **Step-by-Step Mail Merge Wizard**. The Mail Merge task pane is displayed, as shown in Figure 12-3.
3. In the Select Document Type area, select one of the following options:
   - **Letters** are form letters designed to be sent to multiple people.

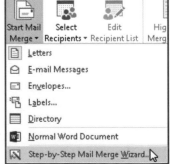

- **E-mail Messages** are form letters designed to be sent to multiple people via e-mail.

- **Envelopes** are envelopes addressed to multiple people.

- **Labels** are labels addressed to multiple people.

- **Directory** is a collection of information regarding multiple items, such as a parts catalog or phone directory.

4. Click **Next: Starting Document** at the bottom of the Mail Merge task pane.

5. In the Select Starting Document area, select one of the following options:

- **Use The Current Document** uses the currently open document as the main document for the mail merge (it can initially be blank).

- **Start From A Template** uses a template you designate as the basis for the main document of the mail merge.

- **Start From Existing Document** uses an existing document you can retrieve from your computer or network and designate as the main document for the mail merge.

6. Click **Next: Select Recipients** at the bottom of the Mail Merge task pane.

Mail Merge ▾ ✕

Select document type

What type of document are you working on?

- ⦿ Letters
- ◯ E-mail messages
- ◯ Envelopes
- ◯ Labels
- ◯ Directory

Letters

Send letters to a group of people. You can personalize the letter that each person receives.

Click Next to continue.

Step 1 of 6

→ Next: Starting document

Figure 12-3: The Mail Merge task pane is where you begin the merge process.

Select Recipients

The names and addresses of your recipients must be compiled into a list, which is a data source. A data source has two parts: fields and records. A *field* is a category of information. For example, in a mailing list, First Name, Last Name, and Street Address are examples of fields. A *record* is a set of information across the fields for an individual. For example, in a mailing list, the record for John Doe would include information for all the relevant fields for this individual—his first and last name, street address, city, state, and ZIP code.

To set up a name and address list, continuing from the previous section:

1. Having clicked **Next: Select Recipients** at the bottom of the task pane, you now have the following options in the Select Recipients area:

- **Use An Existing List** Allows you to browse for an existing name list that you have already created.

- **Select From Outlook Contacts** Provides an opportunity for you to choose a Contacts folder from your Outlook contacts to use as a starting point in establishing your data source.

- **Type A New List** Allows you to create a new list. This is the option we'll continue to describe, since many of the steps in using existing lists or contacts are used here as well.

2. Click **Type A New List**, and then click **Create** in the Type A New List area. The New Address List dialog box appears, as shown in Figure 12-4.

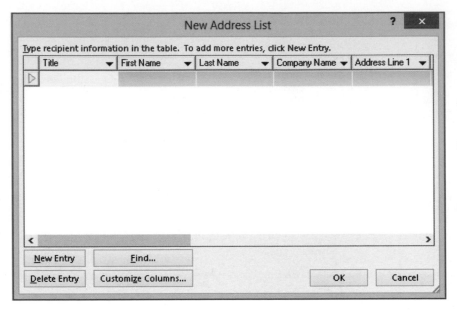

Figure 12-4: Use the New Address List dialog box to create your mailing list.

3. You have these options as you enter the information for the first record in the fields you want to use:

- To begin, click in the first field and type the title.

- Press **TAB** to move from field to field, or press **SHIFT+TAB** to move back to the previous field. Scroll to the right to see more fields.

- Click **New Entry** to add a new record for the next entry.

- Click **Customize Columns** to add, delete, or rename some of the columns or reorder them to facilitate entering data.

- Click **Delete Entry** to delete an existing, selected entry.

- To correct an incorrect entry, just click in the field and change it.

- Click **Find** to find a particular entry, perhaps to see if you've already entered that name.

4. Repeat entering names and addresses until you have added all the records you want to your list. When you are done, click **OK**.

5. A Save Address List dialog box appears. Type a file name for the list, select the folder on your computer where you want to save it, and click **Save**.

6. The Mail Merge Recipients dialog box appears, as shown in Figure 12-5. You have these choices:

- To delete names you do not want to include in the list, clear the check boxes next to those recipients.

- To make further changes to the name list, select the file name in the Data Source list box, and click **Edit**. When you're finished, click **OK** to close it, and click **Yes** to update your recipient list.

- To sort the recipient list using multiple fields, click **Sort** to open the Filter And Sort dialog box, and then click the down arrows next to the sort levels to specify the order of the sort. Click **Ascending** or **Descending** for each sort level. Click **OK** to return to the Mail Merge Recipients dialog box. (See the Tip for sorting single fields.)

- Click **Filter** to open the Filter and Sort dialog box, to select certain records to include in the list—perhaps you only want to include people within a particular business or ZIP code. Click **OK** to close the dialog box.

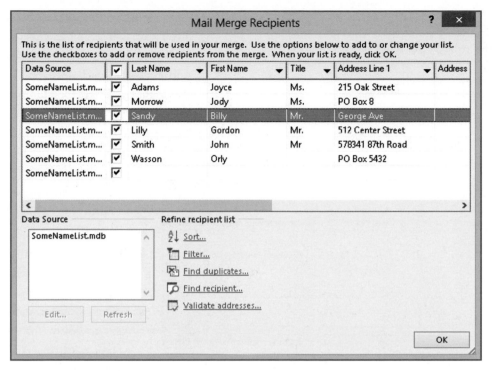

Figure 12-5: Use the Mail Merge Recipients dialog box to manage your mailing list prior to completing the merge.

- Click **Find Duplicates** to open the Find Duplicates dialog box to see if you have included more than one record for a recipient. Click **OK** to close it.

- Click **Find Recipient** to find the record for one entry by using the Find Entry dialog box.

- Click **Validate Addresses** to verify your address. To do this you'll need special software installed. Click this option to find out more.

7. Click **OK** to close the Mail Merge Recipients dialog box.

8. Click **Next: Write Your Letter** at the bottom of the Mail Merge task pane.

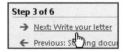

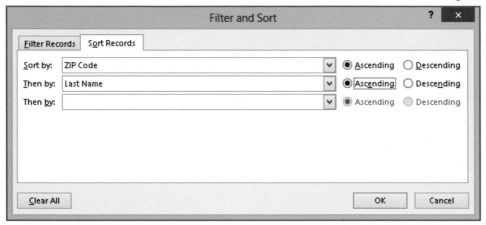

- Click one of the three items in the top of the Mail Merge task pane if you want to insert a predefined block of merge fields, such as a complete address or a greeting line. For example, if you click **Address Block**, you'll open the Insert Address Block where you specify the contents of the address block. Clicking **Greeting Line** opens the Insert Greeting Line dialog box where you manage the contents of the greeting. With both dialog boxes, you can preview the block by clicking the **Preview** arrows, shown in Figure 12-6. When the block is the way you want it, click **OK**. If you select the third item in the task pane, **Electronic Postage**, you receive a message telling you to install software.

- Click **More Items** (the fourth item in the task pane list) to insert an individual merge field. The Insert Merge Field dialog box appears. Verify that Database Fields is selected, and then select the field that you want to insert (for example, First Name or Last Name). Click **Insert** to insert the merge field into your document. Click **Close** when you are done inserting all the fields you need.

Finalize the Main Document

After creating the data source, you need to finalize the main document and insert the merge fields. This section will tell you how, after creating the main document, to insert merge fields. The example uses a letter; additional sections will show you how to use merge fields when creating envelopes and labels.

1. Continuing from the previous two sections, having clicked **Next: Write Your Letter** at the bottom of the Mail Merge task pane, write the body of the letter in the document pane, if it has not already been done—don't necessarily worry about the addressee and the greeting until you're satisfied with the text (although you *can* enter the fields and text together if you find it makes more sense to you).

2. Place the cursor in the document where you want to insert a merge field, such as the name of the addressee. Do one of the following:

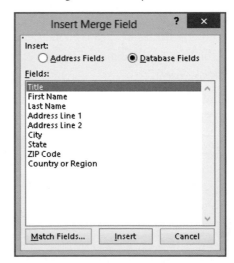

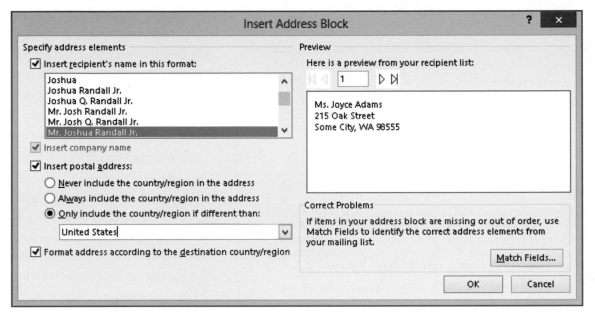

Figure 12-6: You can customize the predefined field blocks to meet your mail merge needs.

3. Add commas, spaces, and other punctuation marks to the address as needed. If you have some conditional fields that are printed only if some condition is met, like printing the country if it isn't "United States," see the section "Use Rules." Figure 12-7 shows an example of a business open house with merge fields inserted.

4. Click **Next: Preview Your Letters** at the bottom of the Mail Merge task pane.

Preview the Merge

Prior to actually completing the merge, the Mail Merge task pane presents you with an opportunity to review what the merged document will look like. This way, you can go back and make any last-minute changes to fine-tune your merge.

To preview a merge:

1. Continuing from the previous sections, click **Next: Preview Your Letters** at the bottom of the Mail Merge task pane.

2. Use the right- and left-pointing arrow buttons under Preview Your Letters in the Mail Merge task pane to scroll through the recipient list.

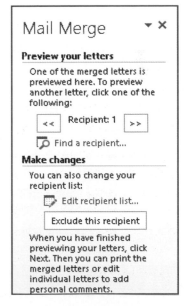

Microsoft Office 2013 QuickSteps *Printing, Using Mail Merge, and Working with Graphics* **311**

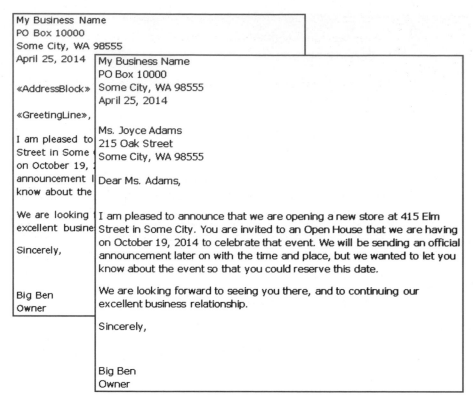

My Business Name
PO Box 10000
Some City, WA 98555
April 25, 2014

«AddressBlock»

«GreetingLine»,

I am pleased to
Street in Some
on October 19,
announcement l
know about the

We are looking
excellent busine

Sincerely,

Big Ben
Owner

My Business Name
PO Box 10000
Some City, WA 98555
April 25, 2014

Ms. Joyce Adams
215 Oak Street
Some City, WA 98555

Dear Ms. Adams,

I am pleased to announce that we are opening a new store at 415 Elm
Street in Some City. You are invited to an Open House that we are having
on October 19, 2014 to celebrate that event. We will be sending an official
announcement later on with the time and place, but we wanted to let you
know about the event so that you could reserve this date.

We are looking forward to seeing you there, and to continuing our
excellent business relationship.

Sincerely,

Big Ben
Owner

Figure 12-7: Merge fields are a convenient way to create a form letter for multiple recipients.

3. If you want to merge to a single name, click **Find A Recipient** to enter
   a recipient name and search for it in all fields or a particular field.

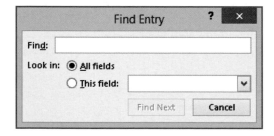

4. If you want to exclude a particular recipient from the
   merge, while that recipient is displayed, click **Exclude This
   Recipient**. (You can add the excluded recipient back by
   placing a check mark next to the name in the Mail Merge
   Recipient dialog box, which is displayed when you click
   Edit Recipient List.)

   –Or–

   Click **Edit Recipient List** to edit a particular recipient's
   information. If you click this link, the Mail Merge
   Recipients dialog box appears again (see Figure 12-5).
   Click the file name in the text box beneath Data Source,
   click **Edit**, modify the information, click **OK**, and click
   Yes to update the recipient list. Click **OK** again to close
   the Mail Merge Recipients dialog box.

5. Click **Next: Complete The Merge** at the bottom of the
   Mail Merge task pane.

Complete the Merge

The last step in performing a mail merge is to complete the
merge; that is, to accept the preview of how the merge will
look and direct Word to perform the merge. The result of
this step is a document assigned to a particular recipient list, which you
can save, print, modify, and use again in the future.

To complete a merge:

1. Continuing from the previous sections, click **Next: Complete The
   Merge** at the bottom of the Mail Merge task pane.

2. If you wish, click **Edit Individual Letters** and select the letters to edit.
   You would use this to make unique changes to specific documents.
   The merged letters will appear as their own document in a new Word
   window, where you can make any changes you want and then print
   and save them as you normally would.

3. Click **Print** in the Merge area to open the Merge To Printer dialog box.

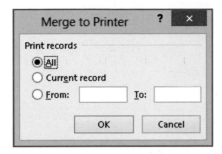

4. Select one of the following options:

- **All** prints all records in the data source that have been included in the merge.

- **Current Record** prints only the record that is displayed in the document window.

- **From/To** prints a range of records you specify. Enter the starting and ending numbers in the text boxes.

5. Click **OK** when ready. The Print dialog box appears.

6. Select the print options you want, and click **OK**. Your merged document is printed.

7. When you are ready, click the **File** tab and then click **Save** to save your merge document.

 Use Rules

Rules (also called *Word Fields*) apply to merge fields or static text if certain conditions are met. One of the most common rules applied to variable fields is the If…Then…Else rule. The If rule performs one of two alternative actions, depending on a condition you specify. For example, consider the statement "If the weather is sunny, we'll go to the beach; if not, we'll go to the museum." This specifies a condition that

must be met (sunny weather) for a certain action to take place (going to the beach). If the condition is not met, an alternative action occurs (going to the museum).

This is an example of how using an If rule in Word looks with the field codes turned on:

{IF { MERGEFIELD City } = "Seattle" "Please call our office." "Please call our distributor."}

This works as follows: If the current data record contains "Seattle" in the City field, then the first text ("Please call our office.") is printed in the merged document that results from that data record. If "Seattle" is not in the City field, then the second set of text ("Please call our distributor.") is printed. Using a rule is easy and doesn't require writing such a complex statement at all.

To insert a variable field into a merge document:

1. Position the insertion point where you want the rule.

2. In the Mailings tab Write & Insert Fields group, click **Rules** and select the rule you want (for example, If…Then…Else…) in the drop-down list.

3. The Insert Word Field dialog box appears. Fill in the text boxes with your criteria, and click **OK** when finished.

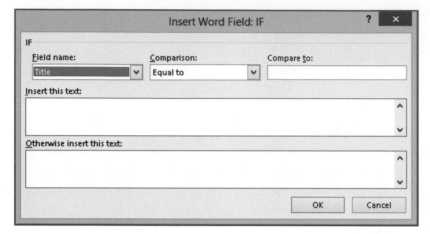

Merge to Envelopes

The process for merging to envelopes is similar to that for merging to letters; you must first define your envelope, type your return address if you don't have one defined, find your source of recipient addresses, insert the merge fields, preview your envelope results, finish the merge, and print the envelopes. This can be done with the Mail Merge Wizard, as described earlier with letters, or by using the options on the Mailings tab.

The following steps use the options on the Mailing tab.

1. In Word, open a new document. In the Mailings tab Start Mail Merge group, click **Start Mail Merge** and then click **Envelopes**. The Envelope Options dialog box appears, as shown in Figure 12-8.

2. Select the options you want from the Envelope Options and Printing Options tabs. Click **OK** when finished.

3. An envelope will appear with your default return address in the upper-left corner (if you have entered one) and, if you have Show Paragraph Marks turned on, an indented paragraph mark where you

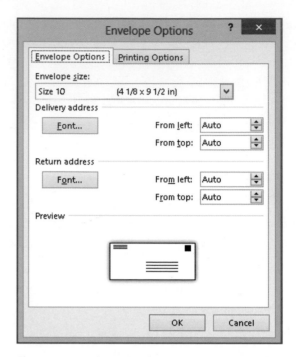

Figure 12-8: Word provides almost as many envelope sizes as it does paper sizes that you can use in printing.

will put the addressee. Type a return address, if needed, or make any changes you want to the return address and any other static text that you want. This will be printed on all envelopes.

4. In the **Mailings** tab Start Mail Merge group, click **Select Recipients**, choose the type of list you are using, and follow the steps needed to identify or create the list; see the earlier section "Select Recipients."

5. When you have your recipient list ready, click in the addressee area of the envelope. You'll see the address text box defined. In the Mailings tab Write & Insert Fields group, click either **Address Block** or **Insert Merge Field**, depending on whether you want to work with the address as a single predefined block or a set of discrete elements, and complete the steps needed to place the merge fields on the envelope. You may need to insert spaces and punctuation after you've inserted all the merge fields. If you need help, see "Finalize the Main Document" earlier in this chapter.

6. In the Mailings tab Preview Results group, click **Preview Results**. Your envelope should look similar to that shown in Figure 12-9. Use the **Previous Record** and **Next Record** arrows in the Preview Results group, or type a record number in the text box between the arrows, to look through your merged envelopes.

7. When you are ready, in the **Mailings** tab Finish group, click **Finish & Merge**. If you want to make changes to some of the envelopes before they are printed, click **Edit Individual Documents** and the data will be merged to a new document that can then be modified. Otherwise, click **Print Documents**. Choose the records to be printed, and click **OK** to open the Print dialog box, where you can choose your printer options.

 Merge to Labels

The process for merging to labels is similar to that for merging to letters and envelopes, and can be done with the Mail Merge Wizard, as described earlier with letters, or by using the options on the Mailings tab, as described with envelopes. The following steps use the options on the Mailings tab.

Figure 12-9: You can see how your merged envelope will look when completed, prior to printing it.

1. In Word, open a new document. In the Mailings tab Start Mail Merge group, click **Start Mail Merge**, and then click **Labels**. The Label Options dialog box appears.

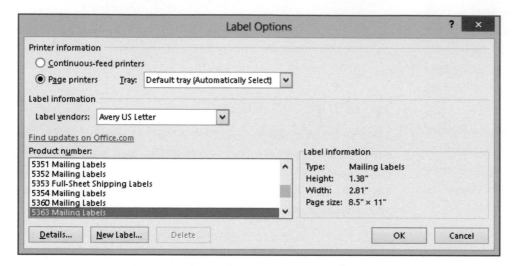

2. Select the options you want. Be sure to identify in the Label Vendors drop-down list box the label vendor you want for the specific label, or click the **New Label** button for a custom one. Click **OK** when finished. A page formatted for labels will appear in Word—you may not see the formatting just yet.

3. In the Mailings tab Start Mail Merge group, click **Select Recipients**, choose the type of list you are using, and follow the steps needed to identify or create the list; see the earlier section "Select Recipients." The page should show "Next Record" merge fields.

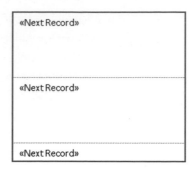

4. When you have your recipient list ready, click in the empty space for the first label. Then, in the Mailings tab Write & Insert Fields group, click either **Address Block** or **Insert Merge Field**, depending on whether you want to work with the address as a single predefined block or a set of discrete elements, and complete the steps needed to place the merge fields on the envelope. See "Finalize the Main Document" earlier in this chapter.

5. In the Mailings tab Write & Insert Fields group, click **Update Labels** to copy the fields in the first label to all the labels, as shown in Figure 12-10. In that case, the individual address fields are treated as one block.

6. In the Mailings tab Preview Results group, click **Preview Results**. Your labels should look something like this:

Ms. Joyce Adams	Ms. Jody Morrow	Mr. Billy Sandy
215 Oak Street	PO Box 8	George Ave
Some City, WA 98555	Far City, OR 97555	Some City, WA 98555
Mr. Gordon Lilly	Mr John Smith	Orly Wasson
512 Center Street	578341 87th Road	PO Box 5432
Some City, OR 97555	Some City, Wa 98555	Big City, OR 97432

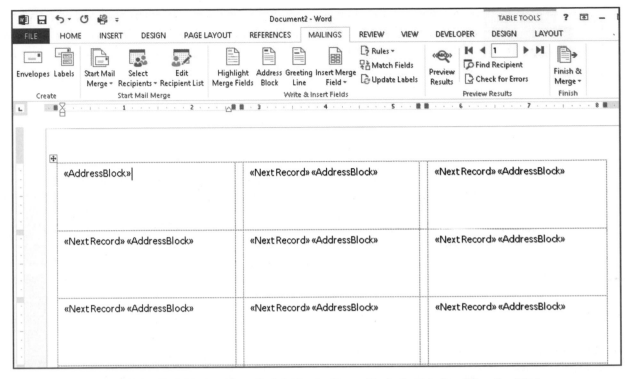

Figure 12-10: You can replicate the fields (or Address Block field, as in this case) in the first label to all the other labels.

7. When you are ready, in the Mailings tab Finish group, click **Finish & Merge**. If you want to make changes to some of the envelopes before they are printed, click **Edit Individual Documents** and the data will be merged to a new document that can then be modified. Otherwise, click **Print Documents**. Choose the records to be printed, and click **OK** to open the Print dialog box, where you can choose how the envelopes will be printed.

WORK WITH GRAPHICS

Graphics is a term used to describe several forms of visual enhancements that can be added to a document. In this chapter you will learn how to insert, format, and manage graphic files (*pictures*), such as digital photos

and clip art images. Pictures or graphics can be manipulated in a number of ways once you have them within an Office program. You can organize your clip art collections, resize images, and move the images into the exact positions that you want. (You can work with graphics in Word, PowerPoint, Excel, and Outlook messages.)

Pictures are files that are produced by a device, such as a digital camera or scanner, or that are created in a painting or drawing program, such as Microsoft Paint or Adobe Illustrator. In either case, the files are saved in a graphic format, such as JPEG or GIF (popular formats used on the Internet) or TIF (used in higher-end printing applications). You can find a Microsoft Office 2013 page that lists the supported file formats at http://technet.microsoft.com/en-us/library/dd797428.aspx?.

Add Pictures

To add pictures, you can browse for them, use the Clip Art task pane to assist you, or drag them from other locations.

Browse for Pictures

1. Place your insertion point in the Office document where you want to insert the picture.

2. In the Insert tab Illustrations group, click **Pictures** to open the Insert Picture dialog box, shown in Figure 12-11.

Figure 12-11: The Insert Picture dialog box displays thumbnails of picture files accepted by Office programs.

3. Browse to the picture you want, and select it. (If you do not see your pictures, click the **Change Your View** down arrow and click **Large Icons** or **Extra Large Icons**, as shown in Figure 12-11.)

4. Click **Insert**. The picture is displayed in the document.

TIP You can add a caption to inserted pictures to give a uniform appearance to your picture identifiers. Right-click a picture and click **Insert Caption**. In the Caption dialog box, choose a label (create your own labels by clicking **New Label**), the position of the caption, and a numbering format (by clicking the **Numbering** button). You can also have your Office program use AutoCaption to automatically add a caption based on the type of picture or object inserted.

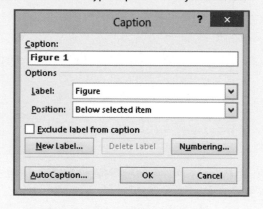

Drag Pictures from the Desktop or Folders

Besides using the Insert tab Pictures command in an Office program to add pictures, you can drag picture files from the Desktop or Windows or File Explorer into an open document.

1. In the Office document you're using, find the location where the image is to be inserted.

2. Using Windows or File Explorer (or on the Desktop), find the image to be inserted.

---

3. Drag the picture from Windows or File Explorer (or the Desktop) to the location in the Office program document where you want it.

 NOTE Often, when you insert a picture or illustration, it is not the size that you want it to be. To easily make a picture the size you want, click it to select it (sizing handles are displayed when a photo is selected), and then drag the sizing handles to resize or rotate the image. The pointer turns into a crosshair icon while you are dragging to resize the picture.

Add Clip Art

You can search for clip art and other images online or in your SkyDrive or computer. If one possibility doesn't provide the results you want, try another one.

1. Place your insertion point in the document where you want to insert the picture.

2. In the Insert tab Illustrations group, click **Online Pictures** to open the Insert Pictures dialog box. You have these options:

   - **Office.com Clip Art** To search Office.com, type a category of clip art you want to find in the Search text box, and click the **Search** icon to find free clip art online. You'll see the results of the search, which contain both photos and drawings, as shown in the example in Figure 12-12. Select the image you want, and click **Insert**.

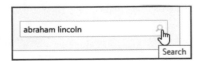

 TIP Add something like "drawings" to your search category to find just graphic images rather than photos.

- **Bing Image Search** To search the Internet, type your search criteria in the Search text box and click the **Search** icon. You'll see the results of the search. Select your image, or type another criterion and try again. When you find the one you want, click it.

- *Yourname* **SkyDrive** To search your SkyDrive folders, click **Browse**. Find the folder containing the image you want and double-click it.

- **Also Insert From** To search your photos and videos in Flickr (a website for storing and sharing photos and videos), click the **two-dot** icon. You will be allowed either to search your Flickr account for an image or to sign up for an account if you don't have one. You can also connect with Facebook. Clicking the **Facebook**

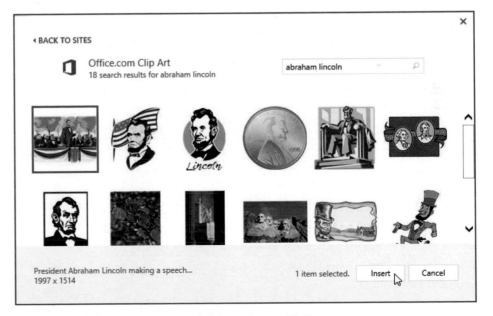

Figure 12-12: You can search the online library for clip art and photos.

icon lets you connect your e-mail address with your Facebook account to see all your photos and videos.

Also insert from:

3. After inserting the image you want, you can resize or rotate it as needed (as described later in the chapter).

> 💡 **TIP** After you embed a picture within the text, you can specify how you want it to be positioned (for instance, with or without text wrap). Click the picture, and then click the Layout Options icon that appears to the right of the picture. Choose your layout options. (You can't use this feature in Compatibility Mode.)

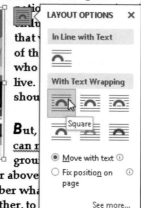

*F*our score and seven years ago our fathers brought forth on this nation, conceived in Liberty, and dedicated to the proposition th equal. Now we are engaged in a great civil war, testing whether

struggled here, have consecrated it, far above world will little note, nor long remember wha they did here. It is for us the living, rather, to

LAYOUT OPTIONS ✕

In Line with Text

With Text Wrapping

Square

◉ Move with text ⓘ
○ Fix position on page ⓘ

See more...

▷▷ Remove Unwanted Areas

You can remove unwanted areas from a picture by using the Crop tool on the Picture toolbar. If you change your mind after you complete the cropping, click **Undo** in the Quick Access toolbar or press **CTRL+Z** to reverse the cropping.

> ✓ **QuickFacts**
>
> **Using the Picture Tools Format Tab**
>
> Pictures are manipulated primarily by using the Picture Tools Format tab, shown in Figure 12-13. This ribbon tab differs slightly in PowerPoint and Excel. The Format tab automatically appears when a graphic image is selected in a document. The tab's four groups allow you to adjust the characteristics of an image, determine its style, arrange an image on a page or in relation to other images or to text, and size an image. In addition, the Picture Styles group task pane launcher and the Size group dialog box launcher provide a number of other settings.

1. Open and select the picture you want to crop. See "Add Pictures" earlier in this chapter.

2. On the Picture Tools Format tab, click the **Crop** icon in the Size group (not the down arrow). The picture redisplays with eight sizing handles on the corners and sides, and the mouse pointer becomes a move icon when inside the picture, as shown in Figure 12-14.

3. Drag the cropping handles where you want the edges of the picture to be. Once you've done that, you can use the pointer (the move icon) to drag the underlying image around beneath the crop-defined area. This allows you to get the positioning exactly right.

4. When you release the mouse button, you can see the area of the picture that will be cropped. To do the actual cropping, press **ESC** or click outside of the image to turn off the Crop tool.

> 💡 **TIP** You can crop to a shape to create some interesting effects. After selecting the picture, click in the Picture Tool Format tab and then click the **Crop** down-arrow in the Size group. Choose **Crop To A Shape** and select a shape from the menu. (If you don't see the Crop down-arrow, create the shape in a blank document and drag it to the current one.)

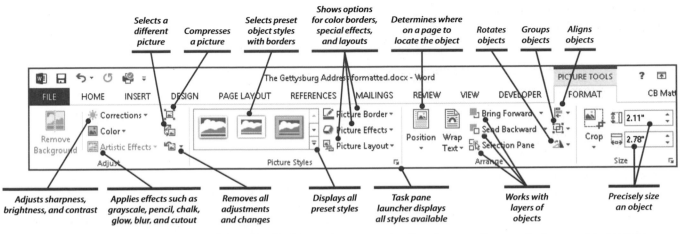

Selects a different picture

Compresses a picture

Selects preset object styles with borders

Shows options for color borders, special effects, and layouts

Determines where on a page to locate the object

Rotates objects

Groups objects

Aligns objects

Adjusts sharpness, brightness, and contrast

Applies effects such as grayscale, pencil, chalk, glow, blur, and cutout

Removes all adjustments and changes

Displays all preset styles

Task pane launcher displays all styles available

Works with layers of objects

Precisely size an object

Figure 12-13: The Picture Tools Format tab, from Word in this case, is your one-stop shopping venue for accessing image-related options.

Figure 12-14: Cropping removes the gray area of a picture outside the sizing handles.

Add Shapes

Shapes are small, prebuilt drawings that you can select, or you can create your own by modifying existing shapes or drawing your own freeform shapes. You access the prebuilt shapes and the tools for creating your own either from the Insert tab Illustrations group or from the Drawing Tools Format tab Insert Shapes group.

1. In the Insert tab Illustrations group, click **Shapes** to open the Shapes drop-down menu.

2. Choose a shape by doing one of the following:

   • Click a shape from one of the several categories.

   • Click one of the lines or basic shapes to begin your own shape.

   • Drag the mouse crosshair pointer in the approximate location and size you want.

▷▷ Create a Diagram

You can quickly create and modify several different types of diagrams, some of which are easily interchangeable. One type, an organization or hierarchy chart, provides special tools and features that streamline the structuring of this popular form of charting.

1. In the Insert tab Illustrations group, click **SmartArt** to open the Choose A SmartArt Graphic dialog box, shown in Figure 12-15.

2. Click **Hierarchy** in the left column, and then double-click the organization chart, which is on the top left. The start of an organization chart, as shown in the example chart in Figure 12-16, and the SmartArt Tools Design tab will be displayed. You can then personalize your chart by doing one or more of the following:

   - To simply restructure the organization chart, click the highest level, or *manager*, position in your chart, and in the SmartArt Tools Design tab, click **Layout** in the Create Graphic group

to open a menu of hierarchical options. Click the structure that best matches your organization.

- To apply another layout style to the organization chart, click the chart and then, in the SmartArt Tools Design tab Layouts group, click the **More** down arrow. As you mouse over the layout options, you'll see how each affects your chart underneath. These layouts offer a way to add "pizzazz" to your charts.

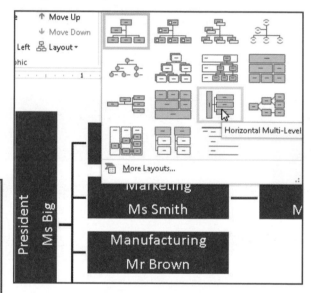

- To add a new position to your chart, click a current box that the new one is related to on the chart. In the Create Graphic group, click the **Add Shape** down arrow and select the type of new position you want to add to the current structure. For a higher level, click **Add Shape Above**; for a subordinate level, click **Add Shape Below**; for a co-worker level, click either **Add Shape Before** or **Add Shape After**; and for an assistant, click **Add Assistant**.

Figure 12-15: SmartArt allows you to easily create a number of diagram types, such as organization charts.

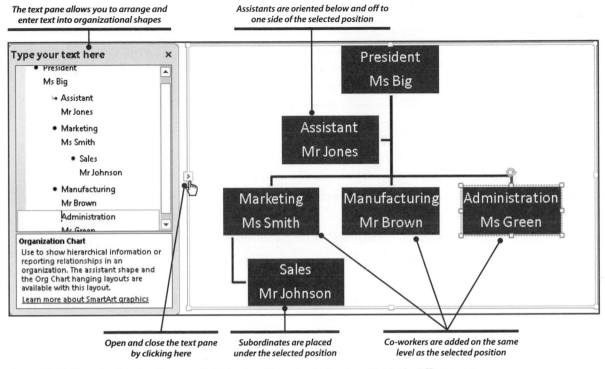

The text pane allows you to arrange and enter text into organizational shapes

Assistants are oriented below and off to one side of the selected position

Open and close the text pane by clicking here

Subordinates are placed under the selected position

Co-workers are added on the same level as the selected position

Figure 12-16: Organization charts are easily laid out and formatted using SmartArt in the Office programs.

- To place text in a shape after adding a new shape or selecting one, simply start typing. You can also enter text in the text pane. If it is not already displayed, click **Text Pane** in the Create Graphic group, or click the **Text Pane** icon shown in Figure 12-16.

- Type the name, title, and/or other identifiers for the position. The font size will change to fit the text box. Press SHIFT+ENTER after each line for a subordinate line (like a position after a name) that is spaced close to the previous line, or press ENTER for a second line equally spaced in the box. Format text in the shapes as you would standard text, using the Home tab and its associated options.

- Click **Right To Left** in the Create Graphic group to flip the entire chart so the names and shapes on the right are switched with the ones on the left. (You can switch it back by clicking the button again.)

- Click **Promote** or **Demote** in the Create Graphic group to move a shape and its text up or down in the organization chart.

- In the SmartArt Styles group, click the **More** down arrow to access some styles to apply to your layout.

- In the SmartArt Styles group, click **Change Colors** to vary the look with color.

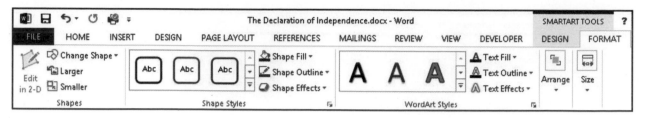

Figure 12-17: Use the SmartArt Tools Format tab to quickly redesign the overall appearance of your organization chart.

- If you make a "permanent" change, as just described, you can return to the previous layout, color, or style by pressing **CTRL+Z** or by clicking **Reset Graphic** in the Reset group.

- To select a group of shapes and their text so that they can be acted upon all at once, hold down **CTRL** while clicking each shape (including the connecting lines).

- Click the SmartArt Tools **Format** tab to display several options for changing the shape and its text, as shown in Figure 12-17.

 NOTE Diagrams are really just combinations of shapes that fit a specific need. As such, you can, for example, delete an element of a diagram by selecting it and pressing **DELETE**. Or you can delete the entire diagram by selecting its border and pressing **DELETE**. See "Modify Graphics" to learn how to format the overall diagram, as well as how to change various components of shapes.

 Take a Screenshot

Office allows you to take a screenshot and insert it into your document. You can also insert a partial screenshot through clipping.

Insert a Full Screenshot into Your Document

1. Click in the document where you want the screenshot inserted.

2. In the Insert tab Illustrations group, click **Screenshot**. (In PowerPoint, Screenshot is located in the Images group.) A menu

of the windows currently open on your computer screen will appear.

3. As you mouse over the thumbnails, a screen tip identifies which file it is. Click the thumbnail of the window for which you want a full image inserted into your document.

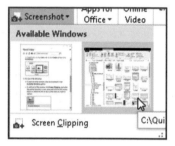

Insert a Partial Screenshot into Your Document

When you insert a partial screenshot, it might seem that the steps are in the incorrect order, since you first select your primary document, then the window you want captured (which overlays all other windows), and then you click the primary document again for the command to capture the image (which puts it back on top of other windows). But it works out!

1. Click in your document where you want the partial screenshot to be inserted.

2. Click the window you want to be captured in the screenshot. It will temporarily be placed on top of the document.

3. In your document, click the **Insert** tab, and then click **Screen Clipping**. The window you want to capture will be placed on top again, and the screen will be obscured by a white film.

4. Drag your pointer over the part of the window you want captured, as shown in Figure 12-18. When you release the pointer, the selected part of the window will be inserted into your document.

Figure 12-18: You can capture a full or partial screenshot with the Screenshot command.

MODIFY GRAPHICS

Pictures (those that use an absolute positioning layout) and shapes or drawings share a common Format dialog box, although many of the features and options are not available for every type of graphic you can add to an Office document. This section describes formatting and other modifications you can apply to graphics.

 TIP Right-click a graphic (on the handle), and click **Format Shape** (or **AutoShape** or **Object**, depending on the graphic) to open a task pane that makes available only the options that pertain to that type of graphic. For example, if you right-click a rectangle shape you inserted, the Arrows area of the Line Style option is unavailable because this is not an action you can do with this type of graphic.

Resize and Rotate Graphics Precisely

You can change the size of graphics by setting exact dimensions and you can rotate graphics. (You can also drag handles to change them interactively. See "Use Handles and Borders to Position Graphics" later in this chapter for ways to resize and rotate graphics with a mouse.) The dialog boxes for size differ slightly between Word, PowerPoint, Outlook messages, and Excel.

1. Click the graphic you want to resize or rotate to select it. In the Picture (or other graphic type) Tools Format tab, click the **Size** dialog box launcher in the Size group. (For some graphics, such as an organization chart, you may have to display the Size menu in order to select the Size dialog box launcher.)

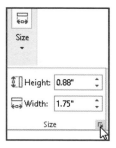

2. Click the **Size** tab, and, if it isn't already selected, check the **Lock Aspect Ratio** check box to size the graphic proportionally when entering either width or height values.

3. Under Size And Rotate (depending on the graphic, the option may be Height And Width), enter either the height or the width dimension, or use the spinners to increase or decrease one of the dimensions from its original size.

   –Or–

   Under Scale, enter a percentage for either the height or the width to increase or decrease it, or use the spinners to increase or decrease the percentage of the original picture size.

 QuickFacts

Understanding Graphic Positioning in Office Programs

When you position a graphic (picture, clip art, drawing, or shape) on the page, the position can be *inline*, or *relative*, to the text and other objects on the page, where the graphic moves as the text moves, like a character in a word. The alternative is *absolute* positioning, where the graphic stays anchored in one place, regardless of what the text does. If the graphic uses absolute positioning, you can then specify how text will wrap around the graphic, which can be on either or both sides, or along the top and bottom of the graphic. Also, for special effects, the text can be either on top of the graphic or underneath it. See "Position a Graphic Relative to Areas in a Document."

4. To rotate the graphic, under Size And Rotate (or Rotation), enter a positive (rotate clockwise) or negative (rotate counterclockwise) number of degrees of rotation you want.

5. Click **OK**. The picture will resize and/or rotate according to your values.

 CAUTION Enlarging an image beyond the ability of the pixels to span it can cause unwanted effects.

 TIP After you change a picture from its default style of being inline with the text to a style that supports absolute positioning, it is difficult to return to the default style. It's easiest to just delete the picture and reinsert it.

Position Graphics

Graphics (including pictures that use absolute positioning) can be positioned anywhere in the document by dragging or setting specific values. In either case, the graphic retains its relative position within

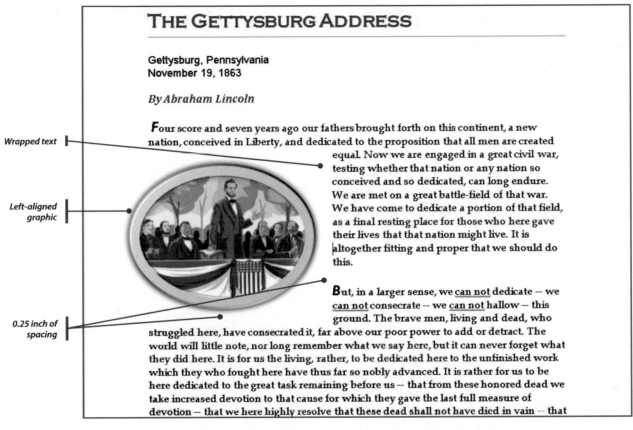

Figure 12-19: *You can easily arrange text and graphics in several configurations using dialog box options.*

the document as text and other objects are added or removed. You can override this behavior by anchoring the graphic to a fixed location. You can also change how text and other objects "wrap" around the graphic. Figure 12-19 shows several of these features.

Position a Graphic Relative to Areas in a Document

Besides dragging a graphic into position, you can select or enter values that determine where the graphic is placed in relation to document areas.

1. Click the graphic that you want to position to select it. Click the icon to the right of it. (You can also click **Text Wrap** in the Format tab Arrange group.) A menu is displayed.

2. Click **See More** (or **More Layout Options**) to open the Layout dialog box.

3. Verify that the **Position** tab is selected. Select or enter the horizontal- and vertical-positioning entries by selecting them from the drop-down menus, entering the values, or using the spinners to increase or decrease distances, as shown in Figure 12-20.

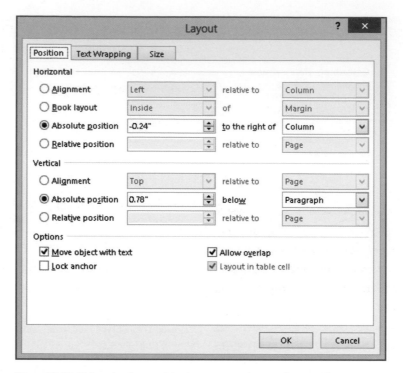

Figure 12-20: Using absolute positioning, you can choose where to place a graphic relative to other objects in the document.

4. To anchor a graphic in place, regardless of whether other content is added or removed—for example, a graphic you want in the upper-left corner of a specific page—check the **Lock Anchor** check box and clear all other options.

5. Click **OK** to close the Layout dialog box.

Use Handles and Borders to Position Graphics

Graphics are easy to manipulate using their sizing handles and borders.

● **Select a graphic**   Select a graphic by clicking it. Handles appear around the graphic and allow you to perform interactive changes. Two exceptions include text boxes and text in text boxes.

 TIP When a graphic uses absolute positioning, an anchor icon may be displayed. If the anchor is locked, a padlock icon may also be displayed. If you don't see the anchor icon and the graphic is using absolute positioning, click the **File** tab, click the **Office Program Options** (Word and PowerPoint), and click **Display** in the left column. Under Always Show These Formatting Marks, click the **Object Anchors** check box. Click **OK** to display anchor icons in the document.

- **Resize a graphic** Drag one of the square or round (if using absolute positioning) sizing handles surrounding the graphic—or at either end of it, in the case of a line—in the direction you want to enlarge or reduce the graphic. Hold **SHIFT** when dragging a corner sizing handle to change the height and length proportionately. (You can proportionally resize a graphic without pressing **SHIFT**. Click the **Picture** or **Drawing Tools Format** tab, click the **Size** dialog box launcher, and click the **Size** tab. Then select the **Lock Aspect Ratio** check box.)

- **Rotate a graphic** Drag the small circle or dot on top of the graphic in the direction you want to rotate the graphic. Hold **SHIFT** when dragging to rotate in 15-degree increments.

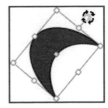

⏵⏵ Work with Graphics

While graphics can be positioned absolutely by simply dragging them or choosing placement relative to other objects in a document, Office also provides a number of other techniques that help you adjust where a graphic is in relation to other graphics.

Move Graphics Incrementally

Select the graphic or group of graphics (see "Combine Graphics by Grouping"), and press one of the arrow keys in the direction you want to move the graphic by very small increments (approximately .01 inch).

Reposition the Order of Stacked Graphics

You can stack graphics by simply dragging one on top of another. Figure 12-21 shows an example of a three-graphic stack. To reposition the order of the stack in Word, Excel, or PowerPoint, select a graphic, click the **Format** tab, and then click the **Bring To Front** or **Send Backward** down arrows in the Arrange group. You'll see a menu. Then click one of the following:

- **Bring Forward** moves the graphic up one level (same as Bring To Front if there are only two graphics in the stack).

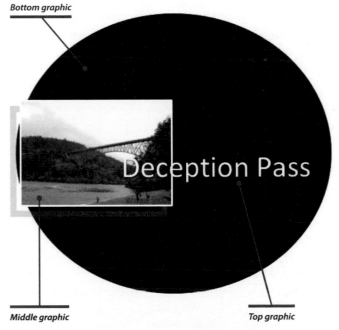

Figure 12-21: You can change the order of stacked graphics to achieve the look you want.

- **Bring To Front** moves the graphic to the top of the stack.
- **Bring In Front Of Text** moves the graphic on top of overlapping text.
- **Send Backward** moves the graphic down one level (same as Send To Back if there are only two graphics in the stack).
- **Send To Back** moves the graphic to the bottom of the stack.
- **Send Behind Text** moves the graphic behind overlapping text.

> **NOTE** To change the order of layered graphics, or to reveal one hidden by another, right-click the graphic you want to change and click **Bring To Front** or **Send To Back**. If you don't see the stacking options on the context menu when you right-click one of the graphics in a stack, click outside all the graphics, and then click one of the other graphics.

Align Graphics

To align two or more graphics relative to one another, select the graphics by holding down **SHIFT**. Then click the **Align** command in the Format tab Arrange group, and click an option.

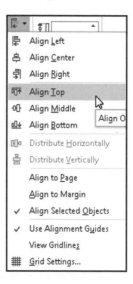

Evenly Space Graphics

Select the graphics by holding down **SHIFT**. In the Format tab Arrange group, click **Align** and then click **Distribute Horizontally** or **Distribute Vertically**, depending on their orientation.

Combine Graphics by Grouping

You can combine graphics for any number of reasons, but you typically work with multiple graphics to build a more complex rendering. To prevent losing the positioning, sizing, and other characteristics of the individual components, you can group them so that they are treated as one object.

- To group graphics, select the graphics to be grouped by clicking the first graphic and then holding down **CTRL** while selecting other drawings and pictures. In the Tools Format tab Arrange group, click **Group** and then click **Group** again; or right-click one of the selected graphics, click **Group**, and click **Group** again. A single set of selection handles surrounds the perimeter of the graphics. Coloring, positioning, sizing, and other actions now affect the graphics as a group instead of individually.

- To separate a group into individual graphics, select the group. In the Tools Format tab Arrange group, click **Group** and click **Ungroup**; or right-click the group, click **Group**, and then click **Ungroup**.

conditional formatting
    comparing cells, 169–172
    Rules Manager, 172
contact groups, creating, 296–297
Contact window, displaying, 293
contacts. *See also* Outlook 2013
    accessing in Outlook, 280
    Actions group, 293
    adding, 294–295
    adding images, 295–296
    adding items, 296
    changing images, 295–296
    Communicate commands, 293
    copying from e-mail, 295
    creating messages from, 295
    editing, 295
    Names commands, 294
    Options commands, 294
    Show commands, 293
    Tags commands, 294
    Zoom command, 294
context menus, opening, 5
copies of documents, saving, 12
copying
    animations in PowerPoint, 231
    Clipboard items, 26
    comments in Excel, 134
    data in Excel, 121
    formulas, 164
    page formatting, 80
    slides, 205, 208
    text, 40–41
    text boxes in PowerPoint, 219
    text in PowerPoint, 223
    worksheets, 153
copyright (©) character, shortcut key, 44
correcting info automatically. *See* AutoCorrect
corrections, modifying in Excel, 125–126
counting
    characters, 51
    words, 51
cropping pictures, 320–321
currency symbol, adding in Excel, 114

Custom Views, using in Excel, 17
cutting text, 41

D

data
    copying in Excel, 121
    entering in Excel, 108
    finding in Excel, 123–124
    linking, 164
    moving in Excel, 119
    pasting in Excel, 121–123
    records, 108
    replacing in Excel, 124
    series, 116–117
    tables, 108–109
data bars, using to compare cells, 169
data types, using in Excel, 108
dates
    entering in Excel, 111–113
    formatting in Excel, 113
    managing in Excel, 115–116
decimal places
    adding in Excel, 114
    decreasing in Excel, 114
decimals, converting to fractions, 114
default printer, setting, 302
Delete button, caution in Excel, 118
Deleted Items folder, emptying in Outlook, 291–292
deleted text, recovering, 42
deleting
    cell contents in Excel, 118–119
    cell styles in Excel, 145
    cells in Excel, 131
    columns in Excel, 131
    comments in Excel, 134
    footers, 98
    footers from slides, 217
    formulas, 163
    headers, 98
    highlighting, 52
    items on Clipboard, 26
    messages, 291–292

named cells, 160
    rows in Excel, 131
    section breaks, 93
    slides, 208
    slides from Slide Sorter, 203
    styles, 87–88
    text, 42
    text boxes in PowerPoint, 219
    worksheets, 153
dependent cells, tracing, 176
desktop, pinning shortcuts to, 2–3
diagrams, creating, 322–324
dialog box launcher, identifying, 14
disabilities, using Accessibility Checker, 28
display controls, setting in PowerPoint, 261
document pane
    enlarging, 12
    I-beam mouse pointer, 32
    identifying, 13, 32
    insertion point, 30, 32
Document Properties panel, displaying, 19–20
documents. *See also* files; main document;
  subdocuments; templates; Word 2013
    adding identifying info to, 19–20
    backing up, 11
    closing, 12
    creating in Word, 30–36
    deleting styles from, 87
    importing, 36–37
    locating existing, 7, 9
    master, 103
    navigating, 44–46
    opening, 7
    opening existing, 7, 9
    saving as copies, 12
    saving as templates, 12
    saving automatically, 11
    saving for first time, 10–11
    saving manually, 33
    selecting, 39–40
    starting Office programs, 33
    terminology, 5
    translating, 24–26

double-line spacing, setting, 70
Draft view, using in Word, 17, 37
drop caps, creating, 64–65
duplicating slides, 205

E

Editing group, displaying, 30
em (—) dash, shortcut key, 44
e-mail. *See also* messages; Outlook 2013
    checking for manually, 275
    filtering junk mail, 277–278
    HTTP (HyperText Transfer Protocol), 270
    MAPI (Messaging Application Programming
      Interface), 269
    Message window, 277
    POP3 (Post Office Protocol 3), 269
    reading, 277
    receiving automatically, 276
    Send/Receive Groups dialog box, 277
en (–) dash, shortcut key, 44
endnotes
    changing, 100
    converting to footnotes, 100–101
    deleting, 100
    Go To command, 99
    inserting, 99
envelopes, merging to, 314–315
equal sign (=), using with formulas, 160–161, 173
euro (€) character, shortcut key, 44
Evaluate Formula feature, accessing, 178
even vs. odd pages, differentiating, 96
Excel 2013. *See also* cells; formulas; functions;
  worksheets
    active cell, 108–109
    adding backgrounds, 148–149
    adding cells, 131
    adding columns, 130–131
    adding comments, 133–134
    adding data quickly, 116–117
    adding rows, 130–131
    adjusting column width, 129
    adjusting row height, 128–129
    Alignment tab, 147

AM and PM, 114–115
applying formatting, 135–136
applying styles, 144
applying themes, 144
attaching formatting, 150
AutoComplete feature, 116
automatic corrections, 125–126
canceling cell editing, 118
caution about Delete button, 118
cell styles, 142–145
cells, 108
Center Across Selection, 147
centering text, 147
changing alignment, 146–148
changing cell borders, 132–133
changing cell styles, 145
changing fonts, 145–146
changing orientation, 146–148
completing entries, 110
consistent look and feel, 142
constraining text, 110
Context option, 148
conventions for times, 114–115
copying data, 121
copying formatting, 149–150
currency symbol, 114
custom colors, 139
custom fonts, 139
custom themes, 141–142
customizing styles, 144
data entry from lists, 117
data types, 108
dates and times, 115–116
decimal places, 114
decimals to fractions, 114
default column width, 129
direct formatting, 135–136
Distributed (Indent), 147
editing cell contents, 118
entering dates, 111–113
entering numbers, 111
entering sums, 175
entering text, 108–110

Error Checking feature, 176
file formats, 126
Fill Color button, 148
Fill option, 147
finding data, 123–124
finding specific objects, 124–125
Flash Fill, 117
Format Cells dialog box, 113
Format Painter, 150
formatting comments, 135
formatting conditionally, 169–172
formatting dates, 113
formatting numbers, 113–114
galleries on Quick Access toolbar, 144
Go To option, 124
grid layout, 109
heading fonts, 139–140
hiding columns, 130
hiding rows, 130
Justify option, 147
left indent, 147
Left To Right option, 148
locating comments, 125
locking columns, 150–151
locking rows, 150
maximum columns, 128
maximum rows, 128
Merge Cells, 148
merging cells, 131–132
moving data, 119
Number tab, 113
numbers to percentages, 114
orientation, 148
pasting data in, 121–123
phone numbers, 114
removing cell contents, 118–119
removing cell styles, 145
removing cells, 131
removing columns, 131
removing fill handle, 117
removing rows, 131
removing selected cell contents, 119
replacing cell contents, 118

footers (*cont.*)
 inserting items on, 96
 left page, 98–99
 positioning, 96
 removing, 96
 removing from slides, 217
 right page, 98–99
 switching between headers, 96
 typing text in, 97
 using on handouts, 248–250
 using on notes, 248–250
 using on slides, 216
footnotes
 changing, 100
 converting to endnotes, 100–101
 deleting, 100
 Go To command, 99
 inserting, 99
 skipping pages, 99
Format Painter
 presentations, 215
 using, 80
 using in Excel, 150
formatting
 applying in Excel, 135–136
 revealing, 88–89
formatting marks, turning on, 79
formatting pages. *See* page formatting
formatting text. *See* text formatting
Formula bar
 displaying Cancel button, 163
 displaying Enter button, 163
 displaying Insert button, 163
formulas. *See also* Excel 2013; symbolic formulas
 calculation of, 161
 canceling editing, 163
 canceling entering, 163
 cell references, 161–162
 copying, 164
 defined, 160
 deleting, 163
 editing, 163
 entering, 161

evaluating in pieces, 178
external references, 164–166
functions as, 160
mathematical operations, 161
moving, 163–164
recalculating, 164
reference cells, 155–160
replacing with values, 163
using, 163
using = (equal sign) with, 160–161
values, 160
viewing, 155
forwarding messages, 287–288
fractions, converting decimals to, 114
functions. *See also* Excel 2013
 argument values, 175
 arguments, 173
 AutoSum technique, 175
 components, 172–173
 entering, 173–175
 formula identifiers, 172
 inserting, 174
 names, 172
 preceding with equal sign (=), 173
 SUM, 162
 typing, 173–175
 using quickly, 173

G

Gabriola font, using, 63
galleries, placing on Quick Access toolbar, 144
General preferences, setting, 19–20
Go To command, using, 45
grammar, checking, 27
graphic effects, changing themed, 91, 141
graphics. *See also* images; pictures; SmartArt
 graphics; themed graphic effects
 absolute positioning, 328
 aligning, 330
 anchoring, 328
 choosing in SmartArt, 322
 defined, 301, 317

grouping, 330
inserting into slides, 195–196
moving incrementally, 329
positioning, 326–329
repositioning stacked, 329–330
resizing, 329
resizing precisely, 326
rotating precisely, 326
spacing evenly, 330
task pane, 325
ungrouping, 330
groups, using in ribbon, 14
Gutter spinner, accessing, 81

H

handout master
 changing, 244–245
 using with presentations, 234
handouts
 creating as Word documents, 259
 headers and footers, 248–250
 printing, 251
 removing borders from, 251
hanging indent
 example, 66
 keyboard shortcut, 66
 making, 69
 removing, 69
 setting, 70
Header And Footer tab, closing, 96
headers. *See also* footers
 aligning, 96
 creating from menus, 97
 creating from scratch, 97
 deleting, 98
 editing, 96–98
 inserting items on, 96
 left page, 98–99
 positioning, 96
 removing, 96
 right page, 98–99
 switching between footers, 96
 typing text in, 97

using on handouts, 248–250
using on notes, 248–250
Heading level keyboard shortcuts, 66
Help icon, identifying, 13
Help system, accessing, 22–23
highlighted text, finding, 13, 52–53
highlighting
applying, 52
removing, 52
highlighting color, changing, 52
horizontal lines, adding, 77
horizontal scroll bar, using, 45
HTTP (HyperText Transfer Protocol), 270
hyperlinks
inserting into presentations, 215
managing in messages, 284
removing from presentations, 215
hyphenation
automatic, 53
manual, 54

I

I-beam mouse pointer, identifying, 30, 32
icon sets, using to compare cells, 169
identifying information, adding, 19–20
Illustrations group in PowerPoint
Chart, 247
Shapes, 247
SmartArt, 247
illustrations, adding to notes, 248
images. *See also* graphics; pictures
adding to notes, 248
enlarging, 326
Images group in PowerPoint
Online Pictures, 247
Photo Album, 247
Pictures, 247
Screenshot, 247
importing documents, 36–37
indent levels, changing for lists, 69
indenting
first line, 68–69
paragraphs, 66–67

indents. *See also* paragraphs
hanging, 69
left, 68
right, 68
setting for lists, 69
unindenting, 68
using ruler for, 69–70
index entries, tagging, 101
indexes
generating, 101–102
updating, 102
insert mode, using with text, 38–39
inserting
endnotes, 99
footnotes, 99
section breaks, 92–93
insertion point
identifying, 30, 32
moving with keyboard, 38
moving with mouse, 38
using with text, 38
intersections, referencing in Excel, 158
italic shortcut keys, 57
italic style, applying, 58

J

junk mail, filtering, 277–278
Justified keyboard shortcut, 66

K

kerning, using, 61
keyboard
entering special characters, 43
entering symbols, 43
navigating documents, 45
selecting text with, 40
keyboard shortcuts. *See also* program shortcuts;
shortcuts
bullet (•) character, 44
contacts, 294
copying data in Excel, 121

copying slides, 208
copying text, 41
copyright (©) character, 44
cutting text, 41
double-line spacing, 70
em (—) dash, 44
en (–) dash, 44
entering dates in cells, 112
euro (€) character, 44
filling data into active cell, 117
finding data in Excel, 123–124
Go To command, 45–46
hanging indent, 69
inserting slides, 207
left indents, 68
lowercase, 64
Name Manager, 160
paragraphs, 66
pasting text, 41
pound (#) character, 44
presentations, 207
redoing actions, 42
registered (®) character, 44
removing highlighting, 52
removing slides, 208
single-line spacing, 70
text formatting, 56–57
trademark (™) character, 44
underlining text, 59
undoing actions, 42
unindenting hanging indent, 69
unindenting paragraphs, 68
uppercase, 64

L

labels, merging to, 315–317
landscape orientation, determining, 81
languages, translating words into, 24
layout masters, editing, 234–238
layout slides, numbered lists, 238
layouts in PowerPoint, explained, 185
leaders, using with tabs, 96

PowerPoint 2013, 181, 185, 190–192
  previewing, 33–34
  saving documents as, 12
  searching for, 34–36
  using, 8, 33
  using with Excel, 142
  viewing, 8
text
  adding borders, 77–78
  adding shading, 77–78
  adding to slides, 194–195
  aligning in PowerPoint, 223–224
  aligning with tabs, 94
  changing to WordArt styles, 219
  copying, 40–41
  copying in PowerPoint, 223
  cutting, 41
  deleting, 42
  entering, 38
  highlighted, 40
  inserting, 38–39
  moving, 40–41
  moving in PowerPoint, 223
  pasting, 41
  replacing, 48–49
  resetting, 60
  selecting with keyboard, 40
  selecting with mouse, 39–40
  typing over, 38–39
  undeleting, 42
  underlining, 59
text boxes
  changing fill color, 220
  copying in PowerPoint, 219
  deleting in PowerPoint, 219
  positioning precisely, 220
  rotating in PowerPoint, 220
  using in PowerPoint, 219
text effects, using, 61–62
text formatting
  align left, 57
  align right, 57
  all caps, 57

bold, 57
bulleted list, 57
center, 57
change case, 57
character formatting, 57
explained, 55–56
Font dialog box, 56–57
font name, 57
font size, 57
italic, 57
shortcut keys, 56–57
small caps, 57
subscript, 57
superscript, 57
symbol font, 57
Text toolbar
  displaying, 15
  using, 15
theme color
  changing, 90
  creating, 92
theme fonts, changing, 90. *See also* fonts
themed colors, changing in Excel, 136,
  138–139
themed fonts, changing in Excel, 139
themed graphic effects. *See also* graphics
  changing in Word, 91
  changing in Excel, 141
themes
  applying in Excel, 144
  applying to slides, 194
  assigning to documents, 89–90
  changing in Excel, 136
  customizing in Word, 91–92
  customizing in Excel, 141–142
  explained, 84
  in PowerPoint, 185
  previewing, 91
  searching in Excel, 142
Thesaurus feature, using, 22–23
thousands separator, adding in Excel, 114
time conventions, specifying in Excel, 114–115
times, managing in Excel, 115–116

timings
  clearing in PowerPoint, 267
  recording in PowerPoint, 267
  rehearsing, 268
title bar, identifying, 13
title masters, creating, 239
toolbar. *See* mini toolbar; Quick Access toolbar
touch vs. mouse commands, 5
trademark (™) character, shortcut key, 44
transitions
  editing in PowerPoint, 229
  using with slides, 228–229
translating
  documents, 24–26
  words, 24–26
Trust Center
  opening, 167
  security settings, 167
typeface, defined, 58

U

underlining text, 59
undo actions, redoing, 42
undoing actions
  in Excel, 118
  in Word, 42
unions, referencing in Excel, 157
uppercase, toggling to lowercase, 64

V

values, using in formulas, 160
vertical alignment, setting, 82
videos, creating for presentations, 257–258
View buttons
  Draft, 37
  Outline, 37
  Print Layout, 37
  Read Mode, 37
  Web Layout, 37
views in Excel
  Custom Views, 17
  Normal, 17

views in Excel (*cont.*)
    Page Break Preview, 17
    Page Layout, 17
views in PowerPoint
    described, 185
    Normal, 17
    Notes Page, 17
    Outline View, 17
    Reading View, 17
    Slide Sorter, 17
views in Word
    Draft, 17
    Outline, 16
    Print Layout, 16
    Read Mode, 16
    Web Layout, 16

W

Watch Window, using with cells, 177–178
Web Layout view, using in Word, 16, 37
Widow/Orphan Control, accessing, 72
wildcard characters, 48. *See also* characters in words
    asterisk (*), 48
    at sign (@), 48
    backslash (\), 48
    [!c-c], 48
    [c-c], 48
    [cc], 48
    left angle bracket (<), 48
    {n,}, 48
    {n,m}, 48
    {n}, 48
    question mark (?), 48
    right angle bracket (>), 48
windows
    closing, 13
    maximizing, 13
    minimizing, 13
Windows 7, starting Office programs in, 2–3

Windows 8, starting Office programs in, 3–5
Word 2013. *See also* documents; templates
    clearing styles, 87
    columns, 93–94
    creating documents, 30, 32
    creating styles, 86
    endnotes, 99–101
    file types, 37
    footers, 96–99
    footnotes, 99–101
    headers, 96–99
    indexes, 101–102
    modifying styles, 86–87
    Office screen, 5–6
    opening documents, 6
    outlines, 105–106
    preview of styles, 88
    recent files, 6
    section breaks, 92–93
    Start screen, 29
    Style Gallery, 88
    Style Inspector, 88–89
    style sets, 85–86
    table of contents, 102–105
    tabs, 94–96
    template searches, 6
    themes, 84, 89–92
    using styles, 84
Word Count feature, using, 51
Word screen, returning to, 37
Word views
    Draft, 17
    Outline, 16–17
    Print Layout, 16
    Read Mode, 16
    Web Layout, 16
WordArt styles, changing text to, 219
words
    counting, 51
    finding synonyms for, 22–23

replacing parts of, 48
searching for, 46
selecting characters in, 40
translating, 24
workbooks
    changing automatic link updating, 168–169
    changing display of, 154
    comparing, 154
    saving, 164
    using in Excel Web App, 126
    viewing worksheets from, 154
Worksheet tabs, coloring, 153
worksheets. *See also* Excel 2013
    adding, 153
    changing default number, 153
    column headings, 108–109
    copying, 153
    defined, 108
    deleting, 153
    entering text in, 108–109
    grid layout, 109
    headers, 108–109
    moving, 153
    moving through, 154
    renaming, 153
    row headings, 108–109
    splitting, 152–153
    tables of data, 108–109
    viewing from multiple workbooks, 154
writing aids
    building blocks, 50–51
    Highlight feature, 52–53
    Hyphenation feature, 53–54
    Word Count feature, 51

Z

ZIP codes, formatting in Excel, 114
zoom, using in PowerPoint 2013, 207
Zoom buttons, identifying, 13